The Delight Makers

The Delight Makers

Anglo-American Metaphysical Religion
and the Pursuit of Happiness

CATHERINE L. ALBANESE

The University of Chicago Press
Chicago and London

The University of Chicago Press, Chicago 60637
The University of Chicago Press, Ltd., London
© 2023 by The University of Chicago
All rights reserved. No part of this book may be used or reproduced in any manner whatsoever without written permission, except in the case of brief quotations in critical articles and reviews. For more information, contact the University of Chicago Press, 1427 E. 60th St., Chicago, IL 60637.
Published 2023
Printed in the United States of America

32 31 30 29 28 27 26 25 24 23   1 2 3 4 5

ISBN-13: 978-0-226-82333-1 (cloth)
ISBN-13: 978-0-226-82354-6 (paper)
ISBN-13: 978-0-226-82334-8 (e-book)
DOI: https://doi.org/10.7208/chicago/9780226823348.001.0001

Library of Congress Cataloging-in-Publication Data

Names: Albanese, Catherine L., author.
Title: The delight makers : Anglo-American metaphysical religion and the pursuit of happiness / Catherine L. Albanese.
Description: Chicago : University of Chicago Press, 2023. | Includes bibliographical references and index.
Identifiers: LCCN 2022020579 | ISBN 9780226823331 (cloth) | ISBN 9780226823546 (paperback) | ISBN 9780226823348 (ebook)
Subjects: LCSH: United States—Religion—History. | Metaphysics. | United States—Church history. | BISAC: PHILOSOPHY / Metaphysics | RELIGION / History
Classification: LCC BL2525 .A395 2023 | DDC 200.973—dc23/eng20220723
LC record available at https://lccn.loc.gov/2022020579

*For all the teachers and students from whom
I have learned through the years*

This is the spirit that Beauty must ever induce, wonderment and a delicious trouble, longing and love and a trembling that is all delight.

Plotinus, *Enneads*

The longing at the heart of attraction is for union with the Beautiful.

John O'Donohue, *Beauty*

Thou shall be abundantly satisfied with the fatness of thy house; and thou shalt make them drink of the river of thy pleasures.

Ps. 36:8 (King James Version)

CONTENTS

INTRODUCTION: Lights and Shadows / 1

PART I: GOD SHED HIS GRACE
SECTION 1: DIVINE AND DEVILISH THINGS

ONE / The Metaphysical Cotton Mather / 17

TWO / Jonathan Edwards: Latter-Day Puritan and Metaphysician / 43

SECTION 2: SUPERNATURAL AND NATURAL

THREE / Ralph Waldo Emerson: Supernatural Naturalist / 71

FOUR / Horace Bushnell: Natural Supernaturalist / 99

PART II: THE FRUITED PLAIN
SECTION 3: COMMERCIAL AND UN-UNITARIAN TIMES

FIVE / Albert Brisbane and the Metempsychosis of Sex / 129

SIX / Andrew Jackson Davis and the Matter of Sex and Spirit / 157

SECTION 4: PHYSIC AND METAPHYSIC

SEVEN / Warren Felt Evans: From Methodism to Mind Cure / 187

EIGHT / William James: From Anatomy to the Science of Spirit / 215

SECTION 5: PURSES, PROFITS, AND FUTURES PERFECT

NINE / Minding Money and Market: Emma Curtis Hopkins
and Elizabeth Towne / 245

TEN / Arcanes of Prosperity: The Multiverses
of William Walker Atkinson / 267

ELEVEN: Channeling Delight and Destiny:
The Coming of Seth and Abraham / 287

AFTERWORD: And Crowned Thy Good? / 307

Acknowledgments / 317
Notes / 319
Index / 351

INTRODUCTION

Lights and Shadows

About a year after Richard Nixon resigned as president in 1974, while I was an assistant professor at Wright State University in Dayton, Ohio, the manager in my garden apartment complex in East Dayton discovered my cat. Faced with letting her go or getting evicted, I chose the latter. So began my sojourn in Yellow Springs, Ohio, where my cat and I were both welcome. I spent quite a while in the Village of Yellow Springs, the official name of the town with its some four thousand inhabitants, living there until 1987, when I moved to Santa Barbara. Back in the 1970s and '80s, Yellow Springs was being called the "Fairyland Capital of the Midwest," and I gradually came to see why. Site of Antioch College from 1850, with educational reformer Horace Mann its first president, it was the third college in the nation to admit African American students. Among other aspects of college life, its pioneering work-study program also attracted notice for its innovation and success. In the nineteenth century, Yellow Springs had been home to a water cure and a spiritualist and free-love colony that arose out of it. The water cure had been situated in what was later called Glen Helen—a five-acre nature preserve that still graces the middle of town—and within it flows the healing "yellow spring" (from its high sulfur content) that gave the village its name and the water cure its reason for being.

When I arrived, Yellow Springs was dominated informally by a Quaker establishment, and its historic liberal-left leanings were still continuing. There were two organic groceries in town, *Pravda*—the then-official Soviet newspaper—was sold in the local coffee shop, and crafts everywhere abounded. The local Better Health Co-op sponsored an introduction to Helen Schucman's channeled *Course in Miracles* (1976), and people frequently wore crystals around their necks. With a bad back at the time, I started attending yoga classes, where the Iyengar teacher seemed perpetually to sport a tee shirt that announced, "Just hanging out on this planet." The massage therapist, whom I quickly discovered, regaled me with her philosophy of life, which referred frequently to the "universe" and to the importance of what we thought about for what happened to us. It was fashionable, too, to subscribe to Unity School of Christianity's *Daily Word*, which told readers they had divine natures and reminded them to think positively.

The upshot of all of this is that, before I ever even heard the term "New Age," I had been immersed in it, experiencing an unofficial era of fieldwork that became after a while a spur for my own academic research. I was getting interested in where all of what I had lived with had come from, when and how it had evolved, and how it might have changed yet remained connected to its beginnings. So began my discovery of what I call the metaphysical tradition in American religion (more on that below). Pondering the questions the citizens of Yellow Springs raised for me, I have done various pieces of writing over the years, and this book stands on them. I see it as a deep exploration of what I was already learning, an attempt to open it out and decipher the nuances of its various appearances over time.

Given that background, this is a book of partial readings. It turns on selective journeys into the work of individuals important to the field of American religion, especially in its metaphysical version. It seeks not so much to count in all their ideas but to lift out themes that shed light on a contemporary agenda. My concern is to explain their version of spirituality in the early twenty-first century—a version that, at first, seems disconnected from a traditional religious past.

Especially in the present, the metaphysical religionists whom I track have often tended to avoid conventional Christian language designations such as "God" and "prayer." When acknowledged, their God has been a vast presence living within the universe, an unfathomable intelligence merging with it—an "isness" stirring everywhere *as* it. Some of the thinkers whose ideas populate this book were indeed Christian and others not, but they had all interacted with orthodoxy in ways that moved them afield. Whatever their allegiance to the transcendence of God, they had found divinity immanently present in the natural world. This God or Source, for many, was ever expanding, ever growing into yet more being, and in and through this being's processes, humans found a pulse that translated into divine permission to search and desire. Instead of sin, they could hunt for ways in which the world was shot through with delight and pleasure.

Many of them also liked to declare against the importance of religion. Still, they found alternate languages to express the dimension of their lives formerly and easily tagged as religion. Moreover, as I try to show, the alternate languages used in the present have a past. At a time when pollsters are telling us that formal religion is in decline, this book is looking for ways that contemporary developments are related to past American religion. The people I follow here do not come out of the blue but instead emerge as part of a spiritual lineage, with a chain of ideas and attitudes linking them to generations from decades and even centuries ago. Thinkers and actors as far back at least as early America inform a large swath of the spirituality of the present. And, along with earlier American religiosity and its aftermath, selected inputs from European sources as well as multicultural ones have contributed to a burgeoning spiritual mix. Even further, continuing changes outside the field of formal religion have done their share to repurpose the religious legacy of the past.

Since I have pulled the term *metaphysical* seemingly out of thin air, here is the place to explain further. My book of partial readings questions the relegation of many Americans to a nonreligious homeland devoid of a sense of the spiritual. But the particular form of spirituality I have charted among the many who reject traditional religious rhetoric is distinct and distinguishable from the secular, the agnostic, and the atheistic. Instead, my subjects stand out in their own unmistakable line of descent. As I argue in these pages, names and designations are not the be-all and end-all of a religious stance or signs of its absence. Exploring the limits of language, my story challenges designations such as "atheism" or "agnosticism" as too limited in their conceptual rationalism, too incapable of explaining contemporary forms of spirituality that are complex, nuanced, and nontraditional. Instead of atheism, or agnosticism, or even a secular spirituality without religion, as I have already begun to suggest, the operative theme for this story will be delight. To be truthful, I have borrowed the book's title from Adolph Bandelier's 1890 novel *The Delight Makers*—a fanciful narrative about sacred "clowns" in Pueblo Indian society. With the stolen title and an emphasis on sacred play, though, the similarities to Bandelier's book end.

The "delight" tracked through the partial readings in these pages becomes a way to talk in a different voice about religion. Here religious phenomena traveled through American time and along the way reconfigured as the fulfillment of desire—this in a largely Anglo-American tradition of thought that encompassed related elements. By the middle of the nineteenth century, these elements emphasizing themes of delight and desire congealed in a distinctive religiosity.[1] Beginning with the European Renaissance and incorporating the ideas and practices of Indians, Blacks, Latinx people, and others outside the Protestant mainstream, a third important strand emerged in American religion alongside the mainstream denominational and evangelical strands. Following the language of many of its proponents, I label this third strand *metaphysics* or *metaphysical* (not to be confused with more traditional philosophical usages of the term), and within it I lift out four major characteristics.

First, metaphysics has been built on ideas of mind, and then, second, on ideas of correspondence between higher (divine, natural, cosmic) worlds and our own. Third, it has affirmed the presence and power of energies running from higher to lower worlds. Fourth, it has looked to the salvific, healing nature of those energies for righting whatever is wrong in the human world. In this context, the metaphysical religiosity I track was and is *exoteric* rather than esoteric, open and available to all. And it was and is highly combinative—bringing together material in a grand catch-all of sources to serve its own ends and goals. This last characteristic, in fact, is a large clue to what happened with all American religion in a land of continual meetings of people and traditions, and it is a theme that continues in this book, even as my exploration is mostly limited to Anglo-American thinkers. Of course, there have been and now are other ways to parse the metaphysical dimension of American religious life, and critical scholarship has added to what we can know and how we can interpret its presence. This book, however, will ask what I think are different questions, with answers revealing the metaphysically inclined to be children of an American past who, from the birth of a new nation and before, sought consciously to pursue happiness. So my questions are about resemblance, not difference or (critical) distance.

In other words, I am probing the conceptual universe of metaphysics, especially as it takes its cues from implicit, and often explicit, ideas in the Anglo-Protestant theological tradition and parallel outgrowths. In so doing, I target a growing theology of desire and delight, present from the first and unpacked in various ways in and through the cultural turns of American religion. A word more about desire/delight seems in order here. It is clear that both are inextricably connected to the condition of being in a body and, so, in a material world. In this American version, desire and delight brought with them metaphysical ideas about what materiality meant as a denser, more condensed form of spirit. Here inherited European ideas about a vital principle joining matter and spirit flourished. *Vitalism*, as it came to be called, bridged the gap between mind and body.[2] It taught the existence of a vital, nonmaterial "spark"—an élan vital—that made a being alive rather than inert. Flourishing in the life sciences and especially medicine, vitalism saw living beings as profoundly different from nonliving ones because of the mysterious force beyond their chemical or physical makeup. Leaving its medical origins behind, vitalism came to flourish in a larger cultural context. It took on new life, so to speak, as a force that linked people to a beyond and an above. It functioned as a source of energy from which to draw new power down on otherwise depleted human lives and propel them toward enhancement. As such, it became an overarching concept and language for naming all the sources of desire and delight that metaphysically inclined Americans longed to make present in their lives.

That said, *desire* and *delight* generally signaled three areas of life in which their fulfillment promised happiness—sexuality, health, and personal prosperity. And so it followed easily that, in America, a theology of desire and delight has been preeminently a theology of *abundance*, built on notions of the loving prodigality of a divine or ultimate Source bestowing all that seekers yearned for. "Ask and it is given" became a mantra as these views developed. Affirmations of the abundance of good—the delights of prosperity, exuberant health, and sexual bliss, all ever available for human life—became basic. At the same time, supporting what, on the surface, seems crassly pragmatic and quite superficial, sophisticated cosmologies began to arise. By the late nineteenth and early twentieth century, they took into account a new cultural world in which Asian systems, various ethnic spiritualities, new quantum science, and traditional theological beliefs met and mingled.

But this is to get ahead of the story. As the plot turns, Puritan delight in the Lord and fear of ghosts and spirits, along with views of nature as a source of revelation, left indelible marks on later American culture. In this partial reading of Puritanism, I turn to that formidable Puritan divine Cotton Mather, in all his splendid complexity, and—after him—the equally formidable Jonathan Edwards. With wealth a sign of God's blessing and the wonders of the invisible world ever at hand in the lights and shadows of nature, in unexplained phenomena, and in continuing providences, the Mather-and-Edwards brand of Calvinism did not simply vanish. Instead this Calvinism fell into new times like pieces in a kaleidoscope. In so doing, its sharply chiseled edges began to erode. By the early years of the new republic and in the shadow of ever-present revivals, delight in the Lord could give instant and ecstatic pleasure in conversion experiences. These had grown out of earlier Puritan versions, but a new cultural emphasis exploited and enhanced them. They grew larger and more grandiose. Then, continuing into the mid-nineteenth century, spiritual pleasure came in a new form with proto-holiness experiences of the coming of the Holy Spirit. Here was a second work of grace (after conversion and justification) called sanctification, and it brought with it a growing gospel of perfection. Now conversion was only the prelude to the action of the Holy Spirit that could continue to thrill and comfort the devout believer.

Meanwhile, by the end of the eighteenth century, pervasive early American beliefs about supernatural intrusions into the natural world began to melt away among the learned classes, and the absence of haunts, ghosts, and revivals brought relief to many. Breaking away from the early industrial revolution as part of the budding romantic movement, Americans found that the contemplation of nature mediated spiritual delight on its own. American Transcendentalism, with memorable figures such as Ralph Waldo Emerson, Henry David Thoreau, and later a much-transformed Walt Whitman, heralded a new emphasis on the power of the natural environment to supply ecstasy and delight. Love of nature surfaced in new social forms in the conservation movement, the natural-park movement, and the championship of wilderness and its bio-species that has continued into our own time. Mystical experience became cosmic consciousness, and mountaintops and woodland streams brought seekers into a sense of connection with an All greater than themselves. John Muir became a hero and idol for environmentalist seekers of the spiritual, even as he did more than any other single figure to bring Yosemite National Park into existence.

The Transcendentalists saw nature as the symbol of spirit, and they used the ancient theory of correspondence (copiously present in Puritanism) to ground their ideas. "As above, so below" became their take on the way the ultimate and the everyday were correlated. But they were not alone in their view of cosmic links and connections. Among Christian romantics like Horace Bushnell, a grand analogy of being ran through all things, and language could only hint at, not confine and contain, its presence. Nature and the supernatural belonged to one divine system, and humans stood with God on the side of the supernatural even as they reveled in the natural world and saw in it, like the Transcendentalists, a symbol of spirit.

But not for long. Haunts and spirits resurfaced, and so did a new emphasis on physicality. By the mid-nineteenth century, mass spiritualism brought back the spirits of the dead, who had grown more communicative and more friendly than among their Puritan ancestors. Now meeting spirits, not avoiding them, brought solace and relief. Providing a voice for many, Andrew Jackson Davis, the famed Poughkeepsie (New York) seer, produced tome after tome to articulate a new and vernacular theology of spirit and the spirits. Jackson, taking his cue from the Swedish mystical theologian Emanuel Swedenborg, also taught "conjugial" love—the existence of a perfect partner and soulmate for whom one could divorce a previous partner in the service of true love. Meanwhile, the sexual mores of those who met the spirits grew more permissive, and in their shadow a "free-love" movement celebrated the unencumbered association of humans attracted to one another in their material bodies. Even as the spirits were harbingers of delight from a world other than this one, they brought devotees back to an earth that contained its own sources of pleasure. Often, money trumped sex. The Frenchman Charles Fourier, with his philosophical musings on sexual delight and freedom, came aboard in an American version championed by Davis. But more than for Davis, in Albert Brisbane sexual desire turned financial, and acquisition became true satiation. A committed disciple of Fourier, Brisbane became a one-person engine to create social change through a series of economically independent communities in the style and format advocated by his mentor. That Brisbane's own belief system, like Fourier's, was ultimately preoccupied with sexuality did not deter his politically correct introduction of Fourier to America in economic terms.

Time marched on. The post–Civil War period and then the end of the nineteenth century brought their own religious developments. Religious thought incorporated psychological insights on the layering of consciousness, with—in the classic formulation of William James—a sense of the subconscious world opening into a collective universe that mediated something akin to the divine. Still more, owning the deliciousness of things proved a way to admire the bounty all around and to rejoice in humans as desiring beings—in a world teeming with sources of pleasure. Like part fitting into part, the overplenty in the world was put there to give delight as the full satisfaction of human desire. Now New Thought and Theosophy mined these ideas to yield a conscious theology of desire. Think-it-yourself religious champions ruled the theological day. Figures such as Madame Helena Blavatsky and Henry Steel Olcott in Theosophy were joined by New Thought predecessors, then New Thoughters themselves and their heirs. Individuals, from Phineas P. Quimby and Warren Felt Evans to Emma Curtis Hopkins, Charles Fillmore, and Ralph Waldo Trine, and then Elizabeth Towne, William Walker Atkinson, Napoleon Hill, and Norman Vincent Peale, became well-known worthies. As the old century turned to the new twentieth and continued on, delight could continue to be viewed as the fulfillment of desire. The evolving theology was supported by its own distinctive grammar in New Thought and Theosophical spin-offs; then in the later twentieth century in the New Age movement and in a new spirituality thereafter. The now-current grammar explained the foundational necessity of desire in an expanding universe or universes. Among trance channelers such as Jane Roberts and Esther Hicks, a cosmological vision provided the base for metaphysical religiosity and its theology of delight and desire.

In the context I have described, my story, perhaps obviously, is a story of religious thought or theology breaking free from high-culture traditions and becoming vernacular. The transition worked itself out in gradual stages. First, the reflective impulse spread from learned divines and professional theologians (Cotton Mather, Jonathan Edwards) to preachers or former preachers who theologized as they felt immediate need (Horace Bushnell, Ralph Waldo Emerson, Warren Felt Evans), then to secular professionals (William James) and do-it-yourselfers (Albert Brisbane, Andrew Jackson Davis, Emma Curtis Hopkins, Elizabeth Towne, William Walker Atkinson). Among them came nonprofessionals (often women)—who allowed themselves to be taken over as "channels" by mysterious sources who claimed nonphysical identities and taught their own cosmologies and theologies (Jane Roberts, Esther Hicks). Tracking this process, of course, does not proclaim that all professional theologians and learned divines died and went to heaven; it only notices that other people got involved in doing what the learned previously were understood to be the only ones doing.

On a larger horizon, with unexamined notions that American pragmatism in the tradition of William James and others represents *the* one great contribution of American thought to theology, it is time to question the judgment. Arguably, metaphysics and its theology of delight and desire were as important as the pragmatic turn in theology—in fact, they were its silent partners and consorts. The abundance theology of desire and delight identifies what Americans were often being so pragmatic about. More often than not, pragmatism directed them to the best ways to achieve what they wanted. But it was not from pragmatic systems that they learned to place so high a value on the satisfaction of desire. That move came from received notions that had gradually developed out of a dominant Anglo-American religious past, enhanced significantly as time passed by the presence of other cultures and peoples with their own input. These ideas changed ever so gradually to meet new circumstances in combinative ways.

Noticing the theology of desire and delight has another important consequence, and this outside of its American context. In terms of the study of comparative religions, the metaphysical theology I explore here to some extent upends received categories. Comparative religions scholars can look at the American case, test its dimensions, and ask if it changes their thinking and, if so, how. What does it mean, as a comparative religions scholar, to talk about a theology of delight and desire? How does such a theology of abundance fit with time-honored practices of mortification of the flesh and meditative work to extinguish quests for worldly objects and goals? It is a truism to point to the anti-desire squads who police the world's great religions, with their traditions of asceticism, denial, quietism, and nonattachment. However, if we look again, we can find moods and moments of bliss and the satisfaction of desire in other religious traditions, as in South Asian forms of tantra to cite a key example. And with historical questions in mind, we can look for cultural distinctiveness in an American theology of delight and desire, given its separate evolution and context. As a major part of that difference, we can notice that the Anglo-American liberal theological lineage, as it became vernacularized and touched new people and times, has produced an American hybrid product. This hybrid product is not the same as other hybrids (the Asian one, to cite the same tantric example), and it is this product that calls for interpretation. Resemblances can entice, but they can also deceive. This book argues that something new has been added in our world.

Ironically, in an America in which Buddhism and Buddhists are thriving with a long majority tradition of *ending* desire (the cause of suffering), and the practice of Christian asceticism still lingers, homegrown forms of valuing desire are also thriving. Scrutiny of *New York Times* best-seller lists in the "Advice, How-To, and Miscellaneous" category demonstrates that, again and again, it is metaphysical books teaching the theology of abundance, of desire and delight, that reach top places and stay there. In view of the cultural transformation that these developments signal, searching for the roots of the present becomes an ever more compelling project. So, yet again, this is a book of partial readings of an American religious past that seeks to understand an American present in which the pursuit of desire and delight have impacted the communities we form, the civic engagements we embrace, and the public shape of our privacies.

To do so, part 1 ("God Shed His Grace") of the book is organized around themes of holiness, beauty, and delight as avenues into the Anglo-American liberal tradition. Here, in two sections and four chapters, we look first at the devilish and divine worlds of Cotton Mather and Jonathan Edwards, selecting out of their writings the strands that chart the course of delight from its Anglo-American beginnings. Second, we move into a new time and cultural space with the interwoven themes of nature and the supernatural in the American Transcendentalists, most notably Ralph Waldo Emerson, and the Christian romanticism of Horace Bushnell.

Part 2 ("The Fruited Plain"), in three sections and seven chapters, turns more explicitly to the theology of desire and delight with its focused metaphysical connections. Here the entrepreneurial Albert Brisbane—significantly *the* American disciple of the eccentric French thinker Charles Fourier—shares an economics of sexuality with the sexualized spiritualism of Andrew Jackson Davis—who claimed he never read a book. In the two chapters that follow to explore mind cure, first comes the erudite former Methodist minister Warren Felt Evans, who read many books and perpetually rehearsed their contents and wrote about them. If for Davis, being spiritual *and* religious *and* sexual were of a piece, for Evans, seeker culture became idealism as he tried religious stance after stance in a quest that led to Swedenborgianism and then mental healing. Meanwhile, Harvard professor William James, who had moved from medicine to philosophy and finally psychology, looked with interest at New England's burgeoning mental healing movement in New Thought. He did not stop there but became intent on pursuing psychic research, spending hours and years studying a spiritualist medium named Leonora Piper.

As New Thought exploded into late nineteenth-century cultural consciousness, healing your body turned increasingly toward healing your purse. A new section, with three chapters, pursues that narrative. Now more of the self-ordained denizens of the new gospel arrive in the initial chapter in the persons of New Thought teacher of teachers Emma Curtis Hopkins and New Thought's major publisher Elizabeth Towne. A second chapter charts the prodigious output of New Thought champion William Walker Atkinson, with his adherence to the Law of Attraction (from the mid-nineteenth century, the version of the law of correspondence that attracted metaphysical devotees). A final chapter on channeling in the trance productions of Jane Roberts (who introduces us to "Seth") and Esther Hicks (who engages with the group entity called "Abraham") explores delight and destiny as twin partners of the spirit. Here the theology of abundance, in what is perhaps a strange transformation, reaches its most sophisticated form—brought to consciousness by nonexperts in their own channeled version of process theology.

Although merely skimming the surface of so very much and shamelessly acknowledging its partial readings, this book comes to its major conclusion: The theology of desire and delight *is* American theology. Not to be relegated to an evangelical subculture of prosperity preachers and seekers with Pentecostal and faith-cure leanings, it is a pervasive kind of intellectual labor within the space of metaphysical religiosity. Alongside William James's pragmatic theology, about which we have heard so much, it represents the warp and woof of American theology. Open to a crass materialism at every turn, it yet tantalizes with its aesthetic take on religion and the things of spirit. It hints that art and intuition—more than science—are a productive way to think through American religion.

To say this is perhaps to invoke a venerable University of Chicago ancestor. In 1973, William Clebsch saw his *American Religious Thought* appear in the Chicago History of American Religion series edited by Martin E. Marty.[3] The book took on moralistic readings of American religious thought and, as an alternative to them, sought to track a (clearly liberal) history centered on the contributions of three religious figures: Jonathan Edwards, Ralph Waldo Emerson, and William James. Instead of an ethical reading of the tradition, Clebsch argued for an aesthetic one, with a vision of humans feeling their way into a harmonious at-homeness in the universe. There were problems with the work to be sure—hanging *all* of American religious thought on three figures was one; elitism a second; ending with Reinhold Niebuhr, in a section that proved inconclusive, a third. Still, the work pointed in an important direction with its turn to aesthetics. As Clebsch laid out his thesis, with its evocations of harmony and at-homeness, it was clear that "delight" was everywhere, and metaphysics was present, at least by implication.

Unfortunately, the book never generated much continuing scholarship. So this book, in a new time and intellectual space dominated by the landscape of American metaphysics, is a step toward resuscitating the aesthetic insight in Clebsch's work. In the American metaphysical world that I seek to explore, beauty generated delight, which generated the fulfillment of desire and the sweet happiness of success. As time passed, it was true, beauty as a conscious category seemed to fall away. Things got more complicated. Physicality—the condition of being in a body—could open one to sexual pleasure. It could also bring a whole lot else in personal health and healing as well as the delights of material possession and wealth. *The Delight Makers* is most bent on pursuing all of this in an introductory way. The lights and shadows of its project are emblems of our human materiality, and they orient us to visions of beauty that become background for celebrating desire and its fulfillment in delight and abundance.

To point to the shadows, too, is to acknowledge a night-time vision in the aesthetic project. Aesthetics become delight and the fulfillment of desire can move into ethically problematic territory, as my afterword suggests. It can start to look much like what Christian theology called sin and what other theological traditions labeled as evil. In her often-quoted prayer "The Great Invocation," twentieth-century channeled author Alice Bailey—well-known in the theosophical diaspora—asked heartfully that the "Plan of Love and Light" would "work out" and "seal the door where evil dwells." Sealing the door where evil dwells was not a project that delight makers who came after the Puritans were generally good at. But they sensed the fearsome presence that lay beyond the door. In Platonic fashion, they could call evil the absence of good that ought to be present—thus lack, thus the need for yet more abundance, thus more pursuit of delight and desire. The Platonic answer, though, never seemed to be enough. To switch metaphors, evils rose in the garden of delight like so many weeds, and the weeds got large enough to threaten the good. What to do? The theology of abundance never produced a satisfactory answer. As with pragmatism, so with desire. There was a large hole in the vision. The shadow side remained.

This book has no answer to the problem of evil. Enough to raise it. Enough to acknowledge that, as with any human project, the project of the delight makers had large and manifest flaws. We need to own up to them even as we explore the creative and pleasurable spiritual universes they created. Sealing the door where evil dwells seems a project that never works completely. Ugliness seeps through, and pain persists. But that does not wipe out delight—or end pleasure and beauty.

PART I

God Shed His Grace

SECTION 1

Divine and Devilish Things

Most people accept stereotypes without much question. They make the complex simple, the ambiguous graspable, the rough places smooth (to echo scripture). Perhaps nowhere are these judgments more the case than for New England's Puritans as they are recalled in the conventional culture of our time. Especially when their seventeenth- and eighteenth-century world is summed up in the person of key and memorable figures. Consider, for example, Puritan divine Cotton Mather, who comes down to us as stern and dour, buttoned-up, superstitious, and half-crazed—on his horse at the Salem witchcraft executions declaiming against minister George Burroughs about to be hanged. In Boston cloth merchant Robert Calef's account, Mather declares Burroughs to be "no ordained Minister," adding dismissively that "the Devil has often been transformed into an Angel of Light."[1] Or consider that latter-day Puritan divine Jonathan Edwards, driven by reforming Calvinist zeal as he preaches at Enfield in 1741 at the height of the Massachusetts revival that had begun in his own Northampton church in 1734. In a sermon favored several centuries later for consumption in high school and college English classes, Edwards solemnly intones, "The God that holds you over the pit of hell, much as one holds a spider, or some loathsome insect over the fire, abhors you, and is dreadfully provoked: his wrath towards you burns like fire."[2]

If such snapshots make intellectual life seem easier, aside from the gravity of their moral lapse, they thoroughly fail to grasp the complexity that permeates Puritan culture and the characters of its individual actors. Like all humans, Puritans lived at the center of intersecting passions, desires, insights, and contradictory messages about things earthly and beyond. Even in the partial readings in which this book engages and even viewed through the prism of two Puritan leaders—Mather and Edwards—stereotypes crumble in the multifaceted thought worlds that emerge. We turn first to Cotton Mather and then to Jonathan Edwards, seeking hints and clues of what the future of the theology of desire and abundance would hold.

ONE

The Metaphysical Cotton Mather

Cotton Mather, who lived from 1663 to 1728, descended on both sides from Puritan divines who spread their culture's religious ways declaratively. His mother, Maria, was the daughter of John Cotton (1583–1652), the minister who in his preaching took an active theological stance in favor of grace as a free gift of God to all (instead of only to a predestined select group). Cotton had also preached human passivity in its presence, and his mysticizing sermons had sparked the controversial Anne Hutchinson's antinomian rejection of all law in matters of spirituality. His father, Increase (1639–1723), was the son of Richard Mather (1596–1669), both of them key players in the Massachusetts Bay Colony. Richard, whose second wife was the widow of John Cotton, worked prominently to shape models of ecclesiastical polity for New England Congregationalism, authoring important broad-gauged directives. Increase, who published some 125 works in his time, took an active role in the governance of Massachusetts Bay, the administration of Harvard College, and—most notoriously—the Salem witch trials. With such a pedigree, Cotton Mather had a path charted for him from birth and early childhood into adulthood and maturity.

The producer of a bibliography of probably more than 450 items, Mather could surely boast of exceeding the authorial bar of his ancestors. At fifteen years old, he was the youngest Harvard graduate up to his time. After graduation, he studied medicine, overcame a speech impediment, and by 1680 preached his first sermon and began assisting his father at Boston's Second Church. Five years later, he was his father's full colleague at the Second Church and continued at the church for the rest of his life. He outlived two wives and married a third, producing fifteen children, only two of whom survived him. As the Salem witch craze permeated Bay Colony life, Mather was ambiguous enough to warn against "spectral evidence" (from visions or dreams) in court cases for accused witches but never publicly countered the courts when they ignored his advice. He adamantly believed in devils, witches, and angels, and he thought that their influence on human life was not to be denied. Meanwhile, Mather's views about requirements for admission to communion in church services were decidedly conservative. Thoroughly immersed in the politics of the colony and of Harvard College, he has likewise been cited for his intellectual prowess. He has been called a herald of both the Enlightenment and the Great Awakening, and a transitional thinker who synthesized and fused the medicine and theology of his day. Natural philosopher, major historian of Massachusetts Bay to his time, and ever-curious scientific thinker, as well as medical experimentalist (it was Mather who championed smallpox inoculation and introduced it to Boston), Mather in effect lived many lives.[1] He was also privately tortured by all sorts of psycho-emotional conflicts even as, publicly, he was clear and compelling in reasoned arguments when he preached and wrote. In short, Mather's complexity will probably never be fully sorted out. In what follows, instead of trying to do so, I focus on the hints he provided for a later American culture of delight makers and their quest for abundance.

An obvious place to begin is with the idea of prosperity, a significant part of Calvinist thought and upheld clearly in Mather's writings. For Puritans, among them Mather, material prosperity was not evil; indeed, it functioned as an unambiguous sign of God's blessing. A. Whitney Griswold remarked as early as 1934 that Mather was one of the first to teach American businessmen to serve God by making money. Far from being medievalists in their economic views, Puritans thought of business as a divine calling. Merchants in Massachusetts Bay cited God on their invoices, expressing gratitude for their profit and writing off losses as a function of his greater glory. Mather capitalized on what was there, and his own reading of Puritan themes, argued Griswold, provided "the true moral foundations for rugged American individualism." Two generations after Griswold, Sacvan Bercovitch did not disagree. He called Mather "the pioneer in American letters of the rags to riches formula, worthy of the title of father to the New World success story." Bercovitch thought that Mather's accounts of self-made business success in New England struck "a distinctly modern note" and one closely connected to a central literary theme on the nation's cultural landscape.[2]

Perhaps it is not too much to say that Mather championed a code of living in which God desired Bostonians to be rich. Here is Mather himself on the point. Writing in 1701 in his *Two Brief Discourses*, Mather announced unequivocally that "Every Day, we shall have Occasion for a *Promise* of a *Supply* for all our wants in the Day." Still more, "Every Day, we shall have occasion for a *Promise* of *Success* in our Affairs." Beyond this general declaration, Mather affirmed as much for a Christian's personal and specific calling. Here Christians should be distinguished by their *"Usefulness"* because God had made each a *"Sociable* Creature." So every Christian should have "some *Settled Business."* Such business callings offered various services to a Christian's neighbors, including some that served "their *Delights."* Nor should Christians be without personal delight, since Mather instructed readers that "a Christian should have it contrived, That his *Calling* be *Agreeable*, as well as *Allowable."* Moreover, Christians should get ahead. Ambition for success was godly and good, even as it meant hard work. "Would a man *Rise by* his Business? I say, then let him *Rise to* his Business." Citing Proverbs 22:29 ("Seest thou a man diligent in his business? He shall stand before kings, he shall not stand before mean *men*"), Mather exulted at the "marvellous things" that business diligence would bring. Reiterating his message about the positive rewards of business success, he emphasized the "Contentment" the Christian's personal calling should deliver. It was the "singular Favour of God, unto a man, That he can attend his *Occupation* with *Contentation* and *Satisfaction."* "Stick to your *Business*," Mather urged, "and leave it with God, how you shall succeed in your *Business."* There was no need to fear "Starving," for God was there, and so the *"Harvest"* would come.[3]

Returning to at least part of the message of *Two Brief Discourses* in *Bonifacius* (1710), Mather offered substantive advice to the rich. As one would suspect, given his own spiritual commitments, Mather emphasized that the rich should be rich in doing good. It was God who gave *"Power to Get Wealth,"* a *"Sovereign GOD"* who had "bestow'd" distinguishing riches. Thus, it followed that, familiarly, wealth was a sign of blessing. Still further, those who knew intuitively how to acquire property and possessions should be busy getting rich. Speaking directly to the wealthy who might be reading, Mather told them "That the Riches in your possession are some of the Talents, whereof you must give an Account unto the Glorious LORD." *"Whoever buries his Talent,"* Mather cautioned, *"Breaks a Sacred Trust."* All of a rich person's estate should, obviously, be put to *"Honest Uses,"* but, more, part of it should go to *"Pious Uses."* Hence, tithes or "tenths" were the order of the day in Mather's advice. He did not fail to notice, too, the frequency with which tithers had "been Rewarded with a strange Success, and Increase of their Estates." They had "even in this World" experienced the fulfillment of scriptural promise. To wit: *"Cast thy Grain into the moist Ground; for thou shalt find it after many dayes.* And in another biblical word: *Honour the Lord with thy Substance; so shall thy Barns be filled with Plenty."* Mather, in effect, was doling out advice on how to get richer—just tithe and then some, and you will reap your material reward. "This I will tell," he confided, that "they who have conscientiously employ'd their *Tenths* in *Pious Uses*, have usually been Blessed in their Estates, with a very Remarkable Providence of God."[4]

Mather's assumptions regarding wealth as divine blessing are scattered throughout his writings, often as asides to other points he was making. As early as 1689, for example, Mather's published sermon *The Way to Prosperity* (which in keeping with Mather's own commitments consistently spiritualized the idea of prosperity) still could give its nod to the earthly version. Mather was preaching to a convention of the governor, council, and representatives of the Massachusetts Bay Colony, and he carefully quoted scripture to make his point that "if the Lord be *with* a people, they shall prosper in all their Affairs." "In every *Expedition*," he declared, "they shall come off with Satisfaction; and they shall not miscarry in any of their *Applications*." More than two decades later, as Mather spoke for exuberant prosperity in Salem and other towns, he invoked "*Mighty Angels*," "a *Multitude of the Heavenly Host*," and "the Enthroned JESUS" to affirm the "*Showers of Blessing from Heaven*" that would "be always falling." When God took up his habitation there, he would "grant much *Prosperity* to such a Town." It was clear in what followed that the riches Mather had in mind were spiritual, but nonetheless prosperity remained a good thing. Similarly, in *A Man of Reason* (1718), as Mather declaimed on "Assertions of *Practical Religion*," he moved from acknowledging "a GOD, the *Maker & Ruler* of the World" to Reason's message that "all our *Enjoyments*, are the *Blessings* and *Favours* of GOD."[5]

It is true that Mather was not always so sure. Indeed, David Levin's searching study of Mather explored the tension between Mather's celebration of divine blessing and prosperity, on the one hand, and his testimony to decline (or "declension") and tribulation on the other. The year following the death of his father, Increase, for example, the bereaved son published a biography of his famous father (1724). Grief was surely prevailing in Mather's emotional register as he lamented that "our SAVIOUR has no where promised a *Temporal Prosperity*, unto a Life of Piety." Instead, Jesus had "bid us look for the Discipline of the *Cross*, and . . . told us, *That through much Tribulation we must enter into the Kingdome of GOD*." As Levin shows, during Mather's later years, as he experienced his own personal time of declension, he projected the personal onto the public and political. But Mather's bipolar view was not simply a product of his own decline. As Levin argues, Mather's "fundamental uncertainty" influenced his monumental history of New England from 1620 to 1698, grandly called *Magnalia Christi Americana* and published in 1702. The uncertainty underlined a "pattern of alternation" already noticeable "in Mather's personal view of New England's fortunes during the first thirty years of his own life." Levin, however, went on to acknowledge that "faith in the progressive destiny of the Lord's people" predominated. "Even the jeremiad," he remarked, assumed "that God will restore His favor if His people truly reown their covenant with Him."[6]

Prosperity, moreover, leads implicitly, and sometimes explicitly, into the territory of desire. Writing for another century and in another context, Kate Bowler still had words to say that apply to Mather and his prosperity project. In the midst of inner dissonance regarding material abundance, he had, as Bowler said of certain twentieth-century American Protestants, "found a religious language of desire." It was a language in which desire was "coupled with the comfort that God ordered both the supernatural and mundane"—in his own life and in the life of his society. That desire was best when it was satiated and fulfilled. Mather once told a convention of ministers that living usefully meant living *"Pleasantly."* "There is a virtuous *Epicurism* in *Usefulness*," he sermonized. "No *Epicure* can swim in such Delights, as the Man that is *useful* wherever he comes." The theme of service as source of delight (desire fulfilled) seems a far cry from concerns of delight makers in a twenty-first-century world. But the Epicurean reference signals an aspect of Mather's vision that moved substantially beyond stereotypical portrayals and points a way to a coming theology of abundance and in-the-body pleasure. Robert Middlekauff, in fact, began the section devoted to Cotton Mather in his three-generational study of the Mathers with a chapter called "The Virtuous Epicure," citing Cotton Mather's own words in this sermon.[7]

The language of desire opens gates to an entirely different side of Mather than do portraits of him as an Enlightenment-leaning polymath. As Middlekauff points out, Mather's phrase "the desire for Grace argues the Presence of Grace" was a frequent refrain for the supposedly emotionally restrained Puritan. Still more, Mather wrote in a context in which some views of desire deemed it a physical phenomenon connected to the bowels in the human body. For Mather, with his unconventional use of psychological ideas about human faculties, affectional—or emotional—transformation became evidence of an inner change in which reason taught the will, which in turn led the affections. Desire for grace that was in itself grace became the external sign of inner conversion—a kind of sacrament of a rebuilt self. Beyond that, desire was joined to love. As Middlekauff remarked, "a true longing for salvation did not transpire in a selfish spirit." Involving "a profound yearning for union with God," so-called "pious desires" became the work of "the Holy Spirit of God." They reflected an "aching need" to be merged with the divine. *"Oh! Could I so far be swallowed up in Him, and with His Love, as to be glad when He is Glorified, tho' there should be much of my own Misery and*

Confusion in it." And "Here *Life* comes on. The *Love of* GOD brings on the *Life of* GOD."⁸

Mather, indeed, had reservations about the scope of human reason and, as Middlekauff noted, urged the importance of feeling. By the time Mather got ready to publish *The Christian Philosopher* in 1715, he was expressing his reticence. Argued Middlekauff, Mather hoped "that experience might reduce men's pride, stimulate them to reform society, and lead them into the Christian Union that would greet the return of Christ. Experience would do all this—but not the experience of the creatures, nor the experience grasped by reason, rather the direct and immediate experience of the Holy Spirit."⁹

We have arrived at the territory of evangelicalism and pietism. Here it is that Richard F. Lovelace's memorable study details a persuasive case for Mather as "the leading synthesist of the Puritan past in America and the most representative pre-Revivalist during his lifetime." Mather, wrote Lovelace, was "a passionate enemy of the new rationalism, although he was willing to use some of its terminology in order to reach and hold his audience." Surveying "the total context of Mather's statements about the use of reason," Lovelace concluded unequivocally that Mather was "not a rationalist in the eighteenth-century sense." He was following in venerable historian Sidney Mead's footsteps, since Mead saw Mather's work fanning the spark that would engulf the Northampton pulpit of Jonathan Edwards as pure revival flame.¹⁰

In this vein, even a casual perusal of Mather's *Christian Philosopher* underlines the part of its subtitle that reads *"with Religious Improvements."* Chapter after chapter ends, not with reason, but with ecstatic affirmations of the God who made it all to be. The prose of affirmation is, ostensibly, deist in tone, with virtually no reference to Jesus the Christ or the mysteries of Christian redemption. Still, withal, its tone is, to use the evangelical term, pietistic in its emotional expressiveness and exclamations of heartfelt praise. Perhaps the pietism is nowhere more clearly demonstrated than in Mather's chapter on "man," whose very body is called "a *Machine* of a most astonishing Workmanship and Contrivance!" So astonishing, in fact, as to induce Mather's enthusiastic expression of praise (one of many in this ever-effusive work): *"My God, I will praise Thee, for I am strangely and wonderfully made!"* Thus, even as Mather provides technical information on the human body, his chapter is couched throughout in language of rapture and profound feeling. So it is no surprise, really, that as capstone for his literary creation, at the end of *The Christian Philosopher* Mather quotes British physician, philosopher, and almost-psychologist George Cheyne: "Thus from what occurs throughout the whole Creation, *Reason* forms an imperfect Idea of this incomprehensible Mystery."[11]

Underlining this revelation of Mather's inner life, early twentieth-century authors Ralph and Louise Boas observed that his writings reveal a Mather who used his religion "to rationalize his desires." They see his lengthy and searching diary as not "a record of what happened" but rather "a record of what he felt." And fifty years later, David Levin could remark that by 1679 the early Mather was already "an impassioned agent of pietism," linking the pietism to his concern for doing good.[12] Moreover, such doing of good concerned Mather seemingly endlessly—perhaps nowhere testified more than in his *Bonifacius*. Still further, the theme was present almost continuously in sermon after sermon that pointed meticulously to the "uses" of Mather's message.

But, to return to *The Christian Philosopher*, there is another trajectory we can follow—away from deeds of virtue and toward an aesthetic sensitivity. Read from this perspective, for all its invocations of science and analysis of facts and figures on the natural world of Mather's day, *The Christian Philosopher* is a celebration of divine beauty. By seeing God in the details, Mather created an encyclopedic panorama as a hymn to the beautiful as much as, or more than, to factual knowledge. Detail became a homeopathic aid to reveal the stunning symmetry and aesthetic intricacy of the world. Discerning the aesthetic "plot" of the work, as early as 1907, historian of philosophy I. Woodbridge Riley acknowledged that *The Christian Philosopher* had "not the cold tone of extreme rationalism." Rather, it exhibited a "phase of deistic development" that made the "external world" a site of "growing interest." "Because of the author's love of mysticism," Riley declared, "that interest is less scientific than aesthetic." Mather, Riley summarized, possessed "a thorough appreciation of the beautiful." In effect, well before Perry Miller ever drew a line from Jonathan Edwards to Ralph Waldo Emerson, Riley was drawing one from Mather to the American Transcendentalists. *The Christian Philosopher* "with its scientific arguments for design, fell flat," Riley observed. "But its aesthetic element lived on; it anticipated by a century the transcendentalists' love of nature for its own sake. In fine, Mather would have agreed with Emerson when he said, 'Come into the azure and love the day.'"[13]

Riley, in fact, elaborated in ways that set the stage for Miller. "From Edwards to Emerson there is a line of Platonizers who looked at the natural through the bright lens of the supernatural," he explained. These were "'analogy-loving souls'" with their penchant for seeing "double meaning in all events." Theirs was "a poetic spirit of interpretation" that "impregnated the New England mind for two hundred years." Where, for Riley, could it be found? On his short list was, as we might expect, Mather's *Christian Philosopher*.[14]

It is not difficult to locate Mather's controlling scheme within this aesthetic framework. First, Mather provided an exposition (heavily based on the work of a small stable of scientific worthies) of the empirical knowledge of the day regarding each natural phenomenon. Then, as point of it all, he searched for a message of moral improvement, and, finally, he expressed abundant praise for the God who made each part of the world—hailing through it all the beauteous splendor of nature. For example, there was the case of fish. After a recitation of technical information on these creatures of the sea, Mather was ready for moral improvement and then for praise. He remembered a *"Crassus"* who tamed a fish in a pond to come when called. What did this anecdote tell Mather? "I shall have a Soul deserving *his Name*, and be more stupid than the *Fish*, if I do not hear the Calls which the *Fish* give to me to glorify the God that made them; and who has in their *Variety*, in their *Multitude*, in their *Structures*, their *Dispositions* and *Sagacities*, display'd his Glories."[15]

With the aesthetic dimension clearly visible (as the fish show), a preference for analogy—based on the age-old theory of correspondence between the large world of the macrocosm and the small, microcosmic world of humans—shot through Mather's thinking. One conceptual place to which such analogical thinking leads is deism. If, in symmetry with Platonic idealism, the supernatural may be seen within the natural world, God need not act by miraculous intervention in the natural order. Divinity is simply reflected in nature's established course. Still, as we will see, Mather's vision extended beyond the Platonic logic and, for his age, its deistic result. His ambivalence—his straddling of pietism and deism—could work because a more basic synthesis was controlling his mentality. His particular way of thinking about correspondence shaped his abiding vision of cosmology, history, religion, and personal existence in a body. More to the point here, although the fact is not often recognized, thinking analogically meant thinking aesthetically. In a Western culture shaped profoundly by ancient Greek notions of harmony and proportion, the theory of correspondence provided a framework to impose upon the data of material existence—on events and substances and all that lay between. Even for disruptive and decidedly unlovely occurrences and attitudes, thinking in terms of correspondence colored reality with an artist's brush. Like an hourglass turned prism turned rainbow, a fundamental beauty lurked beneath the ugly and rendered it, in a strange way, satisfying and pleasing.

To cite only a few examples of this analogical process (and its underlying aesthetic), typically Mather applied doctrinal notions of providence and punishment to contemporary happenings and even autobiographical ones. The poetry implicit, for example, in a thunderbolt striking a sinner who had blasted fellow humans through greed and hate could work deistically or not, but its fundamental aesthetic persisted. When the Boston meetinghouse burned in a terrible accident, Mather linked the fire to the "fiery sins" of Bostonians before the catastrophe. More personally, when his *Diary* revealed that he suffered "tormenting Pains" in his "*Teeth* and *Jawes*," he asked himself, "Have I not sinned with my Teeth? How? By sinful, graceless excessive *Eating*. And by evil Speeches, for there are *Literae dentales* in them?"[16]

Mather's writing exuded correspondence with a vengeance. As a small gem that crystallizes his way of looking and seeing, we can examine Mather's "Appendix Touching Prodigies," which he published at the end of his sermon *The Way to Prosperity*. Meaningful coincidences abounded in the short appendix, and the prodigious was, in short, synchronistic. An "*Earth-quake* in the "*Southern* Parts of the Countrey" presaged "our late Vexations." Meanwhile, "in the Summer of the Year, 1688, just before the first eruption of our unhappy War, we had growing in *Boston* a Cabbage Root, out of which there sprouted . . . very wonderful Branches." One of them exactly resembled "a *Rapier*," and another was "extreamly like to the *Club* used by the *Indians* in their Barbarous Executions." Manifestly, nature was telling of war, and one did not need to read tea leaves when such signs were writ large in the cosmos.[17]

To emphasize the point, the winter of the same year brought "a *Red Snow*, which lay like Blood on a spot of Ground, not many miles from *Boston*." Ever the analogist—even in historical terms—Mather could not resist adding that "the *Bloody Shower* that went before the suffering of the ancient *Britains* from the Picts, (a sort of People that painted themselves like our *Indians*) this Prodigy seem'd a second Edition of." Then, on October 1, 1689, additional unmistakable prodigies appeared, "not unlike those which *Pliny* mentions as *presages* to the *Cimbric* Wars of old." It was on that morning, with a sky too clear to suggest any approaching thunder, that "there suddenly Blazed a *Flame* in the fashion of a *Sword*; which Blaze after a continuance, far longer than that of an ordinary *Lightning*, expired in a smoke that gave Terror unto the Beholders of it." And there was more. Immediately came "very terrible and Repeated Noises, exactly like *Volleys* of *small Shot*, not without *Reports* like those of *Great Guns* superadded thereunto." People more than a hundred miles away saw and heard the same thing, confided Mather. "*This* was a Scene which all the Colonies of this large Countrey, and

Thousands of People, at once were Spectators of, carrying in it, *something*, beyond the *known Laws* which ordinary *Meteors* are Conform'd unto." He assured readers that, even with the follies of the human imagination of which he was well aware, in this case "no small Numbers of Gentlemen, who do not use to be *imposed* upon" were surprised enough to say "as with one mouth" that *"The Finger of God was here."*[18]

In short, from the inscrutable majesty of the skies to graphic details concerning his own body, Mather saw the world under the rubric of correspondence. And all of it taught, in its fundamental aesthetic, of divine things. To underline the point of just this sort of comprehensiveness, we can do no better than to look to Mather's unpublished "autobiography," *Paterna*, which he wrote ostensibly for the instruction and edification of his son Increase. Unembarrassed by bodily processes, *Paterna* contains, for example, this piece of enlightenment in the service of righteousness: "I Resolved, that my Attendance on the Excretory Necessities of Nature, should be Still accompanied, with some Holy Thoughts of a Repenting and an Abased Soul." Because "Urinary Excretions" happened "often" daily, Mather was grateful for not suffering from "Nephritic and Ischuriac Miseries" [i.e., kidney and bladder troubles]. As well, the "Humiliation" that Mather linked to these processes led him "to think with wonderment" of the Savior's work in his behalf. "Wherefore, when I am obliged at any time, unto ye Urinary Discharges," he confessed that he would think on both of these themes. "My God, I bless thee for Saving me from ye terrible Diseases of the Wheel broken at the Cistern." And then, "IESUS; Wilt thou ever bring this Vile Body, to the glories & the Blessings of the Heavenly places!"[19]

Premonitions especially assumed importance in Mather's analogical way of thinking. Like his father Increase, he employed the term "Particular Faith" to identify the way that God used the synchronous and even the visionary to foreshow favorable events to follow. David Levin explained: "Both father and son called the favorable version of such specific premonitions a Particular Faith, a conviction that Providence would allow the faithful believer a particular benefit." Levin went on: "Those who experienced the Particular Faith took pains to distinguish it from more nearly ordinary premonitions or coincidences."[20]

Correspondence, thus, controlled vision, and—to move to the social dimension of the rubric—vision controlled history, or more properly history writing. Mather's monumental *Magnalia Christi Americana*, which I cited earlier—his far-reaching ecclesiastical chronicle concerning the Massachusetts Bay colony and nearby New England settlements—is a large-scale exhibit of Mather's way of thinking and of writing history. Outside the intimate world of "Particular Faith," *Magnalia* still brought much more than linear and developmental history. It was episodic and often biographical in its account of events, containing material from diaries and extant manuscript histories by William Bradford and William Hubbard as well as Mather's father's correspondence and his own sermons and other publications.[21] More than that, its overall framework was built on analogy, premonition, and correspondence, rendering the whole an aesthetic composition.

Mather's epic vision for a narrative was captured in his grandiose opening, which echoed the ancient Roman poet Virgil's *Aeneid*: "I sing of arms and the man, who first from the Trojan coast, exiled by fate, came to the Lavinian shores." As Mather initially proclaimed, "I WRITE the WONDERS of the CHRISTIAN RELIGION, flying from the depravations of Europe, to the American Strand." With classic scope and baroque magnificence echoing in his authorial plan, Mather—no doubt aided by the sporadic and piecemeal nature of his sources—wandered elsewhere. The general introduction to its seven books already suggests that this epic narrative would be far from seamless. If Divine Providence had "irradiated an Indian Wilderness" as Mather declared, the story of what happened as outlined here seems more like a stage play with various separated acts and intermezzos than a developmentally connected tale.[22] That tale began well enough—with a first book titled "Antiquities" that offered an account of the original settlement of New England, not without attention to ominous warnings and divine deliverances constructed according to the familiar rubric of correspondence. These were already expressed in Mather's sources, the William Bradford account of Plymouth colony being the most familiar to twenty-first century audiences.

But Mather's general introduction already indicates that he intended to tell the story of the American settlement with special attention to its leaders. He would occupy a series of books introducing actors who were preponderantly magistrates and especially ministers. They were trotted on stage in biographical format—not without confiding "Remarkable Occurrences" (read analogical events) in their "exemplary" lives. Next came the "Notables of the only Protestant University that ever *shone* in that hemisphere of the New World," as Harvard's leaders stood for their bow. Only after acquainting readers with a seemingly endless cast of important characters did Mather shift his gaze in his fifth book to study collective events. Here were the "*Actions* of a more eminent importance," the work of synods and the evolution of church discipline, with Mather's signal that the drama would become explosive. He warned of "the Disturbances, with which they have been from all sorts of temptations and enemies tempestuated," even as he soothed readers with allusions to "the Methods by which they have still weathered out each horrible tempest." Then, as if he had come too close to a narrative and developmental story, Mather introduced a sixth book to tie the drama securely to an aesthetic frame of divine-human correspondence: "Into the midst of these Actions, I interpose an entire Book, wherein there is, with all possible veracity, a Collection made of Memorable Occurrences, and amazing Judgments and Mercies befalling many particular persons among the people of New-England." Mather's final book, on "the Wars of the Lord," returned to a collective chronicle as he recounted "Afflictive Disturbances which the Churches of New-England have suffered from their various adversaries; and the Wonderful Methods and Mercies, whereby the Churches have been delivered."[23]

It is Mather's sixth book of *Magnalia*, which he titled significantly enough "Thaumaturgus," or "performer of miracles," that especially must occupy us here. Mather's table of contents notified readers that "it contains many Illustrious Discoveries and Demonstrations of the Divine Providence, in Remarkable Mercies and Judgments on many particular persons among the people of New-England." Running 148 pages of the 651 in the Hartford edition of 1853, the hefty size signaled the importance of what Mather needed to tell. And as if to underline the correspondential rubric that governed it, the seventh chapter of this book—titled *"Thaumatographia Pneumatica"* and telling of "the Wonders of the Invisible World, in Preternatural Occurrences"—contributed 41 pages to the total.[24] No doubt the extended nature of this sixth book and its final chapter was encouraged by the circumstances of *Magnalia's* origins. Initially, Mather's father, Increase, had been preoccupied with constructing a history of New England, and others had urged him to do so. By 1694, Increase along with the president and fellows of Harvard University and other ministers, had issued a call for material for such a history. In the instruction that went out, proposals asked for "the things to be esteemed *memorable*" and then spelled out what they were: "especially all *unusual accidents* in the heaven, or earth , or water" along with *"deliverances," "mercies,"* and *"judgments"* as well as the fulfillment of scripture. Accompanying all of this should be *"apparitions, possessions, inchantments,* and all extraordinary things wherein the existence and agency of the *invisible world* is more sensibly demonstrated."[25]

Like father and his ministerial tribe, like son. Aesthetic symmetry would permeate Cotton's production, as even a casual perusal of its pages suggests. Of his entire sixth book, Cotton Mather intoned, "We will now write a book of rare occurrences, wherein a blind *fortune* shall not be once acknowledged." Indeed, "the use of it shall be confuted, as well as avoided, in the book now before us, wherein all the *rare occurrences* will be evident operations of the Almighty God, 'whose kingdom ruleth over all.'" Mather's organizational plan for the chapters of this book seems at first glance odd. He introduced, first, wonders relating to sea deliverances, then a catch-all chapter of "Remarkable Salvations" for others who were not "Sea-faring," and after that a chapter "Relating to Remarkables done by Thunder." From heaven back to earth, Mather now explored the phenomenon of the prodigal returned to divine alignment (i.e., correspondence) with tales of "Remarkable Conversions." Criminals and offenders came next in this catalog, as divine judgments matched and upended their deeds, and their dying speeches reflected the grand analogy in which, through their heinous actions, they had participated. Indians trailed not far behind in the next chapter, as if to balance the work of evil with the success of the gospel among native peoples. Here, with special attention to Martha's Vineyard, Mather offered an appendix "relating Things Greatly Remarkable, fetched from one little Island of Christianiz'd Indians." At last now, Mather was ready for his extended capstone "*Thaumatographia Pneumatica*," his spiritual grab-bag of all that he could not insert elsewhere, with witchcraft figuring prominently in the contacts between the invisible world and New England everyday life.[26]

Closer attention to this seemingly erratic plan, however, reveals its aesthetic grid, its bared "plotline" that began with cosmology—the mysterious sea, which was a place where the event-centered world of human society gave way before the inscrutable and uncontrollable. On land, too, the cosmological made its mark in symmetry with God's saving power. There were "*swarms of caterpillars*" to devour fields. There were "desparate maladies" and "*droughts* or *floods*" to ruin harvests but "remarkable rescues from death." With Indians read as a force of nature, the ending account of Hannah Swarton's deliverance from them became an instance of the power of the gospel to match and tame.[27]

From this vantage point, the return to the heavens with a chapter on thunder seems no return at all. Cosmology gave an opportunity to see the plan of correspondence written with unmistakable letters. "The remarkable effects of thunder have been memorable subjects, upon which the pens of historians in all ages have been employed," Mather wrote. "And indeed, though the natural causes of the thunder are known unto us, yet there are those notable voices of the almighty God, often sensible in the directing thereof." New England, for Mather, had experienced its "mischiefs" aplenty, and "if things that are smitten by lightning were to be esteemed sacred, this were a sacred country." "Rarely a summer passes," he added, "without some strokes from the thunders, on the persons, or houses, or cattel of our people." He noticed, too, that "our *meeting-houses*, and our *ministers*' houses have had a singular share in the strokes of thunders." These observations provided the occasion for Mather to insert his own sermon *Brontologica Sacra: The Voice of the Glorious God in the Thunder* into the text of the *Magnalia*.[28] The divine symmetry was immediately apparent: "Let not your attention to the thunder at this instant *abroad*, interrupt your further attention to the greater and louder thunder here-within." "The 'voice of God,'" Mather declared, was "far beyond that *voice* which is now making its rapid peals in the skie."[29]

It was only after detailing the hand and voice of God in a cosmology that moved from sea to sky that Mather paid closer attention to the poetics of evil. Here entered the prodigal sons, offenders, criminals, "savage" Indians—whose "powaws" had "familiarity with infernal spirits"[30]—and then witches and evil spirits among white New Englanders. In each account, we read of the wonderful providence of God, matching the offense with its symmetrical counterpart in disruption and danger, often as an aesthetic ploy to transform the situation and the sinner. If, for example, we dip into the final chapter of thaumaturgies, Mather's underlying vision was transparent. He confided to readers near the beginning that "the Christians who were driven into the American desert, which is now call'd New-England, have to their sorrow seen Azazel dwelling and raging there." With devils thus occupying the land, "molestations from *evil spirits* . . . have so abounded in this countrey, that I question whether any one town has been free from *sad examples* of them."[31]

If Mather was putting Salem village into larger context, he had abundant material for the task. Linking Leviticus 16:8–10, with its declaration of a scapegoat for sin sent into the wilderness to the fallen angel Azazel, Mather had found Azazel's demonic home in the rocky soil of New England. There was Ann Cole of Hartford, with the witch who possessed her executed, and Elizabeth Knap of Groton, who cried out upon the evils instigated by a neighbor woman. Knap had "taken after a very strange manner; sometimes weeping, sometimes laughing, sometimes roaring, with violent agitation, crying out 'Money! Money!'" There was, too, William Morse of Newberry, who seems to the modern reader the victim of poltergeist phenomena. "*Bricks*, and *sticks*, and *stones*, were often by some invisible hand thrown at the house, and so were many pieces of wood: a cat was thrown at the woman of the house, and a *long staff* danc'd up and down in the chimney." Similarly, Nicholas Desborough of Hartford "was very strangely molested by stones, by pieces of earth, by cobs of Indian corn, and other such things, from an invisible hand, thrown at him." And George Walton of Portsmouth experienced "showers of stones" that "were thrown by an invisible hand" upon his house. The catalog of infamy and insult continued, incorporating in its thirteen examples (the witches' number?) a lengthy account of the four children of John Goodwin of Boston. They had been religiously "educated," and known to all for their "piety, honesty and industry," but became possessed by "something *diabolical*." Mather had taken the eldest child into his own household, and there she was finally exorcised by him with the help of other ministers and their prayers and fasts.[32]

The laundress to the Goodwin household, Irish and Catholic, became a new scapegoat, enduring confusion, blame, and ultimately execution as a witch.[33] As in the case of Indians, Mrs. Glover had revealed the unconscious fears of New England's culture. Cut off from old England and cast into an uncontrolled wilderness that howled and roared, Mather and his allies found "invisible" forces of evil and their embodiment in real people—some as malicious agents of the diabolical and others as their victims. The stories Mather told were, typically, narratives of confrontation between good and evil. They were pitched battles in which good ever triumphed, often after long and anguished combat. At the same time, their aesthetic frame is clear. Wild New England country corresponded to biblical evil. Wild Indians and Catholics echoed the savage horrors of the landscape. And among New Englanders, the presence of collective sin, as in biblical times, weakened good Christian folk and rendered them vulnerable to alien forces.

It is a short step, if a step at all, into the territory of metaphysical religiosity. Both the *Magnalia* and *The Christian Philosopher* are maps of Mather's mind, and much—if not most—of that mind was metaphysical. Mather saw portentous (and demonically mediated) signs in astrology and in the predictions of fortune tellers. His accounts of New England's governors—to take one example—were filled with observations and asides that witnessed his ideological leanings.[34] With the theory and practice of correspondence a central and controlling insight, Mather was primed for visitations from the invisible world, as their energies rained upon the land and people of New England. Here the power of mind ruled supreme, channeled and funneled for Mather and his ministerial colleagues by the Christian practice of prayer. Still more, the prayer of devout Christians became a salve to soothe away the wilderness and its frights, to heal the ruptures and fissures that separation from old England had created. No surprise, therefore, that Mather spent time not only with demons in the person of witches and their victims in Salem and elsewhere but also with angels. In fact, the stereotype of Salem witchcraft that has so colored Cotton Mather's portrait in the popular record leaves his equal and stronger traffic with angels mostly unnoticed and underexplored.

"Let the Heart be full of *Heaven*," Mather wrote, "and it won't be full of Satan . . . Let us be *filled* . . . with Meditations about the *Fulness* and Glory and Beauty that is in the Almighty God." Mather's counsel pointed toward an aesthetic of angels that was an aesthetic of light—and that also acknowledged the dark. Seen from the encompassing perspective of the complete Christian mystery, "good" angels signaled the profound contrast with darkness and evil that lurked in the demonic kingdom. In fact, Mather's invocation of the *"Fulness* and Glory and Beauty that is in the Almighty God" came in the context of a sermon he called *"Batteries upon the Kingdom of the Devil."* So there were evil angels, and Mather saw their spirits and acts in the witchcraft he discovered seemingly everywhere. But in the words of Richard Lovelace, who alluded to the "mystical dimension of Mather's thought and experience," contact with the supernatural was a given in his personal universe. "Mather felt that vital spiritual experience involved not only the sensible awareness of contact with God himself through the ministry of the indwelling Spirit but also the apprehension of other spirits, both good and evil," wrote Lovelace.[35]

According to Lovelace, too, Mather's view of angels was founded on his view of Jesus—"as Jehovah, the Lord of Hosts, surrounded and worshipped by a heavenly court containing innumerable gatherings both of natural and supernatural creatures." Such ideas already hint of what would become characteristic views of a mediated divine presence—that is, mediated by figures other than/more than Jesus—that shaped nineteenth-century Swedenborgian adoptions and later metaphysics. For Mather, though, what mattered most was the experiential. He wanted to contact angels, and he wanted to do that strongly. By 1693, a year after the Salem witchcraft epidemic had swept Mather's world, he began longing for communication with angels as never before. He had lived through a long and arduous connection with one Mercy Short—possessed and warning Mather of demonic assaults on himself and his family, and then depossessed with the aid of good angels. Now Mather prayed and fasted to attract angelic favor. Kenneth Silverman has remarked that Mather's prayer work to attract angels was "highly unusual for a Puritan," because, as he explains, "since the time of Christ, according to the general Reformed [Calvinist] position, good angels, but not evil angels, had ceased to appear."[36]

Reformed tradition, however, did not deter Mather. And he began to get results, at first experiences of angelic guidance and protection—and then more. In September or October of 1693, Mather recorded in his diary "'*Res Mirabilis Et Memoranda*,' a strange and memorable thing." Mather saw an angel "whose face shone like the noonday sun. . . . His garments were white and shining; his robe reached to his ankles; and about his loins was a belt not unlike the girdles of the peoples of the East." The diaries would be employed again. Writing for the edification of his son Increase (and no doubt others), Mather confided his passion and something of its results in *Paterna*. "On a certain Day of <u>Prayer</u> with <u>Fasting</u>, which I kept in the Thirty-first year of my Age [ca. 1693–1694], my <u>Special Errand</u> unto the Lord was, <u>This</u>: That whereas His <u>Good Angels</u> did by <u>His Order</u>, many <u>Good Offices</u> for His people, He would please to grant unto me, the Enjoyment of those <u>Angelical</u> Kindnesses and Benefits, which use to be done by <u>His Order</u>, for His <u>Chosen Servants</u>."[37]

In the perennial manner of mystics, Mather would only share the edges of his experience: "<u>My Son</u>, It is <u>not Lawful for me to utter</u>, the marvelous and amazing Favours, which I have Since received from ye Blessed ANGELS. I have Seen, and felt, most wonderful Effects of their <u>Ministry</u>. . . . I have as infallible Demonstration of the Existence and Agency of those <u>Heavenly Spirits</u>, as I have to prove any matter of <u>Sense</u> in the world." Mather could not say more. He could not forget his "promise of <u>Concealing</u> Such Things as are not proper to be Exposed." He also recounted an instance in which he believed an angel had kept him out of harm's way by striking him with temporary illness so that he could not board a disease-infested ship squadron from the West Indies to preach. Thereafter, in Latin, he alluded to the resplendent angelic vision of his diary. "At another time, and in another place," Mather declared, "tis possible, <u>My Son</u>, I may tell you <u>more</u>. All that I will here Say, is: Be Sure to Beleeve, That there are <u>Holy Angels</u>, and Behave yourself So Holily that ye <u>Good Angels</u> may take pleasure to do you Good." He went on to warn that Increase should "keep close to the <u>Written Word of God</u>" and should "affect not <u>Extraordinary Dispensations</u>," which might bring "Delusions and Confusions, of ye worst Consequence imaginable."[38]

As Silverman wrote regarding the angelic incident, the visitor brought a multiple message, but in its midst the caller prophesied Mather's great work for the church at a revolutionary time. Still more, Mather's angelic preoccupation shared the stage with his father's. Increase Mather, needing to decide on an invitation by Governor William Phips to represent Massachusetts in England, started reading avidly about angels and preached a series of sermons on angelology that lasted until February 1694. Cotton Mather took notes.[39] So began a nearly ten-year period of what Kenneth Silverman called "heightened psychic awareness." As Silverman assessed, it was not clear whether Mather's angelic visitor returned during the time. Mather was wary of confiding such experiences to paper, and his diaries for 1694 and 1695 are lost. But, wrote Silverman, whether or not they appeared, the angels "at least came close." In 1697, on his birthday, Mather felt the rapture of a quasi-mystical experience testifying, apparently, to angelic support for his ministry, and on another occasion he felt that he had received the promise of a future angelic visit.[40]

It was, in fact, in this time of heightened interest in angelic experience that Mather had become preoccupied with premonitory Particular Faiths, which, as we have seen, he held to be different from ordinary intuitions or coincidental happenings. Bound up with angelic energies, Particular Faiths assumed millennialist proportions. By 1711, "late strange Extasies and Prophecies" in Britain and southern France moved him to an impassioned desire for divine intervention. If God would but "order a Descent of His holy *Angels* to enter and possess His Ministers, and cause them to speak with the Tongues of Men under the energy of *Angels*, and fly thro' the World with the *everlasting Gospel* to preach unto the Nations, wonderful Things would be done immediately." Writing thus brought to Mather's mind a "strong Impression." "*They are coming! They are coming! They are coming! They will quickly be upon us; and the World shall be shaken wonderfully!*"[41]

In the midst of Mather's premillennial euphoria—his belief that Jesus would come before the millennium, when the world as we know it would end—we need to acknowledge, too, that he saw angels as both good *and* evil. Significantly, he construed the bad ones as evil spirits who often kept witches in league with themselves. Mather confessed at least once in a sermon to his congregation regarding the possessed Goodwin children that there was "Mention of Creatures that they call *White Whitches*, which do only *Good-Turns* for their Neighbours. I suspect that there are none of that sort." As Ralph and Louise Boas remarked, Mather spent considerable time "circumventing the wiles of the devil, whose evil presence he forever suspected, especially at those times when he was inclined to be most happy." For him, good angels, devils, and God himself were all of a cosmological piece. If he denied one, he jeopardized the entire theological system.[42]

Such acknowledgments lead in two directions. On the one hand, they burrow us deeply into the journal-keeping and other spiritual acts that structured Mather's spirituality—not too different, if probably more intense, than the practices of his New England contemporaries. On the other, they enlarge our critical vision to grasp the quasi-vitalistic underpinnings of Mather's mind. His theological system was a construction in which spirit and matter were intricately and luminously connected.

Mather's journal-keeping—his voluminous diaries—reflect a Puritan practice inherited from a medieval spirituality that cherished mystical contact and self-scrutiny as a step toward attaining it. By journaling daily,

Mather examined his life and spiritual success (or not) repeatedly. But he also aimed to cultivate the feeling states that could usher him into something more than his own mind. Thus it was that, outside the confines of his diaries, he repeatedly employed ejaculatory prayer—short affirmative declarations of connection to God's presence, power, and grace and pleas for divine intervention. Mather had learned the practice from his father, and it is important to note that it carried social ballast. Mather told his diary that "it has been a frequent Thing with mee, to redeem the *silent*, and otherwise, *thoughtless*, Minutes of my Time, in shaping Thousands of *ejaculatory Prayers* for my Neighbours. . . . In passing along the *Street*, I have sett myself to *bless* thousands of persons, who never knew that I did it." On the basis of such reflections, Lovelace wrote that Mather's ejaculatory practice was "a simple expression of faith focused outward in a very real concern for others." In fact, Mather's *Paterna* spoke extensively to the point, as Mather detailed for his son outlines of the practice and provided pages of examples. Later, he instructed Increase in ways that transformed prayer petitions into "Ejaculatory Thanksgivings unto the Lord, upon all the Occasions which offered themselves unto me." He went on to edify his son with accounts of days of "Secret THANKSGIVINGS." On one such day, he endeavored "to fetch out of all sorts of Objects, that occasionally occurr'd unto me, occasions for Ejaculatory Thanksgivings. And perhaps many Scores of Hallelujahs were thus formed in the Intercalar, and Intervening Thoughts of the Day."[43] We have already seen an extension of this practice in the writing habits Mather employed in his *Christian Philosopher*, praising the almighty effusively after he reported on what was known technically about each natural phenomenon. The poetics of praise in his work were prolonged ejaculations meant to elicit corresponding feeling states in Mather and his readers.

Even more, as Lovelace assessed, Mather's "machinery of prayer" was pulling him out of Puritan insularity. It "almost led him beyond the wall separating Protestants and Catholics in his era and pointed the way toward the larger ecumenical sympathies of the future."[44] To specify in terms of a developing metaphysical religiosity, the shift from petition to thanksgiving to unconditioned praise in Mather's prayer work augurs what would happen in late nineteenth-century New Thought. Now spiritual seekers would shift from petition to thanksgiving to affirmation, along the way employing the practice of gratitude affirmatively. Prayer would become a stated declaration of the result intended, and the gratitude expressed would be an acknowledgment of divine favor as already granted, with a cultivation of the feeling state that accompanied a positive answer to prayer. In this world of metaphysical possibility, meaningful coincidences and synchronicities—like

Mather's Particular Faiths—would reign supreme. The "law of attraction" eventually would become a restatement of the law of correspondence as a metaphysical mantra.

Mather, though, already knew about synchronicities, and—if a rose by many names would smell as sweet—he also knew about the law of attraction. Kenneth Silverman with some bemusement wrote of Mather's "strange intimations and providential favors, sometime less cosmic than comic." Among them, weather cooperated when Mather traveled—with expected storms delayed until he reached home—and once when "Hundreds" of bears mysteriously swarmed the road to Ipswich, Mather met not a one. Suffering from heartburn, the idea occurred to him to apply a plaster to his chest, and the pain vanished. When Mather could not afford a new cloak, reflecting on Jesus stripped of his garments enroute to crucifixion and telling himself that he (Mather) would never be without a covering, "a woman in his congregation surprised him with a present of a handsome and costly cloak."[45]

So it went. In *The Christian Philosopher*, however, such personal favors were subsumed into a grand vision of design. Implicitly, the comic reveals itself to be governed, indeed, by the cosmological. With abundant help from George Cheyne, Mather reiterated Isaac Newton's three laws of motion and a corollary that concerned attraction. In Mather's exposition, "*Every Part* of every Body *attracts* or *gravitates* towards *every Part* of every other Body: But the *Force* by which one Part attracts another, in different Distances from it, is reciprocally as the *Squares* of those Distances; and at the same Distance, the *Force* of the Attraction or Gravitation of one Part towards divers others, is as the Quantity of Matter they contain." Nor did Mather forget. Later in his work, explaining the phenomenon of cohesion again with the help of Cheyne, he told readers that "the *Cement*, which hinders the Separation of Bodies, when the Points of their Surfaces are brought into Contact, . . . can be nothing but the *universal Law of Attraction*, whereby all the Parts of *Matter* endeavour to embrace one another." With this explanation, Mather had "gotten within a little of the Glorious GOD" and was ready for "the very *next Step*." We learn that "our *Globe*" was "kept well together by this wondrous Contrivance of the Creator, *Gravity*, or the *Power of Attraction*." The aesthetic of harmony and proportion is not hard to find in Mather's words: "By this Power also all the Parts of the *Globe* are kept in their proper Place and Order; all Bodies gravitating thereto do unite themselves with, and preserve the Bulk of them entire."[46]

Still further, there was magnetism—as Mather notes, "a Principle very different from that of *Gravity*." With its "Operations" mostly "discovered in the communion that *Iron* has with the *Loadstone*," he offered a long essay on the phenomenon, clearly fascinated by what he had found. We need not follow him through the essay's intricate reportage to arrive with him at its outcome. Here the law of attraction became, as I have already begun to suggest, a different expression of the law of correspondence. "In the *Loadstone* drawing and lifting up the *Iron*, behold thy *Saviour* drawing us to himself, and raising us above the secular Cares and Snares that ruin us."[47] The magnetic, the gravitational, and the powerfully attractive assume deep theological import beyond their testimony to the glory of the creator when we juxtapose them to Mather's Particular Faiths and meaningful coincidences. There was a power—a glue—linking and connecting all things material and mental in Mather's universe. He had learned, in a way, to operate it. And he had also learned, as we will see, to name it.

The inner work of journaling and praying incessantly, on the one hand, and the outer work of comprehending and celebrating the design in the universe, on the other, led Mather to a metaphysical vitalism that explained all. Now Mather could make sense of how the universe and all its functional parts and practices fit together and how personal life events and the workings of his own body were enclosed within a larger order. It was here that Mather's elegant bridging between spirit and matter dominated his thought and his world, and it is here that we encounter his Nishmath-Chajim. Simply put, the Nishmath-Chajim begins in Hebrew and in the biblical Book of Genesis as one of the names of God. In the King James Version, we read that "the LORD GOD formed man *of* the dust of the ground, and breathed into his nostrils the breath of life; and man became a living soul."[48] "Nishmath-Chajim"—the one who breathed life—became elided with the "breath of life" and its results in creating human beings as living souls (and by implication in creating other life forms).

For Mather, the Nishmath-Chajim provided an all-encompassing answer—a go-to construct—to deal with abiding questions concerning nonrational phenomena. Robert Middlekauff has observed that such phenomena included apparitions of the dead, witchcrafts and possessions, the Holy Spirit, and even "the puzzling capacity of birds to build nests without any apparent instruction."[49] Thus the expository power of the Nishmath-Chajim landed Mather squarely in the territory of divine immanence, of a mystical theology of presence that was tangible.

Mather reached the territory through circuitous paths. As early as 1693, as Kenneth Silverman noted, Mather's *Wonders of the Invisible World* was explaining witchcraft in a nontraditional way. Instead of simply construing it as a covenant with the devil, Mather invoked a "plastic spirit." "*Witchcraft* seems to be the Skill of Applying the *Plastic Spirit* of the World, unto some unlawful purposes, by means of a confederacy with *Evil Spirits*." Later that year, Mather encountered the possessed seventeen-year-old Mercy Short and speculated on the nature of "a Substance that seem'd like a Cat, or Dog" in her room. He saw it in terms of "an Innate Power"—a presence that could "attract suitable matter out of all Things for a Covering or Body, of a proportionable Form and Nature to itself." Then, by 1695, in the fallout from the witch trials of 1692 and his own compromised role in them, the embattled Mather sparred with Robert Calef—the same Calef who claimed to quote him at George Burrough's execution. As part of their exchange, Mather tried an indirect assault, writing a long letter ostensibly to another. In the treatise that resulted, Mather again identified a "plastic spirit" to explain the workings of the invisible world in that of flesh and matter. "There is a *Plastic Spirit* permeating of the World," he wrote, "which very powerfully operates upon the more corporeal parts of it." He added that the "*Angels*, both good and bad, are on the account of their *Natures*, the most Able of all creatures, to Apply that *Spirit* unto very many and mighty purposes."[50]

What was this plastic spirit, and how did Mather come by it? Silverman remarked that "the notion of a plastic spirit—essentially an old idea new-named, similar to classical ideas of a vegetative soul—had the allegiance of nearly every important thinker in England at the time. As a last hold on the supernatural, it appealed to those who, like Mather, recognized the new mechanistic picture of nature but clung to Christian belief."[51] Evidently the idea fascinated Mather, and he would continue to think with it and develop it. Over two decades later, we catch a fleeting glimpse of the result in Mather's *Coheleth* of 1720. Here he told readers that the "Departing soul" carried off with it "some Fine, Rare, Material *Vehicle*," which was "such as what the *Angels* do seem cloathed withal." It is in Mather's *Christian Philosopher* of the same year, however, that we gain a better sense of the process by which he arrived at his long-held conviction of a quasi-material substance joining body and spirit into one unified field.[52]

In a clear statement of his intellectual debt, Mather acknowledged as one of his two principal sources the English naturalist and sometime Anglican priest John Ray (1627–1705), a physico-theological thinker and writer who speculated on the "plastic nature" by means of which God executed the laws of motion. Building on seventeenth-century English Platonists at Cambridge, Ray looked to an immanent vital principle infusing the physical universe. For Ray, the "*plastick Nature*" explained why a stalk of fennel could not become an oak. Mather's twentieth-century editor Winton Solberg identified Ray as "the leading spokesman of biological vitalism." He remarked further that Mather's ideas of "the contrivance of God in the vegetables which grow on the earth was largely shaped by the biological vitalism of the Cambridge Platonists." Solberg especially named Henry More (1614–1687) and Ralph Cudworth (1617–1688) for their notion of "a spirit at work in the material world as a means of combating materialism and atheism."[53] Ray, Solberg declared, made the idea his own, and it confirmed the direction in which Mather had already been running.

By 1722, the plastic spirit had a name, and it was now the Nishmath-Chajim, effectively linking vitalism with its plastic spirit to a biblical source. Mather expressed his idea of the Nishmath-Chajim in his medical pamphlet *The Angel of Bethesda* of 1722—named for the angel of John 5:2–9, who at times visited the Jerusalem pool of Bethesda, charging the water so that it healed the first diseased person who entered thereafter. Mather's preoccupation continued. Two years later he pulled together material on medicine that had appeared in various places to produce a longer work that he also titled *The Angel of Bethesda* (unpublished during his lifetime). Later, in his "Triparadisus" of 1712, he explored the role of the Nishmath-Chajim in a "Second Paradise."[54]

As Mather's writing history already suggests, the medical utility of the Nishmath-Chajim became for him one of its central appeals. Indeed, John Ray was not the only vitalist in Mather's intellectual life. As Otho Beall and Richard Shryock observed, Mather's early reading included the work of English physicians William Harvey (1578–1657) and Nehemiah Grew (1641–1712), as well as Belgian physician Jean Baptiste van Helmont (1577–1644). All three were exponents, in one way or another, of philosophical vitalism. And Grew had already been one of Mather's five leading sources in his *Christian Philosopher*.[55]

But Mather took the reading and reconstructed it, integrating it thoroughly into his own thought world. His *Angel of Bethesda* of 1722 already told the comprehensive tale, announcing in its first-page title: "Nishmath-Chajim. The Probable SEAT of all Diseases, and a General CURE for them." "There is *a Spirit in Man*," Mather declared, "A Wonderful Spirit, which from very good Authority may be called, NISHMATH-CHAJIM, [Or; *The Breath of Life:*] And which may be of a *Middle Nature*, between the *Rational Soul*, and the *Corporeal Mass*; But may be the *Medium of Communication*, by which they work, upon one another. It Wonderfully receives also *Impressions* from *Both* of them; And Perhaps it is the *Vital Ty* between them." Thus, spirits—even the spirits of devils, as Kenneth Silverman noted—were made of "the finest imaginable materiality, light and invisible, capable of being detached from and infused into more solid substances."[56]

With the Nishmath-Chajim, Mather had arrived at a metaphysical construct that would foreshadow the developing metaphysical theology of more than a century later. Silverman assessed it as "his fullest elaboration, after years of pondering the notion, of the plastic spirit." It was "an attempt to harmonize his scientific and religious ideas, his understanding of matter and of spirit, his natural philosophy and pneumatology [i.e., his theology of spirits], his vitalistic and mechanistic views of the universe—Mather's own unified field theory." Mather, to be sure, had not found all the answers. He wondered about each person's Nishmath-Chajim and "by what *Principle* the Particles of it, which may be finer than those of the *Light* it self, are kept in their *Cohesion* to one another." Be that as it might, the Nishmath-Chajim had work to do, not only in uniting spirit to flesh but also in overseeing the operations of the body. Mather explained that the Nishmath-Chajim was the *"Spirit* of the Several *Parts,* where it has a Residence; and it is the *Life* by which the Several Parts have their *Faculties* Maintained in Exercise. *This* tis, that *Sees,* that *Hears,* that *Feels;* and Performs the *Several Digestions* in the *Body.*" More than that, it was the Nishmath-Chajim that was "more Eminently the *Seat* of our *Diseases,* or the *Source* of them." Citing Plato, he averred that "all *Diseases* have their Origin in the *Soul.*"[57]

This knowledge held immediate practical implications for would-be physicians—again in an idea world that would be replicated over a century later in the American metaphysical tradition. "MOST Certainly, the Physician that can find out Remedies (particularly in the *Mineral* or *Vegitable* Kingdom) that shall have a more Immediate Efficacy to Brighten, and Strengthen, & Comfort, the *Nishmath-Chajim* will be the most Successful Physician in the World. Especially, if he can Irradiate the Spirit in the *Stomach,* he will *do Wonderfully.*" Quoting adages on heart heaviness making the heart "stoop," a "Good Word" making it glad, and the medical value of a "Chearful Heart," Mather argued that the "Invigoration, or the Debilitation of the *Nishmath-Chajim,* is that wherein these ancient Observations are accomplished."[58]

In his longer work of 1724, also titled *The Angel of Bethesda,* Mather cataloged a series of disease conditions and recommendations for their treatment, mingling pastoral with medical advice. But he did not forget to repeat and build upon material regarding the *Nishmath-Chajim* from his earlier pamphlet. Devoting his fifth chapter, entitled "Nishmath-Chajim: The probable SEAT of all Diseases, and a general CURE for them" to that subject, Mather—as in the first pamphlet—summarized the ancients on whose views his own hung. "SOME *Rays of Light* concerning this *Nishmath-Chajim,* have been darted into the Minds of many Learned Men," he owned. There followed Mather's short list, including at its head Jean Baptiste van Helmont and someone he only named as "Grembs," probably Franz Oswald Grembs of Salzburg, who was van Helmont's "devoted disciple," according to medical editor Gordon Jones. No one on the list, though, invoked a Nishmath-Chajim, and Jones called it an example of one of Mather's "armchair theories." If so, the Hebrew term lifted from the creation story of Genesis was a brilliant verbal symbol to bring together Mather's abiding passions for religion, philosophy, and science. It is worth noting, too, that Mather's first chapter in this lengthy, putative medical work began with "The Grand CAUSE of SICKNESS," which was "SIN."[59]

Mather's seamless connection between religion and philosophy on one side and science on the other was already apparent in his *Angel of Bethesda* of 1722. With "secular" science cast into a temporary closet, Mather expanded on his observations on the quasi-materiality of the soul at death. As he instructed readers, "It is Probable, that when we Dy, the *Nishmath-Chajim* goes away, as a Vehicle to the *Rational Soul*; and continues unto it an Instrument of many Operations." In fact, this condition of fine and gossamer materiality became for Mather the evidence of a physical place in which the soul resided after death. He continued: "Here we have some Solution for the Difficulties, about *Place*, and the *Change* of it, for such an *Immaterial Spirit* as the *Rational Soul*; And some Account for *Apparitions* of the *Dead*." Thus the after-death visions of souls that the living claimed to have experienced came by means of the Nishmath-Chajim, with its minute particles linking spirit to flesh. And so, too, spirit/soul "transportations"—what by the twentieth century would be called astral travel—came by the same means. "Yea, We are certain of it," he enthused. "That Persons before they have *Died*, upon strong Desires to Visit and Behold some Objects at a Distance from the *Place* to which they were now Confined, have been thrown into a *Trance*." In that state, they lay "some Considerable While without *Sense* or *Breath*; and then Returning," they "reported" what they saw. To corroborate, "incontestable Witnesses have deposed, that *in This Time*, they were actually Seen at the *Place*, which they affirmed they had gone unto."[60]

Mather's geography of the heavenly realms grew more complex as he pondered the role of the Nishmath-Chajim, especially for souls after death and their purported physical locales. In his account, wrote Middlekauff, "the souls of the departed entered the Second Paradise." This was "the next to the highest apartment in Heaven," but the divine worship in which the soul therein engaged did not preclude its earthly visits, with the Nishmath-Chajim rendering the visits possible. Reiner Smolinski's edition of Mather's *Triparadisus* confirmed yet again Mather's vision. In it, Mather posited first, second, and third paradises, and it was in the second that we find one more time his Nishmath-Chajim. Apparently not willing to let his expository theory die, Mather repeated material from the *Angel of Bethesda* of 1722 and the later comprehensive version of 1724.[61] Clearly, in the Nishmath-Chajim Mather had found an answer to nagging questions about matter and spirit and the mysterious links between them.

It is not hard to see in Mather's "armchair theory" prefigurings of the spiritualism that would emerge full-blown by the middle years of the nineteenth century. Here the theology of a finer matter that constituted spirit—most clearly advanced by spiritualist thinker Andrew Jackson Davis—was paramount. Here, too, Emanuel Swedenborg's earlier eighteenth-century cartography of three heavens (different enough from Mather's millennial version) would be transformed for Davis and other spiritualists into a series of seven heavenly spheres in which the souls of the dead resided. Swedenborg's celestial, spiritual, and natural heavens and Davis's Summerland, or Second Sphere, were places Cotton Mather would have liked. At the end of the seventeenth century and the beginning of the eighteenth, however, the Nishmath-Chajim was Mather's culminating concept in his explanatory search for a vital principle. It was a concept that carried medical implications and provided a path to healing, but it was also a concept that, as Silverman rightly noted (above), countered mechanistic theories for Mather and others. "There are indeed many things in the *Humane Body*, that cannot be solved by the Rules of *Mechanism*," Mather had written. "Our *Nishmath-Chajim* will go very far to help us in the Solution of them. Indeed we can scarce well subsist without it."[62]

Mather, in short, had provided a rich template for later metaphysicians. It was a long journey from ideas of prosperity as divine blessing to the Nishmath-Chajim, but it was a journey aesthetically toned and elegantly described. Mather's remarks disdaining the "Rules of *Mechanism*" are key in understanding the genuine delight and fascination he found in the natural world and the way he connected it without rupture to a spirit within and beyond it.

TWO

Jonathan Edwards:
Latter-Day Puritan and Metaphysician

More than a generation removed from Mather, Jonathan Edwards shared with him twenty-five years of New England living alongside at least several remarkable connections and coincidences. Edwards, who lived from 1703 to 1758 and died before he was fifty-five, was dispatched by the smallpox inoculation that Mather had earlier championed and fostered. Like Mather, he had inherited a clerical mantle. His father, Timothy, was a minister and also tutored young boys for college. His mother, Esther, was the daughter of the controversial Solomon Stoddard, who at his Northampton (Massachusetts) church had opened communion to congregants baptized as Christians but yet not able to experience personal conversions. Like Mather, too, Edwards would be both pastor and theologian for most of his adult career—although his life as scholar and thinker foreclosed much of the civil political activity that compelled Mather.

Not surprisingly, Timothy Edwards home-schooled his son—the fifth of eleven children, of whom the other ten were daughters. The child early demonstrated prodigious intellectual powers and a penchant for study and scholarship that would remain with him to the end of his life. By 1716, just before he reached thirteen, the younger Edwards was matriculating at Yale College, and by 1720 he became a Master of Arts student in theology there. In the midst of these MA years, he underwent a period of intense religious experience and later reminisced on the conversion he had known—in some ways, as we shall see, different from the prevailing pattern. Meanwhile, he began the practice of keeping notebooks in which he would work through his wide-ranging thoughts on theology, philosophy, and even natural science. The notebooks in some ways would be the seedbed for the towering intellectual and theological treatises that he would author throughout his life.

Jonathan Edwards's ministerial life began early as well. For a short time—a series of months from 1722 to 1723—he acted as supply-preacher at a church in New York City, and then, for another series of months from 1723 to 1724, pastored a congregation in Bolton, Connecticut. Thereafter he returned to Yale as a tutor, and later, in 1726, received a call to the Northampton church of his grandfather Solomon Stoddard. In another year, he would marry Sarah Pierpont, and their family would eventually grow to include eleven children. Two years later on the death of his grandfather, Edwards assumed the full pastorate at Northampton. It was there that he presided over one of the most well-known episodes in the Great Awakening, and in nearby Enfield, he delivered his perennially reprinted sermon "Sinners in the Hands of an Angry God." It was in Northampton, too, that he chiseled out much of his Reformed theology in works that bowed before a Calvinist God and yet incorporated the ethos of his personal, more heart-centered religious experience. But carried forward by his Calvinist conviction, Edwards's relationship with his congregation eroded as he began to contest the open communion his grandfather had preached. Finally, in 1750, after a bitter and contentious political battle with congregants, Edwards was dismissed from his church.

The next year found him in Stockbridge, Massachusetts, where he worked as pastor and missionary to the Indians. The politics of Stockbridge also turned out to be contentious, and when Edwards received an invitation in 1758 to become president of the College of New Jersey (now Princeton), he accepted, after some caveats. He had hardly begun his new appointment when he decided to be inoculated against smallpox. Edwards died of the complications. His written legacy, however, ensured that he would be hailed again and again as America's greatest theologian.[1]

Edwards had read John Locke from his early days at Yale, and he greatly admired Isaac Newton. He also apparently devoured the latest and most groundbreaking works in English and European thought. So it is perhaps not remarkable that Edwards's early notebooks would reveal his ponderings on such topics as "being" (1721) and "mind" (1723). We can begin exploring Edwards as a delight maker by searching through these first writings to lift out themes that keep him in the sometime company of Cotton Mather and also forward him toward an American metaphysical future. We can fan out from there to pursue a series of themes as we look for the spiritual contours of Edwards's life that identified him with pleasure, delight, beauty, divine immanence and expansiveness, mysticism, and the experiential realm.

"Of Being" was no doubt influenced by Cambridge Platonist Henry More, part of the group of English seventeenth-century philosophers linked to the

University of Cambridge. There were echoes, too, from earlier Catholic and Reformed ideas, and Edwards's writing already displayed the spaciousness and sense of compelling mystery that continued to distinguish his work.[2] Indeed, early in his musings, Edwards announced to himself that space was "this necessary, eternal, infinite and omnipresent being." "But I had as good speak plain," he added. "I have already said as much as that space is God." Edwards seemed to be on a roll. It was utterly clear to him "that all the space there is not proper to body, all the space there is without the bounds of the creation, all the space there was before the creation, is God himself."[3] Into that eternal space that was God, as we shall see, humans could engage in what later the founders of the new United States would call "the pursuit of happiness." Although the phrase would not emerge for more than fifty years, and although, in its context, it can best be described as public happiness, in the Edwards spiritual universe it was already beginning—parsed as beauty, proportion, delight, and a kind of devotional pleasure.

Still, Edwards was careful. Not more than a year or two after the declaration of God's spaciousness, Edwards penned a miscellaneous entry in his notebooks. It was, he wrote, "gross" and "unprofitable" to think of God as "infinitely extended throughout the immense space," such "as bodies are." Just as the human soul's "greatness" did not consist "in any extension," so for its maker. God was not "a sort of unknown thing that we call substance," but instead "omnipotence, perfect knowledge and perfect love." The words were in a way a clarification, but Edwards had previously hinted the same thing in "Of Being," asserting that an "infinite and omnipresent being cannot be solid." It was, he observed, a "gross mistake" to "think material things the most substantial beings." "Spirits only," he declared, "are properly substance."[4]

The vision was grand, and it did not consist merely in the quasi-declaration that God was spatial. In "The Mind" (ca. 1723), we catch a further glimpse of where it was heading. "Being" narrowly examined, Edwards told his notebook, "is nothing else but proportion." Since only spirits had "a proper being," his thought moved consistently toward idealism, even as he refused to negate what we see and sense. In the divine mind exist "his [God's] determination, his care and his design that ideas shall be united forever, just so and in such a manner as is agreeable."[5] Yet what we see and sense became, for Edwards, the beginning of wisdom. Already, he was asking about excellency and about beauty—considerations that would persist abundantly in his later writing.

E. Brooks Holifield has remarked that the "sense of the glory of God" constituted Edwards's religious center. Obviously, this sense of God's glory resonated strongly with his Calvinist background. But what happened as well in his thought world points to his immersion in extra-Calvinist readings and reconstructions—something, as I have remarked, already apparent in "Of Being." For Edwards, influences abounded from such sources as Cambridge Platonism, Dutch philosophy, and British ethical thinking. This was because he used the language of "excellency" to explain the majesty and mystery of God. In turn, writing of excellency brought themes of "harmony, symmetry, or proportion," as Holifield notes. "By associating excellency with mathematical relations like proportion and harmony, and by linking those concepts to the notion of beauty, he [Edwards] carried New England theology into the mainstream of seventeenth-century philosophy and eighteenth-century aesthetic and ethical theory."[6]

"Proportion," wrote Edwards, "is complex beauty." Moreover, "all beauty" consisted "in similarness, or identity of relation." Edwards thought that such "correspondency, symmetry, regularity and the like" could be "resolved into equalities," and he thought further that such equalities in complex beauty were too numerous to be detailed. George Marsden, in fact, has compared Edwards's view of "excellency" and "beauty" to music, citing his affinity for the term "harmony" and his connection of harmony to "proportion." Marsden elaborated: "To fully appreciate this analogy one should recall that Edwards was writing at the time when J. S. Bach (1685–1750) was at the height of his creative powers. . . . Though Bach was Lutheran and German, he and Edwards were working in similar worlds of discourse where ineffable beauties that pointed to the divine were found in the harmonies of complex relationships." It was true that, as Marsden noted, "Edwards probably never heard the works of Bach." Still, "he had heard other eighteenth-century music and knew enough about it to understand how complex harmonies, both challenging to the intellect and overwhelming to the affections, could point toward the divine."[7]

For Edwards, even the "pleasures of the senses" were the "result of equality." Such pleasures, though, as Marsden affirmed, paled before the landscape of spirit. The material world with its "consent of bodies to one another, and the harmony . . . among them" was "but the shadow of excellency." What followed, though, was fundamental to spirit. Its secret glue, for Edwards, was love—no contest. But important here, the spiritual with its excellency and love brought joy and delight. "If we would get a right notion of what is spiritual," Edwards reflected, "we must think of thought or inclination or delight." Yet even as "aesthetics and the structure of beauty" constituted a subject line for Edwards's "Mind," as John E. Smith, Harry S. Stout, and Kenneth P. Minkema have said, it is clear that *delight* was its signal subtext. In place of the sinner's guilt and plea for mercy, the business of contemplation was less penance than pleasure.⁸

The road of consciousness to delight and pleasure, significantly, traveled through Edwards's personal experience of conversion and the striking incidences of divine delight he recorded. From his childhood, Edwards confessed in his "Personal Narrative," he had been troubled by the doctrine of the sovereignty of God, especially its negative aspect, in which the deity had consigned some souls to eternal hellfire. Finally, the young Edwards had come to an intellectual acquiescence—seeing, somehow, "justice and reasonableness" in the teaching of predestination, so that his "mind rested in it." Abiding in his consciousness, however, was another take on divine sovereignty, a sense of it that was implicitly subversive. Edwards's conversion would upturn the conventional template because he had often, after his mental breakthrough, had a *"delightful* conviction." Divine sovereignty "very often appeared, an exceeding pleasant, bright and sweet doctrine to me." Edwards recalled that pleasure and delight in the divine came to him strongly when he was reading 1 Timothy 1:17: "Now unto the King eternal, immortal, invisible, the only wise God, be honor and glory forever and ever, Amen." The verse resonated so intensely that he pondered "how happy I should be, if I might enjoy that God, and be wrapt up to God in heaven, and be as it were swallowed up in him." And then Edwards recalled that he chanted: "I kept saying, and as it were singing over these words of Scripture to myself; and went to prayer, to pray to God that I might enjoy him." Now the natural world appeared to him in startling splendor. As he beheld the "clouds and sky," he saw in them "the sweet glory of God." "And while I viewed," he remembered, "I used to spend my time, as it always seemed natural to me, to sing or chant forth my meditations; to speak my thoughts in soliloquies, and speak with a singing voice."⁹

Here were echoes of Bach to be sure—and more. Instead of being overwhelmed with a conviction of personal sin, Edwards was lifted into a stratosphere of divine delight. His personal testimonies were filled with this sense of delight in the divine, of raptures and transportings that energized his spiritual and scholarly life with a passion that was more than purely rational. From childhood, Edwards recollected, he was preoccupied with religion. He met with other boys "to pray together" and "experienced I know not what kind of delight in religion." It was his "delight to abound in religious duties." In fact, he and some of his schoolmates built a secret prayer place—a "booth in a swamp." This was not enough for the young Edwards, though, and he owned that he "had particular secret places . . . in the woods," where he could be alone. After his conversion, too, he spoke of new "delights" felt "in things of religion." Different from his boyhood memories, "they were totally of another kind"—more inward, pure, soul-animating, and refreshing." "Those former delights," he compared, "never reached the heart; and did not arise from any sight of the divine excellency of the things of God; or any taste of the soul-satisfying, and life-giving good."[10]

Nor was this all. The sense of the divine kept coming and growing. The eroticism of his confession is hard to avoid. Edwards's "longings after God and holiness" broadened into a language of tactile pleasure. Holiness was "ravishingly lovely" and brought "ravishment to the soul." Edwards noted his own earlier words gleaned from meditation. At that time "the soul of a true Christian" seemed like "a little white flower, as we see in the spring of the year; low and humble on the ground, opening its bosom, to receive the pleasant beams of the sun's glory, rejoicing as it were, in a calm rapture." Calm and pure his vision was, he reassured himself a number of times, but the language, for a twenty-first-century reader, is charged. In fact, after his conversion, verses from the *Song of Solomon* (or, as Edwards called it, *Canticles*) repeated themselves to him again and again. "Reading and meditating on Christ; and the beauty and excellency of his person, and the lovely way of salvation," words from *Canticles* 2:1 were, he told, "abundantly" with him. "'I am the rose of Sharon, the lily of the valleys,'" he quoted. "The whole book of Canticles" was "pleasant" to him, and he "used to be much in reading it." Like a heavenly earworm, *Canticles* had made a home in his consciousness. And once, in 1737, when he had ridden into the woods, he saw the glory of the person of Christ with an absorption and intensity that continued, he judged, "about an hour." He remained "in a flood of tears, and weeping aloud." Edwards wrote pointedly of the experience: "I felt withal, an ardency of soul to be, what I know not otherwise how to express, than to be emptied and annihilated; to lie in the dust, and to be full of Christ alone."[11]

In her biography of Edwards, Ola Elizabeth Winslow remarked that, in his early days as a preacher, Edwards selected texts from *"Solomon's Song"* among several other biblical books, more than he did later. She suggested, too, "many correspondences" between these early sermons "and his own personal experiences." With a more specific focus, Smith, Stout, and Minkema have drawn a link between Edwards's courtship of Sarah Pierpont and "the beauty and almost sexual intimacy that he used to characterize the saint's relationship to Christ." In one miscellaneous notebook entry in 1724, Edwards exclaimed, "How greatly are we inclined to the other sex!" He went on to connect sexual attraction to Christ's love of "the church, which is his spouse." Meanwhile, he also thought that stronger sexual passion went with stronger spirituality. "The more exalted the nature is, the greater love of that kind that is laudable is it susceptive of; and the purer and better natured, the more is it inclined to it."[12]

Perry Miller in 1948 addressed the "revolution in sensibility" that characterized Jonathan Edwards. Instead of using nature to elucidate scripture, he said, Edwards was quoting scripture the better to understand nature. In this endeavor, Miller declared, Edwards had made "nothing less than an assertion of the absolute validity of the sensuous." Edwards himself corroborated with his musings reproduced in *Images or Shadows of Divine Things* (more on this later), leaving out scripture altogether. "The whole material universe is preserved by gravity or attraction, or the mutual tendency of all bodies to each other," he wrote. "One part of the universe is hereby made beneficial to another; the beauty, harmony, and order, regular progress, life, and motion, and in short all the well-being of the whole frame depends on it. This is a type of love or charity in the spiritual world." Later echoing the message, William Clebsch observed that Edwards "made religious experience so outwardly palpable that these Christian truths and the realities for which they stood became sweet to the taste, symmetrical to the eye, harmonious to the ear, pleasant to the touch and the smell." They "became for their own sakes lively to the senses, enlightening to the mind, and delightful to the heart."[13]

So *eros* was a type of divine love, and everywhere—in heaven and on earth—delight and pleasure functioned as signposts of alignment with the divine energy that flowed through all things. Edwards may have turned to the *Song of Solomon* less frequently after the time of his conversion, but its message of sensuous delight in the things of the spirit followed him. It emerged in his sermons and even in the carefully argued treatises he produced on a plethora of theological subjects. In "A Divine and Supernatural Light," for example—a sermon Edwards preached in 1733 and published the following year—he addressed "*a spiritual and divine light, immediately imparted to the soul by God, of a different nature from any that is obtained by natural means.*" What was this light? Edwards instructed listeners and readers that it consisted in "a true sense of the divine excellency of the things revealed in the Word of God," which meant, in effect, "a sense of the loveliness of God's holiness." More specifically, instead of merely intellectual knowledge, Edwards extolled "the sense of the heart." Here there was "a sense of the beauty, amiableness, or sweetness of a thing," with the heart "sensible of pleasures and delight in the presence of the idea of it." There arose a "conviction" of "truth and reality" that led the mind to dwell upon "divine objects" with "delight." In an often-quoted reflection on his premise, Edwards explained that there was "a difference between having a rational judgment that honey is sweet, and having a sense of its sweetness. A man may have the former, that knows not how honey tastes; but a man can't have the latter, unless he has an idea of the taste of honey in his mind." As Winslow has remarked, "'It would be worth the while to be Religious if only for the Pleasantness of it,' is quite as typical a sermon theme as that of the familiar *Eternity of Hell Torments*, upon which his preaching reputation so securely rests."[14]

In a series of sermons on *Charity and Its Fruits* that Edwards delivered in 1738 (published in 1765 posthumously), Edwards carried his gospel of sweetness into an essentially ethical domain. In the fifteenth in the series, he turned his thoughts to heaven and announced that it was a *"world of love."* With God "a full and overflowing and an inexhaustible fountain of love," he asserted, Father and Son were united "in an infinitely dear and incomprehensible mutual love," while the Holy Spirit flowed out and was "breathed forth in love." "There," Edwards mused in quasi-erotic language, "this glorious God is manifested and shines forth in full glory, in beams of love; there the fountain overflows in streams and rivers of love and delight, enough for all to drink at, and to swim in, yea, so as to overflow the world as it were with a deluge of love." As if to underscore the pleasurable nature of what he contemplated, Edwards added that "there the Holy Spirit shall be poured forth with perfect sweetness, as a pure river of water of life, clear as crystal." The lingering sweetness of heaven's love clung throughout Edwards's sermon. The love made heaven a place of peace, and, he asked rhetorically, who could "express the sweetness of this peace?" "Love," he continued, was "a spring of sweetness." With heavenly music intermingling with his own earthly rapture, Edwards beheld the rapture of the saints. "Every saint" was "as a note in a concert of music which sweetly harmonizes with every other note." In metaphors he had used repeatedly, Edwards declared, "All shall stand about the God of glory, the fountain of love." As it were, they would open "their bosoms to be filled with those effusions of love which are poured forth from thence, as the flowers on the earth . . . open their bosoms to the sun to be filled with his warmth and light, and to flourish in beauty and fragrancy by his rays."[15]

For another and arresting example, if we jump ahead to 1755 and Edwards's ethical treatise, *Dissertation Concerning the End for Which God Created the World* (published posthumously in 1765), Edwards argued almost like a contemporary process theologian. He labored to show that God created the world "that there might be a glorious and abundant emanation of his infinite fullness of good *ad extra.*" The very perfection of his nature "moved him to create the world." Since creatures were not yet there, the creation of beings was "a disposition in the fullness of the divinity to flow out and diffuse itself." Just as, in a tree, "the root and stock" would "diffuse and send forth its sap and life," so with the divine being. Behind the diffusing act, as in a tree, lay not simply the production of fruits, but rather "its disposition to communicate itself, or diffuse its sap and life in general." To the point here, "God's value for and delight in the emanations of his fullness in the work of creation" argued "his delight in the infinite fullness of good there is in himself, and the supreme respect and regard he has for himself." In short, God's delight in his "diffusive disposition" was what "excited" him "to give creatures existence." To state the matter explicitly, God *desired*.[16]

More than that, as divine teacher, God used his works to educate his creatures. Edwards, in fact, understood God's works as "a kind of voice or language of God to instruct intelligent beings in things pertaining to Himself." "We know," Edwards enthused, "that God hath so much delighted in this way of instruction." To invert the message, Clarence Faust and Thomas Johnson expressed the long, lingering effect of Edwards's personal experience on his later life and work. "Edwards's whole thought life," they wrote, "was centered about the deep conviction of the all-sufficient, all-encompassing power of God which had mastered him as a young man. This power he delighted to contemplate and made it his chief purpose in life to proclaim." If God delighted, in keeping with the law of correspondence, Edwards also delighted. And if Edwards delighted in the world, then other humans must do the same. With the world's "sweetest and most charming beauty" because of "its resemblance of spiritual beauties," almost all were held fast in its presence. The reason that even people who seemed to be "miserable" loved life was "because they cannot bear to lose the sight of such a beautiful and lovely world." They harbored "ideas, that every moment whilst we live have a beauty that we take not distinct notice of, but bring a pleasure that, when we come to the trial, we had rather live in much pain and misery than lose."[17]

The world was indeed a beautiful place—more on that later—but the desiring, expanding nature of God bore theological implications that need to be explored first. Marsden perhaps best summarized them when he mused that, for Edwards, the universe was "an explosion of God's glory." If we follow the logic of that statement, we need to return to *End for Which God Created the World*, in which, as Edward's pondered the world, he told readers that in it "the emanation or communication of the divine fullness" related both to God and the creature. God was the "fountain," since it was he who emanated. And then the comparison: "As the communication itself, or thing communicated, is something divine, something of God, something of his internal fullness; as the water in the stream is something of the fountain;

and as the beams are of the sun." At the most basic, Edwards was pointing more to divine immanence than transcendence—and in a philosophical ethos that bore Platonic and Neo-Platonic resemblances. At a further remove, we can begin to wonder, as some scholars have, if Edwards were indeed a pantheist (believing all was God) or panentheist (believing all was *in* God). Thus, Henry Bamford Parkes's 1930 biography of Edwards assessed its subject as a "pantheist schoolboy" and "a pantheist of a type very uncommon before the romantic movement." Not to be outdone, Miller in 1949 cited early Unitarian William Ellery Channing saying that "by making God the only active power of the universe, Edwards annihilated the creature" and "became in effect a 'pantheist.'" And in 1962, Faust and Johnson thought that one passage in Edwards's "Personal Narrative" was "more pantheistic than its author was perhaps consciously aware," pointing toward "the Wordsworth who wrote 'Of splendor in the grass, of glory in the flower.'"[18]

Miller had been careful enough to distinguish between the naturalism of Ralph Waldo Emerson, which he declared Edwards "would have scorned," and Edwards's own intensity in "his love for a universe that divinity had made and in which divinity was immanent."[19] The horror of the label "pantheist" for an eighteenth-century late-Puritan divine cannot be denied. But Edwards might have been dancing with angels on a pin as he gloried in the presence of God animating all creation. Whether or not he understood the precariousness of his theological situation, it is not difficult to find its full message translated in nineteenth-century times by Emerson and other Transcendentalists and later, far less subtly, by radical proponents of an unorthodox theology called New Thought.

In the world of the immanent God whom Edwards cherished, however, as his observations have already suggested, earthly (and heavenly) delight came from the experience and reality of beauty. Beauty was God's other name, and Edwards never let readers or listeners forget this. As long ago as 1907, American philosopher I. Woodbridge Riley pointed to Edwards's "high aesthetic interest." Later, American religious historian William Clebsch was more direct. Reflecting in the context of Edwards's posthumously published *Nature of True Virtue* (1765), he stated flatly that "the leading category of religious experience became not salvation but beauty." Edwards's treatise, he argued, "shifted the effects of religion from duty to beauty, from ethics to esthetics." It would be difficult to disagree. Edwards announced his vision at the very beginning of his treatise. "Whatever controversies and variety of opinions there are about the nature of virtue, yet all (excepting some skeptics who deny any real difference between virtue and vice) mean by it something *beautiful*, or rather some kind of *beauty* or excellency." With distinctions between "particular" (more limited) and general (universal) beauty, Edwards launched into a reflection on "true virtue." It was "love to Being in general" and also "the beauty of an intelligent being." Invoking "spiritual beauty," he called it "*consent* and *union* with Being in *general*." Nor was all of this simply ideational. Edwards was at pains to present the beauty of virtue in the sensate register of humans. "The way we come to the idea or sensation of beauty," he wrote, "is by immediate sensation of the gratefulness of the idea called 'beautiful.'" It was "not by finding out by argumentation any consequences . . . anymore than tasting the sweetness of honey, or perceiving the harmony of a tune, is by argumentation on connections and consequences." With honey again Edwards's comparison, true virtue involved, always and ever, the felt experience of beauty.[20]

Edwards's companion treatise to *True Virtue*, *End for Which God Created the World*, linked beauty to the desire that, for him, propelled divine creation. Written in 1753 or 1754, most probably before he composed *True Virtue*, *End for Which God Created the World* exhibits familiar concerns regarding the moral realm. So much is this so that Paul Ramsey, Yale series editor for both works (originally published together in 1765), remarked of the two that "the one is the mirror image of the other; the 'end' for which God created the world must be the 'end' of a truly virtuous and holy life." No surprise, therefore, to find Edwards extolling the "infinite fullness of all possible good in God," citing it for "all excellency and beauty" and continuing with a vision of the expanding deity—an eighteenth-century prototype of an expanding universe. "As this fullness is capable of communication or emanation *ad extra*," Edwards wrote, "so it seems a thing amiable and valuable in itself that it should be communicated or flow forth, that this infinite fountain of good should send forth abundant streams, that this infinite fountain of light should, diffusing its excellent fullness, pour forth light all around." Edwards found it "fit" for the light to "shine forth" since, as there was "an infinite fountain of holiness, moral excellence and beauty, so it should flow out in communicated holiness." Beauty and excellence, for Edwards, ever repopulated themselves. Without limit or exception, he proclaimed "*a disposition in God, as an original property of his nature, to an emanation of his own infinite fullness.*" This, nothing less, was "*what excited him to create the world.*" Thus it was "*that the emanation itself was aimed at by him as a last end of the creation.*"[21] The God of beauty and the God of desire, in Edwards's theological statement, existed in tandem with one another—a different version of the "mirror image" that Ramsey had observed.

In Edwards's end, moreover, was his beginning. Significantly, his considerations of beauty and declarations of excellency began as early as his notes on "Mind." In fact, Edwards began his series of notebook entries on the "Mind" with a reflection on "excellency," which he complained had no proper definition. Throughout the series of notes, he continued to connect excellency to beauty. "Excellence," Edwards thought, "is that which is beautiful and lovely." He went on to add, "That which is beautiful with respect to the university of things has a generally extended excellence and a true beauty." It is not difficult to see where he was tending, and in Edwards's reading true, whole, and complete beauty was always divine. It was, as he reflected in another note, "being's consent to being," with the subtext that real and total being was the being of God. What we saw with our senses was "but the shadow of excellency," and it was pleasant because it was "a shadow of love." In a musical metaphor that, for a present-day reader, evokes Marsden's allusion to Bach, Edwards told his notebook that "when one thing sweetly harmonizes with another, as the notes in music, the notes are so conformed and have such proportion one to another that they seem to have respect one to another, as if they loved one another." Foreshadowing his final agenda in his *Nature of True Virtue*, Edwards could think through his theme in terms of excellency and love. "Wherefore all virtue, which is the excellency of minds, is resolved into love to being," and "love to being" meant love to God.[22]

More than twenty years later, in the midst of concerns regarding revivals, Edwards, in his *Treatise concerning Religious Affections* (1746), again made the case for divine loveliness. With a vitalistic template that echoed that of Cotton Mather, he addressed the "laws of the union which the Creator . . . fixed between soul and body," positing a connection between "any lively and vigorous exercise of the will or inclination of the soul" and its effect on the body. "The motion of the blood and animal spirits begins to be sensibly altered," he explained, "whence oftentimes arises some bodily sensation, especially about the heart and vitals, that are the fountain of the fluids of the body." The mind ruled, but now under a new name: it was "called the *heart*," and from its "vigorous and sensible exercises" came the "*affections.*"[23]

No doubt there were echoes here of John Locke and his philosophy of "sensationalism" in which humans gained understanding by way of their senses. But Edwards crafted his own more spiritual version and was at pains to distinguish between the supernatural region in which his "sense of the heart"—for it was that—dwelled and the mere sensate Lockean model. Still, "true religion must consist very much in the affections," Edwards wrote, as he continued to invoke "animal spirits" like a theological mantra. "As was observed before," he reminded readers, the body affected the mind. Indeed, "so subject" was "the body to the mind, and so much do its fluids, especially the animal spirits, attend the motions and exercises of the mind, that there can't be so much as an intense thought, without an effect upon them."[24] We are back in the territory of desire, with a creator who has shaped creatures to imitate the original divine longing, the original divine centrifugal energy that seemed more like emotion than like thought.

Where did this reality lead humans? It brought them to a hidden place that was also ethereal. The "sense of the heart," with the Spirit of God dwelling within, meant inner holiness, and holiness was, in a familiar theme, "the beauty and sweetness of the divine nature." Now the soul became a "partaker of God's beauty." Morton White perhaps best captured the train of thought that Edwards was following. Being religious meant "holy affections," and such affections arose from a "certain kind of idea in the understanding. What kind of an idea? Edwards said that it was the idea of God's loveliness or excellency, which could not come through the normal five senses and therefore had to come through what he called the Sense of the Heart." With this extra sense, a truly religious person could affirm "that God is lovely, just as a man previously blind can know that the sky is blue when he comes to see."[25]

Underlining the significance of Edwards's appeal to beauty, Roland Delattre, in his now-classic *Beauty and Sensibility in the Thought of Jonathan Edwards*, declared for "the aesthetic aspect of Jonathan Edwards' thought and vision." Delattre argued that beauty and sensibility provided "a larger purchase upon the essential and distinctive features of his thought" than "any other aspect, such as the idealist, empiricist, sensationalist, Platonist, scholastic, Calvinist, or mystic." "Edwards was convinced," he stated unambiguously, "that beauty is the reality in terms of which the Divine Being and the moral and religious life of human beings as well as the order of the universal system of being, both moral and natural, can best be understood." Thus, for Edwards, beauty was "fundamental" and the "first principle of being, the inner structural principle of being-itself." To emphasize the daring of the Edwardsian theology, Delattre cited the formidable twentieth-century Reformed theologian Karl Barth. In his monumental *Church Dogmatics*, Barth warned that, because of its connection to "ideas of pleasure, desire and enjoyment, . . . the concept of the beautiful seems to be a particularly secular one." It was "not at all adapted for introduction into the language of theology, and indeed extremely dangerous."[26]

Edwards, though, did not seem to worry much about "ideas of pleasure, desire and enjoyment," nor about the experience of them in a spiritual context. Wrote Delattre in a summary declaration: "The experience of the beauty of divine things constituted for Edwards the most intimate and fullest communion with God."²⁷ Still more, not only did beauty meld into divine union, but it was also, in a collective sense, profitable, as Alan Heimert once argued. Some of the mystery that was linked to Calvinism after the Great Awakening "was attributable to a commitment to social goals which were ultimately aesthetic." So it was that the Calvinist Edwards envisioned the beautiful society, whole and intact, as it was led by God in a "pursuit of happiness" that was, "almost by definition, a quest for the great community." Heimert went so far as to posit that "in substance, the God of Jonathan Edwards was a supremely excellent Christian commonwealth." To be sure, as George Marsden has noted, Edwards lived his life as a social conservative with authoritarian notions of ministry and an embedded sense of divinely ordered hierarchy. That acknowledged, Edwards's social vision of beauty endured the more. With "beauty" and "excellency" Edwardsian synonyms, beauty signified, over and over again, harmony, symmetry, and proportion. Summarizing this circular theology (with its implied social logic), Holifield argued that when Edwards linked excellency to proportion and harmony, and then "to the notion of beauty, he [Edwards] carried New England theology into the mainstream of seventeenth-century philosophy and eighteenth-century aesthetic and ethical theory."²⁸

We do not have to travel the entire distance with Heimert in order to notice that Edwards's pursuit of happiness and beauty was public. We can affirm, with Holifield, too, that Edwards's theology of beauty was utterly basic to his theological project. Even history had its beauty, as Holifield has shown, since with the millennial thinking that inhabited Edwards's mind, he saw "the 'beauty' of Providence as God ordered all events toward a common end." Thus, the verbal trinity of excellence, proportion, and beauty, as in the rest of Edwards's theology, colored his millennialist descriptions. Adding to the assessment from his own Reformed and evangelical perspective, Mark Noll declared "the unifying center of Edwards's theology" to be "the glory of God depicted as an active, harmonious, ever-unfolding source of absolutely perfect Being marked by supernal beauty and love."²⁹

If the public Edwards extolled beauty in the pursuit of the divine, his more personal writings revealed the same aesthetic preoccupation—something briefly noticed earlier. Writing to Lady Mary Pepperrell on the loss of her son in 1751, he consoled her by asking her to think with him "a little of the loveliness of our blessed Redeemer." Edwards counseled her to "rest in him," and to "have sweet complacence and satisfaction of soul in his excellency and beauty whatever else we are deprived of." He continued by calling the Redeemer "the image and exhibition of the infinite beauty of the [Deity], in the viewing of which God the Father had all his infinite happiness from eternity." "Like the light of the morning, as a morning without clouds; as the dew on the grass, under whose influence the souls of the people are as the tender grass," so the "beams of his beauty and brightness" were "fitted for the support of the healing and reviving of the afflicted." Indeed, Edwards's first "Miscellany," written around the time that he was working on his notes on "Mind," affirmed that holiness was "a most beautiful and lovely thing." There was "nothing in it but what is sweet and ravishingly lovely"—words that he remembered and reiterated years later in his "Personal Narrative," as we have seen. George Marsden remarked astutely on this personal side of Edwards, declaring that "an overwhelming sense of the wondrous beauty and love of the triune God . . . remained the polestar of his life and thought." Marsden underlined the point repeatedly as his biography of Edwards unfolded. Significantly, its last line returned to the same theme of the beauty of the Redeemer that Edwards had used to comfort Lady Pepperrell. Those among humans—the majority by far—"seeing the beauty of the redemptive love of Christ as the true center of religion . . . will love God and all that he has created."[30]

Many years before Marsden wrote, Miller was saying something similar, even as he pointedly noted the tension beneath the aesthetic vision. Edwards, he thought, "was striving, against immense handicaps, to express a new vision of the world in which the conflict of the spirit and the flesh, of the divine and the rational, which had shattered and still shatters European culture, could be resolved into a single perception of beauty." Conflict or no, the beauty that was harmony, proportion, and excellency had a still deeper foundation—the foundation that, for all its Calvinist moorings, was intrinsic to Puritan culture. This was the strong and seemingly illimitable perception of a universal correspondence in physical, cosmological, moral, and spiritual life. Mather had been grounded in it, and so was Edwards. Thus, Miller's classic edition of *Images or Shadows of Divine Things* was predicated on Edwards's fondness for typology, both in scripture and the natural world. Nothing was completely discrete, and the lines of connection were everywhere, with one piece of the physical or moral world replicating another and yet another endlessly. Edwards understood quite explicitly what his worldview of correspondence (for it was that) entailed. Early on in *Images or Shadows*, he hailed the "great and remarkable analogy in God's works." There was, he thought, "a wonderfull resemblance in the effects which God produces, and consentaneity in His manner of working in one thing and another throughout all nature." He saw the link clearly in the "visible world." Still more, his observation led to a charged rhetorical question: "Why should not we suppose that He makes the inferior in imitation of the superior, the material of the spiritual, on purpose to have a resemblance and shadow of them?" It was, truly, "reasonable to suppose He makes the whole as a shadow of the spiritual world."[31]

As for Mather, so for Edwards. Nature's productions in its microcosm pointed the way to the macrocosm of spirit. In turn, that larger, grander macrocosm held the key to discerning the meaning of nature's shadowed reality. Countering and, more, denouncing a "mechanical philosophy"—reductionistic in explaining how nature worked solely through the laws of matter and motion and led nowhere but to itself—Edwards understood mechanistic doctrine as a restriction on divine power. God, rather, taught through the "shadows of divine things," and the "voice of God" through them conveyed "instruction to our minds." "Wherever we are, and whatever we are about," Edwards concluded, "we may see divine things excellently represented and held forth."[32]

Nor did the theory of correspondence—with nature as shadow of spirit—end with the Puritan culture that Edwards so stunningly epitomized. As early as 1889, estimating the significance of Edwards's often-cited sermon "A Divine and Supernatural Light," his early biographer, Alexander Allen, thought that it resembled "so closely the later transcendental thought of New England as almost to bridge the distance between Edwards and Emerson." And as Emerson's early gospel *Nature* (1836) so clearly demonstrated, the theory of correspondence was key to the way he and the other nineteenth-century New England Transcendentalists saw the world.[33]

Between Edwards and the Transcendentalists, though—as we shall see—if there was a bridge, there was also a gulf. Edwards, with his Puritan and Calvinist moorings, still held to the "book of Scripture" as the "interpreter of the book of nature." If, for Edwards, all things physical and embodied were the pale correspondents—the "shadow" of the world of spirit—it was scripture that declared exactly what "spiritual mysteries" were "signified and typified in the constitution of the natural world." Scripture even went further, and sometimes it could be found "making application of the signs and types in the book of nature as representations of those spiritual mysteries." Still, the resonances between microcosm and macrocosm were never one way. As Edwards himself suggested and Marsden wrote, in Edwards's world, "a complex language of God" was being uttered. It ran a gamut from nature and direct experience all the way to the highest forms of abstraction. Perhaps this was why Edwards exhibited such ease, in his early sermons especially, in moving from his own spiritual experience to universal truths and teachings. At the other end of the spectrum from experience to ideation, there was Edwards's own leaning toward idealism—which, from yet another perspective, expressed the theory of correspondence. Edwards had observed in his notes on "Mind" that "the existence of the whole material universe is absolutely dependent on idea." Marsden has translated the Edwardsian idealism as a repudiation of belief in the ultimacy of everyday experience. It was a "failure of imagination" to think that "commonsense experience was ultimate."[34] In other words, there was the here and now, and—beyond it—the "over there" of mind and imagination. Humans used imagination to create and shape images of things, and the images were as large or as small as their prejudgments and sense experiences.

In his early note, "Of the Prejudices of Imagination" (ca. 1721–1722), Edwards minced no words. "Opinions arising from imagination take us as soon as we are born, are beat into us by every act of sensation, and so grow up with us from our very births; and by that means grow into us so fast that it is almost impossible to root them out." Thus people "come to make what they can actually perceive by their senses, or by immediate and outside reflection into their own souls, the standard of possibility and impossibility." In this reading—a perceptive comment on psychological process—the human microcosm had fallen out of alignment with a greater macrocosm of ideas. Edwards deplored the result. "Imaginations of this kind among the learned themselves, even of this learned age, hath a very powerful secret influence, to cause them either to reject things really true as enormously false, or to embrace things that are truly so."[35] In the wings waiting—if we want to get ahead of the story—lurked the subversive injunction of the late twentieth and early twenty-first century: If you do not like the way things are, then create your own reality. Use your imagination, as some trance channels would advise, to align yourself better with the grand ideational complex they called Source. From that act and connection, delight and abundance would flow.

If we turn to Edward's moral universe instead of the twenty-first century, correspondence and analogy also ruled, and nature told the tale. Consider water. Edwards deemed it "a type of sin or the corruption of man and of the state of misery that is the consequence of it." Water was akin to sin in its "flattering discoveries." Its surface appeared "smooth and harmless," and "as if it had paradise and heaven in its bosom." Not so, Edwards warned; it was "all a cheat." Descending into it, "instead of finding pleasant, delightfull groves and a garden of pleasure and heaven in its clearness, we should meet with nothing but death, a land of darkness, or darkness itself." By contrast, nature proclaimed the soul in virtue. "How great a resemblance of a holy and virtuous soul in a calm serene day," Edwards wrote appreciatively. "What an infinite number of such-like beauties is there in that one thing, the light; and how complicated an harmony and proportion is it probable belongs to it." In their turn, while the sun shone "serenely and undisturbedly upon them," fields of plants and flowers resembled "every grace and beautiful disposition of mind" and, still more, "an inferior towards a superior cause, preserver, benevolent benefactor, and a fountain of happiness." As the sun itself suggested, even on a cosmological scale, moral analogy prevailed. There was a "resemblance of a decent trust, dependence and acknowledgment in the planets continually moving round the sun, receiving his influences by which they are made happy, bright and beautiful."[36]

Just as "light, or our organ of seeing" prompted an excitement—"an harmonious motion" that began in the "animal spirits" and was "propagated to the brain," analogy came with its own propagating logic. If everything in the world could be enlisted as testimony to natural and divine law, then the language of resemblance escalated with ease into a further proposition. When everything was like everything, could it be that all participated in the same one reality? And if that were so, and one moved in the direction of experience more than theology (i.e., the theology of pantheism or panentheism), then the groundwork had been laid for mysticism. At least in the West, mystical experience has been seen as a gradual event, or better, ascent. By medieval times, the standard template was a three-stage process that began with purgation or renunciation and continued into an illuminative state of divinely impressed knowledge beyond the logical and rational. The culminating event in the mystical life, at its third stage or state, was a unitive experience in which one merged with the divine (or, in later years, the cosmic energy of nature or the deep inner recesses of the self).[37]

Turning back to Edwards, if we pore through his reflections and published writings, it is not hard to find him signaling his intimate acquaintance with the mystical life. Scholarship regarding Edwards has been less than enthusiastic about applying the "m" label as a major way to understand him. Yet, as early as 1889, Edwards biographer Alexander Allen found the "unmistakable marks of the mystic" in Edwards's writing—"union with God, absorption as it were into the inmost essence of the divine." By 1907, philosopher I. Woodbridge Riley was incorporating a similar sense of Edwardsian mysticism. Referring to three phases in Edwards's life, Riley linked the earliest to the mystical. He discerned "a certain intellectual duality" between Edwards as philosopher and Edwards as theologian, but in Edwards as an "ecstatic," he saw "little variableness." Indeed, a "common element, like a subterranean stream," flowed "steadily beneath the entire field of his speculations." Still more, Riley thought that Edwards's "type of piety" was "thoroughly the mystic type, the enjoyment of God in complete self-surrender to His Spirit and the communication of God himself to spirits directly by an immediate illumination."[38]

Eight years later, in the chapter "Early Idealism" in his *American Thought*, Riley included a subhead on "Jonathan Edwards, Mystic." There he argued that to see Edwards as a "relentless logician" illumined "only one side of the picture." The public Jonathan Edwards was a "pitiless professional theologian." But in private, matters were different. Citing the experiences of Edwards's boyhood and youth, Riley turned likewise to the mature years. It was then that Edwards wrote *Religious Affections* (1746), describing "the true believers' soul[s] as receiving light from the sun of righteousness in such a manner that their nature is changed, that they become little suns partaking of the nature of the fountain of their light." Riley went on to cite the traditional Western, three-stage mystical ascent—from purgation to illumination to union—in order to chart the mystical spirituality of Edwards. Diving deeply into Edwards's early thought, he discovered a religious seeker who acknowledged a three-stage process on the mystical path. "First . . . great and violent struggles" enabling "a spirit to part with all things in the world." Then "a kind of vision or certain fixed ideas and images of being alone in the mountains or some solitary wilderness far from all mankind; finally, a thought of being wrapt up in God in heaven, being, as it were, swallowed up in Him forever."[39]

For his part, White, echoing Riley, believed that he found in Edwards support for the proposition that "a man may be both a logical thinker and a mystic." Other scholars, from Parkes, with his allusion, in 1930, to Edwards's "mystic experience" and "God-intoxication," to Philip Gura, in 2005, with his reference to Edwards's "mystical thoughts" from 1723 to 1733, acknowledged a mystical Edwards, however fleetingly. For all this, there are many silences in the biographical literature on Edwards regarding a putative mysticism. Meanwhile, Winslow was at least careful about mystical assertions, and Miller, in his turn, adamantly dismissed any consideration of Edwardsian mysticism. Winslow had apparently read mystical literature, and she aimed for exactness. With references to the Edwards of the "Personal Narrative," she compared him to classic European mystics such as Jakob Boehme, Brother John of Parma, and Richard Rolle. She owned, too, that *mysticism* was a "dangerous word." Still, without a "more precise term," she was ready to link Edwards during his college experience to "this strangely diverse company." She also thought that, afterward, "he spoke their language to the letter." Yet she veered away from attributing to him the total, unitive experience of a Boehme, whom, she said, could forget analogy and "look into the very heart of things."[40]

For Miller, though, there was no room at all for ambivalence. Using a literary lens that could incorporate philosophical theology but brooked no interchange with comparative religions, Miller looked to Edwards's understanding of emotion. "I believe," he declared, "how utterly incorrect it is to call him, as he is often called a 'mystic.' At least, in any sense that would imply the merging of the finite individual with a distinctionless divine." Miller went on to connect a decidedly unmystical Edwards to Lockean sensationalism. "By redefining the historic Christian concept of grace as 'a new simple idea'—acquired through sensation and entirely dependent upon sensation—Edwards was asserting in the language of Locke the indestructible particularity of the individual experience."[41]

Yet, *pace* Miller, it is the religious *experience* of Edwards himself, as recorded in unpublished personal writing and then translated into the language of theology in his sermons and treatises, that tells another tale. Consider, especially, Edwards's narrative of the very private religious events that befell him from boyhood through the time of his conversion. I have already touched on these to some extent, but the Edwardsian account bears repeating in greater depth. Even as a boy, as I noted, Edwards had known "delight in religion." Beginning with a pleasure principle that would accompany his developing religiosity, Edwards moved further and further into the domain of the mystical—with much less attention to renunciation than promoted in classic Calvinist conversion experiences. Reading 1 Timothy at the point of his conversion, we recall, he had longed to be swallowed up in God. Going beyond the purgative way of penance and regret, he clearly entered on an illuminative path, remarking on the inward delights of contemplation, on the inner space in which he knew "a calm, sweet abstraction of soul from all the concerns o[f] this world." He envisioned being "far from all mankind, sweetly conversing with Christ, and wrapt and swallowed up in God." It was vision at this point, to be sure. But Edwards repeatedly invoked the language of ineffability that haunts the testimonies of Western mystics. There came "an ardor of my soul, that I know not how to express" and, walking in his father's pasture, "a sweet sense of the glorious majesty and grace of God, that I know not how to express."[42]

Still more, he entered into what Richard Maurice Bucke, much later in 1901, would call cosmic consciousness. With a "sense of divine things" that "gradually increased"—in a passage cited by Faust and Johnson for its pantheistic quality—divinity seemed to be almost everywhere in the natural world: "in the sun, moon and stars; in the clouds, and blue sky; in the grass, flowers, trees; in the water, and all nature." Foreshadowing by many years the contemplative habits of a Henry David Thoreau, he "often used to sit and view the moon, for a long time; and so in the daytime, spent much time in viewing the clouds and sky." And then there was the year 1737, as we saw, when Edwards had ridden into the woods for his health. He left his horse and began to walk. Then he saw, in a way that he thought "for me was extraordinary," a "view" that turned into a signally mystical event. "The person of Christ," Edwards recalled, "appeared ineffably excellent, with an excellency great enough to swallow up all thought and conception. Which continued, as near as I can judge, about an hour; which kept me, the bigger part of the time, in a flood of tears, and weeping aloud." He longed to "be emptied and annihilated; to lie in the dust, and to be full of Christ alone." "Several other times," he acknowledged, he had experienced "views very much of the same nature, and that . . . had the same effects."[43]

Edwards had paid his dues with "affecting views" of his "sinfulness and vileness," and he had worried that he did not have enough of a sense of sin. Still more, his dues seemed to become larger as he aged. Yet in terms crucial to this reading, he owned that "in some respects I was a far better Christian, for two or three years after my first conversion, than I am now." How did he know? He had "lived in a more constant delight and pleasure." Meanwhile, as he moved into the time of his writing, he confessed to "a more full and constant sense of the absolute sovereignty of God, and a delight in that sovereignty." By 1738 or 1739, he had felt so intensely "how sweet and blessed a thing it was, to walk in the way of duty" that he broke "into a kind of loud weeping," a state that lasted so long that he was "forced" to shut himself in and "fasten the doors." Edwards's response to his condition was telling. "I could not but as it were cry out, 'How happy are they which do that which is right in the sight of God! They are blessed indeed, they are the happy ones!'" He experienced "at the same time, a very affecting sense, how meet and suitable it was that God should govern the world, and order all things according to his own pleasure." He "rejoiced in it," he told the pages on which he wrote, and so he ended his revealing narrative.[44]

Whether or not we can posit full unitive experience for Edwards—although the hour that passed in 1737 when he walked in meditation and was swallowed up in Christ argues strongly for that—his mystical path led through flowers more than weeds. Instead of a glorification of suffering and an account of seemingly endless dark nights of the soul, Edwards walked in the way of joy and delight. His early mystical process was, manifestly, one of pleasure. At least five years before he wrote his narrative, he had delivered his often-cited sermon "A Divine and Supernatural Light," in which he publicly proclaimed, as we have seen, the "sense of the heart." Besides heart and emotion, though, the metaphor of light pointed to the visual and the visionary, and the sermon is significant in its repetitive invocation of the light-beyond-rational that God imparted to the Christian believer. Here was the illuminative way for the pious laity, the good news for those who experienced the emanation of God's excellency and beauty. Divine knowledge, it was "rational to suppose," had been "given immediately by God, and not . . . obtained by natural means." The "spiritual wisdom and grace" that God bestowed was a gift beyond others. "No gift or benefit" was "in itself so nearly related to the divine nature" and contained "so much a participation of the Deity." It was "a kind of emanation of God's beauty," and was "related to God as the light is to the sun." It was "nextly from himself, and by himself, according to his sovereign will."[45]

More than that, the light brought joy. There was nothing in human knowledge that compared "to that joy which arises from this divine light shining into the soul." This light illumined things that were "immensely the most exquisitely beautiful, and capable of delighting the eye of the understanding." Even beyond the joy, though, came a declaration of passage. The Christian could move from the illuminative way to the unitive experience of the divine. The light changed "the nature of the soul." Human nature was assimilated "to the divine nature," and the soul was transformed "into an image of the same glory that is beheld." Citing 2 Cor. 3:18, Edwards invited listeners to the fullness of divine encounter. "'But we all with open face beholding as in a glass the glory of the Lord, are changed into the same image, from glory to glory, even as by the Spirit of the Lord.'"[46]

More than a decade later, in 1746, Edwards's *Religious Affections*—which had provoked Miller to argue against the mysticism of its author—if read a different way (Riley had briefly done so), charted, within its emotional matrix, a short course on mystical theory. With the treatise's focus on affections, Edwards needed to clear a path for the higher and the more that might lie hidden behind the exuberance of "animal spirits." Because mind and body were knit together by "laws of union," the mind could "have no lively or vigorous exercise" without affecting the body. "So subject is the body to the mind, and so much do its fluids, especially the animal spirits, attend the motions and exercises of the mind, that there can't be so much as an intense thought, without an effect upon them." Even so, the affections and the heart could convey the *"spiritual, supernatural* and *divine."* For "true saints," the "Spirit of God" influenced the heart "as a principle of new nature." The "Scriptures" showed the Spirit as "dwelling" in the saints "as his temple, his proper abode, and everlasting dwelling place." Still more, the spirit was "represented as being there so united to the faculties of the soul" that it became "there a principle or spring of new nature and life." Put another way, Edwards was invoking the unitive state at the apex of mystical theory.[47]

But Edwards went further. With his own experience of beauty and delight coloring his mystical theology, he explained that holiness was "the nature of the Spirit of God" and that holiness was "as it were the beauty and sweetness of the divine nature." This, in fact, was "the proper nature of the Holy Spirit," just as heat was "the nature of fire, or sweetness was the nature of that holy anointing oil, which was the principal type of the Holy Ghost in the Mosaic dispensation." Now the soul became "a partaker of God's beauty and Christ's joy," truly in "fellowship" with father, son, and spirit. Though "infinitely less in degree," Edwards insisted that "the grace which is in the hearts of the saints, is of the same nature with the divine holiness"—just as "the brightness that is in a diamond which the sun shines upon, is of the same nature with the brightness of the sun." The transformation brought the mind what "some metaphysicians" called "a new simple idea." Taking John Locke to new places, as I have already suggested, Edwards posited "a new spiritual sense" within the mind, a sense so profound that the soul could be "compared to a raising of the dead, and to a new creation." The new spiritual sense came with "new dispositions" that were "new principles of nature." Manifestly, there had been "a new foundation laid in the nature of the soul."[48] Edwards had, in effect, argued that his new spiritual sense imbued the receptive Christian with a heretofore unknown capacity for mystical union with the divine—a union that brought with it thrills of delight and overwhelming perceptions of beauty.

Mystical theory disclosed mystical fact in Edwards's *End for Which God Created the World*, which, we recall, was one of the two capstone treatises at the end of his career. Reiterating analogies of emanation and flowing that had appeared in earlier writings, *End for Which God Created the World*, like all of Edwards's published works, stood out for its highly reasoned and meticulously argued tone. But its burden soared far beyond the rational in its intuitive grasp of the core of mystical experience, binding that experience securely to God's own purpose in making a world. Edwards declared the implicit mystical truth of total union as the divine object. Laboring intensively through six earlier sections of his exposition, in the seventh he was ready to count his gains. The end of creation, stated succinctly, was—familiarly—the glory of God. And without the creation, God had a problem. His glory was purely internal, and to be complete it required an audience—an external register for glory. So the glory of God, "when spoken of as the supreme and ultimate end of the work of creation, and of all God's works," was "the emanation and true external expression of God's internal glory and fullness." Uncomfortable, however, with a total distinction between internal and external glory, Edwards, the wordsmith, tried harder. An unexpressed "exercise of God's perfections," on the one hand, and "the creature's high esteem of God, love to God, and complacence and joy in God; and the proper exercises and expressions of these," on the other, were not "entirely distinct things." "If we more closely consider the matter, they will all appear to be one thing," he wrote. They were "but the emanation of God's glory; or the excellent brightness and fullness of the divinity diffused, overflowing, and as it were enlarged." The divine exercise of inner perfection in creation was "not distinct from the emanation or communication of his fullness." This meant that there was "nothing" in "this effectual exerting of God's perfection, but the emanation of God's internal glory."[49]

As I have already suggested, Edwards's language has raised questions for some regarding pantheism or panentheism. Without cheering for those in the camp of extreme immanentism, however, it is safe to observe that, if words could walk, Edwards's language here was walking a fine line between orthodoxy and something very different. But my point now is to move past that particular theological issue to point to the mystical foundation and follow-through from Edwards's words. And I aim to underscore it by recalling his own early mystical experience as one unavoidable basis for the positive theology he had now embraced. Whatever the relation between God and the universe in general, in the case and quality of the individual soul, the divine infusion meant that union with God was not only the soul's highest goal but also, at some level, its implicit state. In other words, a soul could not be—exist—without an abiding divine presence. God and every human soul were intrinsically one.

It is worth quoting Edwards closely on the issue: "In the creature's knowing, esteeming, loving, rejoicing in, and praising God, the glory of God is both exhibited and acknowledged; his fullness is received and returned. Here is both an *emanation* and *remanation*. The refulgence shines upon and into the creature, and is reflected back to the luminary. The beams of glory come from God, and are something of God, and are refunded back again to their original. So that the whole is *of* God, and *in* God, and *to* God; and God is the beginning, middle and end in this affair."[50] This is hardly the language about the divine nature of humans coming from the Unity School of Christianity and other New Thought movements in the late nineteenth-century and beyond. But it does, however careful and sophisticated its formulation, bear a family resemblance to the brasher assertions of later times.

In the Edwardsian implicit and explicit mysticism, we catch a glimpse, always, of the joy in the divine that infuses his particular slant on theological issues and on the spiritual life in general. Edwards was a man with a mission, and his mission was to announce the sweetness, delight, and beauty of divine life and of human life in tune with it. Using Christian—in fact, Calvinist—language to articulate his message, he still kept true to the early experiential grid through which particular ideas had flowed. The affections and animal spirits were there and would never go away. But in Edwards, they soared into a realm where both eroticism and a sense of the heart fused inseparably with a divine energy beyond what he was able—with all his words—to say. Edwards had approached the ineffable, and he would not be turned back.

Mather and Edwards were surely men of their times—Calvinist Christians who believed fiercely in all that the rhetoric of religion had unfolded for them and had woven inextricably into their lives. Moreover, I have already observed briefly some of the ways that their lives and experiences overlapped in key external ways. But here I want to lift out the internal character of their thought worlds and the experiential bases on which they rested. For both—perhaps surprisingly because of the Puritan stereotypes we have all inherited—certain themes emerge that would continue to characterize an American fascination with metaphysical religiosity. Themes such as a preoccupation with delight and beauty are easy to find in both, although Edwards surely had the edge on these. Likewise the cosmological theory of correspondence provided a framework for both aesthetic and everyday meaning-making. Platonism cast its long reflection for both, and they shaped their theological and philosophical discourse with its assumptions ever at hand. Still more, evangelicalism was not foreign to either. Indeed, it birthed a fundamental and profound episode and aftermath for Jonathan Edwards in the time of awakening in which he preached and wrote.

With all of these similarities, what stands out in the particular template into which each cast his spirituality was the primacy of the visual for Mather and of the affectional for Edwards. (In terms of the five senses, the tactile comes closest for Edwards—emotions "touch" us and arouse our "animal spirits" one way or another.) Mather *saw* visions and recounted narratives—seemingly endlessly—about others who told of startling visions with sights of strange and disrupting things. He had befriended history. Edwards, by contrast, *felt* his way to the truth he could tell, and he told it preferably in abstract terms—his thirty sermons on *A History of the Work of Redemption* (1739) notwithstanding. There was a pronounced circularity to his thought, a symbolic closeness that marked it, making it difficult, indeed, to pull apart as here I have tried to do. The heart did not wink or smile, or come to him in a former-day vision. Still, for both men, the truth that could be seen or told contained huge inputs for the aesthetic and the delightful. A theology of abundance characterized them—for Mather, with his pragmatic attention to wealth, prosperity, and political success; for Edwards, with his more emotionally charged renditions of the wealth of the spiritual world.

Beyond these markers, what needs to be noticed is the current of vitalism that ran through each man's words and works. For Mather, that current was encapsulated in his concept of the Nishmath-Chajim; for Edwards, it came through metaphors of emanation, flow, and the fountain-like activity of the divine. For both, it told of a distinct preference for energy and robust movement over the contentment of standing still. For the metaphysical future, the energetic dimension would grow stronger, even as early statements of the theology of abundance would mark Mather and Edwards as important embodiments of delight making, influenced by overseas voices but also very much homegrown. They had planted seeds. It would be left for later people and times, with inputs from a changing world and its increasing news from abroad to hybridize their message.

SECTION 2

Supernatural and Natural

"A foolish consistency," Ralph Waldo Emerson famously remarked, is "the hobgoblin of little minds."[1] If so, as the eighteenth century and the late-Puritan world of Jonathan Edwards faded into at least partial oblivion, new voices began to speak in an Anglo-American theology of desire. The voices—like Emerson's often-quoted words—were the product of less consistent theologians. They came from persons tied in one way or another to the clerical profession but—unlike Cotton Mather and Jonathan Edwards (who were, after all, active clerics throughout their days)—less rigorous in their take on theology. This is not to make too large a point of difference. But it is to suggest the gradual changes that became visible with time—its erosions and reconstructions as one era yielded to another.

The personalities of individual actors cannot be taken as stand-ins for an age, but something palpably new *was* abroad in the land by the middle years of the nineteenth century. Emerson himself probably nailed it best when he told a Boston Masonic Temple audience in 1842 that his Transcendentalism was "an age-old way of thinking" fallen "on Unitarian and commercial times." Perry Miller, as others before him, had connected the dots between Edwards and Emerson, but the pungency of Emerson's own insight regarding "Unitarian and commercial times" cuts to the core of the cultural changes afoot.[2] Both Unitarianism and commerce introduced distance into the pieties of preceding centuries. With deism and theological naturalism as viable options for an intellectual elite and with America's growing fondness for the business of business, not to mention the mobilizing industrial revolution, the delights of divinity had to be re-imagined and reconstituted—not only for Unitarians but for other Christians, too. In this context, the approaches worked through by the former Unitarian minister Emerson and the continuing Congregational cleric Horace Bushnell are instructive.

THREE

Ralph Waldo Emerson: Supernatural Naturalist

If we count both sides of his family, Emerson (1803–1882) had come from eight generations of "emphatically clerical stock." Liberal tendencies had already been visible in his grandfather William Emerson, who—in a controversy over Edwardsian theology—became minister to the Arminian faction of the church in Concord, Massachusetts, rejecting the Calvinist doctrine of predestination. Later he would die as an army chaplain in the Revolutionary War. William Emerson's son, also William, moved to Boston in 1799 to pastor the First Church there. He did not abandon his father's religious leanings, earning a reputation as the most liberal preacher in the city and also delving into numerous community-oriented projects. Yet, like many elite Bostonians of the period, he was a social and political conservative, valuing societal hierarchies, dubious about change, and deeply suspicious of the French Revolution. Meanwhile, he married Ruth Haskins, the daughter of a well-heeled distiller, and soon their family grew to include eight children. Only five—all sons—lived into adulthood, with Ralph Waldo the second oldest. The child was not quite eight when his father died of stomach cancer, and so death—of father, of siblings—confronted him from childhood. So did poverty. After William Emerson died, Emerson's mother ran a boarding house to support the family, and they entered a time of hardship. Yet Ruth Haskins Emerson valued education, and she saw promise in her son Ralph Waldo. At nine, he was matriculating at the elite Boston Latin School, and at fourteen, in 1817, he was admitted to Harvard College. Seven Emersons in five generations had preceded him there, and although the young Emerson would later rail against the curriculum of "Latin, Greek, and Mathematics," which the "Good Spirit" left as "shells high and dry on the beach," he graduated in good standing in 1821. He had never been at the top of his class, but he was noticed enough to be class poet, and he also began the practice of journal-keeping, something he would continue for more than fifty years.[1]

Politically, the young Emerson at first emulated his father with conservative values, and he became a Federalist (later a Whig). Religiously, also like his father, he was a liberal—now a Unitarian. He had already been teaching during the summer while still a student at Harvard, and after graduation he continued teaching, although he did not really like what he was doing. He turned, then, to divinity, pursuing theological studies at Harvard. He became ordained to preach in 1826, and later accepted ordination at the Second (Hanover Street) Church in Boston. Ironically enough, it was the pulpit that Increase and Cotton Mather had formerly inhabited. Three years later, in 1829, Emerson had become a married man, wedded to the still-teenage Ellen Tucker, fragile already with tuberculosis. Ellen would die two years later at twenty, from the same disease that would kill his brother Edward in 1834 and Charles, the youngest, in 1836.

Emerson himself had already experienced lung trouble since 1826 but traveled south and then recovered his health for a time. Later, following Ellen Tucker's death and its aftermath of crippling grief, theological and pastoral problems arose for him, even in the liberal context of Unitarianism. He objected to the administration of the Lord's Supper (the communion service). Still more, he was not exactly at his ease being a bedside comforter for the sick and dying. Awash in continuing turmoil, Emerson resigned from his ministry and, still suffering from weak health, began a European "tour"—something often accomplished by young men of a certain social class at the time. Traveling in Italy, Switzerland, France, England, and Scotland, he met, among others, Samuel Taylor Coleridge, William Wordsworth, and especially Thomas Carlyle, with whom he began a lifelong correspondence.

When Emerson returned home, he accepted invitations as guest preacher for empty pulpits but increasingly immersed himself in a career as an independent lecturer and poured himself into his writing. His speaking engagements moved out from New England into the mid-Atlantic states, the Midwest, and even—by his later years—the city of San Francisco. He became, in effect, a traveling sales clerk for the spirit. Prosperous in his new career, he had married Lydia Johnson in 1835, and a year later their first son, Waldo, was born. A banner year for Emerson, 1836 also saw the formation of the often-cited "Transcendental Club" and the publication of his small book *Nature*, which became the gospel of the emerging Transcendentalist movement. Two daughters came later—Ellen in 1839 and Edith in 1841—but in 1842 misfortune struck suddenly when Waldo died from scarlet fever. Edward Waldo, a second son, arrived in 1844. He grew to adulthood and eventually took charge of his father's literary legacy, collecting much of it and producing the widely used centenary edition of his father's works in 1903 and 1904.

Visitors frequented Emerson's home in Concord, among them a series of social reformers whom he received genially. By this time, Emerson—who would never exactly be a flaming liberal—had shifted noticeably from the social conservatism of his forebears, embracing such causes as antislavery and peace. He especially warmed to fellow Transcendental travelers—people like Bronson Alcott, Henry David Thoreau, (William) Ellery Channing, Margaret Fuller (ambivalently), and others who shared informal membership in a so-called Transcendental Club. By 1840, they were producing a literary periodical, *The Dial*, and after two years Emerson became its editor until the magazine folded in 1844. By this time, too, early collections of his essays began to appear, including a first and second series in 1841 and 1844 respectively. Two years later came a book of his poems (1846), and by 1849 he had published *Nature, Addresses, and Lectures*. The 1850s and 1860s saw the publication of still more collections of essays: the seven-lecture *Representative Men* (1849 and 1850), and *English Traits* (1856), followed by *The Conduct of Life* (1860), more poetry, and *May-Day and Other Pieces* (1867). Not to let his published works stand as they were, by 1870 Emerson had revisited the first six volumes of his prose to produce a volume titled *The Prose Works* as well as still another essay collection called *Society and Solitude*. Then in the 1870s his daughter Ellen, with James Elliot Cabot, transformed his lectures into *Letters and Social Aims* (1875), and subsequently Emerson collaborated with them for his *Selected Poems* (1876).

This steady stream of publications followed Emerson until a half dozen years before his death, leaving a formidable literary record that was also a quest of the spirit. He had been part poet and part philosopher, immersed in the details of living in his age but keeping one eye on the "self" of each individual and likewise on a horizon that shaded off into eternity. With an outer life that was comfortable, regular (except for lecture-driven travel), and thoroughly middle class, Emerson in his journaling told another tale of high spiritual adventure. In fact, a door swung both ways between his journals and his lecture-essays. In the journals, he recorded materials he had come across in his reading, mundane details, personal observations and complaints, and even sometimes dreams. Thus partial readings of Emerson can explode in a variety of directions, colors, and energies. His inbetweenness invites pursuits that lead here, there, and everywhere, seemingly limited only by an interpreter's intent. So as I follow Emerson along paths of delight and pleasure, love of nature and beauty, and supernature and analogy—alongside juxtapositions of prosperity and mysticism, and of vitalism and compensation—there is copious material for partial readings. Always, I argue, the key to making sense of him is to understand that at base his thinking was circular, evoking the title of one of his early essays. Emerson wrote in concentric circles—so much so that it is usually possible to enter an essay as one enters a movie theater, not worrying that one is halfway through a film. The alert viewer can still figure out, often exquisitely, what is going on, can discern the moral of the story, and then go back and view the first part with extra awareness. That done, the viewer—now Emersonian reader—can begin to discern that the circles are actually spirals, and at their own leisurely pace they are going somewhere—somewhere important to explore.[2]

Consider, if you will, Emerson's pithy essay "Circles," published as part of his first series in 1841. "The eye is the first circle," he announced. "The horizon which it forms is the second; and throughout nature this primary figure is repeated without end." Humans were not forgotten in the endless circularity, as the "eye" first suggested, and the circles of nature were woven into the circles of their lives. But the circles were going *somewhere*—they were hardly standing still. Already in his introductory paragraph, Emerson wrote declaratively that "every action admits of being outdone." "Our life is an apprenticeship to the truth, that around every circle another can be drawn; that there is no end in nature, but every end is a beginning; that there is always another dawn risen on mid-noon, and under every deep a lower deep opens." Applying the moral explicitly, he could tell readers a few paragraphs later that "the life of man is a self-evolving circle, which from a ring imperceptibly small, rushes on all sides outwards to new and larger circles, and that without end." But because the circles were going places, the concentric merged into the spirallic. In a belief later echoed by spiritualist Andrew Jackson Davis as he wrote of the spheres through which a soul traveled after death, Emerson proclaimed that "every ultimate fact is only the first of a new series."[3]

What Emerson called the "law of eternal procession" meant that the "natural world" might be understood in his familiar "concentric circles" as part of a system. But as so many tectonic plates, they shifted: "We now and then detect in nature slight dislocations, which apprize us that this surface on which we now stand, is not fixed, but sliding." Not only was this true outwardly but also inwardly, in the place where virtues formed and got expressed, for the law of eternal procession extinguished each "in the light of a better." Just to be clear on where all of this led, both within and without, Emerson admonished his readers, reminding them that he was "only an experimenter." Perhaps like a theological version of an earthquake report, he declared that he had no intention of settling anything "as true or false." "I unsettle all things. No facts are to me sacred; none are profane; I simply experiment, an endless seeker, with no Past at my back."[4]

Emerson's gospel announcement smacked of vitalism, and even, as we shall see, of a sublimated eroticism—a defiant thrust against death and deformity in the service of ever-unfolding life. Perhaps the ghost of Cotton Mather, who had preached from the Second Church's pulpit that Emerson left, was whispering intuitive news of the Nishmath-Chajim to the now secular Emerson. Perhaps it was Emerson's own visceral confrontation with the disintegration of what he held dearest or even a sluggish quality to his own life energy, which required continual pumping up. At any rate, like nature itself, which—as he said—abhorred the "old," with "old age" counted as "the only disease," he celebrated the young and their propensity for love. Even those who computed their biological age at seventy should become "organs of the Holy Ghost." "Let them be lovers," he enjoined. "In nature," he continued, "every moment is new; the past is always swallowed and forgotten; the coming only is sacred. Nothing is secure but life, transition, the energizing spirit." Now his words hinted subtly of Emanuel Swedenborg (see below), with his doctrine of "conjugial love" and twinned souls (which Emerson would later publicly renounce), and of Andrew Jackson Davis's coming message of marriage reform with the need for divorce. "No love can be bound by oath or covenant to secure it against a higher love," proclaimed Emerson. "People wish to be settled: only as far as they are unsettled, is there any hope for them"[5]

More than that, the concentricity of circles as they transmuted into spirals signaled the "insatiable desire" that lay at the base of human experience. The "one thing" that powered such desire was the urge "to forget ourselves, to be surprised out of our propriety, to lose our sempiternal memory, and to do something without knowing how or why; in short, to draw a new circle." This vitalistic impulse that proclaimed circles-become-spirals and exploded stasis into growth had already been announced in 1836 at the start of Emerson's revolutionary book *Nature*. If we jump ahead to its 1849 re-issue, a new epigraph notified readers unmistakably: "*A subtle chain of countless rings / The next unto the farthest brings ; / . . . And, striving to be man, the worm / Mounts through all the spires of form.*"[6] Still more, if we look at the revolution announced in the entirety of *Nature*, we see the nucleus of the first circle that would explode into all the other circles in Emerson's writing. It is here that the spiral began and here that we need to look further.

From the first paragraph of the introduction to *Nature*, Emerson was beating down tradition and his own "retrospective" age, which was building "the sepulchres of the fathers." With nature's "floods of life" streaming "around and through" his readers, he challenged, "Why should we grope among the dry bones of the past, or put the living generation into masquerade out of its faded wardrobe?" The sun was shining "to-day also." There were "new lands, new men, new thoughts." Nor did the vitalistic announcement of the powers of nature end with the first paragraph. As Emerson developed his theme, he assured readers that for the "lover of nature" an "intercourse with heaven and earth" became part of "daily food." The charged language continued, proclaiming that "in the presence of nature" such a lover knew a "wild delight" running through, with "every hour and season" yielding "its tribute of delight." Emerson wrote, apparently, from experience. In the woods and "standing on the bare ground," he had felt "the currents of the Universal Being" circulating through him. He had become "part or particle of God," a "transparent eye-ball"—that "first" sphere later extolled in "Circles"—that could "see all."[7]

Emerson was not finished magnifying circles. Such was the "plastic power of the human eye" that "primary forms"—like "the sky, the mountain, the tree, the animal"—gave "a delight *in and for themselves;* a pleasure arising from outline, color, motion, and grouping." Thus the "simple perception of natural forms" counted as "a delight." With vision ever primary, Emerson affirmed that the world existed "to the soul to satisfy the desire of beauty." The present time of nature, with its vital energy, gave the lie to a dead past in which humans could not fruitfully dwell. It followed that "a life in harmony with nature," with an attendant love of "truth and virtue," would "purge the eyes to understand her text." The reality of Emerson's era, though, was different. Humans were dwarfs of themselves, used but half their powers, and trusted only their understanding, which yielded a "pennywisdom." The world needed restoring to its "original and eternal beauty," and "the ruin or the blank" that humans saw when they looked at nature was in their "own eye." But the eye of the spirit required more. "Love" was "as much its demand, as perception." Neither could be "perfect without the other," and, lamentably, "in actual life, the marriage" was "not celebrated." Even so, it was clear how the marriage should go. Love and perception blurred as nature became the beloved—but a beloved clearly dominated by its human lovers. Vitalism and vision went hand in hand with power *over*—"the kingdom of man over nature" to be entered in a dazzling future with its restoration of "perfect sight" to a blind man. So beauty signaled, as Richard Holmes wrote of Samuel Taylor Coleridge (whom Emerson deeply admired), "an explosion of energy perfectly contained."[8]

Emerson's concentric circles led dizzyingly from one place to the next. Circle and spiral, eye and vision, nature and landscape, beauty and delight, desire and eros, vitalism and energy—all were interspoken. Where indeed were they going? To be sure, as Erik Ingvar Thurin has shown, Emerson was no sexualized "priest of Pan" (the Greek fertility deity), in a phrase from Emerson's essay "History." But as Len Gougeon has explained from a different perspective, Eros was no enemy either for the author of *Nature*. In fact, as Gougeon declared, "Emerson eventually found what he believed to be the center and source of all life: an overarching, mystical and all-encompassing divinity. . . . Eventually, he named this dynamic and transcendent force the 'Over-Soul,' but he also used other names such as Eros, the eternal One, the Reason, Love, or more traditionally, God." Gougeon went on to argue that Emerson thought of Eros "in its most original, mythological sense" as "the most ancient of all the Gods." "His function," wrote Gougeon, "was to coordinate the elements that constitute the universe." Eros, in short, brought "harmony" to "chaos," thereby personifying the "elemental force" that did so. For Emerson, observed Gougeon, "Eros represents the essential cosmic force, the glue that holds the universe and humanity together."[9]

Simply put, the core impulse that generated the vast canon of Emerson's lectures and writings was his ceaseless quest for the vital fluid, the sap of rising energy, that he found so deficient in his age and probably in himself. This is especially apparent in his memorable "Divinity School Address," his unmitigated attack on what he later pungently described as "corpse-cold Unitarianism"—a "thin porridge or cold tea" to the taste—and a death knell to living religion. Invited by a senior committee at Harvard Divinity School to speak at commencement in July 1838, Emerson used the occasion to lambaste ministerial education and its legacy. In truth, he had been especially provoked by the ordination of the Reverend Barzillai Frost, whose preaching left Emerson profoundly dissatisfied at his home church in Concord. Frost was a newly minted product of the Harvard Divinity School, full of knowledge of "higher" biblical criticism but apparently with few rhetorical gifts. As Conrad Wright demonstrated, Emerson cut significant pieces of his senior class address from the larger cloth of his personal journals. In them, he vented his complaints against what he regarded as the dreary and lackluster preaching of his church's new junior minister. "Here," Emerson bemoaned, was "a young man" (he was actually only a year younger than Emerson) who "pitiable & magisterial, & without nausea reads page after page of mouth-filling words & seems to himself to be doing a deed." By March of 1838, Emerson's emotional pitch had escalated, as he compared the efforts of the preacher to the storm-ridden landscape outside. "At Church all day but almost tempted to say I would go no more. . . . The snowstorm was real the preacher merely spectral. Vast contrast to look at him & then out of the window." Three months later and but a few weeks away from "The Divinity School Address," Emerson—without identifying Frost or senior minister Ezra Ripley—contrasted what his church served up with the beauty of nature. "The faith should blend with the light of rising & of setting suns, with the flying cloud, the blooming clover, & the breath of flowers; But now the Sabbath, the priest's Sabbath has long lost the splendor of nature, it is unlovely, we are glad when it is done."[10]

By the time Emerson delivered his July address, he was ready to convert the particular into the universal. Filled with confidence, no doubt, by *Nature*'s critical success and the smooth reception of further work, he felt ready to broadside Unitarian education and its results. To one familiar with his personal journal entries, the opening of Emerson's address sounds acutely familiar. As in the journals, its vitalistic burden is huge. Nature flows with rising energy. The church and its educational system, meanwhile, were to be castigated for being moribund and even worse.

"In this refulgent summer," Emerson intoned, "it has been a luxury to draw the breath of life. The grass grows, the buds burst, the meadow is spotted with fire and gold in the tint of flowers. The air is full of birds, and sweet with the breath of the pine, the balm-of-Gilead, and the new hay." Now he told the class that there existed a "law of laws." "All things proceeded out of the same spirit," and a person must seek "good ends" to be "strong by the whole strength of nature." Perceiving this law awakened the "religious sentiment," which lay at "the foundation of society" and created "all forms of worship." But to access the truth that worship conveyed, a person required "intuition." Faith could not be "received at second hand." When it departed, a person became "an appendage, a nuisance." Instead of the indwelling "Supreme Spirit" acknowledged in all, "the divine nature" was "attributed to one or two persons, and denied to all the rest, and denied with fury." Then came the upshot of the situation: "The very word Miracle, as pronounced by Christian churches, gives a false impression; it is Monster. It is not one with the blowing clover and the falling rain." As he warmed to his subject, Emerson moved on to consider the role of the preacher with words that he had earlier used to condemn the efforts of Barzillai Frost. "I once heard a preacher who sorely tempted me to say, I would go to church no more. . . . A snowstorm was falling around us. The snowstorm was real; the preacher merely spectral; and the eye felt the sad contrast in looking at him, and then out of the window behind him, into the beautiful meteor of the snow." What was wrong with the preacher? "He had lived in vain. He had no one word intimating that he had laughed or wept, was married or in love, had been commended, or cheated, or chagrined." He had not learned "the capital secret of his profession" and did not "convert life into truth."[11]

By contrast, Emerson charged the would-be ministerial graduates with his own vision and dream. "Yourself a newborn bard of the Holy Ghost,—cast behind you all conformity, and acquaint men at first hand with Deity." The remedy for Divinity School death rose from the vital center of nature and eros as Emerson shared his wished-for future. "I look for the hour when that supreme Beauty, which ravished the souls of those Eastern men, and chiefly of those Hebrews, and through their lips spoke oracles to all time, shall speak in the West also." Now came the circle again, as ever concentric. "I look for the new Teacher, that shall follow so far those shining laws, that he shall see them come full circle; shall see their rounding complete grace; shall see the world to be the mirror of the soul; shall see the identity of the law of gravitation with purity of heart; and shall show that the Ought, that Duty, is one thing with Science, with Beauty, and with Joy."[12]

This vitalistic impulse with its undertones of eros pervaded Emerson's writing career, although there is hardly space here to follow it in a systematic way. But the intertwining of vitalism with virtually all of the Emersonian corpus is an issue that cannot be ignored. William Clebsch, in fact, noted Emerson's fondness for the Roman poet Ovid's phrase, "God is in us, and when he stirs we become warm," a characterization that Emerson wrote into his journals four times—in 1826, 1828, 1832, and 1833. Later, Clebsch added, Emerson shaped the idea in his own terms, alternating between humanistic and theological statements. Accordingly, his first series of essays continually stirred readers with images of vital energy. In its opening piece, "History," for example, he seemed almost to be repeating his introduction from "The Divinity School Address." "Upborne and surrounded as we are by this all-creating nature," he asked rhetorically, "why should we be such hard pedants, and magnify a few forms?" Moreover, the primal energy within nature was love, and Emerson remarked that "a mind might ponder its thought for ages, and not gain so much self-knowledge as the passion of love shall teach it in a day." In "Self-Reliance," he objected to "conforming to usages that have become dead to you" because it scattered "your force." He sought the "magnetism which all original action exerts," and extolled the unadulterated life. "Life only avails," he wrote, "not the having lived. Power ceases in the instant of repose; it resides in the moment of transition from a past to a new state, in the shooting of the gulf, in the darting to an aim." In "Compensation," he reiterated the message: human life was "progress, and not a station."[13]

With more development and depth, Emerson's essay "Love" probed vitalistic and erotic themes in subtle ways, conflating love with beauty and transforming the world into a staging ground for a universal celebration of its text. Love began with "the young" but did not forsake "the old," Emerson enthused. It was "a fire that, kindling its first embers in the narrow nook of a private bosom, caught from a wondering spark out of another private heart, glows and enlarges until it warms and beams upon multitudes of men and women, upon the universal heart of all, and so lights up the whole world and all nature with its generous flames." In the "high philosophy of Beauty" that "delighted" the ancients, "the Deity" sent "the glory of youth before the soul" in order that it might "avail itself of beautiful bodies as aids to its recollection of the celestial good and fair." If not over-indulged and "accepting the hint of these visions and suggestions" made by beauty, the soul passed "through the body." Lovers then admired "strokes of character" and contemplated each other "in their discourses and their actions," passing thus to "the true palace of Beauty," inflaming "their love of it, and by this love extinguishing the base affection." By loving the high and noble in one person, the lover came to love them "in all." And so, "beholding in many souls the traits of the divine beauty, . . . the lover ascends to the highest beauty, to the love and knowledge of the Divinity."[14]

This was idealized love, surely, and its echoes of Plato's *Symposium* were blatant. Still more, it without doubt managed to evaporate the erotic in eros, a conclusion that was central to Thurin's study *Emerson as Priest of Pan*. Emerson had, after all, remarked in his essay that young love with its "magical play of charms" was "deciduous." Its best feature was that it put men and women "in training for a love which knows not sex, nor person, nor partiality, but which seeks virtue and wisdom everywhere, to the end of increasing virtue and wisdom."[15] Still, for all that, Emerson's preoccupation with a primal energy that could infuse and empower all of life remained.

Take, for example, "Friendship"—on a related theme in Emerson's first collection of essays. It pointed noticeably to his enthusiasm for conversation, a practice abundantly exercised from 1836 in the Transcendental Club. Applying to conversation the "law of *one to one*" as "peremptory," Emerson thought it "the practice and consummation of friendship." In fact, the "high freedom of great conversation" required "an absolute running of two souls into one." Thurin has pointed out that the word "conversation" contained older meanings than our present usage, and one of them was sexual intercourse. As late as 1870, in his essay on "Clubs," Emerson explored the mysterious and, in fact, titillating nature of conversation in a long sequence of observations. People kindled each other, and Emerson thought that the "best conversation" was "between two persons who can only talk to each other." Even in general, Emerson had observed that "in higher activity of mind, every new perception" was "attended with a thrill of pleasure." "The imparting of it to others" was "also attended with pleasure." By 1875 he had not forgotten his estimate. He would write that conversation, "when it is best," constituted "a series of intoxications."[16]

In 1841, however, the fusion of two souls running into one another was more explicitly addressed in "The Over-Soul." Emerson expressed its source in one of his favorite metaphors—a "flowing river, which, out of regions I see not, pours for a season its streams into me." It revealed him to be "a pensioner; not a cause" and "a surprised spectator of this ethereal water." When he desired and looked up, he knew that "from some alien energy the visions come," with Emerson himself a stand-in for so many others. So he hailed "the transcendent simplicity and energy of the Highest Law"—a law that, to jump ahead to the twentieth century, would be embodied in a trance practice called channeling. But meanwhile, in this first series of essays, Emerson's final piece "Art" linked the mysterious river of Emerson's "Over-Soul" to its own animating principle. "True art" was "never fixed," Emerson insisted, "but always flowing."[17]

Three years later, in his *Essays: Second Series*, Emerson had not laid aside his search for a life energy that would infuse all things. Significantly, he began the series with an impassioned tribute to "The Poet." Complaining about an impoverished perception of beauty abroad in the land, Emerson lamented that people had lost a sense of "the instant dependence of form upon soul." "We were put into our bodies, as fire is put into a pan," he told readers, and then his vitalism sparked and flashed. We were not "pans and barrows," Emerson wrote adamantly, "not even porters of the fire and torch-bearers." Rather, we were "children of the fire, made of it." We were "divinity transmuted," a reality that drew him (and, he thought, should draw readers) to consider "the nature and functions of the Poet, or the man of Beauty." Now he could answer the question about "why bards love wine, mead, narcotics, coffee, tea, opium, the fumes of sandal-wood and tobacco," and "other procurers of animal exhilaration." When the poet let go and spoke "somewhat wildly" without allowing the intellect to take over, he was performing his essential service. "Suffering the ethereal tides to roll and circulate through him," he was "caught up into the life of the Universe." His speech became "thunder"; his thought was "law." The lesson for other more conventional humans was clear. "As the traveler who has lost his way, throws his reins on his horse's neck, and trusts to the instinct of the animal to find his road, so must we do with the divine animal who carries us through this world." Indeed, language itself was once vital and alive, with the poet as "Namer, or Language-maker." But the language humans spoke dragged and drained. It was "fossil poetry," with the etymologist's original "brilliant picture" now become the "deadest word." Death was all around with every passing syllable, and humans needed continually to reconnect and remember a deeper, more vibrant life. "The Universe" was "the externization of the soul." "Wherever the life is," Emerson continued, "that bursts into appearance around it."[18]

The sort of life that would burst into appearance with universal energy was Emerson's constant quest and question. For him, disengaged thought could not be worth its while, since as Gougeon summarized, "thought without passion" was "arid and lifeless." Emerson, noted Gougeon, once confessed to his journal that he was seeking a "spermatic book," and he used the same term to indicate the writings of Plato, Plutarch, and Plotinus. It is no surprise, then, that by 1860 a much older Emerson, with his love of the concentric, could return to reflections on beauty with vitalistic, indeed sensuous, lenses. In *The Conduct of Life*, he pursued a theme that had graced the writing of the much younger man. Beauty was "the moment of transition, as if the form were just ready to flow into other forms." He instructed readers that "to this streaming or flowing belongs the beauty that all circular movement has; as, the circulation of waters, the circulation of the blood, the periodical motion of planets, the annual wave of vegetation, the action and reaction of nature." "And if we follow it out," he added, "this demand in our thought for an ever onward action, is the argument for the immortality." Tracing this continual preoccupation with change, Thurin summarized that "to Emerson the idea that the individual and the universe exist only in transition" was "exhilarating."[19]

Even a dozen years before his death, in 1870, Emerson found ways to express the same subtle eroticism that had graced his younger years. His essay "Books," for example, acknowledged that some books were so important to "private experience" that they ranked "with parents and lovers and passionate experiences." In the seemingly mundane "Domestic Life," he found the "ornament of a house" to be "the Friends who frequent it" and went on to celebrate "Love" as "only the highest symbol of friendship, as all other things seem symbols of love." With age, he reflected, "in the progress of each man's character his relations to the best men, which at first seem only the romances of youth, acquire a graver importance." Similarly, in his essay "Inspiration," published in 1875 as part of *Letters and Social Aims*, Emerson extolled a different form of friendship—the "solitary converse with nature."

"For thence," he wrote, were "ejaculated sweet and dreadful words never uttered in libraries."[20]

Much earlier, in the 1840s, Emerson hailed the inspired poet, as Thurin had it, "at the very center and core of the universe." Characterizing Emerson's thought regarding this figure, Thurin pointed to the Transcendentalist's metaphorical suggestion "that the poet is not so much a token of the love of heaven and earth as the very copula which holds them together *in coitu*, as it were." Thurin also went on to quote an article Emerson published in the *Dial* magazine. Wrote Emerson there: "The poet, like the electric rod, must reach from a point nearer the sky than all surrounding objects, down into the earth, and into the dark wet soil or neither is of use."[21]

For Emerson, as his words here suggest, eroticism was not only vital but also *useful*. So the question becomes, what was the use of the poet and his electric connection to heaven, earth, and all of nature? We can glance, for example. at Emerson's mature essay "Inspiration," which echoed his earlier *Dial* article. Seeking the "fluid" of inspiration, he asked, "Where is the Franklin with kite or rod for this fluid?—a Franklin who can draw off electricity from Jove himself, and convey it into the arts of life, inspire men, take them off their feet?" Again, Emerson's answer uncannily suggested the twentieth-century (and ongoing) category of channeling. Mystic and poet literally became Franklinian lightning rods, as he repeatedly identified a divine connection that made of both instruments for higher knowledge. Citing the celebrated Emanuel Swedenborg (whose persona and writings brought Emerson conflicted feelings, as we shall see), he thought that the eighteenth-century Swedish mystic's "genius" lay in his perception that "'the Lord flows into the spirits of angels and of men.'" "All poets," Emerson emphasized, "have signalized their consciousness of rare moments when they were superior to themselves,—when a light, a freedom, a power came to them, which lifted them to performances far better than they could reach at other times."[22]

One "religious poet," Emerson remembered, "told me that he 'valued his poems, not because they were his, but because they were not.'" If, as Emerson said, the poet claimed "angels" as his source, German mystic Jacob "Behmen" (Jakob Boehme or Böhme) confessed, in Emerson's quotation, to a similar influx. "'All was ordered according to the direction of the spirit, which often went on haste,—so that the penman's hand . . . did often shake. . . . The burning fire often forced forward with speed, and the hand and pen must hasten directly after it, for it comes and goes as a sudden shower.'" Emerson's Boehme quotation continued in unambiguous terms:

"'In one quarter of an hour I saw and knew more, than if I had been many years together at an university.'"[23]

Such talk, of course, was more or less standard fare for mystics, and similar descriptions of high poetic art trail not far behind. Still further, by the twentieth century and beyond, the divinity that flowed into mystics and poets would become radically democratized. Ordinary people, without special religious or poetic gifts, could claim to be vehicles for messages from a world beyond. For Emerson, though, it was sufficient to acknowledge an elite cadre of inspired ones and, at the same time, to point—as in my earlier allusion—to their usefulness. In fact, it was the *use* of such gifts and messages that seemed to keep Emerson grounded in the otherwise sublimated consciousness that Platonic and Neo-Platonic idealism, personal experience, and wide reading and reflection had produced. And it was precisely here that his Puritan background poked through and rendered him, in many ways, a man in the middle.

Emerson's paternal aunt, Mary Moody Emerson, from early in his life provided what Robert D. Richardson Jr. categorically called "the single most important part of Emerson's education." A diarist and avid letter writer, she blended ideas from the Edwards brand of Calvinism with wide and sophisticated reading and visionary insights of her own. She had lived on and off with her brother's family during Emerson's childhood, and her correspondence seemingly never ceased (in fifty years she literally produced thousands of pieces of journal writing and lengthy epistles). Meanwhile, her idiosyncrasies included a notable preoccupation with death. According to Richardson, she slept in a bed constructed with a coffin's shape and, when traveling, clad herself in a burial shroud, wearing out several of them because of her frequent trips. His aunt's Calvinist tinge made its mark on Emerson for a lifetime, and the Puritan heritage of his forebears was in general never lost on him. One wonders if his vitalism, with its overtones of eros, was not at least partially a response to his aunt's obsession with death.[24] Be that as it may—and this is the point here—Emerson always displayed a significant degree of caution and even mistrust for anything that smacked of the paranormal or the occult arts.

The caution and mistrust were already apparent in an early lecture that Emerson delivered at Boston's Masonic Temple in 1839. Titled "Demonology," it stood as the last in a series of lectures titled *Human Life*, and it was surely the most intriguing. Unlike the Puritan Cotton Mather, who had reveled in things occult and ascribed them to supernatural forces, his Transcendentalist heir saw his subject as the somewhat dubious work of natural powers. Here Emerson intended to explore altered states of consciousness, and his reflections on them were at first not negative. He introduced his topic as

"Dreams, Omens, Coincidences, Luck, Sortilege, Magic, and a large variety of facts which are supposed to indicate the presence of some foreign, unacknowledged element in nature that produces exceptions to, if not violations of, the ordinary laws." He also told his audience that "dreams, however monstrous and grotesque their apparitions, have a substantial truth" and thought that his remark could cover "omens, coincidences, presentiments." Emerson did not doubt that a person's fortune might be "read in the lines of his right hand by palmistry,—in the lines of his face by physiognomy, in the outlines of the skull by craniology." His exploration, however, soon turned sour. He observed that "a large proportion of the facts called demonological" were actually "semi-medical questions." Then he turned with a vengeance to mesmerism or animal magnetism. He obviously disliked surrendering one's freedom "by deputy in another self" and went on to castigate: "All these facts are the phenomena of Disease; all these facts are of so fuliginous, nocturnal, and typhoid a character, as to repel rather than invite."[25]

As Emerson lumped together all of "this obscure class of facts," he acknowledged that "some minds" ran "eagerly into this twilight." But it was clear that Emerson preferred the sun. He thought a theory was "greatly to be desired." Obscure facts were "entitled only to a share of our attention and that not a large share." If you would read the famed German occult author Cornelius Agrippa or the work of someone similar, you would be "bewildered and brought into low and noisome alleys and blind lanes that lead nowhere." "Occult facts" were "merely physiological," and they threw "no light and no aid" on the "problem why we live and what we do." It was, Emerson continued, "a false view to couple them in any manner with the religious nature and sentiments and a dangerous superstition to raise them to the lofty place of motives and sanctions." Such ideas would lead inquirers "to prefer haloes and rainbows to the sun and moon." And yet, and yet. Something in him struggled against his Puritan self and encouraged his unsuccessful search for a use in the demonological. He confessed to "the attraction which this topic has had for me."[26]

Emerson allowed that "the numberless forms in which this superstition has re-appeared in every time and every people indicates the inextinguishableness of wonder." A "superstition" pointed to the human conviction— "that behind all your explanations and all your theories, is a vast and potent living nature inexhaustible and sublime which you cannot explain." "Demonology," in short, existed as "the Shadow of Theology."[27] All the same, by the time Emerson delivered his series of lectures entitled "Uses of Great Men" in 1845 and included Emanuel Swedenborg among them, his distance from the demonological had grown larger.

I have already fleetingly cited Swedenborg (1688–1772)—a major figure who will weave in and out of this narrative here and in later chapters. He became one of three Europeans (the others, Franz Anton Mesmer—see later here and in chapter 6—and Charles Fourier—in chapter 5) who most profoundly affected a growing culture of delight makers. Son of a man who by 1718 became a Lutheran bishop, Swedenborg grew to be a polymath with prodigious talents. He completed studies in 1709 at (Swedish) Uppsala University, became Extraordinary Assessor in the Royal College of Mines, and also spent fifty years in the House of Nobles, one of the four bodies that comprised the Swedish legislature. Meanwhile, his scientific discoveries and inventions spanned an enormous range, rendering him a kind of Leonardo da Vinci for the Scandinavian world. He published volumes on algebra, chemistry, and physics, wrote voluminously on both philosophy and scripture, and worked to unify his scientific knowledge and discoveries with his emerging theological and philosophical views. His work on correspondence, on divine influx into the human world, on the Divine Human (and by implication the divinity of humans), on the afterlife, and on similar topics changed the perspective of metaphysical religiosity at a crucial stage in its growth.[28]

Especially important for an emerging metaphysical spirituality, from midlife Swedenborg began to experience a series of trance-produced voice-visions. He became a celebrated champion of altered states, with seemingly endless visits to heaven, hell, and even other planets, and copious written reports of his travels in numerous books. He had become the darling of elite Boston Unitarians, and his disciples in the Swedenborgian church were well-known among Unitarians. So it was that, by 1850, Emerson's essay collection *Representative Men* was published, and Swedenborg, under this more subdued title, was included—the volume's representative of the "Mystic." By now, the youthful enthusiasm that Emerson had entertained for Swedenborg and the Swede's openness to the paranormal had become significantly tempered. Swedenborg, he told readers, suffered from "theological cramp." Swedenborg's "pernicious theologic limitation" was expressed in the doctrine of the "Inferno" and his belief in "devils." Still more, Swedenborg was a "strange, scholastic, didactic, passionless, bloodless man, who denote[d] classes of souls as a botanist dispose[d] of a carex, and visit[ed] doleful hells, as a stratum of chalk or hornblende!" Swedenborg had "no sympathy" (and, we might add, no abiding vitalistic subtext). The Swedish seer, who saw so much and so deeply, "remained devoid of the whole apparatus of poetic expression." "His books have no melody, no emotion, no humour, no relief to the dead prosaic level," complained Emerson.[29]

Acknowledging Swedenborg's reliance on the theory of correspondence (which Emerson had found among the Swedish seer's disciples, including American Sampson Reed), and affirming that Swedenborg "let in nature again," he still found discomfort in his brand of mysticism. Swedenborg's universe suffered "under a magnetic sleep," and it only reflected "the mind of the magnetizer." More than that, Swedenborg's teaching of "conjugial love"—each soul a half with a heaven-ordained soulmate, so that there was marriage in heaven—no doubt shocked Emerson's Calvinist sensibilities, for all Swedenborg's seeming bloodlessness elsewhere. Swedenborg had "unfolded the science of marriage," but his work "failed of success." Although Emerson was circumspect in reviewing Swedenborg's writing on the theme, his conclusion was negative. "Heaven is not the pairing of two, but the communion of all souls."[30]

Emerson's Calvinist roots, however, were expressed in more than simple discomfort with the paranormal, celestial marriage, and—as we have to some extent seen—even earthly marriage. Tellingly, we can raise eyebrows regarding his own marriage on earth. It was true that by the mid-nineteenth century, families had grown considerably smaller than in Puritan days. Even so, by the standards of 1850, six to nine children were common in families, and Emerson's own family of three living children and one who died was small. Add to this that historians have long shown that Puritan aversion to sexuality has been much overplayed and that, within a conventional marriage, New England Puritans generally enjoyed their sex lives. Recall, as examples, that Cotton Mather fathered fifteen children, and Jonathan Edwards, eleven. But certainly an implicit Calvinist perspective must have at least partially shaped Emerson's sexual reservations, which were quite explicit throughout his writings. In a notable example, his essay "Love," in his first series, bore out Thurin's already-noted reservations about the Transcendental leader as "priest of Pan." (Thurin, after a searching chapter on Platonic dialectic and marriage, had assessed that for Emerson "from the point of Platonic dialectic the only perfectly safe women" were "dead women.") Emerson himself, in his essay supposedly concerning the joys and delights of love, had concluded—as we have already seen—that we were "put in training for a love which knows not sex, nor person, nor partiality, but which seeks virtue and wisdom everywhere, to the end of increasing virtue and wisdom." With his strong vitalistic impulse, Emerson had worshipped at the shrine of Eros, it was true, but Eros presided there in idealized form. This was hardly the stuff of conventional eroticism.[31]

On another front, though, Emerson's Puritan heritage, and especially his immersion in it through his close relationship with his aunt—the journal-keeping and epistolary Mary Moody Emerson—meant for him an abiding access to inner experience and its cultivation. In this context, one of his early lectures called religion "the emotion of reverence which the conscious presence and activity of the Universal Mind inspires"—a description William Clebsch cited for its similarity to other Emersonian pronouncements. Clebsch noted, too, Emerson's consistent reference to "the sentiment of reverence or veneration or virtue as the means by which people responded to the stirrings of the divine soul within them."[32]

"Everywhere," Emerson wrote in "The Over-Soul," "the history of religion betrays a tendency to enthusiasm, . . . varying forms of that shudder of awe and delight with which the individual soul always mingles with the universal soul." His entire essay—to which I have already alluded briefly—suggested, however ambiguously (more on this later), that when Emerson talked of religion and the experience of it, he spoke from an inner world. As he would do—and as we have seen—in his much later essay "Inspiration," Emerson addressed, at the outset, "a difference between one and another hour of life, in their authority and subsequent effect," observing that faith came in "moments" only. Yet, he affirmed, "there is a depth in those brief moments, which constrains us to ascribe more reality to them than to all other experiences." He ascribed these miracles of depth to "that Unity, that Over-Soul, within which every man's particular being is contained and made one with all other," and he saw within each person "the soul of the whole" and "the eternal ONE." From this experiential base, he staked out the territory for the rest of his essay: now he was able to specify revelation—"an ebb of the individual rivulet before the flowing surges of the sea of life." "Every moment" when the individual felt so "invaded" was "memorable." This, he affirmed, was the source of enthusiasm. This was the base for giving up questions about the future to live in the present, "accepting the tide of being which floats us into the secret of nature." Hence, he urged all to "work and live, work and live," so that the "advancing soul" would build and forge "a new condition." At that point, "the question and the answer" would be "one."[33]

Comparing evidence such as this regarding Emerson's experiential base to that of Jonathan Edwards, J. August Higgins, not surprisingly, linked both to aesthetics, and he called the Transcendentalist's aesthetics of nature "a form of spiritual practice." For Emerson, it was not simply the idea of nature that was "spiritually transformative" but its "experience." While Edwards turned to the Holy Spirit in his experiential and "onto-aesthetic" understanding, Higgins argued, for Emerson, the crux of all beauty and its ability to generate spiritual experience came from nature. Emerson's challenge to build your own world in his book *Nature*, wrote Higgins, was itself grounded in his conviction that "Nature in its essential unity of spirit exists to be perceived, to be encountered, and to be participated in." Higgins concluded that, for both Edwards and Emerson, there was "an undeniable relationship between aesthetic experience and the structure of reality in its transcendent and immanent dimensions." The relationship provided "the foundation of spiritual experience," and this whether "the object of that experience" was "symbolized as God or Nature."[34]

Emerson's Puritan and Calvinist heritage shone through in other respects as well. For all his apotheosis of nature, pace Higgins, Emerson saw it as a temporary phenomenon only, as demonstrated in an early lecture from 1833. "This, because the whole of Nature is a metaphor or image of the human Mind." If the chance were given to someone, that individual might "study the leaves of the lightest flower that opens upon the breast of summer." Why so? Emerson explained, "in the faith that there is a meaning therein before whose truth and beauty all external grace must vanish." And here was the crucial part: "as it may be, all this outward universe shall one day disappear, when its whole sense hath been comprehended and engraved forever in the eternal thoughts of the human mind." Thurin has remarked that, given observations such as this, Emerson's monism was foreign to a true embrace of science and humanism. Instead, it suggested "an apocalyptic idea of man's redemption rather than a merely millennial dream of a terrestrial paradise of the kind reflected in [romantic poet William] Wordsworth's lines about the wedding of man and nature."[35] Yet the vision here was complex—Puritan and Calvinist distrust of the earthly mixed congenially with the Platonic idealism that had captured Emerson's philosophical perspective.

Moreover, to make matters still more complicated, ultimate monism yielded before an embrace of nature and all things earthly as so many signs and symbols of the spiritually real. Emerson was an inveterate champion of the theory of correspondence that had permeated the thought of Cotton Mather and Jonathan Edwards—their analogical view of the world as a set of spheres pointing forever heavenward. Emerson's gospel announcement of the grand scheme of correspondence in *Nature* (1836) laid the groundwork for the many essays and addresses that followed. The book's fundamental structure was predicated on the conviction that things were both themselves and also signals of other realities, so many sacramental indicators of parts of nature and a supernature—a macrocosm—beyond matter and earth. Such a worldview was not only intimately connected to Emerson's Puritan past but also affirmed, from one front, the Platonic idealism in which material items existed only as copies of truly real ideas. More than that, the doctrine of correspondence had been trumpeted widely in the Swedenborgian teachings rife among Boston Unitarians, and Emerson, as I have already begun to note, read Swedenborg and also his disciple Sampson Reed and other Swedenborgians avidly. From the Puritan side, whereas Mather and Edwards were quick to point to the providential intent of earthly happenings as they acknowledged a biblical God teaching through material means, Emerson's view was more distant and circumspect. Meanwhile, an advancing scientific worldview, from its own side, was promoting a linear logic of cause and effect that would soon make doctrines of correspondence, analogy, and their like the province of poets, prophets, preachers, occultists, and cultural reactionaries.

Within this mélange, there is probably no more startling expression of Emerson's humanistic view of correspondence than his application of it, not in expected terms to nature, but instead to the vast canvas of experience in history. It is not without significance that his essay "History" appeared as the opening piece in his first series of essays in 1841. With the rather expansionist lines that he penned as its epigraph ("I am owner of the sphere, / Of the seven stars and the solar year, / Of Lord Christ's heart, and Shakspeare's strain"), "History" upended any academic practice of the discipline. There was "one mind common to all," Emerson announced. "What Plato has thought," anyone could think; "what a saint has felt, he may feel; what at any time has befallen any man, he can understand." History was the "record" of the "works" of the one mind, and all of the facts of history preexisted "as laws." Each person was "the whole encyclopaedia of facts" so that "Egypt, Greece, Rome, Gaul, Britain, America" lay "folded already in the first man." Emerson was relentless. "Epoch after epoch, camp, kingdom, empire, republic, democracy" were the "application" of the "manifold spirit to the manifold world." And "if the whole of history" resided in one person, it was "all to be explained from individual experience." There was, Emerson stated flatly, "a relation between the hours of our life and the centuries of time."[36]

But there was more to "History" than the invocation of the one mind. Vast as that expanse was, it had its correlative. Side by side and intermingling with mind, nature would not vanish. History needed "to be read and written" from the second fact—after the first concerning the one mind—that nature was its "correlative." Invested with mind and nature, history would no longer be "a dull book." "Every history," Emerson exhorted, "should be written in a wisdom which divined the range of our affinities and looked at facts as symbols." By contrast, he was "ashamed to see what a shallow village tale our so-called History is." In the end, there was far more than human history. Nature trumped it all, and "the path of science and of letters" was "not the way into nature." Children and unschooled farmer's lads stood "nearer to the light by which nature is to be read, than the dissector or the antiquary."[37]

So it is that to nature we can turn to explore Emersonian ideas of correspondence more fully. In his manifesto of 1836—his little book *Nature*—perhaps what is most striking is the distinction that Emerson announced in his introduction. The universe consisted of two entities, "Nature and the Soul." Within this division, the scope of "Nature" was vast and inclusive; it encompassed "both nature and art, all other men and my own body." It signaled all that was "NOT ME." Given this seemingly lopsided distinction, it was clear that the major and ultimate partner for comparison would be the Soul. On the way to the high abode of the Soul, however, there were abundant sites for the repetition of natural and cultural forms that the theory of correspondence invited. "The universe is pervaded with secret analogies that tie together its remotest parts," Emerson would tell a Boston audience in 1839. "The whole world is an omen and a sign," and the "voice of divination resounds everywhere." Even so, Emerson—as *Nature* made so very clear—*used* the natural world. "The beauty of nature reforms itself in the mind," he wrote, "and not for barren contemplation, but for new creation." He thought that "the greatest delight which the fields and woods minister, is the suggestion of an occult relation between man and the vegetable." Still more, the occult relation blossomed into language, a central preoccupation for Emerson throughout his life. "Words," he proclaimed, with not a small debt to Swedenborg and his disciples, were "signs of natural facts." "Particular natural facts" were similarly "symbols of particular spiritual facts." And nature as a whole was "the symbol of spirit." In fact, the original (1836) epigraph to *Nature* was a line from the Neo-Platonic theorist Plotinus: "*Nature is but an image or imitation of wisdom, the last thing of the soul; nature being a thing which doth only do, but not know.*"[38]

From this perspective, the huge canvas of history that Emerson had so obligingly sketched in his essay of the same name begins to assume new significance. Nature was the teacher of Soul, and Soul used nature's lessons to make and unmake history. Emerson had admired Swedenborg because, among other doctrines, he taught and applied the theory of correspondence so consistently, even if Emerson created a large difference between himself and the Swede on other grounds. His essay on Swedenborg in *Representative Men* quoted him ubiquitously, and among the famed seer's "favorite views," Emerson had no trouble acknowledging "the doctrine of Correspondence." Swedenborg, he explained, believed in "the Identity-philosophy." Emerson went on to elaborate. "It is this; that nature iterates her means perpetually on successive planes. In the old aphorism, *Nature is always selfsimilar.* In the plant, the eye or germinative point opens to a leaf, then to another leaf, with a power of transforming the leaf into radical, stamen, pistil, petal, bract, sepal, or seed." If Emerson, not without a Swedenborgian nudge, had pronounced nature the symbol of spirit in 1836, Swedenborg himself—as Emerson quoted him—was more explicit. "'The physical world was purely symbolical of the spiritual world,'" true enough. But more: "'Man is a kind of very minute heaven corresponding to the world of spirits and to heaven. Every particular idea of man, and every affection . . . is an image and effigy of him. . . . God is the grand man.'"[39]

Not only did correspondence work for things of the spirit; it worked for matter(s) on earth. "Money" was "representative," Emerson remarked in his essay on "Wealth" (1860), and it followed "the nature and fortunes of the owner." Enjoining "a few measures of economy," he found the first of these in the pronouncement that "each man's expense must proceed from his character." "As long as your genius buys," he advised, "the investment is safe, though you spend like a monarch." A decade later in "Domestic Life," he repeated the theme. "The genius and love of the man" should be "so conspicuously marked in all his estate, that the eye that knew him should read his character in his property, in his grounds, in his ornaments, in every expense. . . . My expenditure is me." As early as November of 1838, he had written in his journal that "property" was "somehow intimately related to properties of man, & so has a sacredness." Now, in his 1860 essay, he returned to the point more strongly. "The comptingroom-maxims liberally expounded," he told readers, were "the laws of the Universe." Applied to each individual, the "merchant's economy" was "a coarse symbol of the soul's economy." This being the case, the conclusion, for Emerson, was clear. "The true thrift" was "always to spend on the higher plane; to invest and invest, with keener avarice," so that a person might "spend in spiritual creation, and not in augmenting animal existence." Nature—and especially human acquisition—could be good, but coarsely. Spirit was better. And correspondence was total.[40]

So total that Emerson proclaimed in his mature essay "Art" (1870) the "firm law" that "the universal soul is the alone creator of the useful and the beautiful; therefore to make anything useful or beautiful, the individual must be submitted to the universal mind." Moreover, the law came dangerously barbed and produced shattering consequences. The useful arts, at least, needed to conform to the law of nature, or they would "be ground to powder by her omnipresent activity." No static conformity here, unlike the

Swedenborgian version of the doctrine, as Gertrude Reif Hughes has pointed out. Instead, the shattering consequences would arrive because Emerson's correspondence existed as a feature of his vitalism (we are back in that ever-moving camp again!). The "inherent dynamism" of correspondence was so primal, argued Hughes, that it was "dynamic to the point of volatility." It threatened "constantly" to be "unstable" in any relationship, and the threat was "the cost of its regenerative vitality." What was the upshot? As Hughes succinctly summarized, "The *fact* of correspondence" interested Emerson "primarily because of the *act* of correspondence that it presages, requires, and enables."[41] Practice, it turned out—even in the workings of an inexorable law—made perfect.

That dynamism inherent in the law of correspondence required, in Emerson's universe, a colossal balancing law to tame its instability. This was the law of compensation, the bipolar twin to correspondence, and the celebrated source of so much of the comforting side of Emerson's view of the world. Even in the midst of the narrative of correspondence, with all its effervescence and energy, a major force for balance stood strong, not to be effaced by contrary law. If everything secretly, in its most inner being, *was* everything else, everything also bore the imprint of difference and distinction. Hence, Emerson titled the third essay in his first series "Compensation"—and for a fundamental reason. "Polarity, or action and reaction," he declared, existed "in every part of nature." Its presence could be found "in darkness and light; in heat and cold; in the ebb and flow of waters; in male and female; in the inspiration and expiration of plants and animals; in the equation of quantity and quality." It existed as well "in the fluids of the animal body; in the systole and diastole of the heart; in the undulations of fluids, and of sound; in the centrifugal and centripetal gravity; in electricity, galvanism and chemical affinity."[42] Here one could easily argue for the series of correspondences that poke up between the first items and second items in each pair respectively—or for the pervasive vitalism that percolated through—but neither is the point now.

Rather, with all his hymns to identity and correspondence, Emerson was upholding an opposite law of compensation, the law that "dualism underlies the nature and condition of man." "Every excess causes a defect; every defect an excess. Every sweet hath its sour; every evil its good." There was "a crack in every thing God has made," Emerson announced, and he did not attribute the crack to original sin. "That ancient doctrine of Nemesis, who keeps watch in the Universe," kept on working. In a world of eternal recompense, Emerson could be enthusiastic: "This Law writes the laws of cities and nations. It is in vain to build or plot or combine against it." Its truth could be found in "the sacred books of each nation" and was "hourly preached in all markets and workshops by flights of proverbs." "All things" were "double, one against another.—Tit for tat; an eye for an eye; a tooth for a tooth; blood for blood; measure for measure; love for love." Yet Emerson in the end was not going there. After dragging his—perhaps unwilling—readers through the muck of their worldly situation, he was announcing his own good news of salvation. In spite of all that, there was "a deeper fact in the soul than compensation, to wit, its own nature." The soul was "not a compensation, but a life." "Under all this running sea of circumstance, whose waters ebb and flow with perfect balance, lies the aboriginal abyss of real Being. Essence, or God, is not a relation, or a part, but the whole. Being is the vast affirmative, excluding negation." Perhaps ironically, perhaps concentrically, this "vast affirmative" had been foreshadowed by the ever-present law and fact of correspondence. The "universe" was "represented in every one of its particles. Every thing in nature" contained "all the powers of nature." So much so that "the world globes itself in a drop of dew."[43]

In the midst of Emerson's embrace of both duality and unity, there was more to be said. It was true that, as William Clebsch had summarized in his classic work of 1973, Emerson was ever engaged in a balancing act—but, as I noted in the introduction, Clebsch argued for an Emerson occupied not so much with ethical as with *aesthetic* concerns. "The harmony of compensatory and compensating experience became a retreat where Emerson found beauty in whatever happened. Life was a succession of alternations, swayings, ambivalences, pendulum-swings." See-sawing experience led, finally, to "a circle of faith." Seven years before he published "Compensation," Emerson had written in his journal, "When an ardent mind once gets a glimpse of that perfect beauty & sees how it envelopes him & determines all his being, will he easily slide back to a periodic shouting about 'atoning blood'?" If, as Emerson wrote in his 1841 essay "Friendship," "the law of nature is alternation forever-more," and "each electrical state superinduces its opposite," all disjunction was resolved in beauty.[44]

Like Edwards, Emerson cherished beauty as another name for God—even if his language favored a different name for the deity. As I have already noted, Higgins, from a theological and philosophical perspective, has explored aesthetic foundations in the thought of the two in sometimes helpful ways. Moreover, well before Higgins, Clebsch had linked them for their resistance to a Puritan religious heritage of moralism by affirming "the beauty of living in harmony with divine things." This Clebsch called "being at home in the universe." But the rich pungency of Emerson's own words led in its own direction. In the lead essay in his second series, he proclaimed (echoing Edwards) that "God has not made some beautiful things, but Beauty is the creator of the universe." Even earlier, in his first series of 1841, Emerson asked in his essay "Friendship," "Shall I not call God the Beautiful, who daily showeth himself so to me in his gifts?" It was the human act of reflection that disclosed the opaque reality surrounding each individual, Emerson thought, and he began his often-cited essay "Spiritual Laws" (also 1841) with tidings on that reality's nature. "When we look at ourselves in the light of thought," he professed, "we discover that our life is embosomed in beauty." Turning backward, he saw more. "Behind us, as we go, all things assume pleasing forms, as clouds do far off. Not only familiar and stale, but even the tragic and terrible are comely, as they take their place in the pictures of memory."[45]

Yet beauty assumed its most vivid form in present time and space. As Emerson instructed in "Art," "Though we travel the world over to find the beautiful, we must carry it with us, or we find it not." And despite the Clebschian desire to separate beauty from moral themes, in a very real sense Emerson—like Edwards—did not go there. In an early paragraph in his "Divinity School Address," Emerson had declared that "a more secret, sweet, and overpowering beauty appears to man when his heart and mind open to the sentiment of virtue." There was a vitalism, even eroticism—as Gougeon has noted—in this ascription, even as it led to the divine. A person, said Emerson, "learns that his being is without bound; that, to the good, to the perfect, he is born." In his essay "Love," as we have seen, Emerson's "highest beauty" was "the love and knowledge of the Divinity"—but he only reached that place after telling readers that "the ancients called beauty the flowering of virtue."[46]

It is significant that Emerson devoted one entire chapter in his 1836 manifesto *Nature* to beauty. There he posited three aspects of "Beauty" (he capitalized the word often). The "simple perception of natural forms" was "a delight"—a statement that seemed uncomplicated enough. But in a turn that linked his message strikingly to the thought of Edwards, Emerson continued with his second aspect. There existed "the presence of a higher," the "spiritual element" that was "essential" to the perfection of beauty. Emerson made his point plainly. "The high and divine beauty which can be loved without effeminacy, is that which is found in combination with the human will, and never separate. Beauty is the mark God sets upon virtue." Ever the idealist though, Emerson was not content with virtue in and of itself. Beauty related to virtue, true enough, but it also related to thought. Without "the colors of affection" (which moved the will), the intellect searched for "the absolute order of things" as they existed in "the mind of God." Yet the "active powers" (governed by will) were not left behind in an all-Platonic ascent. Instead, the powers of intellect and action seemed "to succeed each other"; the "exclusive activity of the one" generated "the exclusive activity of the other." There was, to be sure, something "unfriendly" about the relationship, and they resembled the "alternate periods of feeding and working in animals," with each preparing and following the other. Still, the will and virtue stood equal and were not overruled. Beauty encompassed all. It was "in its largest and profoundest sense," what Emerson called "one expression for the universe." "God" was the "all-fair." "Truth, and goodness, and beauty" were "but different faces of the same." More than that, as Emerson intimated throughout his long speaking and writing career, the beauty of nature was not "ultimate." It was, rather, "the herald of inward and eternal beauty," and—as for Edwards—"not alone a solid and satisfactory good."[47]

By 1860, when Emerson again turned to the theme in *The Conduct of Life*, he instructed readers that beauty was the "form under which the intellect prefers to study the world." It took them "out of surfaces, to thinking of the foundations of things." It was, as he quoted Johann von Goethe, "'a manifestation of secret laws of nature,'" As we have already to some extent seen, with his abiding circularity, Emerson's beauty, even in his mature years, displayed its vitalistic, even sensuous and erotic side. Reflecting on Cupid "drawn with a bandage round his eyes," he insisted the depiction of blindness suggested that Cupid simply did not see what he did not like. That said, "the sharpest-sighted hunter in the universe" was "love, for finding what he seeks." So in "the true mythology," love existed as "an immortal child," and beauty led him "as a guide." In short, beauty was "the pilot of the young soul." Still, as ever, sensuous delight led further—always a symbol or sign corresponding to "some better health, or more excellent action." Ultimately, beauty needed to speak to the "imagination" and not the sense faculties. "The new virtue" that constituted something beautiful was "a certain cosmical quality, or, a power to suggest relation to the whole world, and so lift the object out of a pitiful individuality." "Every natural feature" had something in it that was "universal," that spoke of the "central benefit which is the soul of Nature." "All high beauty," he reminded readers, contained a "moral element." Emerson concluded by pointing to "a climbing scale of culture" in which "globe and universe" were "rude and early expressions of an all-dissolving Unity,—the first stair on the scale to the temple of the Mind."[48]

That temple of the Mind preoccupied Emerson all his life. His "Over-Soul" was a favored name, but—as we have seen—he also used others to indicate the all-encompassing mystery that so engrossed him. His fascination, in fact, betrayed an erotic quality, but an eros ever seeking, ever desiring, a union that seemed mostly to evade him. With Edwards hovering in the background, it is not difficult to contrast the richly experiential Puritan forebear to his ex-Unitarian heir. Edwards exuded intimacy with the divine; Emerson, like an uncertain lover, seemed to try too hard. Intellectually, his Transcendental philosophy provided all the tools to understand what mystical experience meant. And he certainly seemed to have had his moments—such as his frequently cited out-of-self account in the first pages of *Nature* (see above). There Emerson *saw* in a particularly acute and riveting way. Again, in "The Over-Soul," he deemed the "announcements of the soul" to be *"Revelation,"* a revelation "always attended by the emotion of the sublime. This invasion of the human mind by divinity agitated recipients "with awe and delight." But, in the end, Emerson seemed to be describing a heightened intellectual but not unitive experience. If we follow the traditional Western tripartite division of purgative, illuminative, and unitive ways, the mystical moments that he could claim looked enticingly illuminative but, his words suggest, never quite reached the unitive mystical all. Mostly though, he wrote and lectured about the mystical experience rather than claiming it—in "The Over-Soul," for example, pointing to Socrates, Plotinus, Porphyry, Paul, "Behmen," George Fox, and Swedenborg.[49]

Yet, arguably, there *was* more. Before he finished "The Over-Soul," Emerson could offer heartfelt advice and testimony to readers. He told them that "the heart in thee is the heart of all; not a valve, not a wall, not an intersection is there anywhere in nature, but one blood rolls uninterruptedly, an endless circulation through all men, as the water of the globe is all one sea, and, truly seen, its tide is one."[50] It was circles, once again, and in coming full circle with Emerson, it is difficult not to imagine that he knew, more than conceptually and literarily, what he was recommending for others. Nature, landscape, starry heavens, and blood all identified him as a naturalist. But as my exposition should make clear, the haunting ghosts of the supernatural had refused to disappear. Puritan or not, Christian or not, Unitarian or not, he had touched a layer of human experience and belief that had long been cataloged under the rubric of the supernatural. Emerson liked to use new words to describe old things—his entrenched familiarity with Western and even Eastern classical sources is everywhere apparent. So, discarding overtly Christian language, he still seemed to be putting old wine into his new wineskins. Emerson was a naturalist—and at least a panentheist—surely. But he had subtly and irreversibly brought along a supernatural past, and—without the theological confessions of a Mather or an Edwards—it had happily made itself at home in his new spiritual world. Ralph Waldo Emerson lived his life to the end as a supernatural naturalist.

FOUR

Horace Bushnell: Natural Supernaturalist

At first glance, Congregationalist Horace Bushnell, the liberal minister whose theology dominated post–Civil War Protestant seminaries, seems an anomalous figure to link to Ralph Waldo Emerson. Biographical contrasts are striking—but even a cursory view of some of the details hint at intriguing points of convergence. The two were contemporaries and came from solidly middle-class roots. Bushnell (1802–1876), with an Episcopalian mother and Methodist father, had been born in Bantam in rural northwestern Connecticut and was baptized Episcopalian because that was his village's only church. So, at least initially, his Christianity came in a version softer than orthodox Calvinism. Later, however, in New Preston, Bushnell's parents joined the Congregational church with its lingering Calvinism, even as their farm and wool-carding business went through a period of economic uncertainty that also affected their son. Traditional Calvinist views of sinful humanity and predestination must have resonated with the ups and downs of an anxious Bushnell household.[1]

After graduating from Yale College in 1827, the young Bushnell had some false starts, with stints in teaching, journalism, and law. Then, already familiar with Christian orthodoxy but now distanced from it, he experienced conversion. Significantly, though, it had only been when his "heart" overrode his "head" that his religious turn brought him to the doors of the Congregational church and to Yale Divinity School. So Bushnell's story became largely a tale of Connecticut Congregationalism. Twice a Yale professional school graduate (law and divinity), he had found his spiritual home in the tradition to which his parents had introduced him. Thereafter, Bushnell's Congregational career became the saga of his life. Licensed to preach by the New Haven West Association in 1832, by the next year he was called as Congregationalist pastor of the North Church in Hartford, a position he held until he resigned because of ill health in 1859—much to the regret of his congregation.

Throughout the years of his tenure, Bushnell sparked intellectual consternation among both conservatives and liberals. In 1847, his provocative *Discourses on Christian Nurture* appeared, challenging the revival paradigm of instant conversion with instead an "organic" and gradualist approach that championed the Christian home and family. Then, in 1849, after the publication of *God in Christ* with its lengthy introduction on the metaphorical (i.e., not literal) quality of religious language, "discussions" began among local and larger denominational associations that became, in effect, a heresy trial. Although the Hartford Central Association of Ministers found the "errors" in his book not "fundamental," the Fairfield West Association disagreed. In its 1852 response, the North Church of Hartford withdrew from any affiliation to become an independent congregation, but lingering protests continued from official circles until 1854. In the midst of the controversy, Bushnell published still another book to explain his views. *Christ in Theology* (1851) reiterated his metaphorical views of language and went so far as to admire the mystical (and mythical) Hermes Trismegistus (see below). Seven years afterward, in 1858, after a lecture series he had delivered at North Church, he published *Nature and the Supernatural*, declaring without reservation that both constituted "one system of God" and that humans belonged to the supernatural realm. Throughout his career, Bushnell published volumes of sermons that were generally well received, but he continued to produce single-topic, book-length works that were not without controversy. Like and unlike Emerson and heir, like him, to the Calvinist predecessors who had dominated American life, Bushnell was radicalizing in his take on Protestant theology. He stood between representatives of organized Anglo-Protestant orthodoxy and an emerging community of religionists alienated from it and leaning toward what by century's end would be called metaphysics.

Much earlier though, and before the term was in vogue, this form of American religiosity had incorporated the mystical Hermetic tradition of the West based eponymously on the writings of the legendary Hermes Trismegistus and similar texts and views. The *Corpus Hermeticum* had been rediscovered in the West at the time of the Italian Renaissance, and subsequently its title became a catch-all for other mystical systems that bore a family resemblance. Among them were Neo-Platonism, Gnosticism, and ancient forms of astrology as well as, by medieval times, the Kabbalah, especially in its Christianized form, alchemy, and Paracelsianism. In the early modern period, Rosicrucianism and Freemasonry mingled in the mix. For

Americans, this high-culture Hermeticism combined with a less elite brew that included imported English country magic, Continental mystical species of millennialism, and Native American and African American lore.[2]

These spiritual and cultural influences resonated with the spiritualist movement of the middle nineteenth century (see chapter 6). They also pervaded the culture more broadly through European romanticism, which was making its way in an urbanizing, middle-class American culture. Here—to reference what I have written earlier—an ever-abiding love of physical nature in its wildness existed side by side with Platonic and Neo-Platonic idealizations of nature and with a progressivism that blended in its own way with Christian millennialism. In its turn, metaphysical religiosity was sometimes expressed in and through vernacular forms of Christianity and sometimes not; it largely respected Jesus but was often hostile to organized Christian tradition.[3]

Bushnell himself interacted with this multifaceted and shape-shifting religious growth in Christian terms. This meant his abiding preference for organicism *and* its symbolic look-alike in the world of mind and spirit. It meant, too, his declaration for analogical thinking according to the now-familiar law of correspondence, in which heaven and earth were glimpsed as one mystical whole. It also pointed to his enthusiasm for clairvoyant "miracles" whereby divine energies operated within earthly events. Similarly, it signaled a theology of delight—understood, in the conventional sense, as a high degree of joy and gratification or satisfaction in divine things. Likewise it signaled that delight conferred healing and wholeness—by transforming religion into an aesthetic practice and a spirituality of pleasure. Finally, it signaled a turn toward negative theology, the historic way of expressing the unfathomable mystery of the divine by denying every human characteristic with which it might be associated. None of this made Bushnell an exception or a maverick religiously, although it did get him into trouble with denominational officials. Rather, the language that Bushnell spoke and wrote shared common characteristics with rhetorical forms that—as we have seen in Emerson's case—were becoming powerful mediating symbols in the public conversation of his time. Although, like Emerson, Bushnell could not have known or used the late-nineteenth-century term, metaphysical religiosity was in the air, and Bushnell had breathed its message.

To the point here, Bushnell criticism has from the first read him as a mediating figure. Summarizing the scholarship in 1965, Winthrop S. Hudson hailed the "mediating theology" of Bushnell, who was "both 'conservative' and 'liberal' in his emphases." Bushnell's major biographers, from his daughter Mary Bushnell Cheney and on, multiply the mediations, with his

2002 biographer Robert Bruce Mullin stressing Bushnell's ties to Puritanism and seeing him both as "proto-liberal and proto-Pentecostal."[4] Different from these interpreters, I see a Bushnell who was nudging Protestants into new times because he was charting a path for those beginning to think and speak the language of metaphysics. Bushnell talked the talk familiar to other metaphysicians and also walked their walk, especially in terms of the mystical side to his character. But in the end, there was a fork in the road at which many walked away from Christianity. Bushnell did not, and in his choice *and* his mediation he charted a path for others who would continue to be Christians metaphysically. Still more, when he talked the metaphysical talk, he always brought the working vocabulary home to Christian concepts. For Bushnell, the important words were God, Christ, *sacrifice, sin, atonement, grace, baptism*.

Socially, Bushnell was surprisingly comfortable with many who might themselves be described as proto-metaphysical. Cyrus Bartol, with his Transcendental connections, was, according to Mullin, Bushnell's closest clerical friend during the period of his heresy trial. Still further, Mary Cheney tells us that her father spent an evening in 1843 with Theodore Parker, with whom he discussed the entire terrain of theology, and that he locked arms with George Ripley in a "Bunker Hill Celebration" procession. Both men were members of the Transcendental Club that Emerson led. Still more, Bushnell may also have known Emerson slightly. At least once, in a letter to George Partridge Bradford, Emerson noted that he had seen Bushnell among "other notabilities" in Lenox, Massachusetts, on an 1854 visit.[5]

These personal ties are important and set a frame to Bushnell's published remarks. His 1858 work *Nature and the Supernatural*, especially, can be read as a rebuttal to Parker's controversial views. More specifically, in his 1841 sermon "The Transient and Permanent in Christianity" and in his 1842 *Discourse of Matters Pertaining to Religion*, Parker had supported natural religion and argued against miracles. Wrote Bushnell: "Mr. Parker undertakes to frame a rational view of religion that sets it on the footing of nature. I have undertaken to frame a rational view of religion that comprehends nature and the supernatural as co-eternal factors in the universal system of God."[6] In the case of Emerson, the rebuttal came more crisply. As leader of the "new school of naturalistic literature" and with no one a "finer master of English than Mr. Emerson," a reader would be "surprised to find—who has ever failed to notice it?—that he is disabled ... disempowered, reduced in tone." Because of his reading, Emerson had "no great thought or purpose in him," and his work was, in fact, "somehow mephitic" or noxious. It lacked, for Bushnell, the acknowledgment of the "living God, and objects of faith" so central to his own life.⁷ More than that, Bushnell's understanding of the role of humans in terms of nature represented a direct inversion of Emerson's. Whereas in *Nature* Emerson had seen human technology applied to natural sources as, in a philosophical sense, part of nature, Bushnell thought otherwise. "Nature never built a house, or modelled a ship, or fitted a coat, or invented a steam-engine, or wrote a book, or framed a constitution. These are all events that spring out of human liberty."⁸

Yet—less defensive, less intent on drawing a line in the sand—at the end of his life, Bushnell could hail Emerson in a remarkable note. He clearly resonated to Emerson's Over-Soul. It meant, Bushnell declared authoritatively, "in fact, the Holy Spirit," and Emerson was "writing as one who is captivated by the beauty of his character and office." Bushnell's confident claim to knowledge of the Transcendentalist's authorial intent surprises: "He [Emerson] conceives him to be a kind of all-infolding Soul, communicating God and life to man. . . . He has no questions to raise concerning the universality of the conception. Its beauty proves it, he would say, to be true."⁹

There is yet more. Like Emerson, Bushnell hailed a literary hero in Samuel Taylor Coleridge, whose *Aids to Reflection* in the James Marsh edition of 1829 attracted almost a cult following among those drawn to literature, philosophy, and religion from a romantic perspective. It was from Coleridge that Bushnell drew major components of his "Preliminary Dissertation on Language," which formed the controversial introduction to his 1849 *God in Christ*. The piece searchingly explained Bushnell's own version of the theory of correspondence. Assessing the importance of the "Preliminary Dissertation" for Bushnell, who thought it "key to his line of thought," Cheney went even further than her father. "*Here*, we repeat with emphasis, *is the key to Horace Bushnell*, to the whole scheme of his thought, to that peculiar manner of expression which marked his individuality,—in a word, to the man."¹⁰ Arguably, the most repeated technical term throughout the "Preliminary Dissertation" was *analogy*, a restatement of the idea of correspondence that ran through Emerson's work and that of others familiar with the writings of Emanuel Swedenborg. Bushnell himself used the term *analogy*, favored by his Yale teacher Josiah Gibbs. But the grand theory of language that Bushnell unfolded showed notable, even stunning, similarities to Emerson's in *Nature*, and it is more than likely that Bushnell had read Emerson. Meanwhile, the symbolic thinking of emerging metaphysicals was leading them to the kind of theological permissiveness critics attributed to Bushnell.¹¹

Consider, for example, Bushnell's statement in the "Preliminary Dissertation." "All things out of sense get their names in language through signs and objects in sense that have some mysterious correspondence or analogy, by which they are prepared beforehand to serve as signs or vehicles of the spiritual things to be expressed." As we have seen, in a striking earlier statement, Emerson's *Nature* had proposed that words were "signs of natural facts," that "particular natural facts" were "symbols of particular spiritual facts," and that "nature" was the "symbol of spirit."[12] Bushnell, reading nature apparently in a different way from his later *Nature and the Supernatural*, saw a "logos in the form of things," with the "outer world" a "vast dictionary and grammar of thought" and "also itself an organ throughout of Intelligence." "Whose intelligence?" The answer was clear. It was "God, the universal Author" who stood "EXPRESSED every where." No stack of "treatises, piled even to the moon, could give a proof of God so immediate, complete, and conclusive." "The whole universe of nature" was "a perfect analogon of the whole universe of thought or spirit."[13]

How was divine thought expressed in and from nature? Again, the answer, for Bushnell, was clear. The "words" in nature, like the words on pages and on human lips, were metaphors. Hidden in the etymology of any word was a poetic grasp of meaning derived from the observation of nature. But religious and theological words had been deadened. "Words of thought, though based on mere figures or analogies in their original adoption" in time lost "their indeterminate character." Unfortunately, too, "in a long course of repetition," death came, and the word formula settled "into a literality." It became what was *untrue*. So Bushnell was on a mission to move away from rationalistic theological arguments and into the life-giving realm of poetry and beauty. His disdaining reference to treatises suggested much. Study the scriptures, yes, he said, but do not "be rationalists *over* the scriptures." With methods based on his views of language, "the scriptures will be more studied" and "not as a magazine of propositions and mere dialectic entities, but as inspirations and poetic forms of life."[14] Religious disputes should fizzle away, since no statement about the nature of divinity could be exact. It was feeling, not logic, that brought one to the threshold of the divine, and words could help because they could excite the passions of the soul.

As early as 1839, invited to Andover Seminary to give an address on the occasion of his election to the Porter Rhetorical Society, Bushnell had begun to suggest these views. Invoking "hieroglyphs"—part of the elite language of the day in certain circles—he told the Andover audience that "not the Bible only reveals him but the whole temple of being around us and above is written over with spiritual hieroglyphs all radiant with his light." God had created the "outward world" as "a vast store house of types or images fitted to represent thoughts and be interpreted between man and man." There were words for things and words for thoughts, and humans used the words for things to signal the words for thoughts and the spiritual truths that they sought to express.[15]

Later, after critics panned *God in Christ*, in the midst of his heresy dispute, Bushnell published a revised version of his defense before the Hartford Central Association of Ministers in a new book, *Christ in Theology* (1851). Ironically, again he began with a chapter on language that suggested Transcendentalists and their fellow travelers. A "SINGLE principle," he declared, was the key to what he meant to say: "THAT ALL RELIGIOUS TRUTH, AS WELL THEOLOGICAL AS PRACTICAL, IS AND MUST BE PRESENTED UNDER CONDITIONS OF FORM OR ANALOGY FROM THE OUTWARD STATE." The company he was keeping became clearer as Bushnell admired Sir Thomas Brown, who had embraced the philosophy of Hermes Trismegistus, and agreed with Brown enthusiastically. "It is remarkable," Bushnell enthused, "that this Egyptian Hermes . . . was able, in the depths of nature, and apart from the aids of revelation, to verify it as a truth that 'all things which are in heaven are in the earth, after an earthly manner; and all which are in the earth are in heaven . . . after a celestial manner.'"[16]

As above, so below. It was the central working proposition that had grounded Mather and Edwards, the Transcendentalism of Emerson, *and* a growing metaphysical community. As late as 1869, in an essay that first appeared in the magazine *Hours at Home*, Bushnell reaffirmed the adage, reading the Christian Gospel as a "Gift" to the "Human Imagination" and one that—as metaphysicians would have it—worked in healing, salvific ways. "Every line or lineament" was "traced in some image or metaphor," and the reverberations of that message extended as high as heaven. Urged Bushnell, readers needed to "look into language itself and see how the great revelation of God is coming and to come." Religious truth arrived through images, and the images—to use a term both technical and devotional—were charged sacramentally; they conveyed the very reality they symbolized. The power to create and perceive truth through images—imagination—was "that which dawns in beauty like the day because the day is in it; that power in human bosoms which reads the types of the creation, beholding stamps of God's meanings in their faces." Words themselves were images with faces. They could bring fire and life—"so that a free, great soul, when . . . it cannot find how to express itself otherwise, does it by images and metaphors in flame that somehow body the meaning in imaginative apprehension." In the end, there was one great Logos that was also one great Metaphor. "We can say nothing of Christ so comprehensively adequate as to call him the metaphor of God: God's last metaphor!"[17]

The message of the metaphysicians was all here. The Logos—Mind or Thought—could be found in nature and in language—especially for Bushnell in biblical language. Both were mediating symbols that catapulted a soul into divine presence and life because of the power of the symbolic analogon. If, as in the full theory of correspondence and in metaphysically oriented belief in general, everything was like everything else, everything could *act* on everything else. Here was mystical union as an active principle in the world. Bushnell had entered an essentially magical universe galvanized by divine energy, and the result was healing and salvation. Nor were these connections only theoretical. Like so many who lifted out strands from the religious past and began to reweave them, Bushnell demonstrated the mystical inclinations and experience that followed from the premises—perhaps more than Emerson.

To invoke mysticism, as I have noted, is to speak of direct presence and understanding. To speak of mysticism also invites entry into the paradox at the center of a spirituality grounded in analogy and correspondence. The quasi-dualism of the theory of correspondence (as above, so below) must disappear before the participation in a mystical Whole. Still, the sacramentalism (i.e., the use of the sign as a vehicle to reach the divine presence) implicit in Bushnell's way of seeing language and image hints of another way to understand the paradox. Bushnell's words and images seemed to act as windows into another world, shadowings forth of eternity that could bring the devotee to eternity itself. In the context of a series of challenges in his life—the hostile reception of his work on Christian nurture, the death of his son, and chronic bouts of "throat trouble" (tuberculosis)—he had turned to reading seventeenth-century French devotional literature. For a time he was drawn to the writings of the French archbishop François Fénelon, with his tendencies toward mystical quietism (passively awaiting divine action), as well as the more thoroughgoing quietism of Madame Jeanne Marie Bouvières de la Mothe Guyon as presented in a biography by Thomas Upham. Bushnell's reading, coupled with his ongoing thought patterns and painful life events, all brought him to a mystical result.[18]

Early in the morning in February 1848, Bushnell announced to his wife, Mary Apthorp Bushnell, that he had seen the light, and it was the gospel. "It came to him at last," she wrote, "after all his thought and study, not as something reasoned out, but as an inspiration,—a revelation from the mind of God himself." There had been harbingers to the illuminative moment, though, from Bushnell's days at Yale. In an essay from 1832 that moved from vision to union, he championed moral philosophy in terms that sounded almost Hermetic. By rising to "a steady contemplation of the spiritual," he asserted, one could feel "no longer a clod, but a particle of the divine nature." He was also not without direct experience of the anomalous. As early as his college years at Yale before 1827, in bed and exhausted, he had experienced his body "rising and floating in the air." In the midst of this, "he began to believe that he was dead, and that this was his voyage to the world of spirits."[19]

Bushnell's fascination set him in proto-metaphysical company, a company to which the midcentury spread of mass spiritualism testifies, as we will see in chapter 6. He would never lose interest in such occurrences, and his later *Nature and the Supernatural* would especially speak of them. More typical, though—and more congenial to Emerson's spiritual world—were experiences of extraordinary illumination or union with the divine in nature—with the mediating sign of nature almost effaced in the experience of God. On a trip to Mount Washington (New Hampshire) in 1835, for example, he wrote home to Mary Bushnell: "Every step something glorious opens upon us here. . . . It is not things that interest me, but God. Surely I see God as I never did before." Decades later, natural vistas continued to thrill him and bring him into close proximity with the divine. At Niagara Falls in 1852 and at Lake Waramaug, Connecticut, in 1870, he recounted experiences of divine presence. "I never thought I could possess God so completely," he wrote.[20]

It was, for Bushnell, "altogether, everywhere, lovely." Similar effusive language of beauty and pleasure abounded in these accounts. Moreover, because of Bushnell's vitalism—not unlike Emerson's—he was acknowledging a divine energy flowing through all things. As in the growing metaphysical religiosity of the day, a high doctrine of human nature came with the territory. Humans were the grandest and most complex signs of the work of the creator, even as they embodied creative and healing powers themselves. For Bushnell, the high doctrine, along with his reported sense of glimpsing God—of something akin to mystical certainty and bonding—appeared repeatedly in writings and sermons. In *Christian Nurture*, for example, he scrupled with the idea that humans were "born sinners." "They may just as truly and properly be born saints." In *God in Christ*, he emphasized Christ's divinity by first contemplating humanity. "As the spirit of man is made in the image of God, and his bodily form is prepared to be the fit vehicle and outward representative of his spirit, it follows that his bodily form has also some inherent, *a priori* relation to God's own nature." And in *Nature and the Supernatural*, he explained with apparent approval that Swedenborg and his followers taught "that God creates the world through man." For them, creation was "a purely gerundive matter—God's perpetual act," with God holding "the work *to man*, at every stage." Christ was the metaphor of God because in contemplating him humans saw their deified selves. "Beholding in him as in a glass the glory of the Lord, we shall be changed into the same image."[21]

A felt sense of participation in divine life punctuated many of Bushnell's printed sermons, which were much better received, in general, than his intentionally theological works. Yet titles and lines nuanced a different, metaphysicalizing path that ought to have provoked clerical colleagues. "Christ the Form of the Soul" (1848), the sermon cited by Mary Bushnell in her account of his breakthrough experience of the gospel, already conveyed its message in its title. His text was as definitive. The formation of Christ in the soul was "the grand object of the gospel plan." In "The Immediate Knowledge of God," he saw nonmediated and, it followed, mystical knowledge of God as available freely to Christian souls. Through it, a soul was "raised out of its mere finite speck of magnitude, into the conscious participation of being infinite." In "Our Advantage in Being Finite," he extolled the human situation because in and through it people became creatively involved in the labors of God. They "put their finishes on his works" and so could rightly be called "sub-creators" and "sub-saviours." Much before, in 1852, when spiritualism was in its early heyday, and Mormons were teaching the afterlife rule of humans "as Gods," Bushnell's sermon "God Preparing the State of Glory" offered a parallel. It uncannily aligned with the progressive, unfolding terrain of the post-death experience taught by spiritualist seer Andrew Jackson Davis (see chapter 6) and Mormon prophet Joseph Smith. In the afterlife, Bushnell told listeners, souls would experience their "character and capacity" as "forever rising, growing great and divine." Indeed, "the beings we now call men will at last be raised in volume and rank so as to overtop all our present conceptions of their significance,—kings, priests, principalities, powers, thrones!"[22]

On a larger front, *Nature and the Supernatural*, which managed at once to disturb Andrew Jackson Davis, orthodox clergy, and Unitarian dissenters, coded Bushnell's affirmation of union with God into a word capsule that made it opaque. In rough outline, its message had been part of his thinking for years. As early as 1839, he had told listeners at Andover that "the truth-world having no form, a form-world must be constituted to be its mirror." This was Bushnell's familiar analogical thinking, his statement of the theory of correspondence. However, he went on to address the "intelligence" of the beings who were to receive the revelation in the mirror. These beings could not be "animals," because animals lived "in their senses only." By contrast, "man" was "quickened by the divine principle of intelligence" and so could feel the "mysterious analogy between forms and truths." In an implicit division, on one side were animals and the world of nature; on the other, humanity and the world of truth or God. A decade later, in a letter to Transcendentalist minister Cyrus Bartol, Bushnell talked about the division between the two sides, with an emphasis on the supernatural. There was "a great deal more of supernaturalism in the management of this world than even orthodoxy" had "begun to suspect,—even a systematic, world-ruling, nature-redeeming supernaturalism."[23]

Bushnell's argument in *Nature and the Supernatural* signaled his proto-metaphysical leanings, his sense of the presence of divine and healing energy in the world through the existence and action of humans. The work rested on a distinction between what Bushnell called "Powers" and "Things." The supernatural was the realm of Powers; the natural world, of Things. God, of course, stood on the side of Powers. But most significantly, so, too, did humanity. In almost a theological sleight-of-hand, humans were removed from the world of Things to be reconstructed as the very Powers that altered, shaped, and re-created Things. To put this another way, radically different from Emerson, Bushnell saw nature not so much as a symbol pointing to the divine. Instead, nature represented the world of cause and effect, of regular law that operated in fixed modes. The supernatural, as the domain of Powers, was the world where miracles were made and where nature could be trumped. That being so, humans could stand in the Power of God and participate in divine interventions in the natural order. Thus humans, in Bushnell's theology, had become "as Gods," sneaking into a divine identity by the back door as he closed off the front against critics by condemning naturalism.

But here was the metaphysical rub: Even granted the distinction between Powers and Things, natural and supernatural were not, in the words of William A. Johnson, "two realms worlds apart." Instead, they were "co-factors in the one system of God," both of them "functions of the divine." Deeply concerned lest he be considered a pantheist, Bushnell found his happy solution in a semantic flourish. He could cast diatribes at pantheists and pantheism but still maintain his "one system of God," with natural and supernatural its "necessary phases." Like Emerson's, Bushnell's dualism was not the be-all and end-all of his theorizing, but—unlike his Transcendentalist contemporary—he did not affirm an Over-Soul or its equivalent. As Donald Crosby has explained, in Bushnell's own thinking, he could address the "rigid dualism, as he conceived it, of the conventional theological attitude toward the relation of nature and the supernatural." "The rift between the two realms was healed" when humans were "regarded as standing in dominion" over nature "in keeping with the Genesis account of . . . creation." If, in the words again of Johnson, Bushnell "did not deny a certain antithesis between nature and the supernatural," it was also true that "he defined the supernatural in such a way that the two could be embraced in the one category of nature when viewed as the order of God in creation." So Bushnell was having it both ways—demoting and promoting nature to deliver the metaphysical story he wanted to tell. By implication, words—language—became a ministry of nature, providing matter for mind, ready "to fall under the dominion of spirit." Words thus became "Powers."[24] Out went theologians and rationalists; in came poets and metaphysicians.

In, too, had come another aspect of metaphysical spirituality—its fundamentally magical premise that if everything resonates with everything else, one piece of the world can act powerfully on another in healing ways. Like a latter-day Cotton Mather or perhaps Mullin's proto-Pentecostalist, Bushnell lived his life ever ready to testify to spectacular providential interventions. In this, he parted company with a cadre of radical New Englanders who were battling the existence of miracles. The topic stirred controversy almost automatically among clerics of Bushnell's time and was probably, in 1836, the most significant factor in the separation of the Transcendentalist party from other Unitarians. In brief, Unitarians, especially through the polemics of Unitarian "pope" Andrews Norton, argued that documented miracles offered the strongest evidence for Christianity's claims, grounding their argument on the "sensationalist" philosophy of John Locke. When the Transcendentalists broke away as a self-conscious movement, Ripley, Emerson, Parker, and others insisted that the mind's internal evidence trumped external data. Intuition—far broader than the rationalism of Unitarians—mattered more. We have already met a young and provocative Emerson equating "Miracle" with "Monster" for Harvard's graduating Divinity School class of 1838. As I have noted, Emerson harbored his own ideas of what constituted a miracle and with relish invoked "blowing clover" and "falling rain" for the class. But in a curious earlier inversion, in *Nature* he had detailed "occasional examples of the action of man upon nature with his entire force." These included "the traditions of miracles . . . the history of Jesus Christ; . . . the miracles of enthusiasm, as those reported of Swedenborg, Hohenlohe, and the Shakers; many obscure and yet contested facts, now arranged under the name of Animal Magnetism; prayer; eloquence; self-healing."[25] It was a motley list, to be sure, encompassing traditional sorts of miracles and also others that pointed in the direction of a later-century metaphysical repertoire some would call "occult."

In this context, there are two things to be noticed about Bushnell. First, with his gospel of humans operating on the side of Powers over a nature filled with Things, he had actually been preceded in the declaration by Emerson, his naturalist foil. What is the difference between Emerson's "action of man upon nature with his entire force" and Bushnell's supernatural as "that range of substance . . . that acts upon the chain of cause and effect in nature from without the chain?" Except that Emerson's instances were occasional and people evidently had to try harder.[26] Second, in Bushnell's notion of miracles, he demonstrated a high comfort level with the assorted metaphysical versions favored by Emerson and championed by later enthusiasts in Theosophy and New Thought. He also echoed, in his own way, the providential miracles reported by Cotton Mather.

A "miracle," pronounced Bushnell, was supernatural, "producing in the sphere of the senses, some event that moves our wonder, and evinces the presence of a more than human power." So far so good. But what were specific examples? Stunningly, a large number involved cases of clairvoyance—especially beloved by metaphysicals because of their basis in the worldview of correspondence. In one case, Bushnell recounted the story of preacher Arthur Howell, who met a funeral procession and knew with certainty that the deceased was a woman falsely accused of a crime. At her service, Howell repeated a conversation between the dead woman and her own minister and declared that soon she would be exonerated. The minister, present for the funeral, corroborated, and things turned out just as Howell had said. For Bushnell, Howell's gift echoed that of others, and he remarked on their frequency—"a considerable item in the newspaper literature of our time."[27]

Still more, there was Bushnell's firsthand experience of a clairvoyant during his visit to California. In a Napa Valley hotel, he had encountered Captain Yonut, a West Coast trapper for forty years. The conversation turned "on spiritism and the modern necromancy [communing with the dead]." With hints of a personal story behind the captain's interest, at Bushnell's request, Yonut recounted a dream of six or seven years before. "He saw what appeared to be a company of emigrants, arrested by the snows of the mountains, and perishing rapidly by cold and hunger. He noted the very cast of the scenery; . . . he saw the men cutting off what appeared to be tree tops, rising out of deep gulfs of snow; he distinguished the very features of the persons, and the look of their particular distress." Yonut woke, then fell asleep once more "and dreamed exactly the same dream again." The next morning he told the dream to "an old hunter comrade" who immediately recognized the site "over the Sierra, by the Carson Valley Pass." Captain Yonut quickly gathered "a company of men, with mules and blankets, and all necessary provisions." Neighbors laughed, but the men set out to their destination 150 miles distant. "And there they found the company in exactly the condition of the dream, and brought in the remnant alive."[28]

For Bushnell, the "coincidences of that dream" gave clear evidence of "a supernatural providence." Instances of clairvoyance such as these lined up with sudden and unexplained answers to prayer. In one case, a landlord appeared at a tenant's door demanding the rent, which the renter—a physician—did not have. Then a stranger appeared to pay the physician for "attending me in a fever," and the sum was the exact amount of the rent. There were also reports of speaking in tongues and even of miraculous healings. For example, Bushnell reported an account that smacked of Christian Science to come, when an Englishman wrote about the healing of his son from scarlet fever. Persuaded by another to call a medical professional, the anxious father became convinced he had "fallen into a snare." The doctor came and went, but the father "resolved to withdraw the child, and cast him on the Lord." Instead of medicine, the boy got prayer, and the father got "a mighty conviction that my prayer was heard." Making his way to the nursery, he found that "the boy was sitting up in his bed" and asking for dinner.[29]

Although Perry Miller complained that Bushnell in his book "transcendentalized" Calvinism,[30] his embrace of anomalous happenings was more complicated. In fact, it suggested Mather, as I have argued, even as it shared links with Emerson and also pointed toward the future. If Mather would have nodded his head at the "miracles," metaphysical people would also make them their stock in religious and healing trade but consider them part of nature. Bushnell, in his own stance, had addressed the anomalies with aplomb *and* baptized them in one declarative act by pronouncing them supernatural. Matherized or transcendentalized, it was also clear in *Nature and the Supernatural* and elsewhere that Bushnell knew the metaphysical tribe well (he called them "naturalists")—from pantheists to phrenologists to new enthusiasts for the South Asian "Brama" (read Emerson and friends). For someone deeply immersed in an Anglo-Protestant world, he had read widely outside it, and he knew who his metaphysical "enemies" were or, at least, what their sort of foolishness and wrongheadedness was.

Especially significant here, Bushnell was directly in touch with Swedenborg's theology and displayed an ambivalence toward it. Ironically, the ambivalence left him keeping company with Emerson, although perhaps surprisingly he was less vitriolic about Swedenborg the man than Emerson was. Bushnell even admitted to the portrait painter Frank (Francis) B. Carpenter—attracted to Swedenborg in later life—that the Swedenborgians professed to like his (Bushnell's) books very much. Moreover, Bushnell recalled that he had first been drawn to Swedenborg by hearing of his doctrine of correspondences. But, he continued, "there was broader and better ground for this doctrine than was found in Swedenborg's statements or theories." When Carpenter confessed his inability to "place" Swedenborg, Bushnell thought matter-of-factly that "he must be placed by the side of other theological writers." He also made it clear that he did not enjoy reading the Swede. Bushnell owned many of Swedenborg's works, but found their style so cumbersome, repetitious, and dry that, according to Carpenter, "he could hardly have patience to read." Because Swedenborgianism contained "nothing aggressive," "it could never be preached successfully."[31]

Despite the sharp line that Bushnell had drawn between himself and Swedenborg, similarities with Swedenborg remained, and—just as he had remarked—Swedenborgians continued to notice. Indeed, Benjamin Fiske Barrett—who was called in his obituary "head of the progressive wing of the Swedenborgian church and perhaps the most eminent clergyman of this denomination in the country"—wrote at length on Bushnell. In his apologetic *Cloud of Independent Witnesses* (1891), the prolific Barrett argued for the Swedenborgianism of a series of prominent ministers, and Bushnell ranked among the chosen. Although Bushnell only noted Swedenborg once in his works, Barrett declared, "his writings furnish ample evidence not only of his familiarity with, but of his cordial acceptance of, all the principal doctrines of the New Church as revealed through Swedenborg."[32] In tour de force fashion, he had overlooked the rich and multiple sources of Bushnell's ideas, but the effect of citing doctrine after doctrine in basic agreement with Swedenborg cannot be denied.

As important as the lingering aura of Swedenborg, Bushnell named many of the phenomena he disdained as products of a longing the churches were not addressing. The "necromancy" that preoccupied Captain Yonut, for example, had surfaced elsewhere in his book. Bushnell, of course, was not alone among ministers in condemning spiritualism. But—like Emerson, who had called demonology the "Shadow of Theology"—he linked the "strange zeal observable in the new sorcery of our day" to unfulfilled spiritual yearnings in his time. Why? The "facts and functions of religion" were "reduced to a second-hand character—a reported history, a contrived and reasoned dogma, a drill of observances, where no fire burns."[33]

Fire or not, Bushnell's solution—the "one system of God" containing natural and supernatural—had not worked with critics. The charge of pantheism dogged him continually (the "everything is everything" and "everything is divine" that were embraced by the metaphysically inclined). Even Theodore Munger, who called him "God-intoxicated" like the Jewish philosopher Baruch Spinoza, wrote that Bushnell "was not a pantheist" but was "pantheistic." He did not explain the difference. More provocative still, like Davis and Swedenborg before him, Bushnell acknowledged extraterrestrials. In a sermon of 1852, he preached that God had "planned . . . the work of Jesus Christ, as in all other works in all other worlds." In another sermon in 1857, he was even clearer. These "worlds" were not other earthly cultures. Rather, "the modern astronomic discoveries force it on us, as a conviction not to be resisted, that worlds innumerable exist in habitable order, and, doubtless, that they have their inhabitants." Making sure congregants understood, he repeated later: "Worlds on worlds are reported, their count is innumerable and they appear to be habitable."[34]

Meanwhile, the preoccupation of Davis with Bushnell was telling. The spiritualist scion sent a public letter to Bushnell in December of 1851 through the *Hartford Times*. His message concerned the first of a series of lectures Bushnell was delivering at North Church. Davis, who at the time claimed Hartford as his base, was clearly excited. The announced topic—"On the Naturalistic Theories of Religion as Opposed to Supernatural Revelation"—already gave him "much pleasure." Moreover, Bushnell's way of approaching the subject was "considerably unlike the method pursued by most clergymen," since Bushnell relied on his own "*reason* or judgment" to address "the *corresponding* faculty in the mind of the hearer." Davis went on to propose moving the lectures to a different location and inviting "all parties interested" to "analyze and examine *before the same audience* the various positions." Bushnell did not reply.[35]

On another matter, keenly aware of cultural preoccupation with animal magnetism, Bushnell could comment on the ongoing fascination with it and, as in other cases, glimpse a religious search beneath. In *Nature and the Supernatural*, magnetists figured clearly in Bushnell's introductory catalog of deplorable naturalists. The "magnetists or seers of electricity" had prepared "a religion out of the revelations of natural clairvoyance and scientific necromancy." One wonders here, of course, how Bushnell distinguished "natural clairvoyance" from his own list of supernatural clairvoyant happenings. Still, he explained to readers that the "propensities to mere naturalism" could be linked to "an appetite for things of faith." He seemingly chastised people for "watching at the gate of some third heaven to be opened by the magnetic passes, or the solemn incantations of the magic circles; expecting an irruption of demons, in the name of science." But then, in his own way again echoing Emerson on demonology, he acknowledged that humans "must have mysteries, and believe, and take wings, and fly clear of the dull level of comprehensible cause and substance somehow."[36]

More than that, Bushnell implicitly accepted the magnetic or mesmeric view of the world, with its strong metaphysical implications. For Austrian physician Franz Anton Mesmer (1734–1815), invisible tides swept through individuals, maintaining them in a flow of energy, even as the magnetist/ mesmerist could manipulate the flow so that the individuals became subjects of the magnetist, usually for healing (for more, see chapter 6). In this explanation, the magnetic model was reproducing the metaphysical one of energy streaming from its intangible Source through all things. In similar vein, Bushnell's work on Christian nurture had been based on ideas of unconscious influence from parent to child. His later sermon "Unconscious Influence" (from the 1850s), still addressed the ability of people unawares to affect one another for good or ill. "The most active feelings and impulses of mankind are contagious," he affirmed. "Simply to be in this world, whatever you are, is to exert an influence—an influence, too, compared with which mere language and persuasion are feeble." Yet again, in his "Life, or the Lives," Bushnell rejected the notion that gravity or "chemical attraction," like other laws of nature, represented "only collections, classifications of facts." Instead, gravity was "the intellectual or idealized conception of a *power* by which bodies go towards each other, Chemical Attraction the conception of another kind of power by which atoms go towards each other." As we will see in chapter 6, in his work *The Approaching Crisis* Davis, taking his cue from Charles Fourier and Albert Brisbane, wrote pointedly of the law of "Attraction."[37] Still more, metaphysical generations to come would embrace the law of attraction and run enthusiastically with it—not unlike Mather, who had reflected on it in his own early version.

In Bushnell's case, lamenting "fallen society," he could yet observe that it existed in a condition "far less dreadful than it would be, if the organic force of natural affinities and affections were not operative still."[38] In his earlier work on Christian nurture, he had argued the case for organicism relentlessly. He examined the relation between parent and child and, still in the 1860 version, discovered "something like a law of organic connection, as regards character, subsisting between them." Children were joined "by an organic unity," not with their parents' "instructions" but with their "life." At no age, even adulthood, were people "wholly out of the reach of organic laws" affecting character. "All society is organic," Bushnell stated flatly. Even revivals came because of this law of connection and affinity: "A very great share of the power in what is called a revival of religion, is organic power; nor is it any the less divine on that account."[39]

The argument of *Christian Nurture* had company. Important here was the familial and small-community context in which organic ties brought peace, harmony, and delight. Bushnell's descriptions of family and community life, clad in their idyllic trappings, announced a religion of joy that came with the territory. In his well-known "secular" sermon for the centennial celebration of Litchfield County in 1851, for instance, he memorialized "The Age of Homespun." There were "foot excursions of young people, or excursions on horseback, after the haying," "boatings," "evening schools of sacred music," and "neighbors called in to meet the minister and talk of both worlds together." Most of all, Bushnell recalled "those friendly circles, gathered so often round the winter's fire," the "home circle" to which "a good neighbor and his wife drop in shortly." People took "their recreation, all together, in reading, or singing, or happy talk, or silent looking in the fire, and finally in sleep—to rise again, with the sun, and pray over the family Bible for just such another good day as the last."[40]

Here the law of attraction much to be loved by later metaphysicians meant the magnetism of small societies in which Bushnell reveled. Still further, his delight represented more than nostalgia for a once and former Eden. In *God in Christ*, Bushnell enthused that "when God appears in His beauty, loving and lovely, the good, the glory, the sunlight of soul, the affections previously dead, wake into life and joyful play." By then, he had already begun working out his theology of play and desire with ideas that paralleled others in the proto-metaphysical community. His Phi Beta Kappa oration "Work and Play" (1848) painted the picture of a family setting (again), in which "a man of large meditation" looked down on "his children and a kitten playing on the floor together." There rose "in his heart the conception, that possibly he is here to see the prophecy or symbol of another and higher kind of play, which is the noblest exercise and last end of man himself." "Work," Bushnell explained in a distinction that others have made, "is activity *for* an end; play, activity *as* an end." But there was more. "We play," he told listeners, "because we have in us a fund of life that wants to expend itself." Life began with "muscular play," passed through "the hard struggles of work," and emerged "at last, into a state of inspired liberty and spontaneous beauty." "In short," Bushnell pronounced, "we are to conceive that the highest and complete state of man . . . is the state of play." He did not share Immanuel Kant's philosophical model of "the conquest of desire by conscience," as Barbara Cross has observed. For him, "virtue was the 'play' of the soul, in which inclination and duty merged."[41]

Desire fulfilled, delight, joy—they were all of a piece, and for Bushnell, they summoned the vitalistic impulse that was so strong in Emerson and, as we shall see, also in later metaphysicians. In fact, metaphysics functioned as energy *medicine*, calling forth desire to stir the electric sap of life. It would be 1880 before Thomas Alva Edison filed his patent for the incandescent lamp, but the "electric" precursors, in the wake of magnetism, had already spread their language across the land. Bushnell was a buyer and a speaker. "It is the grand distinction of humanity," he announced in an 1850s sermon, "to receive and entemple the Infinite Spirit; to be energized by him." It followed that "as matter is open to the free access and unimpeded passage of the electric flash," so was "the soul open to the subtle motions of the Eternal Spirit." Disdaining "a certain class of devotees," who practiced "abnegations, penances, macerations, poverties, mortifications, vows of solitude, and complete withdrawment from the world," he preached instead a gospel of blessed longing. Cast in the language of subtle energy, "boundless and divine desires" were "the beginning," he explained in 1848. "To have no desires is to be a stone, not a man," Bushnell insisted. "To fall into God, and there . . . to become inert and cease from all real movement of soul, is Brahminism, not Christ, not Christianity." "Our gospel," he assured listeners in "Christ Regenerates Even the Desires," "even undertakes to intensify the desires, in the highest degree possible, only turning them away from what is selfish and low to what is worthy and good."[42]

Moreover, if Bushnell had relegated "poverties," along with "abnegations," "penances," and "macerations," to his spiritual trash heap, he also had a message to deliver about prosperity as a form of energy and virtuous desire. Foreshadowing the evangelical Gospel of Wealth *and* a New Thought version, he had written in *Christian Nurture* that wealth would "be unfolded more rapidly under the condition of Christian living than elsewhere." "A true Christian society," he observed, had "mines opened . . . in its own habits and principles." "The wealth accruing" was "power in every direction." Even further, with more enthusiasm and fewer caveats than Emerson, he remarked that prosperity was "our duty"—as one sermon from 1847 gave notice. "It is the duty of every man to be a prosperous man, if by any reasonable effort he may," he told his congregation. The same was true for a community: "An industrious, enterprising, hopeful, prosperous community" was "far more easily moved by the demands of duty and religion than one . . . drooping and running down."[43]

And if energy and desire turned outward to bring individual and societal abundance, it also turned inward as prayer. According to Cheney, from early childhood, Bushnell—in an echo of Jonathan Edwards—found spiritual energy and delight in nature, and the delight became a form of prayer. "The religious impressions of childhood . . . were of the simplest and most natural kind, coming to him unforced, often in the fields, and quickened by his delight in nature, impressions . . . in a sense of the divine beauty and majesty." Years later, in 1871, he confessed that he "fell into a habit years ago of talking with God, and it became so natural, that in all my open spaces I do it without thought."[44]

It is surely not surprising that this Edwardsian strain—the contemplation of God in the beauty of nature *and* its spontaneous prompt to prayer—shaped the spirituality of Bushnell, whose background included long familiarity with the Puritan divine. Edwards's "Images of Divine Things" (1728) offered, after all, an early version of the doctrine of analogy or correspondence so championed by Bushnell. Still more, Edwards's sermon "A Divine and Supernatural Light" had set an important precedent with its light in the heart reflecting divine light, and its language of thoroughgoing delight and the energy of prayer playing off each other. Resonating with an Edwardsian past, Bushnell's *Christian Nurture* had insisted that by "the whole economy of prayer" God was "working toward the largest, most inclusive harmony." In terms of the individual, this vast economy became one of enrichment for separate persons, who did not change God or "prevail" with him but instead changed themselves. Although, unlike Mather, Bushnell never reported trafficking with angels, his ideas yet recall in some ways Mather's "ejaculatory thanksgivings." Looking forward as well as backward, his words—like Mather's—seem a harbinger of New Thought ideas of affirmative prayer. Here the affirmation of wished-for results as already present stirred emotional desire and action by the imagination and thus birthed a new situation. In Bushnell's version, he dismissed a God-who-answered in favor of one whose energies could flow freely into human lives because seekers themselves had been transformed. The "precise point" on which the success of a man's prayer "hinged" was "the subjective change or prevailing realized in himself." Still, Bushnell complained that "we only faintly believe in prayer." Defending himself against his critics, he sounded a lot like Emerson. Peppering them with innuendos about living "a kind of second hand religion, a notional religion, which is distant and dry," Bushnell held up instead "the immediate experience of God, in a state of Divine Consciousness."[45]

Read one way, this was heart religion and evangelicalism pure and simple. Read another way and in the context of a concurrent Transcendentalism, it assumed new colors and stripes. It became an early metaphysical message, setting the stage for Bushnell's lifelong war against dogmatism and his refusal to join any ultra-precise theological party. Whereas in *Christian Nurture* he could write enthusiastically on the (divinely connected) organic virtues of the nuclear family, *God in Christ* and later works came up with space and silence. Bushnell found such blessed assurance in his theory of language because it gave him a nineteenth-century, Anglo-American way to negate "that dead body of abstractions, or logical propositions, called theology." "Words of thought or spirit" always affirmed something false because they imputed "*form* to that which really is out of form." Still, there was a *"latent presence"* within words, a "certain power of form" that was paradoxically good. As Bushnell told his readers, because words were "inexact representations of thought, mere types or analogies," language always had to be busy mending itself "by multiplying its forms of representation." Paradox, therefore, came closest to the unknowable truth. Bring in the poets, then, Bushnell urged, echoing Emerson. "If there be any complete science of man to come, they must bring it." The scriptures had gotten it right because they exhibited little of "mere dialectics" but much of "the freer creations of poetry." They were at home in the world of "analogies, signs, shadows, so to speak, of the formless mysteries above us and within us."[46]

Like Emerson, Bushnell had come full circle. Religious language—as metaphor—was an "instrument of suggestion," not of "absolute conveyance of thought." It was at the doorsteps of mystics that seekers could "receive the truth of God" as "an essentially vital power." So mystics and their experience were the end and delight that metaphysical religiosity promised. To be sure, Bushnell counseled readers not to be "apprehensive that the views here offered may bring in an age of mysticism and so of interminable confusion." He soothed them instead with the hopeful news that mystics found secret meanings signaling life "both in words and in things." And he hinted that he stood in good company. Christ and "almost every writing of the New Testament" revealed its mystical element, and readers would do well, he reiterated, to "make a study, to some extent, of the mystic and quietistic writers." Since one could not chop logic to arrive at Christian truth, since every formula turned out to be false, ideas like "trinity and atonement" had "their reality in and through the imaginative and morally aesthetic powers—truths of form and feeling, not of the logical understanding."[47]

Clearly an unrevealed God haunted Bushnell. Although there was no outright evidence that he had read deeply in the classics of the Christian mystical tradition, his words paralleled the language of negative theology, denying every affirmative statement that could be used to name God. The "unrevealed" God was "God simply existing, as spirit, in Himself." "Who, now," Bushnell asked rhetorically, "is God thus existing in Himself? Has He any external form, by which He may be figured or conceived?" The answer was clear. "No. Is He a point without space—is He space without limit? Neither. Is His activity connected with any sort of motion? Certainly not." Bushnell went on with his seemingly endless predicates denied. The unrevealed God was an "Absolute Being" and "the I Am that I am, giving no sign that He is, other than that He is."[48]

Exploring the terrain one more time in *Christ in Theology*, Bushnell pulled at his contradictions further. The link to the unknowable God was language in its analogies and correspondences that led followers into a land of high mystery. Yet the language—the words—were friendly, and, as we have seen, they had "faces." Instead of approaching them with the "logical method" or "mere notation," Bushnell exhorted that they be read "by looking in their faces, as we do our friends." What they would carry "into our soul's feeling or perception, or awaken in it by expression" was "their only truth." That, Bushnell went on, was "a simple, internal state of the soul itself." So when it came to understanding the inner being of God, the faces of words led nowhere except back to ourselves. Negation and silence surrounded the divine. The message, for Bushnell, was clear, and he hammered it home repeatedly. The nature of reality meant that "the best and truest doctrine" would not be "settled by the logical faculty." Rather, it would be discovered "under manifold terms of analogy" when the soul turned to receive God "through simple contemplation, perusing the faces of those words and symbols."[49]

Couched in these terms, Bushnell was saying in his own way what the mystics of the earlier Christian centuries had taught. Within the soul's own self, brought back there by the analogies in words and things, could come the space and energy of revelation. At the same time, Bushnell's words-with-faces were pointing in the direction of end-of-century New Thought. The metaphysical movement, as it developed, distanced God ever more insistently from human comprehension. Late-century metaphysicals often equaled Bushnell in their devotionalism and heart religion (and there are increasing suggestions that many of their rank and file and even major leaders came from evangelical backgrounds).[50] But they clothed God in abstractions—Mind, Truth, Intelligence, Principle, and, in the twentieth century, Source and All That Is. The life of the seeker generally had little to do with any direct rendezvous with so remote an entity, and evangelicals often became come-outers from the churches.

Bushnell's devotion to the person of Jesus meant that he did not join them. His rendezvous was continually with God in Christ. To be sure, he berated those who through their logic-chopping turned faith into "self-management, self-excitement, self-culture, self-illumination." Yet, standing squarely *within* his Christianity, a metaphysical aura still surrounded the rhetoric of religion he employed, and it meshed well with what was to come. "Something in the divine nature called the Word" proved to be the "fountain . . . of all the forms of things" and "the medium of the creation of the worlds." It was "a Form of God, a Mirror of Creative Imagination," and in it God beheld and might "body forth images of his thought."[51] Measured against an emerging metaphysical religiosity, much of it outside the churches, these seemingly innocuous words pointed toward a newer kind of religious world.

There was, however, another way in which Bushnell was teaching negative theology. Metaphysicians in the broad-based Hermetic tradition of the West, with its Neo-Platonic resonances, had defined evil as the absence of good, a failure to understand and make present the virtue that ought to be. So had a number of early Christian church fathers under the general rubric of sin. These thinkers—influenced to some extent by the classical thought of ancient Greece—linked an idea of sin as the absence of good to biblical themes of the Fall, and declared the universal need for redemption in a world that had departed from the good. The view of sin as absence was only one of a number of theological descriptions that sought to elaborate on the presence of evil in the world.[52] Yet significantly, it was this view of evil, cast—as among church fathers—in the language of sin but resonant with Hermetic ideas, that Bushnell adopted and employed. Again, the development was a parallel one, without an unmistakable trail of reading on Bushnell's part to buttress it. Still further, it is likely that Bushnell was being influenced more by Neo-Platonizing translations of Plato. Indeed, scholars of the era have pointed consistently to the pervasive Thomas Taylor translations of Plato, with their Neo-Platonic interpretive stance.[53]

In *Nature and the Supernatural*, as a key case, Bushnell had insisted that the human will belonged to the realm of the supernatural, outside the chain of cause and effect that characterized nature. For him, as William A. Johnson noted, the human dilemma was not occasioned by an "inherent evil" in the will. Yet because humanity belonged to the realm of Powers and not of Things, humans acted in ways uncaused by divine force; in effect, they chose evil—they sinned. Thus they lived "in a condition privative" that involved "their certain lapse into evil." Bushnell hastened to explain that by a "condition privative" he meant a "moral state" that was "only inchoate or incomplete, lacking something not yet reached," which was "necessary to the probable rejection of evil."[54] Still, he had said enough to set the stage for the Christian drama of redemption through Jesus. Moreover, he had done so by means of an argument that, in basic outline, agreed with ideas that pervaded metaphysical religiosity.

Still further, the negative moral state compromised the unalloyed goodness of God's created world. As a consequence of human action, as a result of the "fact of sin," came "a general disturbance or collapse of nature." "What we call nature," Bushnell declared, was "in fact, a state of un-nature induced by the penal or retributive action of causes provoked by sin." So, Bushnell mourned, "the whole field of nature, otherwise a realm of harmony, and peace, and beauty," took on "a look of discord, and with many traces of the original glory left," displayed "the tokens also of a prison and an hospital." Here was metaphysical thinking under the law of correspondence, looking like what was to come after 1875, especially with Theosophy, the movement that attempted to reform spiritualism and so promoted occultism as the power to unlock the secrets of nature and use them to advantage. Humans, as sources of power, had destroyed the order of their world. "The immense power of the human will over the physical substances of the world and the conjunctions of its causes, is seldom adequately conceived," Bushnell told readers. "Almost everything, up to the moon, is capable of being somehow varied or affected by it."[55] But unlike non-Christian Theosophists, who would proclaim the powers of mastery humans in themselves possessed, Bushnell looked to a redeemer. The human power to dis-order things was not, for him, a power to make them right again.

That acknowledged, Bushnell had by his own devices come a long way into a metaphysical thought world that, in his case, was still distinctly Christian. Negative theology functioned to exalt humanity in the scheme of things. Deprived of the good that ought to be present, caught in the web of the First Parents and their wrongful deed, haunted by a continuing human willfulness that struck against the divine, humans—as Powers and not Things—had yet managed miracles. Similarly, Bushnell had managed a rhetorical miracle of his own. He had traveled the same conceptual ground that characterized other metaphysicians who left Christianity. Yet he took it all home to the Congregational church. He saw himself as wholeheartedly a devotee of Jesus of Nazareth. If he was a man pulled by the metaphysical, he had also clearly committed himself to the person of Jesus and the power of ecclesiastical structure. Bushnell loved the church, mourned for sin, and exulted in the vicarious sacrifice and atonement brought by Jesus.

We are back where we began, with Bushnell in the middle—Christian and among the metaphysicians, demonstrating, in fact, an unorthodox and innovating Christianity that could absorb forms of metaphysical religiosity.

Like all readings, of course, this one is partial and needs to be set beside others. The importance of a metaphysical reading of Bushnell, however, is that it teases out the connections between thought worlds, challenging constructions that would place Christian church people and early metaphysicians in hermetically (pardon the pun) sealed worlds, separate from one another. They were not and are not. In the kaleidoscopic richness of theological construction on the ground, leading Christians and leading metaphysicians often inhabited a world that in many ways they made together. That being the case, it is not far afield to call Horace Bushnell a *natural* supernaturalist.

Emerson and Bushnell—at first, a quintessential odd couple—now seem not so odd together. The one, we might say, inverted the other. Celebrating nature, Emerson—with his Over-Soul and dualities become unities—trod cheerfully among cloudy landscapes that those who made fun of Transcendentalism sometimes panned. But the clouds, it turned out, were portals to a heavenly realm that might be described as *super*natural. Emersonian nature was not enough in itself. It was, in Transcendental parlance, the symbol of spirit, and the hierarchical implication was unmistakable. Meanwhile, Bushnell emphatically proclaimed his gospel of the supernatural, with God and the saints, atonement and redemption, sacrifice and eternal reward in a kingdom beyond. Yet, as he placed humans in a supernatural orbit, he was ever invoking nature, treasuring its delights, and discovering in it the preeminent teaching tool for a theology of bliss. Analogons and analogical imagination opened the way, and without them heaven was inconceivable. Supernature, in Bushnell's universe, needed nature.

Beyond the inversion of each with the other, both Emerson and Bushnell stood squarely in a mid-nineteenth-century urban world, rife with new "electric" energies, an industrial revolution, and a rising middle class increasingly attuned to European pundits and trends. Metaphysical thinking was growing ever stronger in their American culture worlds—metaphysics without the late-nineteenth-century name but with a significantly large share of its characteristics. Its presence—sometimes subtle and sometimes strong—left both men wary. Nevertheless, the talk of their respectively radical worlds had been leavened by its presence. Perhaps subversion, perhaps yeasty and exuberant new growth, it refused to evaporate, and the two found themselves picking and choosing from a new array of goods of the spirit. The old Puritan order had surely faded, and younger orthodoxies or counter-orthodoxies were beginning to take hold. Happiness—civil and otherwise—could be found now in different catch basins. Its pursuit, increasingly, was brokering a nature and supernature that fit a changing

American landscape—not just in the clouds but in a built environment of commerce that delight-making Americans were helping to forge. Print sources—like those read and produced by Emerson and Bushnell and like an emerging wave of other writings—were signaling a new and more joyous future than what had been. Mysterious processes of cultural distribution were operating with spendthrift energy. Metaphysics and its delights were erasing the "almost" that Emerson and Bushnell had carefully kept. As Americans rejoiced in their age, it was unsurprising that religion and spirituality would find ways to correspond. A new forever seem to be beckoning with sweet and yet unsettling consequences.

PART II

The Fruited Plain

SECTION 3

Commercial and Un-Unitarian Times

"Once you make a decision, the universe conspires to make it happen." So purportedly wrote Ralph Waldo Emerson; and if he did, probably somewhere in his journals. But a serious Internet search reveals no source. In fact, in the closest approximation, it generates a befuddled discussion on *Wikipedia* (perhaps, suggests one comment, the quotation came from a hymnbook collection and was taken from who knows where?). Even so, the quotation is ubiquitous. Indeed, among other citations, it is advertised for sale as a laminated motivational poster on Amazon.

Emersonian or not, however, the declaration is an early statement of what by the end of the twentieth century and the start of the twenty-first would commonly be called the law of attraction. As a shorthand statement of what I am calling the abundance theology, this "law of attraction" comes bearing the faded trappings of seventeenth-century Puritan culture. Cotton Mather had stated a law of attraction in terms of gravity. Meanwhile, his prose of affirmation, his habit of ejaculatory prayer, and his vitalistic proclamation of the Nishmath-Chajim anticipated a nineteenth-century "discovery" of the subtle human capacity to align with and thus "control" cosmic energy. So did Jonathan Edwards's pursuit of happiness in the contemplation of beauty and the pleasurable delights of spirit. By the nineteenth century, Emerson's stamp had been set on attraction, as the quotation I began with suggests. And Horace Bushnell, with the continual message of his writing, saw the cosmos and its divine force in quintessentially positive terms. What remained, however, was a clear crystallizing of these ideas and, ironically enough, a European input that brought them together in a fresh and incisive way. Now the past and the nineteenth-century European present were being remodeled in newer, Anglo-American terms.

To return to the "Emerson" quotation and its uncertain origins though, the situation comes as no surprise to anyone familiar with metaphysical religiosity. As sociologist and ethnographer Courtney Bender writes in her book-length study of Cambridge (Massachusetts) "mystics," traditional narratives about American metaphysical history were hardly a central preoccupation for her subjects. Their focus was experience. A documented past—thoroughly visible, too, in the Boston architecture of their built environment—did not attract them. Memory was personal and ad hoc. A textbook account was a far cry from what was real and important in their lives.[1] For an American religious historian, however, sources and links loom large. The gradual coalescence of what, by the twenty-first century, has become a formidable presence demands attention. The pursuit of happiness, it turns out, took significant turns in the middle of the nineteenth century and became at once privatized and collectivized. It upended traditional platitudes regarding good and evil. And it sought, on a landscape of social reform, to interweave the pleasure principle in its most physical manifestation—the delights of sex.

Emerson—this time fully documented—had remarked on "commercial and Unitarian times." But as the decades passed, and the times became distinctly commercial, a Unitarian passion for moral philosophy was making room for the regalements of love, both social and highly individualized. "Attractive industry" became a buzzword, while in whispered and not-so-whispered corners, the talk and action leaned toward *free* love." Although he had left his own Unitarian world far behind, a buttoned-up Ralph Waldo Emerson could hardly have been pleased. His latter-day admirer and successor, Walt Whitman, nonetheless, would have no misgivings. Even in the original 1855 edition of his monumental *Leaves of Grass*, he had written that "Copulation is no more rank to me than death is. / I believe in the flesh and the appetites. . . . Divine am I inside and out, and I make holy whatever I touch or am touched from; / The scent of these arm-pits is aroma finer than prayer."[2] Whitman would celebrate both heterosexual and homosexual love in his ecstatic poem, and—through it all—attraction would rule the day and rule the night as well. Notwithstanding, the now-distilled story of the modern law of attraction begins with the far less known American Albert Brisbane and his philosophical attraction to the French philosopher Charles Fourier.

FIVE

Albert Brisbane and the Metempsychosis of Sex

Albert Brisbane, the utopian socialist who straddled the nineteenth century from 1809 to 1890, is a largely forgotten figure in our time. In fact, his obscurity testifies to Courtney Bender's claims about metaphysical oblivion on matters of ancestry and lineage among her Cambridge mystics. Brisbane himself was born in Batavia, New York—a town early settled by his father, who worked as an agent for the Holland Land Company. There he grew up in prosperous surroundings.[1] We know, too, that his father, though Scotch, was an *anti*-Presbyterian and religious skeptic. The entire family was hardly what one could call religious, and—to add to the absence of religion—there were no churches in Batavia for the first seven years of the youngster's life. But Albert Brisbane's English mother was an idealist with one eye on cosmology and the other on social reform. And when Albert was fifteen, with a nonconventional education up to then (he had left what school existed at ten to roam the woods), his father, James, sent him to New York City to study.

It was there that Albert eventually came to be tutored by Jean Manesca, a French-Haitian planter and Santo Domingo refugee. Thoroughly immersed in the tradition of the French Enlightenment, Manesca conveyed an enthusiasm for European philosophical learning to his young charge, and after two years, Brisbane had learned French and persuaded his father to send him to France for further study. In Paris at eighteen, he attended the lectures of Victor Cousin and meanwhile gained fluency in the French language. He studied in both Paris and Berlin, enamored especially with a philosophical idealism that tended toward social concern and reform. During these first years abroad, he also traveled widely, unsatisfied with the philosophical fare he had thus far received. By 1830, he embarked on an extensive tour through Austria, Turkey, Greece, and Italy. We are fortunate that two (of the seven or eight) travel diaries that he kept during this period remain.

Brisbane's travels only heightened his social-reform concerns and his rejection of political solutions to complex societal problems. In the private pages of his diaries, we read lengthy and repeated passages concerning the deplorable poverty, misery, and suffering he encountered, all of which affected him greatly. The diary pages also reveal a young man who wrote stridently as a feminist—bemoaning the sexual slavery of girls and young women especially—but who also regularly indulged his own impulses in bed with prostitutes. Yet even in the midst of his addiction, the feminism was radical. During a visit to Constantinople, recalled Brisbane's *Mental Biography*, he "conceived very clearly the liberty and independence of woman." He "saw that her educational development and moral elevation were primary conditions of social progress in almost every direction." Still further, he argued that "the free association of men and women led to refinement, the desire to please, and also to an effort on the part of man to elevate himself intellectually and spiritually." Even more passionately, he declared that there was "no grandeur for man but in the elevation of woman." "When he drags her down and crushes her, he crushes and brutalizes himself." There was, he declared, "an incontrovertible law that he who would become a tyrant becomes himself a slave."[2] Through passages such as this, the diaries and *Mental Biography* point clearly to the complex persona of his mature years—idealist social reformer and also sexual libertine—both already strikingly visible.

Meanwhile, still searching out philosophical solutions for the social malaise he had encountered seemingly everywhere, he met Jules Lechevalier—a French fellow student who would be notably instrumental in his life. It was Lechevalier who connected the ever-seeking Brisbane to the social-reform teachings and socialist Christianity of Claude-Henri Rouvroy de Saint-Simon (1760–1825) and later to the life-changing work of Charles Fourier (1772–1837). Unsatisfied with the philosophical writings he had studied, including those of Georg Friedrich Hegel, through Lechevalier Brisbane was attracted first by Saint-Simonianism. But he never could fully commit to Saint-Simon's system, and likewise he became disillusioned by developing divisions within the movement and uncomfortable with its religious demands. Then, in the winter of 1831–1832 in Berlin, Brisbane's peripatetic existence as a seeker changed dramatically. Through a book with the underinspiring title *Treatise on Domestic and Agricultural Association* by Charles Fourier, his life spun around. He had been introduced to teachings that truly riveted him, and his enthusiasm seemed wild and boundless. At last, he had found the system that pieced together all the parts of his personality and clearly identified all the parts of the dysfunctional social world he had observed. So from late 1832 Brisbane spent two years in France studying Fourier's system, and he was insistent enough to receive, for a short time, private tutoring from the master.

By 1834, then, he came back home to Batavia with his first wife, Adèle LeBrun. After a period of illness and the return of Adèle to Europe with their surviving son, Brisbane at last recommitted to the intensity of his earlier Fourierism and in 1840 produced *The Social Destiny of Man*.[3] Meant to introduce Americans to Fourier's system, it was a curious work that melded long passages from Fourier's writings, which had only been published in Europe haphazardly, with his own reading of the French philosopher. That reading, as we will see, was a highly redacted product, sanitizing the theories of a radical, extravagant, and—by conventional standards—starkly fanciful and eccentric intellectual to make of them a "practical" program for social change.

The year before, Brisbane had begun to lecture on Fourier's blueprint for productive labor (see below). His enthusiastic addresses and his book, as well as more ephemeral periodical publications and a column in famed reform editor Horace Greeley's *New York Tribune*, kindled a utopian movement. It resulted in the creation of more than forty "phalanxes" (the Fourierist name for intentional communities), the most well-known and successful of which were the North American Phalanx and, in its later years, the Transcendentalist Brook Farm. But despite his enthusiasm, Brisbane found all the phalanxes wanting; they failed to meet Fourierist stipulations for numbers, physical plant, and finances, to name the most obvious problems. In fact, as the would-be phalanxes were exuberantly populating the American landscape, Brisbane left for an eight-month trip to France to study Fourierist manuscripts and to speak with French followers of the movement. He remained totally unwilling or unable to work in practical ways to make Fourierist ideas of social reform take on material success.

By the late 1840s, aspects of the Fourierist system that signaled radical views of sex and marriage began to be published, although the full extent of Fourier's sexual views as well as the more bizarre declarations that were part of his system were never completely acknowledged. Brisbane became something of a Fourierist revisionist in his own way, and he also moved on to other pursuits and interests besides the French master. Meanwhile, in his personal life, counting common-law and claimed relationships, he had four marriages. The legal entanglements of these episodes were huge, as was his sexual appetite. His friend Henry Clay McDougal, in fact, wrote that Brisbane had "been the lawful husband of three wives and in various countries had accumulated nearly as many concubines as the Book credits to the account of the sweet singer of Israel."[4] In his final marriage, his wife, Redelia Bates Brisbane, assisted him in producing an autobiography (*A Mental Biography*) as he told his story in highly romanticized terms, and she wrote it down. Still, if heavily selective and idealized, it represents an important source on what fired him as a distinctive American seeker. Nor was his private quest without huge societal consequences for the century to come and after. By the end of his life in 1890, he had permanently altered the existing metaphysical vocabulary in the nation. Without a material creation beyond his own writing and speaking, he had inaugurated and brokered ideas that would re-mold the shape of inherited metaphysical religiosity.

Broker indeed, as we have already begun to see, he introduced Americans to the thought and social-reform program of Charles Fourier, which came with religious and ethical claims as it looked toward a social revolution both profound and unsettling. It is time, then, to ask, Who was Charles Fourier? And what, explicitly, did he teach that Brisbane found so compelling and life-changing? Born François-Marie Charles Fourier at Besançon, France, in 1772, the French social theorist and philosopher grew up, like Brisbane, in a prosperous family. He was the only son of a successful cloth merchant, and his mother also came from an important commercial family in the city. Like Brisbane, too, his mother exercised a strong influence over him—although she could hardly be called an idealist. Jonathan Beecher and Richard Bienvenu, surveying the literature on Fourier's life, describe her as "barely literate" and call her "stingy, domineering, extremely prudish," with a morbid and obsessive Roman Catholic piety.[5] Moreover, although Fourier's father left him an inheritance if he followed in paternal footsteps, the younger man at first eschewed any connection with mercantile pursuits. Supposedly, as a young child of seven, he had sworn the oath of ancient Carthaginian general Hannibal (against Rome) "to an eternal hatred of commerce."[6] Apparently, the young child lived in a world of his own, with an active memory and aptitudes in music and mathematics, a love of flowers, and a passion for order and arrangement. He studied for a time at the Collège de Besançon, where secular priests taught, but was largely self-taught with not much patience for long and labored tomes.

Beginning in 1789, Fourier's father made various attempts to place his son in the mercantile world (despite the famed Hannibalic oath), and the young man ended up in Lyon and, from there, led a life of work in commerce. But Lyon was also a city that fostered mysticism and a utopian variety of social thought. So the youthful Fourier read the writings of the locals and also began speculating on the problems of the city's economic world. Meanwhile, in the decade of the French Revolution, turmoil came to Lyon, and—after fighting in a local army of sorts—he was nearly executed. Then came a period of more revolutionary turmoil and work as a traveling salesman, until Fourier eventually spent a lengthy period using Lyon, again, as his home base. By the end of the eighteenth century, he was already formulating his overarching philosophy of humanity and society. As Beecher and Bienvenu wrote, "The task which he set himself was to work out a scheme of 'natural association' which would make the gratification of individual desires and passions serve the general good."[7]

Fourier's early exposition of his evolving views came in a piece called "Universal Harmony," which appeared in the *Bulletin de Lyon* in 1803. This was just the beginning of a thirty-four-year career during which he poured out his ideas in a series of writings, many of them unpublished. By 1808, his *Théorie des quatre mouvements et des destinées générales* (1808; *Theory of the Four Movements and General Destinies*) had seen the light of day, if published anonymously and later withdrawn. Then, by 1822, the two-volume *Treatise on Domestic and Agricultural Association*, which so inspired Brisbane, had appeared in print. With a bibliography of newspaper articles, pamphlets, and books that was vast and extensive during his lifetime, Fourier kept writing almost to the end of his days. The two-volume *False Industry, Divided, Disgusting, and Lying, and Its Antidote* came out in 1835 and 1836, and Fourier died the next year in Paris. A posthumous edition of his works—supposedly complete but not actually so—appeared in six volumes in that city from 1841 to 1845.[8]

Important here, Fourier's writings reveal a distinct interest in sexuality. He never married, but as a young man he apparently had many female friends. His definitive biographer, Jonathan Beecher, has called patterns of physical intimacy in Fourier's life "particularly cloudy." Beecher also signaled that Fourier moved easily in and out of numerous relationships with women that were "purely sexual." Apparently, too, he was something of a sexual voyeur, and there were hints that perhaps he played the role of observer for lesbian lovemaking. Yet, as Beecher has demonstrated, he formed abiding friendships with a number of women, some with whom he had experienced sex, and others with whom the relationships were purely platonic. Thus, the overplayed stereotype that has come down to us of an older Fourier who lived as a solitary recluse obscures the very active sex life that he seemed to have enjoyed, especially in his younger days, and also obscures his continuing friendships with women. Still more, just as his American disciple Brisbane would be, Fourier was an adamant feminist. Beecher has argued that he was "the first of the early European socialists to put a thoughtful and rigorous analysis of the situation of women at the center of a comprehensive critique of his society." Fourier was, in fact, admired by "pioneer French feminists" in a rising movement for the emancipation of women in the 1830s and 1840s.[9]

As this rough sketch already suggests, the fit between Fourier, the master, and Brisbane, the disciple in his heyday, was strong. Idealism and interest in social reform led the way, but—like Fourier—Brisbane would prove indifferent to political solutions to social reform, even if he displayed considerable political savvy in the way he introduced Americans to Fourier's thought. Brisbane's passional and, especially, sexual life, likewise, found its gospel advocate in the writings of Fourier, and his feminism was celebrated there as well. Since my concern here is the American transcription of Charles Fourier's ideas mediated largely by Brisbane, my discussion in what follows turns on the Brisbane-Fourier connection. Brisbane's reading of Charles Fourier, as we shall see, was carefully shaped and redacted for an American audience, even as the French themselves were doing the same thing in their European context.

As the reference to the fit between Fourier and Brisbane already suggests, Brisbane's predisposition for Fourierism extended well back into his early life in Batavia. If Fourier's gentle side surfaced in a childhood preference for solitude, a love of flowers and music, and even an artistic flair for drawing, Brisbane, for his part, seemed an unconscious echo of a combined Jonathan Edwards, Ralph Waldo Emerson, and Horace Bushnell. His *Mental Biography* had Brisbane recalling how his "free life" led him "into intimate contact with nature" and made him "a close observer." "With what pleasure," he remembered, "I watched the red-headed woodpecker, his breast against the rotten trunk of a tree into which he would peck, putting his ear down to listen whether the sound of a grub could be heard." Then there was "the yellow-hammer settling on the thistle to pick out its seed, or the robin in cherry-time perched on the cherry-tree." He had "watched the wild squirrel bounding from tree to tree." In the twilight he had heard "the strange mournful voice of the whip-poor-will" and "wondered what spirit was there." He would also "watch for hours the silvery fish as they glided through the village stream." Summing up his childhood experience, Brisbane recalled that "every fact in nature was full of charm to me." "In short," he added, "Nature and I were in unison. I never tired of studying her, and her great book of mysteries read to me like a fairy tale."[10]

From such beginnings, Brisbane nurtured what became, as Lloyd Rohler wrote, an "important concept of the relationship of man to nature." Brisbane "saw man and nature in an harmonious relationship." For him, a human was the "overseer of nature, not her master." Moreover, that reign of harmony (and order) was expressed most succinctly in a keen sense that there was a whole into which humans fitted. In France, studying as a young man in his pre-Fourier days, Brisbane had become interested in philosophical lectures at the Sorbonne, especially those of Victor Cousin. As an American seeker, he was not preoccupied, at this point, by practical problems and "material phenomena." He declared unequivocally that "nothing concrete met my burning desire to comprehend the reason of universal existence and the relation of man to the Great Whole." Here again Brisbane—no doubt unawares—was reiterating the fundamental proposition about the nature of the universe and all life dear to Puritans, Emersonians, and nineteenth-century Protestant liberals alike. "There is harmony in exterior nature, there is a God there," Brisbane had written in his travel diary in 1831.[11]

As for Fourier and, on the American side of the ocean, especially for Edwards, talk of harmony came accompanied by musical analogs. It does not take long reading Brisbane's diaries or his *Mental Biography* to see that he was deeply invested in appreciation of the arts and, notably, of music. Both sources are filled with references, and the Brisbane who emerges through their pages is a clear aficionado, with well-defined tastes and interests in musical art and artists. Remembering thus the Venetian "Place St. Mark with its palace and its basilica" in 1831, he called the Ducal Palace "the music of architecture: presenting contrasts as rich and accords as harmonious as those of the grand symphonies of Beethoven." He had met Felix Mendelssohn in Berlin in 1829 and later spent time with him in Rome. In Paris, he also got acquainted personally with Franz Liszt (who at the time was attracted to the St.-Simonians and told Brisbane years later that he concurred with their general principles).[12]

Correspondence, harmony, music, and—joining them—beauty, all were of a piece. In the midst of his travels as a young man and in the midst, too, of his numerous liaisons with prostitutes, he seemed to be ever reaching, ever searching, and never quite grasping a fleeting reality that circled these themes. While he was in Malta in 1830, he covered his diary's pages with reflections on the nature of art and its connectedness through correspondences. "That real beauty, which should animate a work of art," he thought, was "not the result of simple imagination and unpolished fancy." It was "the result of something higher." And what was that? It was "the result of the Thought having conscience of, and contemplating the beauty in nature, but going out beyond it and idealizing it." Still there was more. It was "the result also of something else besides this, even. But that something," he admitted, "I do not myself know how to define."[13]

Yet for all the abstraction, Brisbane's ideas were joined from early on with what may be described as the beginnings of a social conscience. He claimed that out of his boyhood arose a "second stage" of his "mental development." "I remember," Brisbane told Redelia, "standing on the bridge that crossed the little creek at Batavia one day, and musing as I threw pebbles into the water and observed the widening, rippling circles as they started from the center." The phenomenon evoked for him the "new problems" that were forming in his mind, even though "not yet brought clearly and definitely to the touchstone of consciousness." Tellingly, the questions and problems pointed in a social direction. "What is the work of man on this earth?" he asked. "What was he put here for, and what has he to do?" He decided that he "belonged to a vast army in which each individual had his place and function." He also thought that "those who left the ranks to attend to individual concerns could not advance in the great achievement to which they were destined." "The army was Humanity," he summed up. "I was a soldier in its ranks."[14]

Soldier that he saw himself, Brisbane had found his general in Charles Fourier. Brisbane would cross the ocean back to America to spread the social teachings he had gleaned from the master. Yet the Fourierism that Brisbane brought home to America, as his speeches and public writings demonstrate, underwent a series of transformations. The disciple, it turned out, for all his philosophical musing, was politically quite astute. From the first, Brisbane possessed a sharp intuitive understanding of what his compatriots would buy. And it was, indeed, about buying. The Charles Fourier who flourished in the United States waved, above all, the banner of commerce and industry. Art had become labor, and beauty the fit between worker and work. In a subtle but yet quite revolutionary undercutting of centuries of Christian theology—the banner came printed with the buzz words "Association," "passional attraction," and "attractive industry." In short, Charles Fourier had articulated the fabled law of attraction, and Albert Brisbane was aiming to guarantee that Americans would learn and live it. In the process, they would bury the Calvinism of their collective past; they would leave behind suffering and sin and rejoice in a brave new world of delight and satisfaction.

In this context, the Fourier translations and interpretations that reached an American audience are instructive. Brisbane's 1840 *Social Destiny of Man* greeted English-speaking readers with a veritable barrage of material—some 240,000 words in 480 pages. As Rohler noted, the book addressed the anxiety of the age at the time of the early industrial revolution. "By linking association with efficiency and thrift," Rohler assessed, "Brisbane cannily appropriated to it the character of true hardy American virtues." In terms of content, though, the work weighed in as an authorial hodge-podge. Carl

Guarneri stated outright that one half of it consisted of translations of Fourier's writings, with the second half Brisbane's "own original elaborations and applications."[15] For the first-time reader, discerning which is which presents something of a challenge. Moreover, the book shifts type fonts from chapter to chapter and is also riddled with typographical errors. But Brisbane was a man on fire with a calling, and he would not be stalled by the fine points of publishing accuracy.

Thus Brisbane turned immediately to the periodical press to spread the good news of the new French gospel, contributing pieces on Fourierism in places like the *Democratic Review*, Orestes Brownson's *Boston Quarterly Review*, and the Transcendentalist periodical, *The Dial*. Meanwhile, *Social Destiny* itself garnered several reviews, and by the fall of 1840 Brisbane was at work on a weekly journal of his own. Called *The Phalanx*, it lasted only six weeks, but a successor publication, *Phalanx: Organ of the Doctrine of Association* (a semimonthly), flourished from 1843 to 1845. Brisbane's most important journalistic contact, though, was Greeley with his *New York Tribune*. By 1842, Brisbane had purchased a front-page column in Greeley's daily, and with steady publicity and a sympathetic readership, American Fourierism, Brisbane-style, was off and running.[16]

Still more, after the lengthy and verbose exposition of Fourierism in *Social Destiny*, Brisbane felt the need, perhaps encouraged by his periodical successes, to publish a more succinct handbook of American-inflected Fourierist teachings, now with an emphasis on practical themes. So in 1843 his eighty-two-page (two columns and fine print, to be sure) *Concise Exposition of the Practical Part of Fourier's Social Science* appeared. Other Fourierist authors, too, were joining him—Parke Godwin and his *Popular View of the Doctrines of Charles Fourier* (1844) was probably the best known. As Guarneri reported tellingly, "Instead of simply translating Fourier's works, French and American disciples wrote their own tracts which in the guise of summarizing his ideas limited them to his philosophy of history, theory of the passions [see below], and plan for model communities." Not to be mentioned at first in an American context was Fourier's prediction of a "New Amorous World," the title of a collection of his notebooks on love. These did not appear in print until as late as 1967, even if his *Theory of the Four Movements*, which appeared in translation in 1857 (see below), already prefigured the full Fourierist chapter and verse on love.[17]

By 1848, however, publishing practices had begun to change. Charles Julius Hempel, a Swedenborgian physician who was also an Associationist spoke up in print for Fourier's vision of more freedom in love relationships. Likewise, an Associationist work that addressed only Fourier's theories of sexuality became available—an anonymous translation of Victor Hennequin's *Love in the Phalanstery*. The unknown translator happened to be none other than Henry James Sr., father of William James (see chapter 8) and a follower of Emanuel Swedenborg as well as Charles Fourier. The changes had progressed enough that by 1857 Brisbane felt comfortable publishing Henry Clapp's translation of Fourier's *Social Destiny of Man; or, Theory of the Four Movements*. This was bound together with the French Associationist's *Treatise on the Functions of the Human Passions* and Brisbane's own *Outline of Fourier's System of Social Science*. The work carefully trotted out the master's "system of Amatory Relations," with a caution that it was a prediction for "future ages of Social Harmony."[18]

Then, by 1876, Brisbane tried again—this time with two densely packed volumes in his *Sociological Series, Nos. I and II*. The works recapitulated much from the past but were also more integrative and synthetic, bringing aspects of Brisbane himself in his maturing years into the presentation. He complained in print that Fourier's theory was "not in the least understood by the public in general." He could remedy the situation, he believed, by explaining Fourier's method for readers. Recalling his own 1857 publication, he now thought that he could do better. "Since that date," he confided, "we have made studies which would lead us at the present day to treat the subject with more completeness and with a stricter deduction from Laws." By the time Brisbane arrived at the second volume of the series, he was presenting Fourier's theory of the "Vestalic Body" to which all young girls would belong once they reached the age of puberty—a preparation for the sexual freedom that for them would follow.[19]

Here we can ask in a more systematic way what it was about Fourierist teaching that had so excited and compelled Brisbane. His conversion to Fourier's doctrine was something like the iconic fall from a horse that brought the New Testament Saul, as Paul, forever to Christianity and made him the fiery disciple that he became. In Brisbane's case, the conversion was based in two laws that he found incontrovertible: the law of attraction and its parent law of correspondence. As the "parent" already attests, the two were actually one law—with attraction a subcategory of the law of correspondence (what you think is what you get). We can also look at the Brisbane-Fourier connection in Brisbane's terms and, at the same time, explore the nature of Fourierist teaching, American-style. In what follows, although I will be using the name of Charles Fourier, on the horizon must be the fact that Fourier came to this nation mostly through Brisbane's interpretive lenses and editing practices. With so much of the Frenchman's work available only in manuscript and no other spokesperson so articulate as Brisbane, there was little chance of correcting the mediated version of Fourier to which Americans were introduced.

I have already suggested that Brisbane knew his compatriots well and was keenly aware of what he could sell them. I begin then, with the intellectually revolutionary "law of attraction." Charles Fourier claimed, without bows to others, that he had discovered, as Albert Fried put it, "the principle uniting all things in the universe, from inanimate matter to complex relations" among human beings. Fourier called it the principle of "attraction," and it was, as Fried also pointed out, "an elaborated, extended, and refined version of Newton's law of gravitation." Fourier himself, in his own way, had recognized the connection, paralleling Newton's attention to material attraction with his own talk of the passional version. And, to be sure, he was most likely unaware of earlier American versions of the law of attraction, even as he was homing in on the law in a new way. With Fourier's perspective applied to human society, civilization's failure lay in its suppression of human passions, "the force of attraction native to man." So the reformer's task became one of liberating the passions. What followed was the entire panoply of Associationism, with its communal living in a so-called "phalanx" and its precisely detailed requirements for success.[20]

In his own rendition of Fourier's reasoning, the Brisbane of the *Mental Biography* spoke of Fourier's "discovery" of "the law which governs the action of the human passions, their development and their play in society." Called by Fourier the "law of the Series" (of Groups), as so stated, this law of the Series was but a "technical" expression. Brisbane explained that "the law is that which underlies *all distribution, co-ordination, and arrangement in the universe so far as the creations on the earth reveal the law, and so far as it is revealed in the classifications discovered by man; especially in music.*" Fourier, said Brisbane, contrasted human conflict with the order throughout the universe. He thought that attraction governed the latter and should also rule the former. Hence, reported Brisbane's Fourier, in place of restraint "to compel the passions to adapt themselves to existing institutions," the reverse should be the order of the day. He "proclaimed *Attraction* . . . as the law governing the universe, and demanded its application to human society." Given this law, Fourier had banished "the vast machinery of repression both physical and spiritual: the scaffolds and prisons as well as the hells and purgatories." He had established instead "an order adapted to the real nature of man—to the development of those forces in the soul which shall lead him to obey spontaneously the principles of justice, dignity, moral grandeur, devotion, and heroism."[21]

Where, we might ask, was this celebration of human passion leading, and what were its implications? The challenge to orthodox Christianity is difficult to ignore, with the verbal slam on its "hells and purgatories" (even if, in Protestant America, purgatory had mostly vanished). The libertinism is not hard to find either. That acknowledged, in Brisbane's telling, the liberation of human passions led, with one major part of Fourier's theory, not to sex but to labor and commerce. "Attractive industry," argued Brisbane in *Social Destiny of Man*, meant Association, and Association meant the "detailed subdivision of labour," so that groups of workmen would be in each subdivision "By Attraction, By Charm." Still further, what would result from "combined" and "attractive industry"? Brisbane was enthusiastic. "General and graduated riches," "practical truth in business and social relations," "real and effective liberty," and "constant peace" would come. Even more astounding, there would be "equilibrium of temperature and climate," a "system of preventive medicine," and an "opening offered to all ameliorations and improvements."[22]

If Fourier asserted that "Attraction" was "the only law the Divinity makes use of in governing the Universe" and that humans "must be governed also by attraction," he also declared that attraction was the only law that reconciled "the being governed with the governing power." Practically speaking, human social arrangements must replicate the arrangements of nature, in which the animal, vegetable, and mineral "kingdoms" were "Series of Groups" (here was the law of correspondence subsuming attraction unawares). Not only that, but the planets themselves were "a Serie of a more perfect order than that of the kingdoms." In such a universe, the human echo became the "Passional Serie." There existed "a league of divers Groups, distributed in an ascending and descending order, united passionally from an identity of taste for some occupation either of agriculture, manufactures, art or science, applying a group to each detail of the pursuit, which occupies the Serie." "Attraction alone" must regulate each Group, and in a phalanx, the Groups would form a Serie. How would this all work out? There was nothing to fear, for "the Creator distributes passions and attractions to all his creatures in *exact proportion* to their Destiny"; he had adapted "their instincts and feelings" to the place they would fulfill "in the scale of creation." So important was the point that Brisbane asserted, following Fourier, "The law of Attraction proportional to Destinies" was "an important proof in the question of the Immortality of the Soul." Since immortality was "a *collective* attraction of the human race," a just Creator would not have given humans a desire he had no intention of fulfilling.[23]

On a more mundane level, where Brisbane was preaching human social destiny, the catchphrase for attraction had become "attractive industry." To achieve it, as Rohler summarized, Brisbane claimed that Fourier would "maximize the non-material incentives of labor." This, in effect, was "passional attraction" with no holds barred, even if there was a language problem in that phrase for Americans. In *Social Destiny* Brisbane had urged that the leaders in any Fourierist Association must not only be adept at practical aspects but must also be "perfectly convinced of the goodness of the passions and of the truth of Passional attraction as a social guide." So the refrain of choice was "attractive industry," with "passional attraction" lurking genially beneath and sometimes peeking through. Michael Fellman elaborated that the industrial phrase signified for Brisbane "work made pleasurable through mutual assistance and governed according to correctly understood laws of human behavior." For Brisbane, too, industry could only be dignified and rendered "Attractive" when Associations were large, following Fourier's requirements for an ideal number of 1,800 persons in a phalanx.[24]

Even in this sanitized version without the sex, there were problems for attractive industry in an American setting. Brisbane complained that although his "platform utterances" addressed only the "practical and comprehensible"—"nothing about marriage" (nor "the selfish spoliations of the rich," nor "appeals to class prejudices")—he got in trouble with press and clergy. They "sniffed the danger." They saw that Brisbane's Fourierist gospel of Association "would free woman from the domestic drudgery and despotism to which she is now subjected." Even worse, they (correctly) realized "that the idea of attraction was directly opposed to the spirit of their theology, which looks upon man as a fallen and sinful creature, to be kept in order by constraint and the fear of future punishment." In a theological fling of his own, Brisbane pointed to what was wrong: "They saw that their system of suppression and repression was thus made to appear a positive inversion of the Cosmic truth."[25]

This is not to neglect attractive industry as the revolutionary mantra it was for energizing a radical new approach to labor. Guarneri's definitive study of Fourierism in America identified the importance of its emphasis on attractive work. Fourier's vision, he thought, was "set apart" not just from utopians who fostered work as "social duty" but even "from mainstream nineteenth-century social thinkers who interpreted the urge to work as a form of discipline, self-sacrifice, and productivity." Instead of all this, Fourier promoted work for its ability to deliver "complete self-realization."[26]

More than that, at least in theory, Brisbane had a plan to make results happen. First, he argued, the idea and practice of labor needed to be given dignity. It had to be seen as doing more than simply providing for physical needs. After that, the physical surroundings for labor needed to be made pleasant and even beautiful. The creator who had fashioned humans with beauty and harmony in their physical bodies intended the same thing for the environment in which they dwelled. So the agricultural milieu had to be completely delightful, with fields and gardens that fulfilled the need for loveliness. Similarly, in workshops in which industry was performed—Brisbane called them "Halls of Industry"—the design must incorporate the same kind of elegance that graced agricultural fields. Working people themselves had to be congenial enough to be appealing partners for others, this ensured by an education promoting the arts and sciences in general alongside necessary vocational training. Likewise, they should be incentivized deliberately by material gains and rewards as well as a series of honorary distinctions that could be bestowed. By these means, work would be honored and esteemed. Beyond that, the Fourierist vision of groups and series needed to be made reality. In other words, there needed to be unity with others who felt similar tastes for various jobs. As Brisbane quoted Fourier at his imperial best, "The Series of Groups is the mode adopted by God in the whole distribution of the Universe." "If the passions and characters were not regulated, like the material kingdoms, by Series of Groups," Fourier wrote, "*Man would be out of unity with the Universe*; there would be duplicity of system and incoherence between the *material* and the *spiritual* or *passional* world."[27]

Imperial himself in the social world, Brisbane had declaimed in *Social Destiny* that "Attractive Industry" was "the first remedy to be applied to Social evils." Through it "every individual" would be given "the option of a great many branches of work, with varied and frequent changes, guaranteeing him a sufficiency of food, raiment and lodging, and giving to the material organization of labour the greatest elegance and facility possible." The passions, instead of being riled in war and politics, would become "precious springs of action," with labor "performed by groups of friends, freely united, varying their occupations through the day, to prevent monotony and satiety." Such a situation was an "immense benefit reserved for us by the Creator." Attraction was "in the hands of God," Brisbane enthusiastically summarized, "a magic wand, which enables him to secure from love and pleasure the performance of work, which man can alone obtain by constraint or violence."[28]

Still more, when all was said and done, the magic wand of attractive industry must always and ever be passionate. By 1857, with a nod toward the law of correspondence, Brisbane categorically affirmed that "Passional Attraction" could be "defined as the power that governs the Moral or Spiritual World as gravitation is the power that governs the Material World." One governed "the movements of intelligent beings, the other the movements of material bodies." "God, in requiring of any of his creatures the performance of a work or function, employs no other lever or agent than Attraction; he never resorts to coercion, restraint, or violence in any form." So God governed "the Universe by this power alone," and he impelled "all beings to fulfil their Destiny from the pleasure, the charm, the delight he connects with it, and not from fear of pain or punishment."[29] High among the delights was sex.

Early critics of Brisbane's Fourierist system had already begun to decipher the implications of attractive industry's magic wand, as I have already suggested for press and clergy. When separate kitchens disappeared in a phalanx in favor of community cooperation in cooking, women were thereby liberated from numerous separate tasks to cook and feed their families. Such arrangements already raised questions about couples and nuclear families. The next step for women—and men—might be, could be, sexual freedom in extramarital consensual relationships. Brisbane, of course, had strongly disavowed such activity at first. But with the two Associationist publications of 1848 (Hempel and Hennequin), there were leaks in the dike. Still more, by 1857 and Henry Clapp Jr.'s, translation of Charles Fourier's *The Social Destiny of Man; or, Theory of the Four Movements*, controversial details of the Fourierist system were becoming more readily available. In Brisbane's section of the work—ever aiming to soften the Fourierist teaching as he explained it—he explicitly addressed the "marriage question." "In the whole domain of Social Science," he wrote, "there is no question which is surrounded with so many difficulties as this." Fourier, he stated, was "the only person" who had "made a systematic investigation of this important problem." Indeed, Fourier had "laid down the fundamental principles of the true theory of Amatory Relations," and he had "furnished" their "scientific basis." Careful to distinguish between present and future, Brisbane assured readers that Fourier's ideas applied to "future ages of Social Harmony." Since that fact had been ignored, the accusation had surfaced "that he advocated a system of promiscuity, license, and sensuality," an accusation that was "wholly false." Fourier had been unable to give a "complete statement of his Theory of Amatory Relations." To do so, he would have needed to supply "a full analysis of the passion of Love and its functions." "To explain this Theory . . . to a world having no idea that the Passions can be harmonized, would be," Brisbane thought, "as difficult as to explain to Savages, having no idea that Sounds can be harmonized, the Theory of Music."[30]

Nevertheless, Brisbane was not above trying. Love, like everything else, had been formed into "Passional Series." Furthermore, it was only in "a large Association" that the "Passional Series" could be formed and "Passional

Harmony" realized. Brisbane went on: "The division of the passion of Love into its shades or varieties of amatory sympathy, and their distribution in a Series, constitute the first work to be done in determining the theory of Amatory Harmony, and the true Order that is to exist in the relations of the Sexes." Individuals possessed different kinds of "amatory" characters, and the different types would form Series. Each type would thus be governed by its own set of laws. As Brisbane became more explicit, he told readers that "the Coquettish or Ambitious love, for example, cannot be governed by the same rules and regulations as the Prudish or the Voluptuous love." So those with "the same type of Amatory Character would form a distinct Group or Corporation"—as many groups as there were characters. A series of institutions would correspond to them, and these "would lead to the full, free, natural, and harmonious development of Love." Taken together, they would constitute a single "Institution," and he was willing to call that "Marriage," which was "the complete and natural System for the regulation of the relations of the Sexes." So far the marital principle sounded at least somewhat conventional, but what came next made an unqualified lie of that idea. "In Civilization," Brisbane remarked unhappily, there was but "one mode for the union of the Sexes," and that was "Monogamic Marriage" or, as he specified further, "the exclusive and permanent union of a single couple for life," a union "enforced by law" and "maintained irrespective of Love between the couple," or "their physical adaptation of the procreation of offspring." This was, he declared, "as great an error as to suppose that all persons have the same taste in the matter of food."[31]

What could and should be done in such a civilized world? To answer, Brisbane, like Fourier, was looking ahead to a historical evolution that would advance society well beyond the state of "Civilization." After many bumps in the road, humans had progressed from the nomadic or savage state to the patriarchal era when industry and mental activity dawned. Thereafter came the barbaric state in which agriculture and manufactures experienced their primary development. Only then did the civilized state come into being, and it brought the development of industry on a large scale. It was not, however, a paradisal state, and with all its cleverness of organizational structure, the present condition counted as "imperfect." The human race needed to pass through further ages to arrive at "a State of social Unity, Order, and Harmony" after experiencing "certain periods of social experiment, apprenticeship, and initiation."[32] Fourier's ultimate theory, his "Theory of Universal Unity," or "the natural law of social harmony," beckoned as the end goal of the evolutionary process. Significantly, the author(s) of the preface to the edition Clapp had translated (identified only as "disciples of Fourier") exhorted that "we have not to discuss whether what FOURIER proposes is moral or immoral." The "only question" was "if what he proposes is true or false. If FOURIER'S THEORY is true, if in the domain of Social Science it is conformable to the nature of things, to the Law of Universal Order, and if, at the same time, it is contrary to Morality, so much the worse for Morality."[33] The news was going to be shocking, and Fourier, as he looked ahead to a future age, delivered his version of it.

In his earliest treatise (*Theory of the Four Movements*), Fourier had addressed what he called the material, organic, animal, and social "movements." By the time the 1857 Clapp translation became available, Fourier had made some revisions and, in italicized prefatory remarks, was cautioning readers. "*I confess the necessity of this bond* [permanent marriage] *in Civilization,*" he soothed, and "*I criticize it only in comparison with the new Social Order in which a different form of union between the sexes will require a freedom in love-relations which in the present order is inadmissible.*" As his work progressed, Fourier, like Brisbane after him, deplored the "debasement of women" in Civilization. "Is not the young girl an article of merchandise offered for sale to any one who wishes to negotiate for her possession and exclusive ownership?" he reproached. "Is not the consent she gives to the conjugal tie a mere mockery?" In view of what he saw as essentially human trafficking, he proposed to give women an "*Amatory Majority,*" an age when they would be enfranchised with love relations to their liking. At eighteen, with perhaps four years of puberty behind, there would be ample time for men in the neighborhood to choose a sexual partner. On the part of the women, though, Fourier asked rhetorically if, since they had already waited several years, they should not be permitted to "take lovers legally, *which at present they take without this permission?*"[34]

Reform fireworks did not stop here. Fourier proposed dividing women into two classes—the vestals, who would be under eighteen, and the emancipated, who had arrived at their eighteenth birthday. But more, he looked ahead to a future age and a "system of Amatory Corporations." Instead of the present system of subterfuges with allegations of criminality for sexual behavior out of wedlock, women at their "amatory majority" would divide themselves into three corporations—the Constant, the Capricious, and the Gallant. The first would be home to those "united in permanent marriage according to the Civilized Method." More daringly, the Capricious ones would enjoy "the liberty of divorce," while their sisters among the Gallant would live by "statutes less rigorous still."[35] We can fill in the blanks.

By the last third of the twentieth century, as Fourier's manuscripts were published, the blanks would be filled in more explicitly and completely, and we can understand why the Fourierist writings sat mostly silently in France during the middle nineteenth century. Even so, the published work displays what was, indeed, an odd system. Highly controlled laws governed sexual relations that, at the same time, were supposed to be free and at whim. Meanwhile, it is difficult not to notice that both Fourier and then Brisbane had, in the civilized state, experienced their share of trouble controlling sexual desire. From this perspective, one wonders about their concern for the liberation of women in the phalanx and in society in general. It is also worth noting that, in their time, their respective issues were broadly shared and becoming ever more visible in the nation. The nineteenth century boasted its fair share of solutions to the problem of monogamous marriage—which more or less presented an obstacle to the communally minded as well as the testosterone-challenged. Mormons, for example, practiced polygamy. Shakers and other groups, by contrast, were celibate. And as we look ahead to Andrew Jackson Davis, the noted spiritualist visionary, we also look ahead to a "free love" movement—something that remained on the cusp for Brisbane himself during his lifetime.

Meanwhile, if the law of attraction brought passion to the service of human social arrangements, if it celebrated happiness, pleasure, and desire, and minimized preoccupation with pain and suffering, it also promised abundance for all. Attractive industry drew down wealth, and it brought a plethora of "things" to ensure the dawn of a new prosperity gospel, one only loosely, if at all, attached to Christian moorings. The pursuit of happiness had led to novel turns in an American cultural road, and travelers strode happily. At the same time, the law of attraction could achieve all this because it did not operate alone. Rather, it functioned as the human outworking of a grander cosmic plan reverberating through the planets, the earth and its environs, and finally human society. This, as we have many times seen, was the law of correspondence. No stranger here. From the "remarkable providences" of the Puritans to Transcendental and liberal Protestant connections through heavenly analogies, a vital strand in American culture had inserted the human condition into a greater reality all along. Neither the American Brisbane nor the French Fourier lived outside that sense of a law that told of corresponding existences and movements throughout the universe. Nor would Davis nor other culture brokers who would come later to help with the spiritual labor of making delight.

We have already observed a youthful Brisbane intuiting a cosmic whole and connecting it with the divine—in a move not too distant from what he had absorbed, one might say, from the cultural air that Puritans, Emersonians, and liberal Protestants breathed. For Fourier, Jonathan Beecher and Richard Bienvenu have told us that the "rationale" that shaped most of his "strangest speculations" came from "what he called the 'theory of universal analogy.'" As perhaps the most memorable example, Fourier's declaration of copulating planets turned on his own total embrace of analogy or correspondence. His *Theory of the Four Movements*, from 1808, had explained to readers that "all creation" worked "by the conjunction of the northern or boreal fluid, which is male, with the southern fluid, which is female." That established, a planet was a "being" with two souls and two sexes, and it procreated "like animal or vegetable beings." Planets could copulate with themselves by means of their north and south poles, with other planets "by means of emissions from opposite poles," and even with an "intermediary."[36]

Brisbane did not allude to the copulation. Still, that did not deter him from accepting Fourier's law of universal analogy. In so doing, as Rohler noted, Brisbane reasoned that "since all things in the universe partook of the divine spirit, there must be a correspondence between all," adding that Brisbane "relied heavily upon analogies in explaining his ideas." We see this process at work in many of Brisbane's explanations for everything from human life to the stars. In one example, Brisbane hailed what he had learned from the French philosopher. There was a "unity of plan in the universe." Indeed, the way that humans distributed sound "to produce musical harmony" did not differ "from the manner in which the Mind of the Universe" distributed "worlds to produce planetary harmony." Here the ultimate law was Fourier's "law of universal unity," and its key lay in the near-mechanical outworkings of the Fourierist groups and series that demonstrated the principle of universal analogy. So much so that even the bizarreness of copulating planets was swept up into their place as a group in serial organization.[37]

In his 1843 exposition on *Association*, Brisbane clearly expressed his enthusiasm. Knowing the "laws of Universal Unity," he declared, "Fourier deduced the true and natural system of society, destined for Man, and which, when realized in practice, will produce social Order and Harmony upon the globe—a reflex of the Harmony which reigns in the Universe." Brisbane insisted that Fourier was not offering a "system or plan of his own." His merit was only, as Fourier himself claimed, "having discovered the system of Nature." Nor were the correspondences simply structural. The passions, especially, fit into the grand scheme. In *Social Destiny*, Brisbane, following his mentor, had testified to "a perfect correspondence between the harmonies of the passions and those of the material world." Summing up what Brisbane had appropriated, Guarneri observed the extent of Fourier's grandiose philosophical system. It encompassed "an analysis of the human 'passions,' ideas about the origins and demise of the solar system, a description of the thirty-two stages of humanity's 80,000-year history, and a program of scientific investigation through analogy." In short, Fourier's "new amorous world"—carefully erased from Brisbane's public Fourierism and ranging from vestal virginity to complete sexual liberty—fit into an overarching universe of correspondences and analogous creations. Sexual passion vibrated with the pulse of the cosmos, and Brisbane—at first secretly—could have his lofty reform vision and his free-flung sexual delight as well.[38]

All of this, for Brisbane, was so much soul music. He affirmed ambitiously that "the soul of man being a complete harmony, has within itself the type of the harmonies of the Universe" and so could understand them. He thought that "Passional Attraction" could be seen as "the power that governs the Moral or Spiritual World as gravitation is the power that governs the Material World."[39] Soul equaled world, and world equaled soul. The law of correspondence could have it no other way. Clearly, the times may have been commercial, but they were distinctly more.

It is fair to ask at this point what had become of the divinity who had reigned over the doctrine of correspondence in the visions of Mather and Edwards, of Emerson and Bushnell. If these were un-Puritan and even un-Unitarian times, what were they? And did they have a God who nurtured all? In the new amorous world of Brisbane, the personhood of the deity had clearly receded to a place of virtual nonexistence. But in this regard Emerson had already been a bridge figure. He had, of course, begun his professional religious calling as a Unitarian minister. Yet, as we saw in *Nature*, when he stood on the "bare ground" and felt himself become "part or particle of God," the God he experienced elided with "currents of the Universal Being." Later, Emerson was taken by Asian panentheistic ideas of divinity and also, from his own Western background, was proclaiming the Over-Soul. Given the evolving theological climate, especially for those without formal religious affiliation, Brisbane's, as Fourier's, divinity emerged from a matrix ever more impersonal and, also, ever more mystical.

Hence, in *Social Destiny* Brisbane taught that the universe consisted of three principles. First came the "ACTIVE, or great creating principle," distributing "harmonies" and regulating "the movement of the Universe." This, Brisbane acknowledged, was "GOD." Following on the working of God came the "PASSIVE principle" upon which God acted—"MATTER." Finally came what Brisbane deemed a "NEUTER principle, or the LAWS" followed by the Divinity "in his creations," laws from which there were no deviations. These were precepts "based on principles of mathematical harmony, justice and unity." Humans themselves, following the law of correspondence, were small compounds of the vast universe, with the "soul" as "active principle." However, as Brisbane later continued his theological exposition, he contradicted himself by insisting that Fourier declared for a divinity following not multiple laws, but only one. For Fourier, "Attraction" was "the only law that the Divinity used "in governing the Universe." So it was that humans—unless they were "out of unity with the Divinity," unless they were "isolated and discordant" and "excluded from the advantages" of all creation—had to "be governed also by attraction, the only law." Always, of course, there was correspondence in the great outworking of the Divinity. Like humankind, so the planet. It existed as "link" in "the universal Serie." Here "millions of luminaries performing their mighty work" were "the highest manifestation of the Divinity in his material harmonies."[40]

Scholars have noticed rightly that Brisbane was careful to introduce Association to Americans by linking it to "practical Christianity." But in so doing, he was merely being politically savvy. When one begins to unpack Brisbane's belief, the revelation becomes starkly different. Brisbane's conversion to Fourierism had been profound, and it had shaken him to the depths of his being. As he sought to describe it in his *Mental Biography*, he gave testimony to what Fourier's vision had done for him. "The sublime privilege of participating in the life of the universe; conscious of the Cosmic Spiritual life; conscious of an order reigning in it; conscious of its vast association; feeling its divine life; living its divine life . . . overwhelmed me." Brisbane confessed unabashedly that he "went out from the presence of Fourier so deeply impressed with his magnificent vision, that life on earth seemed . . . utterly empty." "For days after," he recalled, "I was possessed with the strongest desire to get away from this world and to be able by some means to participate in that grand, Cosmic life."[41]

With such unorthodox belief and commitment, it was no surprise that, from the first, organized religion was a bugbear for Brisbane's reform agenda, and it created differences between him and other reformers. His ultimate goal was Universal Unity, and the thin veil of practical Christianity could barely hide what lay behind. Beyond that, when one looks at Brisbane's private musings, his references to practical Christianity play false and hollow. Writing in his diaries, in fact, Brisbane expressed deep antipathy to organized religion. He could tell his journal in 1830 that he felt the "greatest dislike" for the Catholic religion and then go on to say that when religion filled "low and vile minds," it always seemed to get "dirtier by the contact." Religion might be "pure in itself," but existed as "the development of the mind searching out some spiritual or intellectual cause." It was "always in harmony with the state of development" of the society from which it came.⁴² The view from the youthful Brisbane was that the state of society at the time was thoroughly abysmal.

He could, it was true, still name a God figure as he castigated the social world he encountered—a God who had been forced to desert the human enterprise. Brisbane's diary lamented in late 1831 that "at present" there was "no God, no Providence in the world." The harmony that God seemed "to have placed in the universe" was "not in the least reflected in the social world of man." Instead, all was "war, every hatred." In place of "a foresight of love," he found "blind hazard, coupled often with a blind and brutal force." "They who are atheists," Brisbane wrote cynically, "have a foundation to maintain their belief upon."⁴³

By the time a decade and more had passed, though, Brisbane had moved in an increasingly mystical direction, as his original conversion to Fourierism already suggested. In this, he was not unlike like some others in the Fourierist movement who were moving away from practical Associationism. Thus, back in America after his French sojourn, Brisbane recalled for Redelia the "general feeling or intuition which animated me." What he confessed was a far cry from the God of convention or the God of Christianity or the God who had deserted the world. "A great vision floated before my mind," he remembered. "It was the universal association of humanity on this earth. I saw humanity united in a great whole—united in all the details of its material life: unity of language; unity in the means of communication; unity in all its enterprises. . . . I saw this associative humanity working with order, with concert, to realize some great purpose. I had a vivid conception of a great function as the destiny of this humanity; I saw the association of our globe and the humanities upon it with the Cosmic Whole to which they belong." "Far away in the distant future," he enthused, "I saw a globe resplendently cultivated and embellished, transformed into the grandest and most beautiful work of art by the combined efforts of all humanity." It was, he summarized, "a humanity worthy of that Cosmic Soul of which I instinctively felt it to be a part." Divinity, in short, meant a new humanity and a human system infused with the divine that it really was. Divinity meant, above all, the Cosmic Whole.⁴⁴

The vision did not dissipate. Spending part of the summer of 1846 in the Alleghany mountains, Brisbane—like Edwards, Emerson, and Bushnell—felt the power of nature to generate an illuminative mystical experience. One day while he was there, as he gazed at an opening in the forest, he suddenly felt that his mind was receiving "an opening of an intellectual character." He saw "a great intellectual landscape," "a new mental world." Brisbane perceived, as he said, "that there must exist in the universe a *Great System of Laws* which, when integrally discovered, would constitute, like the parts of the human body, a complete whole." Each body part was "the unvarying expression of some force in the Universe." As he gazed, he thought. Just as each of the parts of the human body had "its special function to perform; so must the Laws of the Universe form a body—a great scientific organism." More than that, "a thorough knowledge of these laws" was "indispensable to the comprehension of the phenomena of the Universe, its plan and order."[45]

On the larger front, however, by this time Associationism in Fourierist fashion was not working. It had been overwhelmed by its own mechanics, by its lack of proper planning and funding, by the insufficient size of its phalanxes, and by the realities of human nature as it was. The movement that Brisbane had promoted became ever more inward-turning, with, as Guarneri explained, "a specifically *religious* dimension." So, ironically, it began to acquire the trappings of organized sectarianism—beating the drum of Fourier's ideas on analogy and cosmology, exhibiting hostility to critics of whatever stripe, cultivating a new ritualism as well as what Guarneri called a "clublike atmosphere" for its elite membership. Still, even with the less-than-grand turns and twists in the American Fourierist road, by 1857 and the Clapp translation of some of Fourier's writings, Brisbane could introduce the French philosopher's *Theory of the Four Movements* in cosmic terms. He called the work "a magnificent Epic" and "an Epic of which God and Humanity are the Heroes, and in which the wisdom and the goodness of the one, and the high Destiny of the other are for the first time revealed in the light of absolute Law and Principle."[46]

Given the high references to cosmic life and law that were so compelling for Brisbane, we have to wonder how Associationism fared among the American rank and file. To ask this question is to invite a foray, however brief, into the history of Fourierist communities against the backdrop of a larger blossoming of communitarian societies and utopian experiments in the mid-nineteenth-century United States. Reform movements were spreading because of the new availability of European socialist thought, even as American commercialism was inspiring misgivings for some. The financial Panic of 1837 and an economic crisis that continued into the early 1840s were severely impacting farmers and artisans, while the growth of evangelicalism from the 1830s was arousing new hopes. In this milieu, a bevy of reform movements flourished. Fourierism found fertile soil here, and its Associationist communities sprang up like so many socialist and reformist sprouts.[47]

By 1850 Brisbane's Fourierism had drawn some eight thousand Americans to establish phalanxes on forty-four thousand acres in twenty-six phalansteries from the frontier of Wisconsin to the western region of New York. Even the fabled Transcendentalist Brook Farm in Massachusetts had converted itself into a Fourierist phalanx from 1844 to 1847. But for all the enthusiasm, most of the communities vanished within a year, discrediting Brisbane and his Fourierist ideas. So the boom was brief, and it was marked by criticism. Abolitionists, especially, were unhappy with Brisbane, who saw their emphasis on slavery as limiting and considered the "serfdom of wages" to be the true end of abolitionism. Other reformers likewise felt ruffled by his dismissal of their work as partial. Brisbane, however, did not give up. Even as Brook Farm folded, he was helping to support New Jersey's North American Phalanx, which survived until 1853. Still further, he was involved in plans for a community in Texas in the 1850s, and by the late 1860s, he was lending his sponsorship to a group in Kansas. Guarneri, in fact, has dated the era of American Fourierism from 1840 to 1880. If so, throughout the period Brisbane was the chief protagonist for the Fourierist experiment and its continuing story.[48]

Brisbane, however, suffered a fatal flaw. He was never able to make his vision concrete. He was a compelling orator and writer, but as an organizer, he lacked important skills and seemed actively to veer away from real efforts to build communities. He also as actively discouraged the wildly enthusiastic but ill-prepared attempts to form phalanxes by groups that he thought too small and underfinanced. More than that, though, as Guarneri argued, "utopian socialism proved too similar to the northern capitalist society it attempted to buck." "The painful irony," Guarneri wrote, "was that the very components of American Fourierism's massive appeal made it especially vulnerable to defeat."[49] The fact was that Fourierist communities were never true socialist experiments from the financial end. They counted on wealth to support themselves, relied on joint-stock arrangements, and displayed a clear sense of the difference between capital and labor.

There was, as well, the challenge that communal life and practice posed for the nuclear families who were the backbone of American social life. Community life in a phalanx was simply out of step with years of conventional living on the home-and-family front, and the subversive dangle of a new, though obscured, sexual ethic proved no realistic enticement. As Guarneri commented, "At the height of their movement Associationists walked a tightrope on issues of love, marriage, and the family, balanced nervously between the radical principles of 'passional attraction' and the desire for respectability." "In the late 1840s," he added, "that fragile balance broke down." The strategy of the collective secret—the unannounced gospel of full sexual freedom—could not be maintained. Leakage became ever more blatant; some promoted their own free-love movement; and—as we have seen—the publishing history of Fourierism was offering an abundance of details.⁵⁰

Nor, meanwhile, was there anything resembling a "high culture" in the daily life of typical phalanxes. Like Brook Farm, the North American and Wisconsin experiments were better than others. But especially when placed beside Brook Farm with its population of writers and thinkers, its educational commitment to its own school, and its communitarians who performed plays and music, danced and held costume parties, other phalanxes seemed flat-footed. After work, fun and culture simply did not materialize in lockstep with the Fourierist plan.⁵¹

Allusions to Transcendentalist Brook Farm and to Swedenborgian input in Brisbane's Fourierism particularly suggest the larger cultural matrix in which his ideas were flourishing. Within his circle of friends and supporters and its fellow travelers, an alternative-reality industry grew strong and spread, though not without questions and ambivalences. Emerson was a case in point. From the first, he had avoided a personal commitment to Brook Farm. There was his stand-offish remark in an 1840 letter to English author and critic Thomas Carlyle: "We are all a little wild here with numberless projects of social reform. Not a reading man but has a draft of a new Community in his waistcoat pocket." With his individualism leading, he had specifically questioned the Brook Farm community in his personal journal: "Shall I raise the siege of this hencoop & march baffled away to a pretended siege of Babylon?" Yet despite conflicted feelings about Brisbane and his nonstop efforts at personal and collective evangelization—with all the zealotry that attended the stereotype—Emerson wrote about Brisbane and Fourierism and published some of his material. The July 1842 issue of *The Dial*, for instance, featured Emerson as he took on Fourierism. He observed that "one could not but be struck with strange coincidences betwixt Fourier and Swedenborg" (more on this below). Speaking of Fourier himself (although his knowledge of Fourier had come, of course, through Brisbane), he wrote tellingly, "Our feeling was, that Fourier had skipped no fact but one, namely, Life. He treats man as a plastic thing." In a *Dial* review of Brisbane's *Social Destiny of Man*, Emerson was, however, more sanguine. "The great question, which he [Brisbane] brings up for discussion," the Transcendentalist leader told readers, "concerns the union of labor and capital in the same individuals, by a system of combined and organized industry."⁵²

Great question or not, Emerson's letters to his wife Lidian continued to expose his doubts. He had met Brisbane a few times in the 1840s. After one such meeting, he reported to Lidian that "Mr Brisbane indoctrinated me in the high mysteries of 'Attractive Industry.'" He had already told her more seriously that he could not content Brisbane and his enthusiastic promoter Horace Greeley. "They are bent on popular action: I am in all my theory, ethics, & politics a poet and of no more use in their New York than a rainbow or a firefly." In one journal entry over a year later, he called Fourier's plans "arithmetic with a vengeance" and went on with surgical precision. "His ciphering goes where ciphering never went before, stars & atmospheres, & animals, & men, & women, & classes of every character." Yet as William Hall Brock has observed, there was much that Emerson owed to Fourier as he had come to understand him through Brisbane. "Emerson's vision of a peaceful, harmonious eradication of slavery, his championing of Eros as the motive force for the just society, and his appeal to the humanity of capitalists all distinctly echo Fourier," wrote Brock. He declared, too, that Emerson's "call to the 'great masses' was certainly inspired by Fourier's industrial army."[53]

More than the parallels between Emerson and Fourierism, though, those between Emanuel Swedenborg and Brisbane's Fourier are striking—parallels that would not be lost on spiritualist leader Andrew Jackson Davis as well as many others. We have already met the celebrated Swedish mystic and author through Emerson and another one of his famed ambivalences. Be that as it may, in his work on the Swedenborgian New Church, C. J. Hempel was already announcing that—although Swedenborg had prophesied the new order—its true realization had come with Fourier. Indeed, Guarneri has identified Swedenborgians as perhaps the sectarians closest to Fourierism, pointing out that Swedenborgian ministers had founded two American phalanxes and citing their Fourierist promotion in Ohio, New York City, and Philadelphia. With Fourier achieving recognition as a secular thinker, Swedenborg assumed the mantle of religiosity as his identifiable counterpart. As Guarneri noted, American Fourierists hoped that the linkage of the two figures would bring "religious respectability" to Associationism.[54]

Guarneri also did not hesitate to assess significant connections between Swedenborg and Fourier. Swedenborg had taught that the inner life would be expressed in "uses" on the outer plane even as Fourier declared that the passions formed the basis of all human action. Swedenborg's thoroughgoing theory of correspondence, which had inspired Emerson and so many others, seemed a direct parallel to Fourierist "universal analogy." In addition, both thinkers preached a message of universal unity in a law that was a divine emanation, Fourier with his scientific banner waving, and Swedenborg with his exhaustive study of the Bible. Finally, as Guarneri summarized, both seers "envisioned the kingdom of heaven in remarkably similar terms." Both anticipated a world that had advanced well beyond the one humans knew—Fourier, one in which Harmony reigned, and Swedenborg, a life among the spirits.⁵⁵

Brisbane's contemporary Parke Godwin had wholeheartedly espoused a view similar to the one that Guarneri was echoing. Godwin's *Popular View of the Doctrines of Charles Fourier* had swept Swedenborgian teachings on the theory of correspondence under the Fourierist rubric of "Universal Analogy," enthusiastically linking Swedenborg and Fourier. Together, wrote Godwin, the two had received commissions from "the Great Leader of the Christian Israel, to spy out the Promised Land of Peace and Blessedness."⁵⁶ If so, waiting in the shadow stood yet another figure who would join Fourier with Swedenborg and then declare his own good news of the progressive world of spirit. In the evolving gospel of Andrew Jackson Davis, spirit would for now be in the flesh, so that pursuing happiness could fill the everyday world with pleasure.

SIX

Andrew Jackson Davis and the Matter of Sex and Spirit

If Albert Brisbane, at least at first, traded sex for labor and wealth, Andrew Jackson Davis never shared the inclination. Davis (1826–1910) became famous (or notorious) as the spiritualist scion, trance physician, marriage and divorce-law reformer, and leading light for a movement favoring—among other themes—philosophical spiritualism over the sensationalist séance version.[1] Born in 1826 in Orange County, New York, in a poor and—in twenty-first-century language—dysfunctional family, Davis was named by a heavy-drinking uncle for the hero of the battle of New Orleans and soon-to-be president of the United States. With only a smattering of formal education—five months at a Lancaster school where the children coached each other—he essentially taught himself. As important, from 1838 he showed an aptitude for altered states of consciousness and claimed receipt of a message that helped persuade his family to move to Poughkeepsie. There, by 1843, he was introduced to mesmerism when traveling animal magnetist J. Stanley Grimes lectured in the town. In the wake of the Grimes visit, Davis discovered through the mesmeric experiments of local tailor William Levingston that he was an easy subject. For nearly two years under Levingston's magnetic control, he became a local celebrity with a growing reputation for medical clairvoyance. A brief connection with Universalist minister Gibson Smith at this time yielded the first collection of Davis's trance pronouncements when Smith, in early 1845, produced *Clairmativeness*. Davis would later disown the pamphlet.[2]

The year before, in March 1844, Davis claimed, he had undergone an experience that would change his life radically. Unable to shake off the results of earlier mesmeric work with Levingston, he returned to his boarding house, fell into a deep sleep, and experienced a dream-vision. A voice summoned him to dress and follow; the sleep-walking Davis complied, subsequently awoke and, after further adventures, ended up in a cemetery. There he met the spirits of the ancient Greek physician Galen and the decidedly more recent Emanuel Swedenborg. Galen presented him with a magical staff, later withheld from Davis because of the New Yorker's angry outburst. (He finally received it considerably later.) Swedenborg gave no tangible gifts but offered instruction, telling of visits to "this and other earths" and calling the youthful Davis "an appropriate vessel for the influx and perception of truth and wisdom." Swedenborg himself would illuminate Davis's "interior understanding" and teach him the "laws" that would make him fit to communicate with "the interior realities of all subordinate and elevated things."[3]

Davis lived the Levingston years as prelude. Then, when he met Universalist physician Silas Smith Lyon and two ministers, William Fishbough and Samuel Byron Brittan, Davis broke with Levingston and—now with Lyon in New York City—began a new venture in clairvoyant healing. Fishbough soon followed Davis to New York—to transcribe the trance-produced lectures that Davis began to deliver beginning in November 1845. Lyon would magnetize the "Seer," Davis would speak, and Fishbough would scribe. Davis's 157 lectures appeared in 1847 as *The Principles of Nature, Her Divine Revelations, and a Voice to Mankind*, with copious mesmeric, Swedenborgian, and Fourierist underpinnings (more on these later).[4] The lectures, taken as a whole, were also decidedly anticlerical, and they sounded a note that would continue in Davis's relationship to organized forms of Christianity.

Davis had been particularly taken with Fourier's teaching on the attractive power of love. So it comes as no surprise that, for Davis and his associates, the flame of love burned in more than theoretical ways. The Harmonialists, as Davis and his followers from the 1840s styled themselves, made free love a commonplace; as John Spurlock explained, their "harmony" meant "harmony among people and between the spiritual and the carnal." Davis lived out these views through his marital experiences, seeking what Swedenborg had called "conjugial love" and what, in practical terms, became Davis's search for a soulmate for this world and the next.[5]

Davis's first marital adventure began in the late 1840s in his growing relationship with Catherine DeWolf Dodge, perhaps twenty years his senior and an admirer who brought him the funds to produce *The Principles of Nature*. Davis eventually married Dodge, who divorced her husband (after a claimed vision by Davis) to become his wife—but not before the two were involved in sexual scandal before their official union. Meanwhile, the relationship with Dodge both assisted and nearly derailed Davis's next venture with his friends. This was the publication of the short-lived *Univercoelum and Spiritual Philosopher*, a weekly newspaper that appeared in New York City to advance Davis's views in December 1847 and folded in 1849. Davis continued to write prodigiously (more than thirty books), with his five-volume *Great Harmonia* (1850–1859) an especially ambitious testimonial rejecting the notion of sin and continually calling on nature and its law.[6]

His marital adventures proceeded apace. When Dodge (with whom Davis later declared he had a "fraternal" but not "conjugal" relationship—i.e., of Swedenborgian soulmate quality) died in 1853, he encouraged Mary Fenn Love of western New York to divorce her husband and marry him in 1855. At last, he believed, he had found his true "conjugal" partner in Fenn Love. But twenty-nine years later, his perspective had changed. After he met Della E. Markham, a New York City magnetist and eclectic physician, when he was recovering from an illness, Davis was stating that almost from the first he had known he was mistaken about Fenn Love. Markham had treated him, and Davis had now become convinced that she was his authentic conjugal mate. He divorced Fenn Davis in an "amicable" proceeding (even though she was terminally ill). Thereafter, ostracized by the New York spiritualist community, Davis and his new wife of 1885 moved to Watertown, outside of Boston, where, as a trance physician, he ended his days.[7]

What are we to make of the impressionable and inconstant Davis? What was it that made him a talking, writing encyclopedia and broadcast station for profound changes in his times? And how did he mold these changes so that they flourished through the twentieth and into the twenty-first century? To address these questions, I explore Davis's controversial *Principles of Nature*, the trance-produced work that he would unravel in the books he continued to write.

Even with its entranced status (in the twentieth century, the book would be called "channeled"), Davis's ponderous work possessed a logic and coherence that were obvious. With 782 pages of actual text, the book began with an ambitiously titled 4-page "Address to the World." Next came a relatively short—116-page—philosophical "Key" to what followed and a more than 550-page Swedenborgian-plus-"popular science" division—"Nature's Divine Revelations" proper. Finally, a 103-page "Application; or, A Voice to Mankind" functioned as the point of all that had preceded, instructing people on how to live. Davis was an activist all of his adult life, and this last section dominated his book as the reason for the philosophical scaffold and the citation of other masters. Significantly, the "Application" was thoroughly and unabashedly Fourierist.

Davis's "Address to the World" explained that he had been "impressed to speak" (his words for the entranced state) the material that followed.

Truth was "immortal," and "*Nature* must be the standard" to judge it. Readers must "ask Nature" and their "own superior judgments" what degree of "practical truth" was there "revealed." In so doing, they would "obtain MENTAL HAPPINESS!" Next, in quite logical fashion, Davis laid out what would follow in his "Key" as "a general view of theories that exist" and the "foundation of the philosophy" that he would present in the second section. He called that second part "the soul or basis of the whole superstructure." Finally, the "Application" analyzed human society and presented "an application of previously-revealed principles" for the purpose of "a reformation like unto a new heaven and a new earth." Davis thought, in this regard, that there were "no possible limits to social progress and spiritual attainment and elevation." "Man," after all, was a "*microcosm*, or a combined expression of all the perfections contained in the Divine essence that animates and preserves the harmony of the Universe." No surprise there. The law of correspondence was clearly operating in Davis's world. More confounding, though, was his other piece of counsel for auditors/readers: "Exercise your choicest gift, which is *Reason*—and fear no corruption from truth, though new; and expect no good from error, though long believed."[8] This unambiguous endorsement of Enlightenment rationalism would continue throughout the Davis lectures.

Davis added to the rationalism a natural-history approach that echoed Robert Chambers's *Vestiges of Creation* (1844) and similar works. With this uncritical enthusiasm for the Enlightenment, it was at least mildly astonishing that the main players who shaped Davis's production were Franz Anton Mesmer, Emanuel Swedenborg, and Charles Fourier, hardly grand celebrants at the altar of Reason. Even so, to make sense of the huge book created through Davis's trances, I begin with Mesmer and his magnetic model, which provided its ground and overall structure. (We have already met Mesmer briefly in chapter 4, but here it is important to add more.) Born in Germany, Franz Mesmer completed a doctoral dissertation at the University of Vienna in 1766—*De planetarum influxu in corpus humanum* (On the influence of the planets on the human body). In it, standing at a crossroads between a Hermetic and scientific universe (like his partial contemporary Fourier), Mesmer showed that he had been thoroughly persuaded by Isaac Newton's work on gravitation (1687). But his thesis was also heavily influenced by the writings of Newton's friend Richard Mead, with his insistence on the "influence of the stars." Thus, Mesmer's doctoral work displayed his preoccupation with the transfer of energy from bodies to other bodies, and—from a cosmic perspective—from the sun and moon (understood as planets) to humans. Matter, for Mesmer, was "attractive," and the force causing universal gravitation was "animal gravity." According to this model, as we saw in chapter 4, the heavenly bodies generated "tides" that affected humans in their physicality and influenced conditions of health and disease. When these cosmic energies flowed freely, people felt well; when they were blocked, disease conditions resulted. It became the work of the mesmerist, or animal magnetist, to unclog obstructions and so enable individuals to heal.[9]

So much for science. But Mesmer hastened to weave into his theoretical fabric what he had learned from Hermeticism. Aided by Mead's work on stellar influence, he thought in terms of the ancient idea of the harmony of the spheres. "The harmony established between the astral plane and the human plane," Mesmer wrote, "ought to be admired as much as the ineffable effect of UNIVERSAL GRAVITATION." By its means, human bodies were "harmonized, not in a uniform and monotonous manner, but as with a musical instrument furnished with several strings, the exact tone resonates which is in unison with a given tone."[10] So convinced was Mesmer that he eventually began to play the glass harmonica to assist his patients with a musical prompt, a practice that raised eyebrows as well as questions.

At first, Mesmer enjoyed practical success. He had married a wealthy widow and developed as a flourishing professional in Vienna. But after being accused of fraud by other Viennese physicians, he left the city and in 1778 moved to Paris, again to set himself up as a physician. He did so with style and aplomb, and was consulted by the wealthy and fashionable. Trailing controversy though, he tried but failed to gain approval for his ideas through professional organizations. By 1784, a royal commission investigated him, only to discover no evidence for a physically based magnetic fluid and attributing any positive results to the power of imagination. Finally, in disrepute Mesmer left his Parisian practice and eventually ended his days in Meersburg, Germany, the city of his birth.

An impresario and pragmatist both, Mesmer promoted a nature that managed to fit into the European Enlightenment, with an emphasis on cosmic order and abstract physical laws governing human bodies and minds as well as the inhabited world. But he also added very much more that moved beyond the Enlightenment in his thinking on the harmony of the spheres. In his own work, Davis would adapt himself seamlessly to Mesmer's theoretical perspective, using an Enlightenment base but adding liberally to create a new structure. The "nature" in his *Principles of Nature* left far to one side the landscape delights that had thrilled an Edwards, an Emerson, a Bushnell, a Brisbane, and even a Cotton Mather. What emerged, instead, was a nature that achieved a religious quality in the way that it worked. It was also vast, planetary, seemingly never concrete, and likewise heavily magnetic and "attractive." Always, even with its vapory quality, it was very physical. The *material* being of God—the control factor for nature—formed a basic tenet in Davis's Harmonial creed. Moreover, the God at issue was hardly the human-like being who dominated Christian and Jewish scripture, but instead a source of universal energy that made the present world and all the planets turn. Moving in a universe controlled by the law of correspondence, God, though material, ruled as Great Positive Mind. Here the Enlightenment deity met and greeted Mesmer with his positive and negative magnetic poles—in a brilliant coup that bowed to the Enlightenment and undercut it at the same time. Still more, the "breathings" of the Great Positive Mind, in mesmeric style, "flowed through the ten thousand avenues and forms of animate Nature, until it breathed into man the breath of life, and he became a living soul."[11]

Nature was "merely a *Thought* of the divine Mind," just as "forms" were "the thoughts of Nature." The entire "Univercoelum"—Davis's term for the physicality of the universe—was "necessary as a Form—a Body—of the Great Positive Mind." The magnetic metaphor was clear, for the Great Positive Mind held the universe together by attracting its essentially negative being. Yet—in an apparent contradiction (Davis's thinking was often confused)—the Great Positive Mind as "living Principle" was "the all-producing Cause," and the Univercoelum was "the Universal Effect." This digression into causal thinking did not alter Davis's declaration that, even granted the division between mind and body, matter inhabited both worlds. The sun at the very center sphere of the Univercoelum was a mass of liquid fire and, in a borrowed Newtonian term, the "Sensorium." Still more, even as its fire burned, the sun ruled as an effervescent magnetic attractor—the positive magnetic pole—for all that existed. "In the beginning," Davis asserted, "the Univercoelum was one boundless, undefinable, and unimaginable ocean of LIQUID FIRE!" "It was without bounds—inconceivable—and with qualities and essences incomprehensible. This was the original condition of MATTER." It was "a Whole," and "particles did not exist; but the Whole was as *one* Particle." Without beginning or end and without length, it was "a Vortex of one Eternity." It was also "one infinite Circle," not "disconnected" from power but "the very essence of all Power."[12]

That power, it turned out, was Davis's Great Positive Mind, and he went on to detail the formation of a vast and spectacular universe. Always, the magnetic metaphor had gripped Davis's imagination, and the mystical narrative that emerged was controlled—like a mesmerist controlling a subject—by the force and power of magnetic attraction. Davis repeated the message effusively. He hailed the "Great CENTRE from which all of these systems and Systems of systems emanated." He called it "an exhaustless Fountain" and "a magnificent and glorious Sun" even as it was "an Ocean of undulated and undefinable fire" and "the holy emblem of Perfection."[13]

Now, however, the magnetic and mystical vision dissolved to accommodate a series of popular-science lectures on the formation of the solar system. Then it dissolved yet again to piggyback on the announced planetary travels of Swedenborg. The peripatetic Swede had reported visionary travels to other planets in the solar system and even to "earths" outside it, in which he spoke to the spirits of their inhabitants. Davis followed in the footsteps of his mentor in a travelogue that took him outside the confines of earth and detailed the physical attributes of those who dwelled on other planets. He even predicted an eighth planet six months before the discovery of Neptune. Nature now was indeed vast and cosmological, and delight could be found therein. Reveling in his spirit travels, Davis did not fail to say that he had further and better insights than Swedenborg. He looked to the day when earth-dwellers would experience the "spiritual communion" that was "now being enjoyed by the inhabitants of Mars, Jupiter, and Saturn, because of their superior refinement."[14]

But Davis was not content with that exercise of one-upmanship, and he went on to correct Swedenborg's geography of the spirit world. In his revelatory reports, Swedenborg had collapsed the distinction between matter and spirit. His visits to the spirit world had shown the Swedish seer that three heavens and three hells existed tangibly. So much so that he was able to describe all six with precision and detail. To cite only his three heavens, they were filled with color and odor, and with houses and gardens that resembled those of the Swedish nobility of his time. Spiritual or substantial things, Swedenborg said, formed "the beginnings of material things." Davis had no quarrel with the merging of matter and spirit, as we will see in more detail in his later writings and activities. From the first he had flatly asserted in *Principles* that "all ultimates, to me, are still *matter*." But in his own abiding pursuit of happiness, Davis abolished the Swedenborgian hells. Swedenborg, the entranced Davis told listeners and later readers, had made a mistake in identifying "the first three Spheres as three *hells*, inhabited by lower spirits and angels; while the three higher Spheres were the three heavens in which the higher spirits and angels dwelt." Hell was "true, not in the *absolute*, but in the *comparative* sense." It was "undeveloped," and the highest heavens formed, by contrast, "an unfolded representative." The spirits who lived on different planets likewise exhibited "different stages of refinement." With permission, they could visit "any earth in the Universe, and breathe sentiments in the minds of others."[15] This echo of Swedenborg's doctrine of "influx" could occur even if the recipient were unaware. According to Swedenborg (and Davis), there were always streams of energy that animated humankind and the physical world, both on Earth and elsewhere in the universe. Davis could receive his "impressions" because of influx, which came ultimately from the divine.

Animated by influx, Davis's impressions led him to elaborate with still more tangibility on seven spheres in which the spirits dwelled. The first was the Earth-plane, where spirits inhabited bodies until their deaths. From there they passed to the Second Sphere, or the Summerland, concerning which Davis would later often speak.[16] Thereafter came spheres of increasing perfection, reaching to the seventh. If we subtract the Earth-plane from the count, we are left with the three hells and three heavens of Swedenborg, now transformed in accord with Davis's vision of eternal perfectibility—a vision that Fourier and Brisbane would help him to fashion for Earth itself in the third part of *Principles*. Now, though, he was ready to contemplate what he had seen in trance as an abiding whole. "The whole is BEAUTIFUL," he affirmed. "Everything is perfect in its way and state of being." And all was arranged according to the commodious plan of the spheres. "The earths, or the first Sphere, constitute the germ; the Second Sphere is the roots; the third, the body; the fourth, the branches; the fifth, the buds; the sixth, the blossom; and the seventh is BEAUTY—beauty that blooms with an immortal fragrance."[17]

By the 1860s, however, the beauty of the spheres, however immortal, would be dissolving in a newer vision. Davis would by then be teaching a yet more progressive version of after-death places. When all spirits passed on their respective journeys through the spheres to arrive at the final, Sixth Sphere (note the absence of the former first sphere of Earth in this account), the "Love and Wisdom of the Great Positive Mind" would be "thrown tenderly around them." Then, wrote Davis, the deity would contract "his inmost capacity." The "boundless vortex" would be "convulsed with a new manifestation of Motion." In an echo of Fourier along with Mesmer, the "law of Association or *gravitation*"—in all its materiality—would lead "in the formation of new suns, new planets, and new earths." After that, the "law of progression or *refinement*" would follow, and it would manifest itself "in the production of new forms of life on those planets." Next "the law of Development" would work to create "*new* plants, animals, and human spirits upon every earth prepared to receive and nourish them." Nor would the process stop there, as Davis beheld a universe of unending progress The spirit would have "no 'final home'" because "to an immortal being, *rest* would be intolerable." Instead the spirit would "progress eternally."[18] Swedenborg, in Davis's teaching, stood strongly corrected—in an America that was on the move and on the make—and an America that reveled in its material being.

Before Davis looked to the spheres, for all that, he had been ready to lecture on the natural history of the planet. Here again he did not forget the Great Positive Mind with its attractive force. Ever returning to Mesmer in the midst of his Swedenborgian musings, Davis had especially taken his stab at the Bible and its teachings. Just as in the biblical book of Genesis, humans were created "from the dust of the earth," but then the Davis narrative veered. Humankind existed as a "receptacle of one of the spontaneous breathings of the Great Positive Mind." Still further, the biblical story provided an allegory for Davis's naturalistic synthesis, but—aside from its metaphysical re-reading—scripture did not fare well. Old and New Testaments provided only *partial knowledge*." In contrast with the knowledge of nature, they were seriously wanting. New Testament miracles were "entirely void of all that high and celestial dignity which they would naturally be expected to possess if they were of Divine origin." Organized religion was yet more despicable with its divisiveness, and Davis condemned it for its "dark and turbid waters of sectarianism, into which the light of reason and of divine truth scarcely casts one relieving ray."[19] As we will see in Davis's later writing and thinking, the problems of conventional Christianity and its theology would keep providing a foil for his own evolving theology of materialism and utopian transformation.

Natural history, now as ever, inevitably led Davis to human history and the social miseries that existed alongside the darkness of organized religion. To aid him, enter the third player on his stage. Hiding in the wings was Fourier, via the convenience of Albert Brisbane, to provide a powerful buttress through their gospel of association. Although Davis's first vision had been dominated especially by the spirit of Swedenborg, and although Mesmer's animal magnetism provided Davis's *Principles of Nature* with its abiding metaphor, the Fourierist conceptual universe shaped Davis's world as much. Mesmer's magnetic universe, like Fourier's attractive one, had been inspired by Isaac Newton. Moreover, the law of correspondence (or analogy) ruled clearly in the world of Mesmer as well as that of Fourier. Thus, with the doctrine of correspondence and is sub-doctrine of attraction for guides, it seemed almost inevitable that Davis would absorb and propagate Fourierist views as he came to understand them. After all, in his *Principles of Nature*, Davis had contemplated the "constant attraction existing between all bodies in the vast system of the planetary worlds" through which "Worlds of worlds were made" and "sustained." The future would be even more spectacular. "And thus does, and shall, the great Eternal Laboratory unceasingly produce and reproduce, until all things and all substances shall become rarified, refined, and perfected, and until all will gravitate to spheres of *celestial* attraction and *spiritual* association."[20]

Magnetism notwithstanding, and despite claims to minimal education, Davis had integrated important aspects of Fourierist teaching into his trance-produced *Principles*. In fact, its entire third section was a lengthy recitation of the work of Fourier as it had become available through Brisbane's writings. Tellingly, Brisbane and his followers had been present at a number of the New York lectures reproduced in Davis's book. So, too, had other notables in the radical religious and social culture of the day, among them George Bush, professor of Hebrew at New York University, a minister and a prominent Swedenborgian. So noticeable were the Fourierist and Swedenborgian analogs that some reviewers called Davis's work a plagiarized hodge-podge that came not from the spirits but from his own memory. Nevertheless, whether Davis was remembering, transmitting the words of "spirits," reading audience members' minds, or adapting his message to what they might be disposed to hear, he was reiterating prominent aspects of Fourierist teaching in his mix.

Clearly, Fourier and Swedenborg made good company for each other, and Davis enthusiastically touted Fourier under the banner of the *"law of association."* This law, he proclaimed, existed as "the rudimental principle of Nature established by God, who is LOVE." Even though Swedenborg had "done more than any other person" to bring together a "system" that was "practicable and serviceable to every mind," it could not be "understood or applied so extensively as when the superior Association [would be] formed." "Recurrence to the writings of Charles Fourier" proved "necessary for the purpose of bringing his social system before the world." Moreover, the results would be manifestly more than rational (there went the Enlightenment). "A general revolution is at hand," Davis declared. "Wisdom will fan the sparks into a flame, and this will consume contention and sin." Then, indeed, all would "come forth purified, elevated, HAPPY!" Why? Because this was "the flame of LOVE."[21] Eros here was hardly shy, and, as we have seen, for Davis and his associates, the flame of love burned in ways more than theoretical or celestial. In the *Principles*, however, as in Brisbane's introductory works, Davis was feeding readers a sanitized version of Fourierism, in which sex had largely been exchanged for money and a prosperous economy.

Expanding on his associative views in the third (and last) section of his *Principles of Nature*, Davis appeared to be building on Brisbane's *Social Destiny of Man*. Recall that Brisbane had argued in Fourierist terms for the formation of cooperative communities that would undercut competition and human misery, and instead produce "Harmony"—a term that, to begin, would likely resonate with self-styled Harmonialist Davis. Under the rubric of "association," humans held the key to true reform and unity, and so association was the natural system for social organization. Davis, for his part, followed the party line, transforming it at the same time into a practical metaphysical message that anticipated the language of early New Thought. Humans paid homage to "the Divine Mind" not by means of "prayer and unmeaning supplication." Rather, it was through "harmonious industry and universal ACTION" that they honored the divine. The "misdirected *passion*" of prayer had to be repurposed toward the "constitutional and mutual affection manifested between every particle and compound in being." Such was the "*law of association*." It existed as the "rudimentary principle of Nature established by God," who was—ever and always in Davis's universe—"Love." In this now-Fourierist world, each person lived as "but an *organ* of the great human *Body*." As in music, "*harmony*"—the "representation of divine *Order*"—must be established among all. So each had to be "well instructed and properly situated" in order that each individual's movements might "accord with the movements of the whole" and all would exist "in concert."[22]

Pinning down these lofty ideals and goals, Davis could become more specific. "The cause of all human action," he declared, came from "three things: *Love* (or desire), *Necessity*, and *Interest*." He went on with more detail. "*Desires* are created by the *love*, or bodily requirements. *Necessity* is the desire ungratified, or the requirement unsupplied; and *Interest* is the spring of action, and is a means by which love is rewarded, by which desires are gratified, and necessities supplied." Desire fueled all that Davis would now unpack, just as, for Fourier and Brisbane, *passional* attraction moved all elements of human society. So Davis sought to harness desire, Fourier fashion, in the prescriptive "voice" to humankind he offered. It all sounded familiar. Labor was now "despised and shunned in the human family" since it was "unappreciated." This was why people were poor. If, instead, "universal industry existed, all would be wealthy, and all would appreciate and glorify their existence." Hence, it was "proper that all should be so situated as that industry" might "become a *necessity*." Then its reward might be "legitimate and proportional." Davis was insistent, picking up on the agricultural themes that had first inspired Fourier. The laborer was "entitled to something more than arising at daybreak, going forth into the field and toiling till dark, and then returning to his couch of straw, and awaking again with body prostrated and suffering with hunger." He was not shy, also, about commenting on mechanics and trade as he condemned existing situations. Nor did he leave out the professions, which he roundly chastised. Clergy were the worst of all, as the entranced Davis offered his damning assessment. It was "a deplorable fact that all the miseries, the conflicts, the wars, the devastations, and the hostile prejudices, existing in the world, are owing to the corrupting situation and influence of clergymen." So offensive were the clergy that Davis denounced them in blistering attacks that extended through thirty pages—no doubt enough to make even a Brisbane, if he ever read it, blush at the intemperance.[23]

What, then, should be done? Davis explained smoothly that "human character" was "unfolded, either favorably or unfavorably, perfectly or imperfectly, by the influence of the social and religious conditions that surround it." Humans could not "be good" if the influences around them were "*evil*." Yet they were still children of "Nature," even as Nature was "a child of the Deity." Davis had "proved," he said, that "society and the human race" were "*diseased*," and now he would prescribe the "REMEDY." With Eros helping, he told his audience that humans had "inherited their diversified attributes from the womb of Nature, these having been there deposited and impregnated by the Love and Wisdom of God." The "law of association" had established things this way, and its endowment of "diverse and multipotent characteristics in the race" provided an "indestructible basis" for "the law of reciprocal justice and consequent morality and happiness." Not everybody had the same desires or needed the same gratifications. It followed that "happiness should be dispensed by bestowing blessings in proportion," and always "the divine law of *Association*" must lead the way. This law would bring harmony, and so the musical instrument that was society needed tuning "by an enlightened *Wisdom*." When that happened, there could be no discord. Humans had "no desires" that could not be "gratified." A person had "no peculiarities but what some position would render agreeable and proper."[24]

In familiar Fourierist terms, industry must be made "*attractive*," and then every individual would adopt the "use for which he was destined," so that all "contention" would be "lost in the harmony of the whole." In all this, the Great Positive Mind and its center of liquid fire did not entirely disappear. As Davis interpreted the Fourierist "groups," he saw them as planets in the solar system. "Each group, society, or state," he observed, "as a planet, should be constituted of mutually-assisting particles (or persons), congenial with each other and with the sun or centre around which all societies should revolve." When this was achieved, the human race "would represent the harmony of the Solar System," with no "disturbance . . . because the great central Sun" was "both the parent and governor, whose pervading influence" sustained "an indestructible equilibrium." If the law of correspondence was operating here, it continued to rule as Davis elaborated. Not only could human society "be made to represent the harmonious movements displayed in our Solar System and in the Universe"; it could also "be made to correspond in every possible division and particular to the uniform kingdoms and creations of Nature." Unconcerned about elitism, Davis thought that, depending on capacity, humans would represent the mineral, the vegetable, or the animal world, with subdivisions in every kingdom according to ability. In the midst of the animal kingdom, especially, a central group corresponded to humanity. "Lord" of "all subordinate creations" and possessed of "the wisdom of love," this group would be "a crown of material perfection" and "should manifest all the intelligence and perfection of the whole race concentrated." This might be "the centre of attraction to which all should be inclined" and by which all would be "assisted to attain any degree of eminence possible for Wisdom to desire."[25]

Imitating the Fourierist arrangements of a phalanx, Davis, on much smaller terms, offered an agricultural example of how the new associative arrangements would work. He decided that six men with "farms in proper relations to each other" constituted "the least possible number who could concentrate and produce power among themselves." They would structure a corporation with its own "governor or president, and recording secretary." They would "institute the most searching investigations" regarding what might "beautify their land, and restore fertility to the barren portions," finding "the most feasible plans to arrange and condense their labor for the accomplishment of this end." Davis went on in surprisingly detailed terms—just as Fourier and Brisbane had done—laying out the fine points of the arrangement. Entranced he might have been, but whether bending minds or unearthing memory, he was leaving the cosmic for the terrestrial, and adding a flourish of his own. With finances up front, he foresaw "a mutual deposition of capital, and a corresponding interest," thus making "the whole association an established monopoly," and forcing "a change in the present order of industry, trade, and commerce." He was thinking grandly as he sketched the impact of the six-farm arrangement. "The influence of such an association, properly situated, would extend to adjoining townships and counties, and would be sensibly felt in various portions of the state." With increasing momentum, the association would grow. It would "attract one farmer after another" and "arrest the depreciation of the land, and the decrease of the inflow of wealth from its productions." No individual farmer would be able to compete, "and consequently its influence would continually widen by taking more into its constitution."[26]

Leaving agriculture behind, Davis made his way through the mechanical and trade cohorts and then on to the professions, telling how arrangements would work for all of them. He even prescribed "social festivities" and "gymnastic exercises." When he arrived at the once-maligned clergy, he directed that it shape itself as "an institution for the purpose of moral culture and spiritual progress" and then went on to offer his plan for its reform. The clergy should be "associated in numbers from fifty to seventy-five." Their members must be "so arranged as to produce an harmonious movement." The clergy's task was now suitably monumental. It should be the "seminary for instruction," particularly "in the higher branches of knowledge." Clergy must "understand the depths and widths of natural law and science." They must "bring forth and analyze all the theological *isms* of the land," rejecting evil and preserving good. They must "understand the theology of Nature, and the manifest constitution of the Divine Mind," blending science, theology, reason, and philosophy "into one grand system of education." There must be among them, too, six classes or degrees, "all steps of relative perfection." Then, not content with clerical activities and their rankings, Davis went on to arrange the architecture of their living space, which might "represent in structure externally the combined contributions of art, science, and architecture, and be a standard of magnificence." No detail was overlooked, so that Davis functioned as a spiritualized designer, creating nuance and style much as Swedenborg had done in his reports of heaven and as Fourier and Brisbane had also done in their arrangements for phalanxes. But moving beyond his mentors, Davis's visionary flights landed him in a bizarre rhetorical field, mandating what should be done by "the emperor and his courtiers and counselors" as well as "governors, presidents, kings or lords," all apparently part of the clerical contingent.[27] Given his previous expressed hostility for the clerical profession, these words were odd indeed.

Meanwhile, for an erstwhile proponent of free love, Davis had surely sanitized his descriptions of domestic bliss in the new associations he was planning. "Family forms, sympathies, and relations, it is proper to preserve," he advised. This "inasmuch as it is not necessary to change any of the conjugial attachments that now exist, to successfully establish the principles and movements of an association." He added more subtly that "directions concerning these things will naturally arise from the wisdom and investigation consequent on such a social organization." Women in the associations played a thoroughly conventional role by cultivating and displaying "their conceptions of the beautiful as manifested in any of the delicate arts and sciences." This directive included—in a nod to Fourier—"the floral kingdom." Likewise "in dress and ornament," women should take their cue from the "delicate textures of flowers." From there women could "ascend to the refined arts of painting, embroidery, and all the higher branches as relating to beauty and grandeur."[28]

At last, Davis turned in trance to his teacher, the spirit of Swedenborg, and found his mentor once again wanting. While Swedenborg had "done more than any other person to accumulate, sift, and preserve, the useful productions of each nation," his "system" could not "be understood or applied so extensively" as through the formation of "the superior Association." The more that was needed came through "recurrence to the writings of Charles Fourier," which were "necessary for the purpose of bringing his social system before the world." It was "impossible to escape the conclusion that he revealed many truthful causes and principles of reform that must be in some degree practiced before the kingdom of heaven" could come. Summarizing his vision, Davis extolled the reforms of the day with fervor. In them "the laws of Nature" had been "clearly unfolded," leading to a "code of just and righteous laws of social government," which he had "applied to society" along with directions "for their practice." Davis was sure that he had so arranged the social world that it represented "the material and spiritual creations of the Divine Mind." He spoke grandly of the associative future in which "every child of the Eternal One" was "laboring with pleasure in the field, in the departments of science, in the courts of justice, in the temple of health, or in the sanctuary of peace and brotherly love." Each one was "situated as is prescribed by Nature and her Creator." The Creator's "kingdom" had come, and his will was done on Earth as in heaven.[29]

With all of the spiritualized enthusiasm that Davis displayed in his *Principles*, he had not forgotten his credo that spirit was, after all, simply a highly refined form of matter. The detailed stipulations for the Fourierist-inspired utopia that he prescribed said as much. Still more, the material nature of the spirit world had been his conviction from the first, and he never failed to return to it throughout his long career. Davis's theology of materialism had been thoroughgoing. In his mind's eye, he found matter in the celestial heights even as he envisioned its better, more productive arrangements on Earth. We may well ask how Davis reached this certainty. Was it a function of the many visionary episodes in which he conversed with spirits, learned from them, took their advice, and flourished? And/or did it come from his reading?—a subject that needs to be broached much more than Davis was willing to admit or acknowledge.

At the time he was delivering the trance lectures that became the *Principles of Nature*, he was protesting that he had read only one book in his life—and that a romance. But the "Scribe's Introduction" to his opus (written by William Fishbough) provided telling evidence to the contrary. Fishbough printed a letter from the Rev. A. R. Bartlett, who had been a pastor in Poughkeepsie in the early 1840s. Bartlett implied, in agreement with Davis's standard narrative, that he had been exposed to very little formal education. He did not exhibit "common proficiency in the simplest elements of the English language," the pastor wrote in his testimonial. Even further, Davis "had not an hour's schooling" during the time that Bartlett, now of Chicago, knew him. At that point, however, Bartlett veered away from the Davis account of bookish innocence. Davis, he wrote, "possessed an inquiring mind—loved books, especially controversial religious works, which he always preferred, whenever he could borrow them and obtain leisure for their perusal." In yet another revision of Davis's own story, historian Slater Brown in 1970 suggested that Davis may have "picked up a good part of his information, not from books, but from newspapers," citing evidence for his avid interest in the daily press.[30]

Whether he gleaned his information and ideas from books or newspapers, a popular form of vitalism would have been available to Davis. It is, of course, highly unlikely that he would have been familiar with Mather's homegrown Nishmath-Chajim or Edwards's references to "blood and animal spirits" when he (Edwards) wrote of affections and the sense of the heart. But Davis had already signed on to the mysterious something of the nonphysical, the "force" that breathed life into a physical being and made it to be. Still more, Mesmer's explanation of animal magnetism (which applied to both humans and other animals as distinct from vegetable and mineral entities) was a vitalistic theory. It was thus an easy transition for Davis to move from Mesmer's tides to his own announcement that spirit was a refined form of matter.

Yet another source for Davis's materialist certainty regarding the world of spirit can be found in the teaching of Swedenborg. As the mystical Swede brought together his strong background in the Christian faith with the Hermeticism that also shaped his thought, he wrote of God as the Divine Human. The revolutionary turn of phrase worked to transform the Son in the traditional Trinity into its major figure *and* also turned humans collectively into participants in the divine being. More than that, Swedenborg's belief in divine influx—yet another form of vitalism—envisioned a flow from the divine into the human world—not unlike Mesmer's planetary tides. Given the doctrines of the Divine Human and divine influx, it was, again, only a mild leap to describe the implications by means of the law of correspondence and, by inference, its corollary law of attraction. As in heaven, so on Earth. And yet again, as on Earth, so in heaven. Thus, human practice and cultural arrangements did not exist in isolation. They had their counterparts in the spiritual world.

This being the case, the matter of spirit had become especially basic for Swedenborg in his promulgation of "conjugial marriage," a concept that we have already met in Davis's rendition as "conjugal" marriage. Swedenborg had called his "conjugial" form of marriage a source of nuptial and spiritual bliss into eternity. "A *Universal Conjugial Sphere* proceeds from the Lord," he stated, "and pervades the universe from its first things to its last, thus from angels even to worms." In this cosmic situation, men and women were spiritual equals; they shared a common destiny that had been ordained for them in heaven.[31] So, as we have seen, there were soulmates, and blessed was the person who could find his or hers during life. For Davis himself, as self-made Harmonial philosopher, Swedenborg's hints on the actual physicality of spirit, including its sexual application, offered corroborating testimony for what he probably already believed. After all, the law of correspondence as the law of attraction could be applied not only to cosmic and earthly things but also to the passionate attractions of humans. So the sexual circumstances of Davis's life—his already-noted search for a soulmate—would help to enhance his view of the materiality of spirit. More than even before, it became for Davis a thoroughgoing theological program—and one that was widely accepted by participants in the séance spiritualism of 1848 and after. Here devotees joined a theology of materialism (one could easily talk to spirits who were matter) with an empiricism insisting on scientific "proof" for spirit visits.

Significantly, in the work of Davis himself, the increasing materialization of the Great Positive Mind may be traced through a shift in the language of Davis's cosmology from the *Principles of Nature* to other and later writings. In the *Principles*, gender references were few, perfunctory, and conventional. Nature was blandly "she" in places, and there were references to "her" laws and even her "bosom." Despite the scattered allusions, Davis could declare that "mechanical principles . . . constitute the united action and forces of Nature." The Great Positive Mind was, to be sure, "an everlasting and unchangeable Parent of all things," but it had no identifiable partner in parenting. And while magnetic attraction was an easy metaphor away from sexual attraction, when the universe was invoked for anything even remotely gendered, it was—in a Swedenborgian echo—"ONE GRAND MAN."[32]

Sometime in the late 1840s, however—around the time that Davis's relationship with Catherine DeWolf Dodge grew more intense—the most telling shift in Davis's cosmology came. Now the Great Positive Mind and its magnetically attracted body in the Univercoelum became the sexually attracted "Father-God" and "Mother-Nature." It was the *marriage* of Father-God (wisdom) and Mother-Nature (love) that supported the world, a marriage that began to be described in increasingly graphic terms. By the mid-1850s, Davis was telling readers that "Father-God and Mother-Nature, by their celestial copulations, formed these children." Mind and matter, both eternal, lived together as male and female in "unchangeable wedlock." Perhaps a decade later, Nature stood as "compeer and companion of God—the feminine side of a perfect conjugal union—coextensive, inter-intelligent, co-partners in all departments of life and animation, the two halves of a perfect stupendous whole"[33]

"Celestial copulations" and "unchangeable wedlock" were putting an end to Davis's previous qualified dualism in favor of an unqualified monism. Mother-Nature was "not essentially different from Father-God," as Davis repurposed the older magnetic language, so that Nature became the "negative part of the Positive Principle—even as man's body" became "the negative part of his Mind." There was "not one thing which is body, and another which is spirit," Davis wrote. Neither was there "one thing which is Nature and another which is God." Instead, there was "One Harmonium, illimitable."[34] Now, as in the theoretical imagination that had so commanded the work of Fourier (his copulating planets were yet another echo) and inspired Brisbane, theory offered its practical payoff to the Harmonial philosophy. The theory of correspondence would argue as much. There had to be an empirical manifestation for the cosmic scheme. There must be personal behavior, personal forms of action that "harmonized" with the mystical sexuality of Father-God and Mother-Nature. Because Davis saw himself as teacher and guide to his generation of Americans, personal behavior should have larger parallels in social advice, in forms of moral injunction directed to social issues, not to mention to his own personal behavior of sexual searching.

As with Brisbane, the connection between a feminism that supported social reform regarding women *and* personal sexual proclivities was always hiding in the wings. In a life devoted to the Harmonial version of spiritualism and to social change for women, Davis—as we know—married two women whom he had encouraged to divorce their previous husbands, and he had divorced one woman himself. Nor was his domestic life, in terms of his teaching, an anomaly. For if individuals—men and women—were to be free to seek their true conjugal mates, the legal ties of marriage should not impede. In the best of all possible worlds, in accord with "the nuptial code of Father-God and Mother-Nature," two people who were "parts and counterparts; the two halves of one whole" would find each other, meet, and marry. In the eternal order of things they had been *"born* married." But in the ordinary world, in which people made mistakes, things frequently went awry. So Davis worked tirelessly in his lecturing and writing for marriage and divorce-law reform. He denounced sexual relationships based on anything less, in many ways echoing Fourier and Brisbane. Harmonial marriage, Davis wrote, was "a *blending of the two souls* so absolutely, that no extrinsic influence can dominate over, or in any manner vitiate, the *internal attraction.*"[35]

From Davis's perspective, a true wife should be "the child of love and the woman of intelligence—a friend, a playmate, a sister, a power unto progression, and noble-minded associate, an eternal companion." He condemned government for treating women as "chattel" and called legislators "corrupt and despotic" for denying them suffrage. Arguing that common law destroyed "the legal individuality of woman," he looked to the day when "social re-organization" and a *"universal Republican Government"* would guarantee "Female Elevation, and consequent Liberty." He declaimed against Christian treatment of women and against male physicians. He berated the "narrow enclosures" to which men confined women—the trinity of "kitchen," "bedchamber," and "nursery"—and called the disparity of wages between the sexes a "conspicuous wrong." Still further, Davis expressed dismay for women who spoke against women's rights and considered even marriage degraded because, in a twisted version of his doctrine of conjugal love, women had been "taught to regard *marriage* as the end of all existence." He believed the three "learned" professions—legal, medical, and clerical—belonged appropriately to women as well as men. In a free convention, he thought, a woman's voice should be equal to a man's. Answering a child's question on whether a woman could propose marriage, Davis looked to the day when she could.[36]

Davis got noticed, as we have seen, and he continued his impassioned pronouncements amid accusations of immorality and "Free-Loveism" without giving up.[37] He spoke to aspiring middle-class listeners and readers before and after the Civil War, to new inhabitants of his ideological landscape who were transforming the evangelical demand for perfection before God into a liberal program for the perfect, inner-directed self. In short, he shaped his "spirit" message to the evolving concerns of his followers. Now, increasingly, these "congregants" were acting out the individualism and self-reliance that Emerson had promoted in his lectures of the early 1840s. As another "Transcendentalist" for the times, Davis was legitimating the noncommunal and non-institutionally inclined spiritual direction of so many. As social reformer, he was preaching the perfect society but also, like many other reformers of the era, shifting the argument to the perfect *individual* whose spiritual quest society was supporting. As self-taught theologian of American spiritualism, he condemned organized Christianity in order to champion freedom and spontaneity. And as a private person caught in the workings of larger social forces, he found his way, in part through his marriages, to a world that made sense to him. For him, clear links flourished, connecting his cosmology, his behavior, and his general moral advice. Past was fusing with present, and public with private, in new and combinatory ways.

Davis's clear links were especially gathered in his thoughts on what he called "spiritual republicanism." Midway through his evolution, they were revealed in a series of lectures that brought together his conviction that spirit was matter and matter spirit, his passion for the reform of society, and his utopian plan for the creation of a new Harmonial world. By the early 1850s, he had integrated all of this into his own theological framework through what, as we saw, he had learned from Mesmer, Swedenborg, and Fourier-Brisbane. We gain telling insights into Davis's combinative theology in a series of lectures he directed against Horace Bushnell—who, despite his liberalism, functioned for Davis as a stand-in for orthodox Christianity and its clergy.

I have already briefly noted the connection between Bushnell and Davis when the famed Congregational cleric gave Davis the silent treatment after Davis baited him about his lecture at Hartford's North Church and Bushnell refused to be drawn in. There is much more to the story, however. The spark that led to the book Davis called *The Approaching Crisis* had come after he had sent his provocative public letter to Bushnell through the *Hartford Times* (see chapter 4). The nonresponse to Davis after Bushnell's first lecture in a series he called "On the Naturalistic Theories of Religion as Opposed to Supernatural Revelation," was fuel for Davis's anticlerical fire. His unsubtle letter provided the opening salvo in the first chapter of Davis's self-published work of 1852. The "approaching crisis" of the book was, for Davis, the demise of organized Christianity as he knew it. And the way his work examined its collapse was through a studied argument against the content of five of Bushnell's lectures alongside Davis's presentation of his own vision. Bushnell, as a relatively open and "reasonable" cleric, provided a near-perfect "enemy" against whom Davis could, Don Quixote–like, tilt his sword. Now he could hurl insults at both Protestant and Catholic churches, and he could sweep Bushnell away in his condemnations. So Davis used his lectures to reject all *"unnatural* supernaturalism" in favor of the views of those he called "Liberal Christians and Harmonial Philosophers."[38] The "Harmonial Philosopher" Davis knew best was, of course, himself.

It is instructive to explore Davis's impassioned arguments, which, in a later version in 1868, had stood the test of well over a decade. By then, he was solidly into his forties, and his teaching had settled into a comfortable, if combative, litany of complaints and counter-praises. Davis did go out of his way at first to compliment Bushnell for his "clearness, beauty, and force of expression" and to praise him for being "almost wholly free from that presumptuous and dogmatic style, which most clergymen employ." Bushnell was "frank" and also "noble in his realization of the present colossal proportions of the Progressive Party." Still more, he was "fraternally disposed toward those who think differently from himself." But Davis noticed, too, "some severity toward the Progressive reformers" that was "betrayed" by "the *tone* and alternating modulations of his voice." Davis, however, did not preoccupy himself with tone and voice. His strategy instead was to take on Bushnell's positions, point to what he regarded as their problem areas and yet almost-alignment with his own views, and go on to contrast them more sharply with the good news of Harmonialism. There, contra Bushnell, no "real *conflict* between Nature and Supernaturalism" could exist when both were "properly comprehended." With "a little calm reflection," Bushnell might come to "see truths just *as* and *where*" they were. Then he would "inevitably think better of 'Socialism' so called; better of 'Revelations about the Spheres,' through magnetism; better of 'necromantic conjurations' and spirit-seeing, better of 'Unitarianism.'" Davis was not finished. Now he introduced his own doctrine of progressive revelation. If all scripture was by "inspiration," might it not be that contemporary philosophers, schooled in "the wisdom and experience of the past" and also "receiving the increasing influx of fresher truths from superior spheres" could "bring out a fairer faith?" Might they not offer "a PRINCIPLE of greater saving power, than the *forms* and *faiths*" bequeathed by "superannuated centuries?"[39]

By the time he wrote his assessment of Bushnell's second lecture, Davis had warmed for battle still more. He did not think that Bushnell had *"yet attained* that harmonious moral growth which enables the mind to conduct an honest and impartial investigation." The Congregationalist minister defined supernaturalism "in *contradistinction* to Nature" and so did not differ essentially "from the common orthodox opinions." He was not "truly a reformer *in spirit,* but an iconoclast"—reforming merely the "FORM." Never mind that Bushnell had pronounced natural and supernatural part of the "one system of God" (see chapter 4) and that matters, for him, were hardly simple. Davis churned on with his polemic, which sharply revealed his own theological stance and program. In so doing, he had turned Bushnell's "one system" of supernaturalism upside down to posit his own "one system" of Nature. Here the material creation of the physical universe expanded even further, "embracing all the *future* habitations and realms of the soul" and constituting the "spiritual universe." This, wrote Davis, was the "*definition* of NATURE."[40]

With the definition established, Davis was now ready to take on Bushnell regarding animal magnetism. Bushnell, Davis complained, thought it signaled a longing for the supernatural among people. Such an assessment was "all wrong." In fact, "the *mysteries* of human magnetism" were "simply the normal operations of the natural sympathies of the human body and mind." Davis was bent on unraveling Bushnell's views of nature and supernature, curiously targeting cause-effect statements in Bushnell's lectures when, as we have seen, Bushnell was thoroughly at home in a world of analogy. Bushnell, Davis charged, "connected with the universe of God by a *chain of causes and effects*" and could feel nothing but "the link just above." By contrast, Davis enthusiastically championed his version of the theory of correspondence: "Rationalism, or *Harmonial spiritualism*, sees MAN as a *microscope*—as a *miniature* universe; being perpetually visited by innumerable friends from the four quarters of the firmament."[41]

Bushnell's third lecture afforded Davis still another opportunity to compliment and criticize through his own "one system" of subversion. Bushnell's lecture "manifested considerable scholastic skill and power of intellectual conception." There were "several interesting and well-elaborated passages." Still, "it was no less free from the unskillful ridicule and unnecessary sarcasm which characterized the preceding lectures." Bushnell displayed "peculiar genius," but he suffered from a conflict between his "moral sensibilities" and "his intellectual perception of truth and reason," thus "causing him to draw a strange line of demarkation [sic] between Nature and Supernature." So humanity got depreciated in the crunch, and the human race stood charged with evil and voluntary sin. Davis—probably convinced that the ghosts of Swedenborg and Fourier were cheering—saw a better way. He predicted that the minority assemblage of "*thinking, truth-loving* men and women" he was addressing would, through their journeys, "vicissitudes," and "whirlwinds of public opinion," live to see "the organization of a Spiritual United States." Contrasting the biblical account of creation—"a very interesting myth" and "mainly a *plagiarism*, from the early traditions and cosmological doctrines of the ancient Persians and Chaldeans"—with his own Harmonialism, Davis held forth. The creed of the "eternal Deity" was "written all over the firmament." It was "expressed in the *order, beauty,* and loveliness of Nature." It flowed up "from the depths of the pure soul." "All indications" testified "fully, that the *true religion* is *Justice,* and *joy,* and *peace,* and *beauty."* Davis urged his readers to go forth and "meditate in the open fields." "Let us," he enjoined *"look up,* and contemplate the *works* and *ways* of Nature's God. We are never so *free* and *happy* as when we bring our spirits into direct sympathy with the forms and flowers of nature."[42]

Despite Davis's many abstractions about nature, the pursuit of happiness, it was clear, led him through earthly fields and byways—sources of joy, delight, and all that was good. So whence came evil? The question remained, and it would not be easily banished. But Davis's answer again appealed to the natural instead of the biblical. Children, "by various transgressions of the physical and organic laws," brought evil on themselves, and then they transmitted the "results of the disturbance" by means of "the laws of hereditary descent." Still, the waywardness of children did not explain how evil began—if it meant "the diseases, the wars, the cruelties, the discords in the world." Once again, Davis, with his "impressions," looked to nature. "Evils" were "the *consequences* of a regular system of progressive development in Nature." This was "just as *angular crystals, sharp and craggy rocks, irregular vegetation, cumbrous plants with thorns, huge animals, and imperfect developments of the human species"* were "the steps of a *transcending* law of progress." Davis was taking his cues from Fourier and Brisbane, with their pronouncements on evolutionary stages from savagism up to the still-problematic state of civilization in which humans were mired. People did not know "wrong or misdirection" until they outgrew it. So evil was "local and arbitrary," with succeeding generations altering its meaning "to suit the standard of another generation."[43]

Demolishing orthodox links between evil and the influence of the devil, Davis pronounced "the entire traditional doctrine of the origin of evil" to be "irrational and abhorrent." It cast aspersions on "divine goodness" and "divine power." For the Harmonialist, the idea of "creation," as traditionally understood, was deeply troubling. Rather, the creative impulse emanated from "the divine HEART in the universe" and its "two PRINCIPLES of *love* and *wisdom,"* which were "immutable and invariable." Still more, "the unchangeable principles of Association, Progression, and Development" flowed "from the deific HEART of the UNIVERSE, unfolding worlds, like flowers, and progressively developing the various forms." So in the Harmonialist scenario, evil existed as a way station on the path of growth and goodness. The challenge was, as Davis was "impressed" to say, "to organize ourselves into a form, or body, which shall tend to develop this harmonious condition in our selves and in human society."[44]

By the time he was ready to review Bushnell's fourth lecture, Davis was identifying a "Swedenborgian method of interpreting the [biblical] Word" on the part of his clerical foe. Bushnell's thinking, Davis alleged, seemed to be "slightly tinged by the New Church Doctrine." (Davis may have been on to something here, as we saw in chapter 4.) Bushnell, according to the Harmonial Davis, was still preoccupied with sin and evil—and using Swedenborgian teaching as a support for his traditional views. Since Davis had, for many years, rejected the Swedenborgian hells in favor of his own Fourierist-inspired evolutionary agenda, it was not at all surprising that Swedenborg was doing Bushnell no good so far as Davis was concerned. His lengthy critique of Bushnell and, through him, orthodox Christian understandings of evil was an exercise in rationalist sparring that, point by point, took on and repudiated the Hartford cleric. Davis had found serious fault with Bushnell, who had "not attained the summit of the philosophical argument, in favor of supernaturalism, and against the rationalistic theories of religion." He found it ironic that Bushnell had used "man and nature" to advance his supernaturalist views and had "constantly referred" to both "as living witnesses and demonstrations of the supernatural faith and theory."[45]

Now in his review of Bushnell's fifth lecture, Davis was ready flat out to pull the moorings away from supernaturalism. It had not been proved "a truth," and that for the "manifest reason" that "no universal standard of judgment" could tell what "sin or evil" really was. Case closed, although—to be sure—Davis fought on, demolishing every plank he could in supernaturalism's base. Instead, urged Davis, "progress" was "a law of Nature." The natural came first, and the spiritual followed, for "the fair and beautiful" always unfolded "from the rudest beginnings." The earliest "developments of minerals, of vegetables, and animals" were "universally low and imperfect." But *"True Theology"* stood out as "the holiest and sublimest form of knowledge." It taught that "*every thing*" was "forever progressing in goodness and perfection," was "eternally *growing* more and more lovely, more harmonious, more wise, more happy." Even further, in Davis's "true theology," Nature was "*not limited to this little planet.*" Nor "to the myriads of earths and systems in space; nor to the infinite system of suns in the upper skies." Nature encompassed "the boundless universe" and was "'beautiful' as the Living God." Nature, in short, was cosmic, and landscape loveliness needed to give way before its grandeur. There was always correspondence, true. But the "sweet harmonies of the mid-summer season" only "faintly" typified "the diversified beauties of the Summer Land." The universe was "'beautiful' as the loving God" because it was "his TEMPLE."[46]

As he began to wind down after taking on five of Bushnell's lectures, Davis was ready to pontificate on "Dying Dogmas." "Educated Protestants"—although coming out of Catholicism and rejecting its "graven images and idolatrous ceremonials"—still continued to deal with a bevy of problems. For them, there remained "certain cardinal principles in theology," and Davis would out them. Deposited in the Protestant "theological armory" were "original sin," "the Atonement," "faith," and "free agency"—all of them "idols." Bushnell's alterations of "the theologic faith" could not obliterate the fact that "conflicting elements" lay beneath Christendom's "fair exterior," and it was "now as a slumbering volcano." Davis's truth to replace it brought together the trinity of seers he had come to rely on—Mesmer, Swedenborg, and Fourier. "Man," Davis insisted, was "not the creator of the inexorable laws of his being,"—a rejection of the moral liberty implied in traditional teachings of free will. Instead, humanity was the "everlasting subject" of law, and—as we saw—Davis named the "paramount law" to be "Attraction." Humans obeyed "this law every instant of time; true as the needle to the positive magnet." "No man," Davis declared, possessed "*a will* superior to his attractive or moving principle." The will was "merely the agent, *or fulcrum*, whereby this law, like a lever," moved "the individual from point to point, from attraction to attraction, among the countless contrarieties which make up existence." Finally, bombarded by attractions, humans acted "in accordance with the paramount." This was "all the moral freedom" that existed "in the constitution of things." In the world thus organized, humans were "free to do right" but *"not free to do wrong."* Doing right, people glided "peacefully along with the divine life-currents of this beautiful universe." They were like flowers "on the ocean's bosom." On the contrary, doing wrong was "like an effort to ascend the impetuous tide of Niagara Falls." Always and ever, to end all discussion, the *"chief attraction* of every soul" was "Happiness."[47]

We can leave Davis there, immersed in Swedenborgian influx—an influx that operated magnetically and ever in accord with the law of attraction. In developing his theology of matter, in encompassing both sex and spirit within it, Davis had assembled moving parts to create a middlebrow version of what—from the time of Emerson and Bushnell—was becoming ever more user-friendly. Brisbane had certainly acted as an enthusiastic participant in the move from high to middle. Still more, both Brisbane and Davis were churning out ideologies of democracy and progress that worked in sync with the times. They had resoundingly sought to silence purveyors of sin and evil in favor of cosmic and earthly narratives of delight and destiny, and they had coasted cheerfully from sex to spirit and back again. Together they had constructed a kind of hourglass of ideas to pour new contents into the Anglo-culture of late nineteenth-century America. They had done so with the help of three European thinkers—Mesmer, Swedenborg, and Fourier—bringing to the nation a fresh influx from across the Atlantic to mix into an already strong homegrown brew. Both New Yorkers, Brisbane and Davis had come from decidedly different rural circumstances, the one wealthy and privileged, the other impoverished but clever. Davis, of the two, was the more polemical and also the one better at getting things done. Nonetheless, they had both pursued sex in physical and not just philosophical terms, and they had both surely jumped on the marriage-go-round.

Given the waves they were sending toward a metaphysical future, it was perhaps surprising that in the new world coming, delight would be inverted to announce the need for healing and the easy process of achieving it. When hormone levels were not high because of illness and weakened energy, when vitalistic fluids were not flowing aright, bringing on the good times required effort. Happiness needed to be *pursued*. Always, for delight makers in an attraction-based universe, physical law and human passion worked hand in hand.

SECTION 4

Physic and Metaphysic

While the Great Positive Mind shone with erotic splendor, things were changing rapidly on the American ground. A new field for delight opened—at first challenging, but eventually richly productive. As the nineteenth century soldiered on, and the Civil War came and went, a seemingly out-of-tune nation preoccupied some and spurred others. Clearly the country was facing unprecedented times and frontiers. People were moving toward cities and toward the West, even as ever more immigrants were arriving. Industries were exploding, while opportunities and inventions multiplied, and ruthless businesses practices abounded. Meanwhile, diseases old and new were everywhere flourishing. Let physician George M. Beard be our guide to this last aspect of a world coming to be with his classic tour de force of 1881—a work that he titled *American Nervousness*, with no reference to delight at all.[1]

Beard's book, which he announced as a "supplement" to an earlier one on *Nervous Exhaustion*, told readers that nervousness was "lack of nerve-force," that it was largely a product of the nineteenth century, and that it was especially prevalent in the northern and eastern sections of the nation. He attributed the malady to *"modern civilization,"* as characterized by "steam-power, the periodical press, the telegraph, the sciences, and the mental activity of women." It was an odd conglomeration of factors to be sure, even with Beard's admission of "secondary and tertiary causes." More important than the catalog was his perception that rising out of nerve exhaustion, or what he also called "neurasthenia," came a close relation to "certain physical forms of hysteria, hay-fever, sick-headache, inebriety, and some phases of insanity"—a startling checklist for any professional physician or self-diagnostician.[2]

Beard did not stop there. He went on to detail a number of special influences that affected the nation—"dryness of the air, extremes of heat and cold, civil and religious liberty, and the great mental activity made necessary and possible in a new and productive country under such climatic conditions." Again, from the perspective of our time, the list seems bizarre. But Beard thought that all of the above yielded "a new crop of diseases in America," the likes of which "Great Britain until lately knew nothing, or but little." He was looking at an American original, and—to his unhappiness—he linked it to a series of ills. These included "susceptibility to stimulants and narcotics and various drugs," the consequent need for "temperance," and such other conditions as "neuralgia" and "nervous dyspepsia." Also on the list were "early and rapid decay of teeth; premature baldness; sensitiveness to cold and heat," not to mention "diabetes and certain forms of Bright's disease of the kidneys and chronic catarrhs." The line-up got even more provocative when he complained of the "unprecedented beauty of American women" and the "frequency of trance and muscle-reading." Then there were "American oratory, humor, speech, and language" and even "the greater intensity of animal life on this continent."[3]

Still, Beard could look beyond the nervous situation to see a brighter side for Americans (even if some items on his previous list seemed already "bright"). He estimated optimistically that "increasing wealth" would bring "increasing calm and repose," that "various inventions" would diminish "the friction of nervousness," and that "social customs with the needs of the times" would be "modified." All of this would lead to the development of "strength and vigor" alongside the "debility and nervousness."[4]

We can wonder what it was about the climate of the age that prompted Beard's peculiar categories. From our own point in time, there seems to be little rhyme or reason to them—just an untidy stream of consciousness that posed as a catalog of causes for a worried and anxious professional. That acknowledged, we can leave Beard and his more than three hundred and fifty pages of text with all its quirks and eccentricities. In the midst of them, however, he had put his finger on an evolving complaint that would permeate public and popular culture from the late nineteenth century on. Beyond the major disease conditions that would increase—cancer, heart disease, diabetes, and obesity, to name the most obvious—other chronic sources of misery refused to go away. So there was neurasthenia, or chronic fatigue syndrome, or Epstein-Barr, or hypoglycemia, or the like. Given the realities and woes of their presence, what could delight makers do to mitigate the distress, especially if they themselves were among the afflicted? How could they find joy, abundance, beauty, connection with nature and the universe, not to mention love and pleasure? What could bring them out of their daily pain and into the bliss that delight makers sought for their own lives and the lives of others? Two very different Anglo-Americans—Warren Felt Evans and William James—each found their way to answer these questions. They needed to *pursue* happiness with serious intent. They did, and they ended with legacies that became enduring features in metaphysical religiosity.

SEVEN

Warren Felt Evans:
From Methodism to Mind Cure

Warren Felt Evans, who lived from 1817 to 1889, came before William James. Born in Rockingham, Vermont, he appears to have had a relatively happy childhood on his father's farm and was educated at the district school. By 1835, he said, he turned his "attention to religious things" and became a Congregationalist.[1] In so doing, he inherited a Calvinist orthodoxy that had softened but still stressed human sinfulness and divine selection for salvation. Evans attended Chester Academy in Vermont and then Middlebury College, beginning in the fall of 1837. The following spring found him at Dartmouth College, where he continued until the spring of his junior year in 1839. After that he became a Methodist and began to act as a lay minister.

Evans's reasons for leaving Dartmouth are unclear—perhaps to secure professional status quickly, which he could do in an acting ministry, and this perhaps because of impending plans to marry. The plans materialized in June 1840, when Charlotte Tinker became his lifelong partner. From the scant biographical information available, we know that the couple had at least four children—two boys and two girls. One son, Osmon, died as a toddler. The other, Franklin, like the daughters, survived his father, but was severely wounded in the Civil War. The Evans marriage was apparently quite happy; Charlotte Tinker joined her husband in the spiritual changes he made through the years and eventually in his healing work. The two of them, we are told, were also "accomplished singers."[2]

Evans had been ordained a deacon in 1844 and an elder in 1847, in typical Methodist fashion transferring from one church to another at his bishop's behest every one or more years. At various times, he apparently held eleven different positions for his denomination, mostly in New Hampshire.[3] Then, after twenty-five years of service to Methodism, in 1864 Evans—perhaps shockingly—sent his ordination credentials back to his bishop and joined the Swedenborgian Church of the New Jerusalem. His break, however, had been a long time coming, after years of constant reading, intense prayer, struggle and turmoil, and copious journaling to explore and systematize his thoughts.

Evans's rupture with Methodism and his move in an unorthodox spiritual direction occurred in the midst of chronic "nervous" disease, to use Beard's term. His suffering, sometimes related to digestive issues, had kept him out of the pulpit time after time or led him barely to drag himself into it. Especially, he seemed to become symptomatic in connection with the Methodist conferences that he attended—a clue to what was to come. Over the years in continuing distress, he became convinced through his Swedenborgian reading that the mind controlled the body and its production of health or disease.[4] So in his post-Methodist work, he began a mental healing practice in Claremont, New Hampshire. Then in 1867 he moved to the Boston area and, with his wife, spent more than twenty years practicing and teaching. He charged no fees, accepted only free-will offerings, and from 1869 turned his home into a sanatorium of sorts, where he and his wife welcomed patients. Evans also took to studying medicine and, according to New Thought minister William J. Leonard, "received a diploma from a chartered board of physicians of the Eclectic School, certifying to his qualifications and giving him the title of M.D."[5] After he severed his Methodist ties, Evans had also done some Swedenborgian preaching and acted as a colporteur, distributing Swedenborgian literature. By the time of his death, however, he had thoroughly abandoned a clerical identity.

Not exactly a household name in our time, Evans in the late nineteenth century became an idol and hero for a flourishing metaphysical subculture. Indeed, he was probably the single individual who most shaped the intellectual and practice-oriented direction of what became New Thought. Astonishing in his erudition and in the combinative quality of his thinking, in book after book he churned out an evolving creed that incorporated mental healing (mind cure) and very much more. The books apparently were much read. *The Mental-Cure* of 1869 went through at least nine "editions" and was translated into several foreign languages. *Mental Medicine* of 1872 appeared in fifteen printings that we know of. The copy of *The Primitive Mind-Cure* (1885) that I have used announces itself as a fifth "edition" published in 1886—just one year after its first. Although we do not know the size of the print runs for these works, the reprintings (for they apparently were that) are remarkable for a man who built no organization and, from reports of meetings and activities of the era, kept a low public profile.[6]

Meanwhile, as his intellectual world changed through the years, Evans brought his initial ideas on the power of mind into touch with new ones from a liberal community, often alienated from orthodox Christianity and turning toward Asian religious philosophies and the mystical heritage of Europe. Still more, we can trace the process of spiritual and intellectual change that he underwent. In the years between 1850 and 1865, Evans kept personal journals in which he poured out his reflections on his reading in and out of Methodism and thought it through. Within his journal pages, he also recorded a series of deeply felt religious experiences, many of them quasi-mystical. The journals abruptly ceased, however, in 1865. If Evans continued his journaling practice after that—unlikely because of his escalating career as healer and author—no records have been found. Nor have earlier journals been discovered.

The extant journals, however, provide rich insights into Evans's reading practices and the near-encyclopedic knowledge that he acquired. His recruitment as a substitute teacher in 1852 for the Methodist Biblical Institute in Concord, New Hampshire, already begins to suggest what the journals make abundantly clear. He owned numerous books, read them voraciously, and retained what he learned with a memory that must have been close to photographic. He wrote out Methodist hymn verses frequently and seemingly by heart—many of them by Charles Wesley. Other poetry appeared again and again on journal pages. Much of the material, for a reader in our time, is relatively obscure, and were it not for Internet search engines, many of the sources would be virtually irrecoverable. At times, too, Evans copied long passages into his journals from the works of Augustus Neander, a nineteenth-century German church historian and theologian whom he much admired. When he did so, at times he cited page numbers but never listed editions. He did the same for the writings of Emanuel Swedenborg when he became his follower, and so he did for other writers. He read most of these works in readily available English translations, although he prided himself on his knowledge of New Testament Greek and in several instances lettered Greek words into his journals. The same was true for Latin, which he clearly knew.

During the period when he was writing in his journals, Evans published four short works, often using material from the journals to produce them (a practice followed by many nineteenth-century authors, including Ralph Waldo Emerson). After the journals ended, Evans authored six more books, all widely influential and all on mental healing in a religious context—with a seventh unpublished manuscript (ca. 1883) now in the National Library of Medicine in Bethesda, Maryland. As Evans increasingly saw a connection between the state of the spirit and the condition of the body, it became for him a natural step to address the issue of cure. Supported by Swedenborg's theology, he had come to believe that since humans were "linked to the Great Central Life," "a divine method of cure" had been "revealed" to them.[7]

At first, though, Evans had not turned to Swedenborg. Instead, he found himself attracted to the theological perfectionism advanced in liberal Methodist circles at Oberlin College in Ohio. Moving away from Calvinism, he turned to Oberlin's perfectionist belief that individuals joined their free will to the power of the Holy Spirit to receive a transforming gift of divine grace. This would restore them to the situation of Adam before the Fall. Already Methodist founder John Wesley had expressed perfectionist leanings, and Oberlin had added to Wesleyan thought a self-starting message implicit in its language of will. So perfectionism, for Evans and others, became a kind of theoretical carte blanche for testing the limits of self and spirit, for moving from step to step into new religious territory. Methodists like Evans, in effect, could use their denomination to leave their denomination, and that would be exactly what Evans did.

In the process, Evans was drawn increasingly to narratives of medieval saints and mystics whose extraordinary lives provided compelling examples for a would-be mystic. We read in his journals of Bernard of Clairvaux, Anselm of Canterbury, Richard of St. Victor, Raymond Lull, Thomas à Kempis, and Johannes Tauler, among others, and we learn, too, of English and Methodist models of sanctity. Then, in company with other nineteenth-century seekers, he began to focus on the French quietism of Jeanne de la Mothe Guyon and Archbishop François de Fénelon, the same two figures who for a time had strongly influenced the spirituality of Horace Bushnell.[8] In an about-face from the perfectionism of the Oberlin theology, with its can-do holiness, now Evans would wait on God, stilling himself in a conscious passivity—a practice that later he would come to reject.

Evans's major spiritual breakthrough came, though, when he discovered the writings of Swedenborg. Cautious and hesitant at first regarding any move into the Swedenborgian church, Evans was yet in January of 1859 writing of "Jehovah Jesus" in his journal (Swedenborg's "Divine Human").[9] It became clear, too, that in addition to Swedenborgian ideas on mind-body correspondence, he also accepted spiritualism. Meanwhile, attracted to holiness thinkers such as Phoebe Palmer and William E. Boardman, he moved further away from more traditional Christianity, even as the idealism of Anglo-Irish Bishop George Berkeley grew increasingly important for him. Yet the merger of matter and spirit in both mesmerism and spiritualism left him fudging on how absolute the idealism could be. Eventually, and in his final published book, Evans turned to Theosophy, thoroughly impressed by Madame Helena Blavatsky and advocating what he called "esoteric Christianity."[10]

Reading through the Evans corpus, and especially his intimate confessional journals, it is not hard to track the presence of a series of themes and concerns. We have met them all before. In Evans, the theory of correspondence predominated without contest. So did a love of nature in the mostly rural environments in which he lived. Evans delighted in landscape beauty, reveled on mountaintops, and found in nature's solitary splendor a huge impetus for mystical experience, virtually all Christian in content and tone. He told often of visionary episodes, especially after his immersion in the writings of Swedenborg, with their graphic descriptions of worlds beyond our own. He also recorded sensations of clairvoyance and—as he became a mental healer—shamanistic instances in which he absorbed the illness of a client. His writings were suffused with a sense of vitalism, at home in the worlds not only of Swedenborg but likewise of Franz Anton Mesmer and Andrew Jackson Davis. Through it all, what emerged was the strong attraction—the passion—that he experienced as he pursued the divine as he knew it. Juxtaposed to a life of debilitating ill health, in which he forced himself to fulfill his ministerial duties, came another one of indescribable bliss, a happiness present again and again, even as physically he struggled on. In all of this, Evans had connected the dots between the theory of correspondence, an ambiguous idealism that bridged the divide between body and mind, a vitalism that did the same thing, and, through it all, the law of attraction. What, after all, was the correspondence between mind and body—with mind leading—but an application of the law of attraction? If attraction was a subcategory of the theory of correspondence, it could also take the lead, as the story of mental healing shows.

While Evans began to grow away from his spiritual past, though, more was at stake than theological issues. In June of 1853, he had confessed to his journal that he became a Methodist mostly because his "youthful heart" had "admired that roving life." Now he was grumbling about "a growing dissatisfaction with some features of Methodism" and its piety. Especially what he disliked was the "outrageous financial system, or rather want of system." Evans had not received enough to support his family, and after one promised payment ended with a shortfall of "fifty dollars or more," he thought that a few more incidents like this could lead him back to the Congregational (i.e., Calvinist) church.[11] Evans was no prophet though. Even as the journey ahead would lead finally to Swedenborg, he was eager to recount his many way stations enroute. He detailed all of this in his first book, which he titled significantly *The Happy Islands; or, Paradise Restored* (1860). A tour de force of his journals' pages, the book—with its transparent "plot"—announced that it intended to "analyze some of the higher forms of Christian experience." In allegorical fashion, Evans as unnamed sailor began with the "ancients" (Homer, Plato, and Plutarch) and their references to certain "Fortunate or Happy Islands." He told readers that he became "fully convinced that they were not merely the abode of immortals, but were somewhere in this world" and that "the spiritual state symbolized by them" belonged "to this earthly stage of our redemption."[12]

To get to the islands, however, Evans needed to sail alone. Intent on doing that, he "embarked on board a boat named the Resolute, at a city and harbor called Semivivum [half-alive]"—on a trip that proved "unnecessarily protracted and difficult."[13] He was pleased to detail for readers the seven (was this deliberately the use of a mystical number?) islands he visited—all with allegorical names in a style echoing John Bunyan's *Pilgrim's Progress* of 1678. So did much else about the journey. But the Reformation theology expressed through Bunyan's Everyman named Christian had changed from the moralism of the original into Evans's mystical expedition into the unknown. Catholics were no longer the fearsome presences that they were in the Bunyan allegory. In fact, in certain versions of their spirituality, they lived as venerated residents of the isles.

Evans chronicled his island visits at some length—to places whose Latin names stood for "Entire Consecration, Rest, Full Assurance of Faith, Fulness of Joy, Perfect Love, Liberty and Divine Union." All of the islands were about equally distant from "Divine Union," and, circling it, Evans confided that beneath their surface all "were united, and constituted but one system."[14] As he made his way from one to another, it was clear, too, that his voyage was based on the theory of correspondence fundamental to the Swedenborgian theology that he had already begun to embrace. Each island conformed in its external features to an inner state of soul. Nor was Evans reserved in painting these soul features for readers, displaying the romantic attention to the natural world so apparent in his journals.

On the island called Staurosis, or "Entire Consecration," for instance, he was met by a "Divine Man" on the beach of this "least lovely" of the islands—shaped "in the form of a cross" and "surrounded by high and precipitous rocks" with "no verdure." This island was a required stop because it "contained the only harbor accessible to ships." So Evans found himself, aided by his divine companion, making his way to a summit that "appeared wholly inaccessible." The Divine Man caught him when his foot slipped and sometimes carried the weak but resolute pilgrim. The summit at last gained, Evans felt that he had returned to "the sweet home whose image had followed him in all his roaming." A description followed, telling of a "sequestered vale" and "large flat rock in the shape of an altar, covered with a downy moss, and standing in the midst of flowers." There Evans rested.[15]

In this state of repose, what should surface in veiled and metaphorical form but the so-called "altar theology" of Methodist lay theologian and revivalist Phoebe Palmer, whose well-known *Way of Holiness* (1845) expounded her own brand of perfectionism? "While resting upon this altar," Evans wrote, "there sweetly float out from the soul into the listening ear of a present God the words, 'Here, Lord, I give myself away. I present to thee my body, and my whole inward being, a living sacrifice, holy and acceptable in thy sight.'" Now, as Evans stood refreshed after the altar gift, he beheld the startling sight of a "perpendicular rock" that "rose to a great height." Near the summit he saw an inscription "surmounted by a golden cross: 'Here I relinquish all, and take God, the infinite and uncreated Good, for my sole portion and inheritance.'" Evans's divine guide informed him that anyone who wanted to live in the islands must subscribe to this "New Covenant." The mountain itself was blanketed with names engraved into the rock. Here were "Anselm of Canterbury, Bernard of Clairvaux, Raymund Lull, Thomas à Kempis, Tauler, Ruysbrock, Fenelon, Madame Guyon," as well as John and Charles Wesley, along with more figures whom Evans identified and "innumerable other honored and sainted names."[16]

The list was mostly a catalog of authors cited in Evans's private journals. Etched in rock and recorded in a work for public dissemination, Evans's devotional reading had acquired a proclamatory power that could reflect and legitimate his choices not only for others but for the author himself. In keeping with the theory of correspondence, Evans's *Happy Islands* held a mirror to his inner world and magnified its discoveries as he traveled, like a veritable journeyman of the spirit, from isle to isle. More than that, he was an explicit teacher regarding his theory of knowledge and its cosmological significance. On the island of Euphrosyne, or "Joy," for example, he told readers that there was "a certain experience of heavenly life and bliss which is symbolized by a lofty mountain." Echoing his December 1858 journal, he added that "according to the correspondence which subsists between things in the natural world and the spiritual world, mountains signify a great elevation in the moral and spiritual condition of man." As early as July of 1850, Evans had climbed a mountain near his home and then reminisced in his journal that he had always since childhood "loved to wander in the solitudes of mountains" and "delighted to pray on their lofty tops."

That very afternoon he had "found near a large oak tree, a flat stone, laid upon another stone." What followed told already of an altar theology that—whether influenced by Palmer's 1845 *Way of Holiness* or not—was foundational. "Upon this I prostrated myself after taking off my shoes, rendered thanks to God for his good Providence, which has watched over me all my days; and upon that rude altar I gave myself anew to Christ."[17]

Meanwhile, metaphors of rushing water—so basic to New Thought and made so memorable in Ralph Waldo Trine's much later *In Tune with the Infinite* (1897)—already appeared throughout Evans's *Islands*. Thus, on Plerophoria, or "Full Assurance of Faith" (a "favorite resort"), he called God "the fountain of all life." He went on, in almost Emersonian terms, to declare that "the life of a soul, or an insect, is a stream flowing from that Fountain: and were it not continually supplied from its Source, it would flow away and cease to be." Thus, Evans's theory of correspondence was part of a grand flow—a stream of spirituality that had descended through the times. Moving behind the message was Swedenborg, with his teaching of a divine influx that filled the universe and human life--a conviction that Evans, as I have noted, would increasingly adopt. Always, the influx shaped reality as it flowed, replicating the eternal world of the divine. On the island of Teleia Agape, or Pure Love, Evans could proclaim that "this world, so grand, so glorious, seems but the outward robe of the higher spiritual world." "In the Happy Islands," he explained, "all outward things were arranged in exact correspondence to their spiritual state." "Nature," Evans effused, "seemed a vast harp, struck by angel fingers, which expressed and offered up to God the sweet harmony of holy souls."[18]

By the time Evans's book was being published in 1860—certainly before Evans had become a thorough Swedenborgian—it was clear that he had arrived at the basic belief that constituted mind cure. On the same Teleia Agape on which he was enthusing about angel fingers striking the harp of nature, he had driven his point home pragmatically. If there was "a closer connection between the world of mind and the outward world than many suppose," there was more. Evans noticed that "life was greatly prolonged in this blessed clime, and diseases were fewer than in any other part of the globe." He also observed that "a large portion of the diseases which assail us have their origin in the mind." Calling Christ "the great Physician," he declared his divine work to be "to heal every form of mental disease, and thus to diminish the ailments of the body." "Mind in its different states" was "the body's health or malady."[19] Evans could hardly have been clearer, and if it took him a period of years to realize fully the implications of his island voyage, the sea and the territory had already been marked. We need not follow him further in the isles of bliss to see them as a kind of high-minded raid on his journals. In a new and transformed setting, journal materials functioned as public affirmation of the validity of Evans's insights and their spiritual authority.

Published in 1860 like *The Happy Islands*, the book *Divine Order in the Process of Full Salvation* was most likely Evans's second book.[20] On first reading, this work seems closer than his island allegory to Evans's Methodist spirituality in its perfectionist and proto-holiness wing. Only forty-eight pages in print, the text might be considered an extended pamphlet, beginning with a visionary proclamation that "the Holy Spirit and the Providence of God seem to be moving the members of all Christian churches to seek a higher and deeper experience in religion." Evans complained that the Christian church was "not sufficiently in sympathy with the celestial world where praise predominates," but he also warned that "emotional bliss" was not the same as "holiness" and had "no moral quality." Caught in the dilemma of a failing institution and a flagging spirit, he was ready to announce a way out. "Our first step in the process of full salvation," he taught, was "the renouncement of our own will as the rule of life" (this, tellingly, a different emphasis from his previous Oberlin perfectionism). That accomplished, the next step was "to exercise an appropriating faith," and here—echoing the proto-holiness theology of Phoebe Palmer—Evans called for "laying our whole being upon the altar."[21]

Still, he was on target with what he had taken from Oberlin perfectionism. Evans wanted to renounce his will and yet use it—keeping his sacrifice on the altar without yielding the point. Palmer herself had claimed an experience of "entire sanctification" in 1837, and after that she became a missionary for perfectionist belief and practice that left a role—as in the Oberlin theology—for the human will. She taught that first came the individual's consecration to God. Then came the firm belief that God would be faithful to his promise to sanctify what was consecrated. Finally came the witness to the miracle that God had wrought. Evans, in effect, concurred. As his work progressed, the spiritual community with which it was overtly linking itself became ever more visible. He echoed the language of Boardman, which inaugurated a "higher-life" movement in Presbyterian, Congregationalist, and Baptist churches, seeing the "higher Christian life" as "a life of full consecration and assurance" to advance the process of full salvation. Boardman's book *Higher Christian Life* had appeared in 1858, and announced that conversion was merely the beginning of the Christian life.[22] What continued after that was sanctification, and it came gradually throughout a person's spiritual journey, empowering the individual, through the grace of the Holy Spirit, for a life of service and mission.

With some careful juggling, Evans had managed to combine the *active* passivity of Palmer's altar-bound surrender and Boardman's higher life with the Catholic quietism of Archbishop Fénelon. Distrusting the message of his feelings, he generalized the reflections in his journal to argue that full salvation might "exist when we have no emotion, when the soul is plunged into the night of naked faith." His journal had continued with the affirmation that "naked faith" was "the purest form of Christian love" and was "what Archbishop Fenelon aimed to realize." In his 1860 *Divine Order*, though, the "very essence of love" had been modulated to become acceptance of "the will of another as our will," resolving "that their pleasure be done and not ours." Unlike emotion—"an unsubstantial vapory cloud" and "a mountain of vapor"—love that was "a state of the will" existed as "a mountain of granite."[23]

Beyond this, Evans was making connections that, provoked into fuller consciousness, would become the theology of New Thought. God, who was "love itself," had "a necessary and eternal property . . . to communicate divine good to his creatures." Nothing could stop the divine action "but our want of capacity to receive." The "assurance of faith" brought "full salvation," and faith was the "channel" through which it flowed. Evans was stating, in Christian terms, the proverbial law of attraction. Good begot good; to the person who had, more would be given. When the gift had been experienced, and full salvation was at hand, confessing the new condition, as in Palmer's third step, became "an act of praise."[24]

Evans could not acknowledge, with Palmer, a single act of "entire sanctification."[25] Rather, like Boardman and the higher-life movement, he saw the process of "full salvation" as gradual—a pilgrim's progress through thickets of spiritual dullness and sin. There was "a difference between sanctification in its incipient stage, or infancy, and holiness as a confirmed habit of the soul, a fixed spiritual condition." At first, "an effort" might be "required to do duty." However, "at length, when the law of habit . . . had time to act," then he and others would "become rooted and grounded in love." Finally, "the soul's bent of sinning" would be "destroyed," and the "death of self" would be "complete." The soul "must advance perpetually farther inwards towards God, who dwells there, and lose itself more and more in the divine presence."[26] In this mystical oneness, thus, Evans again—like others in the Wesleyan perfectionist and proto-holiness movement—was entertaining his quietist friends Archbishop Fénelon and Madame Guyon.

Yet for all the holiness-quietist connection, sitting in the next room was a well-known but secret guest. The overt message was clear: Evans had explored a series of ideas congenial to the higher-life movement and, alongside, a related quietist overlay that reflected a devotional trend not unknown in Methodist and proto-holiness circles. Without acknowledgment, though, Evans's theological views also echoed those of Swedenborg. In a lengthy journal entry in December 1861 (well after the publication of his book), Evans extolled Swedenborgian teaching under six heads. In the last of these, he revealed *Divine Order*'s significant secret. "We are taught in the doctrines of Swedenborg, that there is a divine order in the process of a soul's salvation." Criticizing "the current popular teachings of the day in times of revival," Evans thought that the "outward life" was "changed from self-love." But that was not enough for the now-Swedenborgian Evans. Instead, he declared, "our first duty and the first step in the process of our salvation, after coming to the knowledge of evil, is to combat it and put it away as a sin against God." After that the soul could become "receptive of good which flows in from God through heaven." Evans stressed that humans had all they needed to put themselves in the correct disposition toward God. "It belongs to man's free will or free agency, to do this, and he must do it *as of himself*; but all the while acknowledging that it is of God, from whom all good proceeds."[27]

There had been a gap, to be sure, between, on the one hand, Boardman's higher life, Palmer's altar theology, and the earlier, will-oriented Oberlin perfectionism and, on the other, Madame Guyon and Archbishop Fénelon. Evans had tried to bridge the divisions, perhaps better than his predecessors, with language. The fact remained, though, that the idea of "divine order in the process of full salvation"—which Evans found so compelling—came from Swedenborg. It was clear that his pamphlet/book was a theological work in progress, in which Evans was trying to integrate all of his intellectual sources with one another. It was also clear that he had hidden the Swedenborgian aspects of his work from a public whom he had correctly intuited would not be inclined to accept them. Instead, he had cloaked his views in a mantle of pseudo-orthodoxy or something closer to it than Swedenborg, hoping to convert readers to the new ideas. The Swedish seer, he had surmised, would be an unwelcome visitor in the spiritual and theological homes of most of his readers.

By 1862, thoroughly immersed in Swedenborgian doctrine and already an undercover convert, Evans published a third book. *The Celestial Dawn*, like *Divine Order*, tiptoed around the name of Swedenborg, never explicitly citing him, even though the work referenced other Evans journal heroes.

Here were Boardman and Roman Catholic Francisco de Losa, companion and biographer of the mystical Gregorio López, whom John Wesley himself had admired. Alongside them was the more or less nonconformist and nonseparatist Puritan minister Richard Baxter, whose *Saints' Everlasting Rest* Wesley had abridged. And here, too, were Irish Methodist convert Thomas Walsh, who walked city streets rapt in prayer, as well as the enigmatic German Dr. von Cöln. Those with theological savvy were apparently not fooled. Still, even with the icy and censorious reception that the book encountered in non-Swedenborgian quarters, it must have done well enough because it was reprinted two years later.[28]

Reformulating basic Swedenborgian theological themes in terms of his own spiritual odyssey and the reading that had supported it, Evans was ready to offer a comprehensive religious vision to his readers. As in Swedenborg's teaching, the vision was thoroughly interior, and yet it emphatically affirmed human worth in the world. Citing the *Higher Christian Life* (close enough to the Oberlin and Methodist perfectionism with which he had begun), Evans used Boardman's trinitarian teaching, with its acknowledgment of the divinity of Christ. "It will be seen," he wrote, "that the Son is not another God beside Jehovah, but is the Father brought nigh to us." Boardman would no doubt have agreed that far. In the context in which Evans had inserted this reflection, though, orthodox ideas had gone decidedly awry. Already Evans had been instructing readers on the "Divine Humanity of Jesus." Now, instead of the old dispensation—"a dispensation of angels"—the "Divine Humanity" was "the medium through which the celestial influences descend." "Jehovah Jesus" was "the only living and true God." Like Swedenborg, Evans had emptied the fatherhood of God into the sonship and emptied the sonship into humanity. In so doing, he had turned the perfectionism of his past inside out, elevating human life and its projects to a quasi-divine status. It was through the "Divine Humanity" that the "children of God" could find that "the abyss of truth in the divine word" became "luminous to depths never before penetrated."[29] Evans was bringing old saints together with new ones, easing a passage into previously unknown territory that now could be called a spiritual home.

But if heaven had to be "an interior state" before it could be "an external condition," for all his mysticism Evans, like Swedenborg, was pulling readers back to the present world. Heaven needed to be sought in "a domain of thought," but "material substance" could not "be spiritualized." To make his point, Evans could enlist the Scotch commonsense philosophy of Dugald Stewart on the certainty of the existence of mind as well as Bishop Berkeley on the nonexistence of materiality (see below). True enough for

Evans. Yet for all that, the world *was* the reflection of divine reality and, much as for Edwards, shadowed it forth. Natural creations were "types of things in the heavens" and "copies of celestial realities." In the parables of Jesus "by the laws of correspondence the lower creations" were "made to image the higher." The Epistle to the Hebrews, too, recognized and declared "the correspondence between earthly and heavenly things."[30]

As in the emerging theology of Evans's journals, however, correspondence in *Celestial Dawn* led to affirmation, and affirmation became power. Bridging between Edwards's delight in the sensuous world as a type of the heavenly one and a late twentieth-century belief in the power to change material things by one's mind, Evans saw a connection that was in the middle. Mental states affected "the appearance of the external world" and tended "in some degree, to adjust the outward universe in harmony, both in appearance and reality, with our spiritual condition." The "outward world" would be "in correspondence with the world within." Once again, Evans was bringing readers to the doorstep of mind cure. From an idealist perspective that had begun by negating the substantiality of the material world, he had entered by the back door to affirm matter's pliancy to mind. He had implied a human ability to manipulate the world of matter in directions more pleasing to the mind's and heart's desire. The heavenly world, in the end, led back to this one. "In a completed regeneration," Evans told readers—following Swedenborg—humans would be in "the New Jerusalem state." Now their "spiritual vision" would be "purged," and their souls "flooded with the light of a celestial day." The state began now. Its calling card was mind cure.[31]

Evans emerged in public as a full-blown Swedenborgian with his fourth book based on journal materials. *The New Age and Its Messenger* (1864), with a scant 110 pages, was a complete hymn of praise to Swedenborg and an apology for his teachings. Evans had complained to his journal at the end of 1858 that "men, and even the Church" were "buried in the things of sense"—to the point that the "spiritual world" was "a *terra incognita*, an unknown land." He was on fire to find a remedy. He longed for a "genuine rationalism" and beyond it the truly spiritual condition in which the angels existed, with faith as "an intuition, a spontaneous inward perception." Here "celestial love" would predominate. Meanwhile, echoing his journal, Evans's *New Age* contrasted Swedenborg's "open communication with the spiritual world" to a "modern Pythonism" abroad in the land—an allusion to the ancient Greek oracle to refer to the mass spiritualism that flourished through the 1850s. Swedenborg's experience and teaching were, in their "moral influence," as distant from such attempts at contacting the spiritual world as "heaven" was "above hell." Swedenborg's transmissions came "like a beam of heavenly light in our darkness; the other like the dark and deadly vapor of the Stygian lake." The latter made "Christ a mere man, and God a *principle* and not a person." It was "a refined materialism and atheism."[32] Seen in the light of Evans's own spiritual search, his protest and declaration of certainty were ironic. In the years after 1865, his published books would reveal a pilgrim whose theological horizon kept changing until he caught sight of the spiritual landscape that became New Thought and, we can assume, until death cut short his search.

Now though, in 1864, Evans was studying the scripture in light of Swedenborg's law of correspondence. In the process, he echoed Emerson's statement on language in *Nature* (1836), which also shared Swedenborgian roots. Evans was attempting—like Emerson—to use words themselves to make his point. The "Word of God," he said, was "written according to . . . correspondence, and all natural things [were] significant of spiritual things." With a foray into ancient Greek and Latin (Emerson had adhered to English-language meanings and had focused on more general "moral or intellectual fact"), he drove home his confessional message. "The great discovery of Swedenborg, and the grand characteristic of his system" was "the science of correspondence, without a knowledge of which the deep spiritual significance of the Word enclosed within the enveloping letter, cannot be understood."[33]

Evans continued to write enthusiastically throughout his slender volume, which in many ways reaffirmed what he had already declared in *Celestial Dawn*, but now with a significant nametag. He managed to gather some of his journal heroes into the Swedenborgian fold, explaining that "the mystic authors, as Fenelon, Madame Guyon, and Tauler" had experienced "glimpses" of the "spiritual significance" of the Word. This, even if sadly "they had no fixed principles of interpretation" and "groped like blind men along the wall." Especially, though, as his book's title announced, Evans was proclaiming the New Age that Swedenborg had heralded well over a century before late nineteenth-century Theosophists would announce one. With the writing of his journal for support, now his printed pages could speak the newness into being. Even more, Evans could, with Swedenborg, move beyond Earth as he knew it to understand "the God of *all* worlds"—a view that belonged "to the New Age" and was "one of the glories of the New Jerusalem." As we have seen, Swedenborg in his mystical travels had visited other planets; and belief in reputed life in other parts of the universe was also current in the cultural circles in which he moved. Evans was on board for a similar journey. "The extension of the human race, in countless numbers, to all the earths in the stellar universe," he enthused, served "to make man think less of himself as an individual, and thus to weaken that deep-seated love of self" that was "the root of all evil."[34]

Now Evans left his journals behind. Like Swedenborg, who had visited so many worlds, Evans would continue to travel inwardly as he published book after book on the good news of mental healing. In the process, his departure from the purer Swedenborgianism of the late journal years grew ever more obvious. As early as *The Mental-Cure* (1869), Evans's work was revealing his moves outside of Swedenborgian orthodoxy. As Keith McNeil has noted, the Swedenborgian *New Jerusalem Magazine* printed a review of the book that was decidedly chilly. Published by the Swedenborgian-friendly H. H. and T. W. Carter, Evans's book, wrote the unnamed reviewer, could not be regarded as "a successful attempt to throw new light upon the cure of disease from the revelation of spiritual laws made to the New Church." The "general tenor of his book" seemed "more akin to Spiritism than to the New Church."[35]

For all the Swedenborgian chill, this new work—like Evans's later ones—revealed a disciplined, ordering mind and a facility in exposition and argument. Evans was bibliographically responsible in ways that signaled a professionalism and attention to detail not found in his earlier books and in other middlebrow authors. Often, but not always, he parenthetically cited sources for quoted material, giving an author's surname, a short title, and page or pages. Besides the general sophistication of this and later works, and their at-homeness in both religious and scientific worlds, *The Mental-Cure* and succeeding books were nonpolemical. Here was a huge departure from the writing habits of Andrew Jackson Davis and Albert Brisbane—and also from the argumentative Phineas P. Quimby (see below), until recently thought to be Evans's mentor and healer, as well as, for many, the founder of New Thought. Instead, Evans's readers could find affirmation and a catholicity that cheerfully combined sources so that, whatever their maladies, they could pursue the happiness they sought.

What most likely ruffled strict Swedenborgians in *The Mental-Cure* was Evans's comfort with a spiritualist view that resonated with the Harmonial theology of Davis. Mind was an "immaterial substance," even as matter was a substance, one associated with the sense experience of resistance and force. Evans's easy assumptions regarding the real existence of spirits, his citations of the ubiquitous spiritualist Samuel B. Brittan and of the doctrine of spiritual spheres also pointed to his blending of Swedenborg and Davis. So did his understanding of death as a "transition to a higher life" and a "normal process in development." Meanwhile, magnetic references likewise pointed to Evans's familiarity with spiritualist commonplaces. In fact, in the facile way that Evans incorporated "modern spiritualism" into his Swedenborgianism, we can see the ready amalgamation between sources out of which Evans and so many others built their world. Expounding on the "Swedish philosopher" and his doctrine of spiritual influx, Evans saw inspiration and "the commerce of our spirits with the heavens above" as "the normal state of the human mind." In that context, what was "called modern spiritualism" was "only an instinctive reaction of the general mind against the unnatural condition it has been in for centuries." Always though, Evans focused his account on the phenomenon of illness. Bodily dysfunction signaled spiritual dysfunction, and the way to correct the body was to correct the spirit.[36]

Nor was there a conceptual gap between the two in the Swedenborgian universe that Evans inhabited. Echoing the vitalism expounded by thinkers as different as Cotton Mather and Davis, as well as Swedenborg and the New Testament Paul, Evans declared for the existence of a "spiritual body" bridging the gap between the "curious and wonderful" external body and the mind. The spiritual body functioned as one among innumerable "intermediates, through which influx descend[ed] from the higher to the lower"—part of a pattern in all creation. Compounded of "a substance . . . between pure spirit and matter," it was for Evans "a sort of *tertium quid*," literally, a "third thing" that, for many in the developing New Thought movement, would seriously alter the traditional Christian idea of body and soul. Here the (inner) spiritual body became the herald of a series of multiplying bodily spheres that traced a path from gross matter to highest spirit. The spiritual body became, too, the herald of energy pathways that traced the same route; and, already in Evans, the roadmap was ready. "*This inner form,*" he reported, "*is the prior seat of all diseased disturbances in the body.*"[37]

Evans published his second book on mental healing in 1872. *Mental Medicine* placed "psychology" in its subtitle (*A Theoretical and Practical Treatise on Medical Psychology*)—a choice that pointed toward the new conceptual world in which William James would later be making his way. But in the book, Evans's explanation of emanation in terms of the sense of smell suggested some of the more esoteric declarations of Charles Fourier. At the same time, his specific use of a rose as an example and his identification of a spiritual cause for odors and of something like it in the mind all smacked of the writings of Phineas Quimby. Evans had long ago visited him, probably twice, and must have been familiar with some of his ideas. Apparently Quimby had helped to catalyze Evans into growing confidence regarding his own healing ability. More than that, Quimby held essentially Swedenborgian views regarding a distinction between the "natural" and the "spiritual man." He also read the Bible in an analogical or allegorical way, placing him squarely in the theoretical orbit of correspondence so favored by Swedenborg.[38]

Now, as Evans neared the end of *Mental Medicine*, he offered a positive allusion to Quimby's healing practice. He called the Portland mind curer "one of the most successful healers of this or any age" and lauded him for embracing the view that *"wrong belief"* lay at the root of illness. Quimby's work was "an exhibition of the force of suggestion" for "a patient in the impressible condition." Still further, as a former magnetic doctor Quimby could be cited with this much enthusiasm because of the vitalistic substance of Evans's work. Even a casual reading of Evans suggests a steady dose of magnetism, so that the presence of Davis—and of Franz Anton Mesmer standing behind him—was seemingly everywhere. Chapter titles amply reveal the plot. We can point, for example, to "Auto-Magnetism or Self-Healing," "Phreno-Magnetism and its Use in Medical Psychology," and "On the Law of Sympathy and its Application to the Cure of Mental and Bodily Disease." This last suggests how effortless it was for Evans, thoroughly immersed in Swedenborgianism, to feel comfortably at home in a fully magnetic world. It also points to how he could embrace notions of magnetic sleep or somnambulism (recall Davis's episodes in this state), and how he could move from there into quasi-shamanic mode. This, to be sure, may have been part of the appeal of Quimby for Evans in this particular book. The late mental healer (he died in 1866) had written about absorbing a patient's illness to aid in the restoration of health. Evans had already reported the same thing in his journals.[39]

By the time he published his third healing book, *Soul and Body*, in 1876, Evans was declaring his goal as the "restoration of the phrenopathic method of healing practised by Jesus, the Christ, and his primitive disciples." If the neologism "phrenopathy" hinted of former Methodist minister and then spiritualist and magnetist La Roy Sunderland's "pathetism," it signaled, too, a continuing comfort in the language of the older spiritualist community. In a work aiming to be *"scientifically religious,* without being offensively theological," Evans had already, on his title page, quoted from Swedenborg's *Arcana Coelestia* (on correspondences) to set the tone. Still, easy allusions throughout suggested that Evans was immersing himself increasingly in the Hermetic tradition that supported "modern" spiritualism. He acclaimed "John Baptist Van [Jan Baptista van] Helmont," the seventeenth-century Flemish physician and scientist who was also a speculative mystic. He knew German Lutheran mystic Jakob Boehme. And he linked his "spiritual body" to the *"perisprit"* (the subtle body connecting spirit to brain) of the

French spiritualist theorist and mystic Allan Kardec (Hippolyte Léon Denizard Rivail), whose *Book of the Spirits* (1858) he had apparently read. Evans linked it as well to the *"nerve-projected form"* of Justinus Kerner, whose work had brought to public notice the bedridden German mystic and clairvoyant called the Seeress of Prevorst.[40] Arguably, there was nothing here that a widely read spiritualist would not cite or approve.

It was Evans's next book, *The Divine Law of Cure* (1881), that marked his entry into an expanded Western language world to ground his healing practice. Now Evans was reading the Hermetic legacy in idealist terms that, at first glance, seemed more absolute and encompassing, joining his increasingly philosophical brand of idealism to the philosophy of the European Continent and England. Evans's new cast of characters included Bishop Berkeley, whose subjective idealism taught that matter did not exist independently of perception, and that the apparent existence of matter was a function of the divine mind. The new cast included, too, the German idealist philosophers Georg W. F. Hegel, Friedrich von Schelling, Johann Fichte, and Friedrich Jacobi. Adding to the mix, it incorporated the French eclectic philosopher Victor Cousin and the English Romantic poet and theorist of language Samuel Taylor Coleridge—all, significantly, beloved by Emerson and other New England Transcendentalists.[41]

It was true that Evans asserted in *Divine Law of Cure* that he had become a "convert to [Berkeleyan] idealism more than two score years ago" (which would have been during his college years at Dartmouth). Still, the idealism that Evans taught was ambiguous, and it could yet speak to the Harmonial philosophy of Davis and his sympathizers with its spiritual materialism. He agreed with a series of Continental philosophers that "matter and mind in their underlying reality, or substance, are one and the same." Yet, to move beyond Davis, Evans, like Emerson, did not deny the actuality of bodily existence but instead asserted its contingency. Idealists, he told readers, did not deny "the *reality* of external things," but only that they had "any reality independent of mind." That meant that bodily properties were "only modifications of our minds." They were "reducible to feelings or sensations in the soul." "This view of the human body," Evans announced—as he reached still further back—"was held by Jonathan Edwards, the greatest of American metaphysicians, who embraced the philosophy of Berkeley with regard to the external world." Evans went on to quote Edwards. What was the point of all this? Enter Evans's mental healing method to reap the pragmatic benefits of the philosophical situation. Unthought pain was unfelt pain; and disease without wrong thought was as nothing. Banish the thought, and you banished the disease. Here were the "grand remedy, the long-sought panacea," and "the fundamental principle."[42]

Ever evolving, by 1885 and *The Primitive Mind-Cure*, the grand remedy had moved into a new Theosophical world that blended Western philosophy and Hermeticism with Asian texts and ideas. Theosophy was apparently good for idealism, because now the idealism had been ratcheted up a notch or two to become what at first seemed uncompromising. Yet Evans had sensed, perhaps intuitively, the vitalistic uses of idealism. Because he could never totally commit to the nonexistence of the world, Evans's idealism—perhaps like Emerson's—had become a bridge between matter and mind. In a comparative framework that pointed toward New Thought, Evans brought together Berkeleyan idealism, (Jewish mystical) Kabbalistic lore, and a general Hermeticism informed by Neo-Platonism, Swedenborgianism, and explicitly Emersonian references. Even, in his catalog of names dropped and texts quoted, he cited the Theosophical doyen Madame Helena Blavatsky whose massive *Isis Unveiled* had appeared in 1877. But there was also very much more. Evans joined to his expanded Western esotericism a series of references to the Indian Vedas and Vedanta as well as to Buddhism and even to the eleventh- and twelfth-century Persian Muslim mystical philosopher and theologian Al-Ghazali.[43]

Isis Unveiled, although oriented to Western Hermeticism, had provided relatively generous material on Hinduism and Buddhism. Clearly, Evans had been drawn to it in pursuit of the mysterious substance-energy that was now being styled by writers in this post-spiritualist culture as the ether, the astral light, the Hindu *akasa*, or the Kabbalistic "occult air." Blavatsky's authors were Evans's authors. He cited the English occultist "Lord Lytton" (Edward Bulwer-Lytton) and also quoted Éliphas Lévi on the "'universal substance'" (that is, the *akasa*) as the "'great arcanum of being.'" Hermes Trismegistus, in Blavatskian mode, uncritically joined the truth of Asia, even as Evan's citations from the Kabbalah were seemingly everywhere. Always, for him, however, came the pragmatic bottom line. Change the *akasa*/ether, and you changed the person and, so, the outcome of illness. Throughout, Evans's preoccupation with ether was clear. Like Blavatsky, he sought to blend science and Hermeticism, employing his era's Newtonian and scientific concept of the ether and seeing the Hermetic testimony go beyond it. The Hermeticists gave this universal "*aether*" "certain occult metaphysical properties" that modern science knew nothing of; they viewed it as "a divine, luminous principle or substance" present in and also containing all things.[44] Etheric substance, like the subjective idealism that Evans embraced, could span the gap between body and mind, so that well-being would be sparked and established.

To emphasize the point, in his vacillation between the materiality and the immateriality of the cosmic ether, Evans, like Emerson in *Nature*, had struggled with the tension between pure idealism and a material model of the world. But the tension was mediated now by the magnetic universe Evans had inherited and also by the ambivalences of the Hermetic texts themselves. It was mediated, too, by the high Western tradition of idealism and the Theosophical lenses through which he was now reading recent Western idealist philosophers. Natural things were "but representations of things in the realm of ideas"; they conformed to "the old Hermetic doctrine of correspondence" that had been "reproduced by Swedenborg." Indeed, the resemblance between "macrocosm" and "microcosm" was the "key note" of Evans's own "theosophical system." All things in the microcosm preexisted "in the *unseen and real world of light*, the world of ideas," and "after their dissolution they return[ed] to that world."[45]

Yet for all his global combining, Evans wound down his *Primitive Mind-Cure* with a lengthy consideration of Jesus as well as a formal prayer, suggesting the overriding Christian vision that informed his vitalistic journeys through different cultures. By now the historical person Jesus had become separable from the cosmic Christ, a separation that was already being signaled in midcentury magnetic literature of a popular nature. Identical with "the Adam Kadmon of the Kabala," "the Archetypal Man of Plato," and "man as he exists in the divine Idea," this was "the Divine Man, the Christ of Paul, at the same time a divine personage and a universal *humanized principle* of life and light." Echoing Swedenborg's "Jehovah Jesus," or Divine Human, all humanity was included in his being, as individual "weak and imperfect" selves were "merged in the grand unity of the divine-human principle, the divine humanity of the Lord, which is the Christ." Meanwhile, the living "Christ within" purposed to "save even the body."[46]

It was no surprise, then, that hard on the heels of *The Primitive Mind-Cure*, Evans produced as his final published work *Esoteric Christianity and Mental Therapeutics* (1886). Despite the "Christianity" of its title, the book sounded an alarm in even unorthodox Christian quarters. A lead article in *The Christian Science Journal* for August 1886 lambasted Evans in a review, signed only by "A Christian Scientist" (Christian Science founder Mary Baker Eddy herself?). The diatribe—for it was surely that—charged that perhaps no previous theory of the last decade "equalled, in presumption and absurdity, this mad attempt to force Christianity (the hope of the whole human race) into the farcical groves of Occultism." Evans's book had "set before the public gaze a pantomime" with characters who were "dead priests, magicians, and old-time philosophers, whose special hypotheses perished in the same centuries with themselves." Minus the venom, the Christian Science reviewer was not all wrong. Evans had apparently traded Swedenborg for what, said the reviewer, looked "like a twin of Theosophy."[47]

Thus, Evans's preface was telling readers that the author intended his work "to aid the student of Christian Theosophy to explore the inner realm into which his own spirit opens." His first chapter alone referenced Plato, Hermeticism, Hindu adepts, Egyptians, Chaldeans, and the Kabbalah in the service of his theology. Years of combinative thought and practice had produced an Evans who raided the world's spiritual closets unabashedly. He had discovered an implicit metaphysical logic that moved from the theory of correspondence to its corollary in a vitalistic law of attraction and from there to a unified mind-body, in which the mind could call the cards for the body and attract well-being. Yet, despite the Christian Science attack and his inherent Theosophy, Evans called his work *Christian* and managed in his own mind to stay the Christian course. He brought the selective wisdom of a global assortment of religious seers and societies to the New Testament—still in the process finding that "the religion of Jesus Christ" stood "apart from all other religions." Jesus—as "an incarnation of the universal Christ"—could "lodge himself, and incorporate and repeat himself, in his true disciples."[48] Still more, for all the theology, the passion that inspired and drove the book was practice. Like so many Evans volumes, this one had worked hard to legitimate mental healing in order to convert readers.

Perhaps the most striking way to see how far Evans had traveled by the time he wrote *Esoteric Christianity* is to compare his final views of Christ and God to those in *The New Age and Its Messenger* from twenty-two years before. There, as I have noted, he had fought strongly against those who made "Christ a mere man, and God a *principle* and not a person," thoroughly horrified by "a refined materialism and atheism." Now, though, he had upended the Christ of biblical tradition by turning all humans into divine beings and finding the Christ within them. If the way to be saved was to "believe in the Lord Jesus Christ," Evans assured readers that "the Lord, and the Jesus, and the Christ, are all in man as the centre of his being." Christ was not a *mere* man because all people were divine in nature—gods walking the earth. In his own way, Evans was careful. Each individual was "not God, but *a* god" and a "personal limitation of the Universal Spirit," yet still "possessed of all the attributes of its parent source," among them "omniscience and omnipotence."[49]

If humans were elevated here, Christ was surely leveled—not a mere man but still a lot like other people. Evans exalted the "inner I" and "the ever-identical Self." "This unchanging, undying, and identical self is my spirit," Evans affirmed. It was "that which Jesus calls in himself the *I am*, and it is that alone which can say of itself, I Am." This, reiterated Evans, was in all of humankind, for God came to "personal manifestation in the spirit of man." Moreover, as with Christ, so with matter. Instead of "refined materialism and atheism," Evans had transformed matter as he told readers that "in its reality and inmost essence" it was "divine." Only when it took dominion over spirit did it become evil. But matter "in itself, and in its place" was *"an invisible, divine, and immortal substance."* To be sure, this matter was different from what people called matter, which was "unreal and an illusion." Still, Evans's divinized matter was—well—matter. He had collapsed materialism and atheism in a kingdom of God that came "in us, and with saving power." Here "spirit and matter" were "no longer at war" but became "one *substance*," and the "phenomenal" was "absorbed into the real."[50] Was this a realized panentheism? Was it a moral and mystical fusion that left the illusion of separateness behind in a commanding affirmation of unity? Was it, under its skin, pantheism?

Evans did not say, but his attempt to craft his spiritual vision—with threads hanging and rough edges showing—had paid tribute to Swedenborg and yet moved beyond his theology. He had even, at one point, casually corrected him, saying that Swedenborg had "improperly called perception" what Evans now knew as intuition. While he elsewhere cited Swedenborg, referring, for example, to his "grand science of correspondence," it was evident that Evans had vastly expanded his own vision.[51] Swedenborg's voice was one among many in a staggering array that brought Theosophy and even Western philosophy together with a reinterpreted Christianity. Evans, it seemed, was joining everything he had read and pondered into an encyclopedic attempt at a grand synthesis. He had made an intellectual and spiritual combinativeness a habitual way of life.

Evans would die three years later, his life as a metaphysical seeker *and* a delight maker ended. Because of their iconic quality in revealing how religious change happens, I have taken an extended tour of Evans's journals and books. There it is fairly easy to see how he crafted delight out of struggle and well-being out of a dysfunctional body and career. But the question remains as to what it was about his life (and perhaps that of others) that constituted him *so radically* a religious seeker—one who reinvented spiritual connections endlessly and kept leaving a series of pasts in his dogged pursuit of happiness. What made Evans a perpetual spiritual discontent, a journeyer who had to turn over one stone after another to see if any mystery remained? Why did he not settle quietly into an orthodoxy of sorts, even if it was post-Methodist? We can never know for sure. But if we compare him to fellow New Englander Horace Bushnell, to whom he was akin in so many ways, we can perhaps catch glimpses of an answer.

With a life span from 1802 to 1876, Bushnell was fifteen years Evans's senior and died thirteen years earlier. So the two were roughly contemporaries. Both had come from solidly middle-class families, with apparently stable childhoods. Both had committed to conventional Christian denominations. Bushnell's story had been largely a tale of Connecticut Congregationalism, and Evans—after a brief Congregational interlude—chose the "roving life" of Methodism. Both attended university or college, even if Evans never finished Dartmouth and instead continued his learning through an enthusiastic reading habit. Perhaps here lay the beginnings of difference.

Again like each other, both seemed to experience contentment and deep satisfaction in family life, and both also mourned the loss of children. In addition, the intellectual and spiritual journeys of the two led them in similar directions. They came to theology from distinctly pastoral perspectives, and both made religious—and Christian—experience central to their concerns. Both also sparked controversy and endured ostracism from clerical colleagues in their respective denominations. Like Evans, Bushnell had provoked increasing dismay among traditional Christians with his published views. His admiration for Hermes Trismegistus in *Christ in Theology* would surely have delighted the later Evans, and his North Church lectures that had attracted Davis (later Bushnell's book *Nature and the Supernatural*) suggested the metaphysical line he was walking. Meanwhile, both were deeply committed to Christianity: Evans's last book was a concerted attempt to remain a Christian even as revealed himself a global metaphysician.

For the two, the law of correspondence counted as spiritual treasure, with heaven and earth understood as a unified whole, while clairvoyance and vision were alive and well. Both had experienced mystical leanings and felt the presence of the uncanny. Evans's journals testified to his unitive experiences in a resoundingly Christian context. Bushnell could theorize mysticism, as would Evans, and had also known it. On another front, both Bushnell and Evans had been reading some of the same material and were significantly affected by it. Like Evans, Bushnell was attracted for a while to French quietism. Similarly, for both of them, the quietism was linked to experiential themes that leaned in proto-holiness directions in a spirit-filled reading of Christian life. Bushnell's basic insight of the "analogy of being" resonated with Swedenborg's theory of correspondence that had so transformed Evans, and the Swedish mystic's rippling effect, through Emerson and other literary sources, would not go away. Still more, Bushnell was directly in touch with Swedenborg's theology, even if he was coldly analytic regarding it. Despite the line in the sand that Bushnell had drawn between himself and Swedenborg, the similarities remained, and Swedenborgians continued to notice.

Meanwhile, both Evans and Bushnell delighted in the natural world. Like the Evans of the journals, Bushnell had found the footprints of divinity in nature, and he experienced in it, on occasion, extraordinary illumination and a sense of the presence and power of God. For both Bushnell and Evans, too, such experiences were juxtaposed with continuing ill health. Evans's chronic suffering had been a near-perpetual source of discomfort in his ministry, even as Bushnell had his own private plague—"throat trouble" that prevented him sometimes from preaching and eventually forced his resignation from his Hartford church. Like Evans, however, Bushnell pursued the spiritual path of his choosing whatever his physical complaints, and he used the spiritual as an implicit ally in overcoming sickness. Still more, like the route that Evans took, Bushnell's path had skirted what some chose to call pantheism.

Unlike Evans, though, Bushnell refused to see the implications of his own theology—preferring instead to hurl denials at pantheism and pantheists even as he affirmed his "one system of God." Evans, as we know, was far more comfortable venturing into forbidden theological territory as the years passed, leaving it to Mary Baker Eddy and others to throw missiles along with his former Methodist colleagues. So at this point we have a parting of the ways, with denial for Bushnell and affirmation for Evans. We are at the crux of the matter, at the heart of what made the two men—so very much alike—also so profoundly different. How explain what happened on these separate life journeys, both of them in pursuit of delight and happiness? Can we invoke genes and DNA? Can we point to differences between antebellum and postbellum America? Can we find emotional factors to chisel away at their difference?

Whatever the potential for explanation in some of these questions, one social factor stands out. Despite his ill health and his travels, Bushnell remained (literally) firmly attached to one congregation—his North Church in Hartford. He stayed Congregational *and* wore the mantle of a particular pastorate in a particular place. By contrast, Evans, as a committed Methodist, "rode" small-town circuits, moving from place to place as his bishop instructed every one or more years. The Methodist system did not allow a pastor to put down deep or permanent roots anywhere. As a minister, Evans was a sojourner in each small town, ready to leave as commanded. In his second manuscript journal especially, Evans listed the small towns to which he was appointed and gave some sense of his emotional response to each move. It must have been a grueling experience to exit familiar scenes and friendships, and protective defenses must have gone up willy-nilly. It is likely that part of the defense system would have been a cultivated detachment from new people and situations—a willingness to let them in just so far and no more. And if Evans might have learned to be wary of getting too close to people and places, his search for intimacy could lead within.

So the "roving life" must have supplied—or resonated with—a mental template, a grid that could be filled in not merely in outer terms but also in the life of the mind. Evans could internalize external circumstance in ways that made intellectual and spiritual change seem normal and movement from one internal spiritual station to another a continuing part of the inner life. In short, Methodism contributed to metaphysical forms of spirituality for Evans not only by gifting him with a theology of perfection but also by institutionalizing a life of coming and going that made it usual and expected. Methodism also nudged him toward finding within himself the roots that could not grow deep in the outer world. There he could make delight and pursue happiness in a place of promise.

Still other forces were at work in Evans's world that contributed not just to his own situation but to a growing metaphysical movement. Increasingly, these forces made it more likely that even delight makers who stayed home would become, like Evans, *radical* metaphysical seekers who ventured into new territory. For one, as R. Laurence Moore has argued, science and secularization were the twin realities that challenged orthodox Christian religion.[52] If we understand science in the broad sense, it is, of course, difficult to suggest straight-line connections between new forms of knowledge and the expansion of metaphysical spirituality. But there are large questions about possible relationships. For example, what did spreading acquaintance with Darwinian evolution have to do with the turn to metaphysics? What about the burgeoning challenge of biblical criticism emanating from Germany and elsewhere? What did the growth of professional disciplines in history, anthropology, and comparative religions have to do with the erosion of traditional faiths? How much, really, did the increasing availability of Asian texts impact a generation of seekers?

Still more, even if—as Moore suggested—the hold of both science and secularization on the popular imagination has been exaggerated, Americans were living in the afterlight of the Revolutionary War era and the early national period. By Evans's mature years, they had experienced the Civil War and, forcefully reunited, had shuddered through its lingering trauma. They were experiencing the off-key climate of a new world coming and an old one dying, while the sectarian spirit seemed to rise to ever greater heights, and a pervasive unease spread. After the early industrial revolution of the 1830s and 1840s, new and expansive vistas had opened up in both practical and imagistic ways. Still further, in the age of progress, Anglo-Americans were in motion, propelling themselves from place to place, buying up cheap land, and forging new lives that promised blessing but also uprooted traditional moorings.

In the midst of these new realities and their ways of ruffling established patterns, how much did the immigrants pouring into the late-century United States create a climate that relativized old ways and mindsets? How did the phenomenon of urbanization and the percolation of its arrangements and ideas into small-town America change things? How much did increasing social mobility add to the equation? Did the new secular style—as populations moved more and more to follow job opportunities or assignments—make Methodist itinerancy seem a prediction of the future? Did increasing industrialization and the practical technologies that arose—like the telephone and the incandescent lamp—have repercussions that would move beyond the practical? Did new medical discoveries and healing modalities alter the way people saw religion? What about the spread of popular psychology?

We will never know the answers to these questions fully. But the collective changes had to make their mark on what people perceived and felt and what they did about it. Even if much of the intellectual upheaval of the times affected elites more than middlebrow and nonelite populations, change was in the air. Rumor swirled in the nuances of language found in the newspapers and in the commonplace cultural habits that were quietly eroding older ways of being. Many—if not most—dug in and insulated themselves by immersion in received tradition or reinvented tradition, with changes softened into near invisibility. Bushnell surely fitted in here. By contrast, fundamentalism was also not far ahead. Some, however, and not a few, pursued ever-evolving quests to new inner places for spiritual solace and security. Evans was among them. Much more than many others, Evans—like Bushnell—was a thorough intellectual. Beyond that, Evans's Methodist lifestyle only underlined the spiritual climate of metaphysical searching he must have experienced. Both as a major leader of the emerging New Thought movement and as a singular representative of a growing spiritual style, his journals and books shed important light on his culture and times. Evans had etched the lines between the theory of correspondence, the magnetic universe and its vitalism, the law of attraction, and a mysticism that found inspiration in nature and even more in a world within. In reading his story, we get important clues to how delight was created even out of the chronic humdrum of continuing ill health, out of the "nervousness" that George Beard had worryingly discovered as an American pattern.

EIGHT

William James: From Anatomy to the Science of Spirit

If Warren Felt Evans had spent a lifetime moving to different places in New England, William James lived in numerous places in a much larger world. James flourished from 1842 to 1910 and was surely a frequenter of urban landscapes and traveled widely—born in New York City in 1843, he was still a baby when he experienced his first trip to Europe.[1] The oldest of five children—with three younger brothers and a sister who arrived in 1848—he was closest to his brother Henry James Jr., next in the family's chronological order and later a towering figure in American literature. He was close, as well, to his sister, Alice, a complicated woman who—like William James—exhibited abundant symptoms of George Beard's American nervousness. Even so, she would acquire a reputation in literature as a diarist. Family members were deeply tied to one another, and that reality preoccupied eldest son William all his life and through his European travels. He attended school in New York City from 1852 to 1855 and during the next three years studied in institutions and with private tutors in France and England. Fluent in French by the end of this time, like all of the James family, he was deeply engaged in what Louis Menand has called "international hopscotch."[2] So he followed the European sojourn with a year in Newport, Rhode Island, and then returned to the Continent for more schooling and tutoring from 1859 to 1860, this time in Germany and Switzerland. Back to Newport in 1860, he studied painting for a year and then—torn between art and science, and fearing failure in the art world—he entered the Lawrence Scientific School at Harvard. By 1864, he was matriculating at the Harvard Medical School, and the family had moved to Boston to be near him. There were ups and downs in his medical education—including a year on a Brazilian research expedition with Louis Agassiz that convinced him not to be a field naturalist. Finally, in 1869, James received the only degree he would ever work to claim—his MD from Harvard. (He would receive an honorary PhD from Harvard many years later in 1903.)

Not that James ever became a practicing physician. Instead, after a long bout with ill health and depression that brought him close to suicide, he assumed teaching duties at Harvard by 1872—first as an instructor in physiology, then in anatomy and physiology. In 1875 he became an instructor in Harvard's first course in psychology. Appointed assistant professor of physiology in 1876, his academic evolution proceeded apace, and three years later he was teaching his first course in philosophy. The year before, in 1878, he had married Alice Howe Gibbons, and the pair soon produced three sons, although the third one—Herman—died in 1885. A daughter and another son were born later. Meanwhile, in the same year he married, James had contracted to write his groundbreaking *Principles of Psychology*, although the book was not published until a dozen years after, in 1890. By then James was thoroughly ensconced as professor of philosophy at Harvard (1885) and then, from 1889 to 1897, professor of psychology.

At the same time, James was speedily becoming a public intellectual, lecturing widely and eventually publishing a series of books that, as a rule, collected his essays and lectures. Among them were his *Will to Believe* (1897), *Human Immortality* (1898), *The Varieties of Religious Experience* (1902), *Pragmatism* (1907), *The Meaning of Truth* (1909), *A Pluralistic Universe* (1909), and—posthumously—*Essays in Radical Empiricism* (1912). By 1885, too, after his son Herman's death, James had met the trance medium Leonora Piper in a séance facilitated by his mother-in-law. Already interested in psychical research, he cultivated a growing relationship with Piper as the center of what became an abiding preoccupation for the rest of his life. He assumed the presidency of the (British) Society for Psychical Research in 1896 and bonded closely with cofounder Frederic Myers (until Myers's 1901 death) and other founders of the society.[3]

As in his earlier life, James returned to Europe repeatedly and spent a year there with his family from 1892 to 1893. He had also purchased a summer home in Chocorua, New Hampshire, and loved to hike in the surrounding mountains as well as in the Adirondacks. It was there in 1898—the year he retired from Harvard—that James strained his heart while hiking; after that, his weakened cardiac condition plagued him until he died. The physical burden must have increased a deep melancholy with which he struggled from the late 1890s. More than a decade later, he ended his days at Chocorua in the countryside he loved.

What this brief account omits, however, is the profound influence of Henry James Sr. on his brilliant and sensitive eldest son. We have already met the senior James in chapter 5 as a Swedenborgian and Fourierist as well as the anonymous translator of Victor Hennequin's *Love in the Phalanstery*—this last providing a clue to his sometime advocacy of free love. Henry James Sr.—one of twelve children born to a sternly Presbyterian immigrant father—suffered a catastrophic accident at age thirteen when he tried to extinguish a fire caused by a hot-air-balloon experiment. The attempt did not go well, and eventually, because of the damage, his leg was amputated above the knee. Two years in bed did not encourage the Presbyterianism he had inherited. It was not surprising, thus, that although he matriculated at Princeton Theological Seminary from 1835 to 1837, he was not able to commit to a ministerial career. Instead, cushioned by inherited wealth—not without a legal suit—he emerged as a theological and social-reform thinker with ideas radically different from those of his father. Then by 1844, seemingly out of nowhere, James Sr., endured a terrifying and game-changing inner episode that left him utterly anxious, with only "a most pale and distant glimmer of the divine existence."[4] He had been exploring the work of Emanuel Swedenborg since 1841, but after the experience that, in Swedenborgian terms, he would later call a "vastation," his conversion became irreversible.

Even as the senior James spent his days as a Swedenborgian theologian and social critic with reform ideas and sharp opinions, he was an austere man. Devoid of the Calvinism of his own father, he replicated it socially in the treatment of his precocious and sometimes rebellious son William and, in general, in his home. As biographer Linda Simon has remarked, "No one reading Henry Sr.'s passionate paeans to essential human goodness could have suspected the level of violence in his household."[5] On a more philosophical front, with Swedenborg (as well as Ralph Waldo Emerson, with whom he had an on-again, off-again relationship), he championed the law of correspondence. He also held to a passionate belief in the unity of all existence in the divine, with a transcendental oneness the drumbeat for all of his musings. A controlling figure in his family, he bent and shaped his children to depend on the combined intimacy and rigor of his interactions with them. The results would be lasting, and in the case of his eldest son, they would form part of a foundation that the younger James would later reinvent and, in many ways, subvert. Nonetheless, it would be a foundation that could neither be dismantled nor destroyed.

As all of this suggests, the authoritarian legacy of Henry James Sr. molded the emotional life of son William in ways that would persist throughout his life. He became a poster child for Beard's American nervousness or—to give it the technical name that Beard used—neurasthenia. Moreover, as a parallel to—and inversion of—his father's world-shattering "vastation," the younger

James could point all his life to the decisive experience that changed him utterly. At the end of April 1870, in the midst of severe depression, James was reading the French philosopher Charles Renouvier. He had finished the first part of Renouvier's second *Essais* and was earnestly pondering the Frenchman's definition of free will—according to James's diary, "the sustaining of a thought *because I choose to* when I might have other thoughts." James did not think that the definition needed to be "an illusion." So he decided to assume until the following year that it was not. "My first act of free will shall be to believe in free will," he wrote with clear resolve.[6]

The emotional results were radical (if gradual in congealing)—so much so that Gerald Myers thought Renouvier's influence on James was second only to that of the elder Henry James. Still more, Ralph Barton Perry—James's former student and first biographer—declared there could be no doubt that Renouvier was "the greatest individual influence on the development of James's thought." Significantly, James himself before his death had written that without the French philosopher, he "might never have got free from the monistic superstition under which I had grown up." Freedom had come because Renouvier had also argued that no human being could be absorbed into a group consciousness or "one mind." It followed for the Frenchman that human individuality meant free will and self-determination as the bases for moral decision.[7] Throughout his life thereafter, James would be caught in the tension between his father's vision of unity and an alternate vision of pluralism for which Renouvier had provided an initial thrust.

So it was that many years later, in 1897, James would publish a collection of essays as *The Will to Believe*.[8] The title had been taken from the book's lead piece, the text of which had appeared independently the year before, after James addressed the Philosophical Clubs of Yale and Brown Universities. Significantly, the 1896 version featured a preliminary note that acknowledged Renouvier's work. As important, along with other contributions to the volume, the essay revealed a constellation of interests and values that placed James securely in the camp of the delight makers. "Our belief in truth itself," he announced, "that there is a truth, and that our minds and it are made for each other,—what is it but a passionate affirmation of desire, in which our social system backs us up?" He did not mince words as he went on to detail his own outgrowth and reformulation of the work of Renouvier. "*Our passional nature not only lawfully may, but must, decide an option between propositions, whenever it is a genuine option that cannot by its nature be decided on intellectual grounds.*" Breaking with medieval philosophical scholasticism and its aftermath, he was ready to discard objective certitudes that rested on looking back to origins in favor of "the outcome, the upshot" of an idea.⁹ Implicit here were the same existential stalking grounds into which Charles Fourier and Albert Brisbane had made their way—the vitalistic world in which progress and the future charged the present with energy and possibility.

James insisted that "we have the right to believe at our own risk any hypothesis that is live enough to tempt our will."¹⁰ In that context, James's essay highlighted religion as its central concern, a preoccupation that pointed to an intellectual and existential future in which James would increasingly turn toward religious belief. Here already, a careful reader could follow the dots that, by the time James published *The Varieties of Religious Experience* in 1902, would land him among the proponents of mind cure. Were Evans still alive, James could have had an agreeable conversation with him. As James's career unfolded, however, the pull of opposites confronted him in ways that contrasted starkly with the focused struggle and pain that Evans had worked through. After all, the problems and resolutions that faced Evans had at least been consistent, and they had kept his vision ultimately unitive, even as it ranged widely.

For James, though, dramas of difference erupted seemingly everywhere. He moved between his father's idealist conviction of oneness and divine unity, on the one hand, and the path of individualized and radical empiricism onto which he had begun to walk, on the other. He was stretched between a monism that continued to plague him and a pluralism that he championed, tethered to a past that refused to evaporate, even as he looked to a future that he could mold with will and possibility. Meanwhile, James was haunted by religion and things religious, living a life of secularity that still affirmed the possibility and goodness of supernatural belief. How to approach such a complex and divided individual? How to address his evolving mental landscape and find the safe havens that he discovered and bequeathed to generations of seekers in the twentieth century and beyond? If *The Will to Believe* announced a delight maker who was pursuing happiness, how to explain—beyond Renouvier—that state of affairs?

To begin, always and ever in the James universe there was experience. Professionally a scientist himself, James was never ready to throw away insights and ideas generated by experiential means, some of them scientific and some not. With a dual intellectual focus, he thought, in the words of historian Krister Dylan Knapp, that "*personal* experience as much as scientific experiment accounted for understanding the world." On the philosophical front—despite professional tributes to his pragmatic theory of truth (see below)—James himself saw his largest contribution as what he called "radical empiricism" with an in-built pluralism. Against this backdrop, Simon thought that he intentionally came to terms with his identity through "a multiplicity of experiences." "He championed the new," she wrote; "he hungered for astonishment. The next book, the next encounter, the next mountaintop, would reveal, surely, an unexpected vista." Such a vista "could change one's sense of identity." As she clinched the matter, "experience was his salvation, his religion."[11]

In strong respects, James's focus on experience was hardly something to which he had recently arrived. His father's Calvinist and Presbyterian beginnings had ensured that son William would be intimately aware of an earlier American world in which Edwardsian experience reigned in the theology of revivalism. As the years passed, however, James would refine and exalt experience to accord it a new stature. In *The Will to Believe*, he had distinguished between an empiricist and absolutist way of believing in truth. "The absolutists in this matter say that we not only can attain to knowing truth, but we can *know when* we have attained to knowing it; while the empiricists think that, although we may attain it, we cannot infallibly know when." He would split the difference more succinctly in his much-touted theory of truth called pragmatism. In his lectures at Boston's Lowell Institute in 1906 and at New York's Columbia University the following year—gathered by James into his collection titled *Pragmatism*—he declared pragmatism to be "a perfectly familiar attitude in philosophy, the empiricist attitude." He argued, however, that the new pragmatism was "more radical" and yet "less objectionable" than the empiricism of the past. A pragmatist, he observed, would turn away from "a lot of inveterate habits dear to professional philosophers." They included bugbears like "abstraction and insufficiency," also "verbal solutions," "bad *a priori* reasons" from theory to experience, "fixed principles, closed systems, and pretended absolutes and origins." By contrast, a pragmatist turned "towards concreteness and adequacy, towards facts, towards action and towards power." The "empiricist temper" would be "regnant" and "the rationalist temper sincerely given up."[12]

There are shades here of Jonathan Edwards's well-known advocacy of John Locke's sensationalism—his theory of knowledge through the senses—but James was pushing the experiential focus in under-charted directions. Different from Christian evidence for God—inherited from medieval times and based on a testimony to design in the world—James (echoing the intuitive perspective of Emerson and other Transcendentalists) insisted on inner "proof." "I myself believe," he wrote, "that the evidence of God lies primarily in inner personal experiences." Expanded into a comprehensive theoretical statement—"*experiences*," not "experience"—truth became a multiplied noun. "Our account of truth," he attested, "is an account of truths in the plural, of processes of leading." Truths, in fact, paid off by their guidance toward "some part of a system." Meanwhile, truth in the singular was "simply a collective name for verification-processes." "Truth is *made*," James summarized, "just as health, wealth and strength are made, in the course of experience."[13]

James thought that establishing his pragmatic theory of truth was "a step of first-rate importance in making radical empiricism prevail"—the radical empiricism he had seen as most significant in all his work. He argued forcefully that "absolute or no absolute, the concrete truth *for us* will always be that way of thinking in which our various experiences most profitably combine." Where did intellectual reflection fit in? James's ready answer identified truth as a "relation, not of our ideas to non-human realities, but of conceptual parts of our experience to sensational parts. Those thoughts are true which guide us to *beneficial interaction* with sensible particulars as they occur." More specifically, he declared that "the only way in which to apprehend reality's thickness is either to experience it directly by being a part of reality one's self, or to evoke it in imagination by sympathetically divining some one else's inner life." "The immediate experience of life solves the problems which so baffle our conceptual intelligence," he affirmed.[14]

By the time James's mature collection of essays on radical empiricism (published posthumously) had been written, he was defining more precisely what the catchphrase meant. "To be radical," he explained, "an empiricism must neither admit into its constructions any element that is not directly experienced, nor exclude from them any element that is directly experienced." Still more, "*the relations that connect experiences must themselves be experienced relations, and any kind of relation experienced must be accounted as 'real' as anything else in the system.*" James had bestowed the name "pure experience" on "the immediate flux of life which furnishe[d] the material to our later reflection with its conceptual categories," emphasizing that at the core lay experience, not rationality and conceptualization, which came second.[15]

Yet unstated in the full-blown praise of experience lay the reality that certain types of experience generated and compelled James's concern. Throughout his mature writing career, James seemed obsessed with the issue of a something "more." In his short but important book *Human Immortality* (based on his Ingersoll Lecture of 1897), he pointed to the human brain not only for its function in producing thought but also for its *"permissive or transmissive function."* Here he speculated that "at particular times and places" nature's "veil" could "grow thin and rupturable." He wanted readers to admit that *"our brains* are such thin and half-transparent places in the veil." In another metaphor, resistance in the brain could be raised or lowered like the height of a dam, and when lowered the "influx" (favored by Swedenborgians) could occur. "We need only suppose the continuity of our consciousness with a mother sea," he observed, "to allow for exceptional waves occasionally pouring over the brain." When the waves poured, a host of energetically charged phenomena became possible: "Religious conversions, providential leadings in answer to prayer, instantaneous healings, premonitions, apparitions at time of death, clairvoyant visions or impressions, and the whole range of mediumistic capacities, to say nothing of still more exceptional and incomprehensible things." The echo here of Emerson's catalog at the end of *Nature* is uncanny. As I have noted, he had targeted "examples of the action of man upon nature with his entire force." He had gone on to cite "the traditions of miracles in the earliest antiquity of all nations; the history of Jesus Christ; . . . the miracles of enthusiasm, as those reported of Swedenborg, Hohenlohe, and the Shakers." Still more, there were "many obscure and yet contested facts, now arranged under the name of Animal Magnetism; prayer; eloquence; self-healing."[16]

The familiar vitalistic impulse was unmistakable. Arguably, both men had experienced an inner sense of depletion and ennui—in James's case with far more devastating symptoms that pushed harder toward solutions. So vitalism became the secret pulse behind Jamesian experience, and it cannot be ignored. This despite the fact that, as Daniel Bjork has explained, by the late 1860s "new physiological thinking" had "disavowed the vitalism of the mid-nineteenth century that ascribed the functions of living organisms to forces distinct from strictly chemical and physical properties." If the reality of James's continuing vitalistic search requires emphasis, we can notice that as late as 1901 he wrote from Europe in distinctly unphilosophical terms. "What I *crave* most," he avowed, "is some wild American country. It is a curious organic-feeling need." On a European landscape, everything was fenced or planted. By contrast, he yearned for American "wild-animal personal relations" with the natural world.[17]

On the philosophical turf on which he played professionally, James's much-scrutinized pragmatism needs to be seen in terms of the vitalistic impulse that lay beneath its surface. If James had turned the scholastic world of the past inside out, with its preoccupation with the origins and sources of truth, he did so because he was pulled by a future of progressive promises. Thus, pragmatism for James became another piece in his vitalistic agenda. By moving the criterion of truth into the future, by making it a goal-inspired object, he had found a way to generate energy for a present that might be confused, apathetic, depressed, even suicidal. "Not where it [truth] comes from but what it leads to is to decide," he had announced, and so for him pragmatism worked as a vitalistic "attitude of orientation." More emphatically, when James moved the argument toward religion, pragmatic truth refocused theological tradition so that the human vitalistic impulse gave real existence to the unseen. "I confess," he wrote, "that I do not see why the very existence of an invisible world may not in part depend on the personal response which any one of us may make to the religious appeal." The upshot was astounding: "God himself, in short, may draw vital strength and increase of very being from our fidelity." Life itself felt "like a real fight,—as if there were something really wild in the universe which we, with all our idealities and faithfulnesses, are needed to redeem." Our nature, he declared, was shaped "for such a half-wild, half-saved universe."[18]

By the time James published his classic *Varieties of Religious Experience*, he was on the attack against "medical materialism." His weapons were a series of lectures that acted to clear the way for a new take on reality. James's underlying project was to bridge the space between matter and spirit as earlier (and now-discredited) reflections on vitalism had done. Undeterred, he had found an emerging language of conscious and subconscious that—contra any version of materialism—mediated the possibility of God. In the evolving vocabulary James was using, a vital energy from the subconscious could infuse the conscious schemes of the living. A rainbow bridge was beckoning, like the old vitalism, across the great divide. By the time he had reached the end of his lectures, James's conclusions announced without apology the new vitalistic impulse his work was promoting. Living as if religion mattered meant that the "visible world" became "part of a more spiritual universe" from which it drew its "chief significance." It meant, too, that "union or harmonious relation with that higher universe" constituted "our true end." And it signaled that "prayer or inner communion" with "God" or "law" acted as "a process in which work" was "really done" and "spiritual energy" flowed in and produced "effects"—whether psychological or material—"within the phenomenal world." Religion meant "a new zest" that added itself "like a gift to life." It conferred "an assurance of safety and a temper of peace" as well as "loving affections." "Whatever it may be on its *farther* side," James hypothesized, "the 'more' with which in religious experience we feel ourselves connected is on its *hither* side the subconscious continuation of our conscious life."[19]

Always, though, loomed the future. If God added zest to present time and space, the "more" extended into a territory beyond, and that territory beckoned with promise because humans possessed free will. James kept circling the fort, so to speak, defining free will as "a general cosmological theory of *promise*, just like the Absolute, God, Spirit or Design." Free will meant "*novelties in the world*" and "the right to expect that in its deepest elements as well as in its surface phenomena, the future may not identically repeat and imitate the past." In a preoccupation with progress that echoed Andrew Jackson Davis, James hailed the pragmatic method because it plunged forward "into the river of experience." "Design, free-will, the absolute mind, spirit instead of matter," all had "for their sole meaning a better promise as to this world's outcome." When it came to ideas and concepts, the true ones likewise came bearing their hidden vitalistic credentials. True ideas *led*; they brought people into "useful verbal and conceptual quarters as well as directly up to useful sensible termini." The Jamesian rhetoric was unrelenting. Unlike for rationalism, for pragmatism reality was "*still in the making.*" It awaited "*part of its complexion from the future.*" For the one, the universe was "absolutely secure"; for the other, it was "still pursuing its adventures."[20]

Defending pragmatism in *The Meaning of Truth*, James insisted that all experience was "a process" and that "no point of view" could be "*the* last one." Beyond that, "our judgments" changed "the character of *future* reality" by means of the acts to which they led. Contrasting the kind of truth that pragmatism supported with the abstractions that constituted truth in the past, he found "all discarnate truth" to be "static, impotent, and relatively spectral," while "full truth" was "that truth that energizes and does battle." The vitalistic premise continued apace in James's *Pluralistic Universe*. "Reality, life, experience, concreteness, immediacy, use what word you will, exceeds our logic, overflows and surrounds it," he affirmed. "The essence of life" pulsed in "its continuously changing character." In a stark disconnect, concepts were "all discontinuous and fixed." The "only mode of making them coincide with life" was "by arbitrarily supposing positions of arrest therein." Ever in the quest for more experience, James could trash even objects; what "really" existed was "not things made but things in the making." Once they were made, they were "dead." Still more, there beckoned the reality of a grander, better way—a supreme vitalism that pushed beyond the limits of individual identities. "Every bit of us at every moment is part and parcel of a wider self. It quivers along various radii like the wind-rose on a compass, and the actual in it is continuously one with possibles not yet in our present sight."[21]

As all of this emphatically suggests, the vitalistic secret—as for Brisbane and Fourier—was bound to passion and emotion. James, in his own way, had bought into the law of attraction propounded by the Frenchman and his American disciple. His clearest statement came in *Varieties*, as he explored the world of mind cure. He told readers there that most of those who subscribed to mental healing regarded thoughts as "forces." Following a law "that like attracts like," a single individual could draw "as allies all the thoughts of the same character that exist the world over." The results were compelling, and it is not difficult to read James's approval in his description. "One gets, by one's thinking, reinforcements from elsewhere for the realization of one's desires." Indeed, "the great point in the conduct of life is to get the heavenly forces on one's side by opening one's own mind to their influx." Here thoughts were functioning as so many emotionally charged entities, propelling people forward into the completion of their desires. In fact, throughout his career it is not hard to see James's steady stream of tirades against intellectualism and rationalism as the underside of his championship of emotion. If emotions arose from bodily states and changes, as James had argued in his groundbreaking *Principles of Psychology*, and were not "pieces of mental stuff"—in the words of Henry Levinson—then intuition and a series of underexplored psychical states carried new weight. The key was ever the story of blend, mix, combination—what could be called "passion plus"—in a host of nuanced ways and places. The irony of New Thought, at least in the Jamesian version, was that under the table it was a cleverly disguised form of emotion.[22]

Safely within the camp of radical empiricism, religious experiences (James's abiding concern) became "affectional facts," as Levinson had it.[23] Without seeing them as subjective or objective in the conventional division of phenomena, James saw them as active in certain ways and dormant in others. In other words, experiences *worked* in specific directions, and the directions came because of visceral choices—so that the choice of optimism, the choice to be a delight maker, wrapped passion in elemental concern. Religious persons, whatever their doctrinal commitments, stumbled for James upon moments "when the world, as it is, seems so divinely orderly, and the acceptance of it by the heart so rapturously complete, that intellectual questions vanish." Invoking the romantic poets William Wordsworth and Walt Whitman, he acclaimed "ontological emotion"—emotion that concerned the nature of being—as *the* replacement for ontological speculation, "with her girdle of interrogation-marks round existence." "Loafing on the grass on some transparent summer morning" with Whitman in a moment of "energetic living" (vitalism again!), "we feel as if there were something diseased and contemptible, yea vile, in theoretic grubbing and brooding." For the "healthy sense," James wrote, the philosopher was "at best a learned fool."[24]

How, then, could a philosopher—James's calling after all—be reinvented? James's answer, unsurprisingly, put passion ahead of all else. "Things reveal themselves soonest to those who most passionately want them," he argued, because "our need sharpens our wit." So philosophy existed more as "a matter of passionate vision than of logic," and logic only found legitimation "for the vision afterwards." James's own synopsis of the territory ahead may be found in his important essay "The Energies of Men" (1907). A presidential address originally delivered before the American Philosophical Association at Columbia University, the essay posited that people typically used *"only a small part of the powers which they actually possess."* James thought that everybody had days of "feeling more or less alive." People knew that "on any given day" energies were "slumbering," and no incitements of the day could call them forth. With a veiled autobiographical reference, he declared that "most of us feel as if a sort of cloud weighed upon us, keeping us below our highest notch of clearness." Fires were "damped," and drafts were "checked." In an echo of Emerson who, as we have already manifestly seen, lamented that humans applied to nature but half their force, James complained that an individual usually lived "far within his limits." That admitted, how did the "better" people manage their escape? James had a ready answer: "Either some unusual stimulus" filled a person "with emotional excitement, or some unusual idea" induced "an extra effort of will." *"Excitements, ideas, and efforts,"* he affirmed, were "what carry us over the dam."[25]

Meanwhile, as references to Wordsworth and Whitman as well as to wildness suggest, the place where James found the energy to feel totally alive was nature. Gerald Myers has detailed James's habit of fleeing "from human entanglements to nature, solitude, and mystical relief" throughout his mature years. Similarly, Bjork has observed that James found settings in nature "indispensable to his creative life" and that "a wild, unfixed nature continued to figuratively anchor his world picture." As his biographers collectively attest, more than in words, James's love of nature was displayed in the way he typically spent his summers—far from Harvard and immersed in rural settings. Nature, affirmed Perry, with its "wide and unobstructed prospect," imparted to James "the sense of a breathing space, and favored contemplative detachment." Making the point, James's passion for his New Hampshire summer home at Chocorua from 1886 was clear. During the summer that he bought the house, he wrote to his sister, Alice, confessing that "the earth hunger grows on us." Likewise he told his brother Henry that "the more we live the more attached we grow to the country." So, too, his enthusiasm for Keene Valley, New York, in the Adirondack Mountains (where he had spent his honeymoon) was paramount. In fact, Bjork has observed that in the 1890s Keene Valley attracted him most. In one letter from 1895 to his wife, Alice, James confided in words reminiscent of Horace Bushnell to his wife, Mary, "Oh the sweetness of this place dear Alice—such a heavenly peace and happiness have flooded me since I have been here." There was more to say. "I have been happy, *happy, happy!*—with the imperishable beauty of this place, the place I know so well."²⁶

Keene Valley continued to generate heightened moments of bliss in nature. Perhaps the most memorable occurred in 1898 after James had climbed the loftiest peak in New York State, Mount Marcy. That evening, in camp at Panther Lodge, with lingering excitement and the presence of a clear and starry night, he wrote to Alice about what happened. "It seemed as if the Gods in all the nature-mythologies were holding an indescribable meeting in my breast with the moral Gods of the inner life." "It was one of the happiest lonesome nights of my existence," he told her, "and I understand now what a poet is." As Simon declared, in the Adirondacks James "felt an authenticity of being that eluded him elsewhere; here, he could celebrate himself as a rugged participant in the strenuous life. The smell of balsam, the golden afternoon light, the crisp air generated, he [James] said, 'a state of spiritual alertness.'"²⁷

With nature still very much on his mind, during the academic year 1902–1903 James put together a syllabus for a course on "The Philosophy of Nature" emphasizing radical empiricism and pluralism. But the course outline, also, rejected affirmations of the Absolute—upending typical confessions that came with deeply felt perceptions of the natural world. James had already—by 1895 at least—heartily endorsed his perception that "the worship of the God of nature" had "begun to loosen its hold upon the educated mind." He had ventured further, despite "its sounding blasphemous at first to certain ears," that "the initial step towards getting into healthy ultimate relations with the universe" entailed "the act of rebellion against the idea that such a God exists." In his Panther Lodge experience of 1898—what James had called his "regular Walpurgis Nacht," his pagan celebration—he had emphasized to his wife that the Gods of nature-myth and of morality had "nothing in common." The one, he told her, arose from memory, and the other from sensation, even as they whirled together. James could not "find a single word for all that significance" and had no idea "what it was significant of." He called it "a mere boulder of *impression.*" By the time he wrote the lectures that became *The Varieties of Religious Experience*, he was again and memorably identifying "two kinds of Gods." Pluralism and radical empiricism could not be wished away in an all-out affirmation of one God, one Absolute. James Sr. had been severely undercut by his philosopher son.²⁸

Whatever else it meant, James's Walpurgisnacht surely hinted of the mystical. So—with all James's furtherance of radical empiricism—it is a fair question to ask how close he came to mystical experience and/or how much he valued it. The latter is easier to address, especially through his *Varieties*, and in *Varieties* as well there is evidence of his own mystical brinkmanship. James's sixteenth and seventeenth lectures there addressed the theme with an abundance of evidence. The twinned lectures came toward the end of his twenty, and he announced to listeners/readers that the hour had arrived "when mysticism must be faced in good earnest." From all that he had done and said, there were "broken threads" that needed to be "wound up together." To clarify the subject—so often slippery and nebulous—he proposed four identifying marks. James considered an experience mystical if it was ineffable (defying spoken expression) and noetic (exhibiting "insight into depths of truth unplumbed by the discursive intellect"). The experience also had to be transient and unsustainable for long periods. Finally, it must be passive—that is, felt as coming *to* a person "as if his own will were in abeyance."[29]

Even with the emphasis on passivity, James did not hesitate to raise the question of the role of "intoxicants and anaesthetics" in advancing mystical states. Alcohol and nitrous oxide functioned as ready candidates, and James was not shy about rehearsing a previously published report on his own experiment with "nitrous oxide intoxication." "One conclusion" had remained with him as a truth "unshaken." "Our normal waking consciousness" was "but one special type of consciousness, whilst all about it, parted from it by the filmiest of screens, there lie potential forms of consciousness entirely different." Reflecting on these alternate states, James offered a surprising confession in the face of his strenuous advocacy of a philosophy of pluralism and radical empiricism. His own experiences (a declaration that he had been subject to mystical episodes) propelled him "towards a kind of insight" regarding what he called "reconciliation." Tellingly, it meant that "the opposites of the world, whose contradictoriness and conflict" imparted to us "all our difficulties and troubles" were, in the end, "melted into unity."[30]

Filled with a seemingly endless catalog of mystical reports (according to Robert Richardson, fifty-five of them cited or quoted), the lectures underscored the plural experiential emphasis that was in line with the rest of James's classic work. Still more, James's lectures incorporated the voices of both the overtly religious and the secular. Among the religious, it paid attention to Christians as well as to representatives of other world religions as they were available. Any account that James thought credible provided evidence to substantiate the alternate states that he saw as mystical. Meanwhile, his comments were often pithy and illuminating. "The deliciousness of some of these states seems to be beyond anything known in ordinary consciousness," he assessed. Still more, the Jamesian tour de force led to an important conclusion—more significant surely than his four identifying traits. Mysticism, James summarized, was *"on the whole pantheistic and optimistic, or at least the opposite of pessimistic."* It was also *"anti-naturalistic,"* and it harmonized *"best with twice-bornness* [conversion or being "born again"] *and so-called other-worldly states of mind."* James did not stop there though. He went on to add that "in characterizing mystic states as pantheistic, optimistic, etc.," he feared that he had "over-simplified the truth." Classic mystics were privileged cases, and a larger view evaporated the "supposed unanimity" he had earlier affirmed. Even traditional religious mysticism was "much less unanimous" than he had argued. In fact, mystical states could form "matrimonial alliances with material furnished by the most diverse philosophies and theologies." In the end, pluralism ruled in mystical terrain. We had no right "to invoke its prestige as distinctly in favor of any special belief, such as that in absolute idealism, or in the absolute monistic identity, or in the absolute goodness of the world."[31]

James hastened to add that the traditional states associated with religion were "only one half of mysticism." In contrast, mystical phenomena could be dismissed as delusional and linked to "insanity, paranoia," and the diabolical. This admission now provoked James's expedition into "that great subliminal or trans-marginal region of which science" was just "beginning to admit the existence." The region was what has come to be called the subconscious, and of it, James lamented, "so little" was "really known." Religious studies scholar Ann Taves has especially identified the parallelism between the mystical states James described and the psychology of the subconscious, and her insight stands. James, however, did not stop there. He brought his audiences/readers back into sunnier territory than that of insanity as he concluded his two lectures. Mystical states "absolutely" overthrew "the pretension of non-mystical states to be the sole and ultimate dictators of what we may believe." They were "excitements like the emotions of love or ambition, gifts to our spirit." If the mind ascended "to a more enveloping point of view" than that of the rationalist denier, then it ever remained "an open question whether mystical states" might "not possibly be . . . superior points of view." They could be "windows through which the mind looks out upon a more extensive and inclusive world."[32]

Just before he delivered the last of the Edinburgh lectures that became his *Varieties,* James wrote to one correspondent calling mystical experience (using the "m" word "in a very wide sense") the "fountain-head of all religion." Mystical experience, he insisted yet again, belonged "to a region deeper, and more vital and practical than that which the intellect inhabits." He did not soften his stance regarding its importance. Hovering between spirit and psychology, he explained, "I attach the mystical or religious consciousness to the possession of an extended subliminal self with a thin partition through which messages make irruption. We are thus made convincingly aware of the presence of a sphere of life larger and more powerful than our usual consciousness, with which the latter is nevertheless continuous." Nine years later and several weeks before he died, James in the same vein completed an essay on mystically inclined American philosopher and poet Benjamin Paul Blood (1832–1919). As James reflected on Blood—in a piece titled "A Pluralistic Mystic"—he declared that all the "tricks of logicizing originality, self-relation, absolute process, subjective contradiction" would "wither in the breath of the mystical fact." They would "swirl down the corridors before the besom [broom] of the everlasting Yea."[33]

Meanwhile, as nature swirled, whatever else mystical consciousness entailed for James, as a *religious* phenomenon, it generated delight, and its very prodigality signaled an invitation. Already in his second lecture in *Varieties*, James had called the religious state one in which self-assertion fell away and became "as nothing." The time for the soul's "tension" had ended, and "that of happy relaxation, of calm deep breathing, of an eternal present, with no discordant future to be anxious about" had "arrived." Fear had been "positively expunged and washed away." James asserted without hesitation that "this sort of happiness in the absolute and everlasting" was "what we find nowhere but in religion." He owned that "sacrifices and surrenders" were a necessary part of life, but "in the religious life" they were "positively espoused" so that "happiness" might increase. James's conclusion was unambiguous. *"Religion thus makes easy and felicitous what in any case is necessary."*[34]

If the pursuit of happiness animated James in the study of religion, it was likewise an important piece of his academic life as a whole. As his biographer Gay Wilson Allen noted, the aim of all James's "professional lecturing and writing was to promote more abundant health and pleasurable activity in his audience." Moreover, even though based in religion, James's fascination with mind cure and its cultural carriers in New Thought and Christian Science needs to be placed in the framework of his search for pleasure and delight. With his well-known "healthy-mindedness"—the subject of his fourth and fifth lectures in *Varieties*—James used happiness as the catchword for all he there explored. He began his fourth lecture with the direct question, "What is human life's chief concern?" and responded straightforwardly that "one of the answers" would be "happiness." "How to gain, how to keep, how to recover happiness, is in fact for most men at all times the secret motive of all they do, and of all they are willing to endure." It followed that most people regarded the happiness bestowed by a religious belief as "a proof of its truth." He went on in the lectures to elaborate on the different kinds of religious happiness. With a cue from Francis W. Newman's division between once-born and the twice-born people, James restated the idea in terms of the healthy-minded and the sick-minded. Here sick-mindedness described the belief that human life was so filled with misery that a supernatural world was needed to balance and uplift it. Although in the end James would view sick-mindedness as more complete because life tended to be a vale of tears, he was clearly fascinated by the once-born. The healthy-minded whistled down the wind, cheered optimistically, and found in the vale abundant sources of delight and happiness.[35]

James was ready to argue that the "systematic cultivation of healthy-mindedness" was "consonant with important currents in human nature." Christian liberalism had signaled a "victory" over "the old hell-fire theology." Evolutionary theory had laid the ground "for a new sort of religion of Nature." And the "idea of a universal evolution" supported "a doctrine of general meliorism and progress" fitting "the religious needs of the healthy-minded" exceedingly well. But "far more important and interesting," James thought, was the movement that had "recently poured over America" and seemed "to be gathering force every day." He called it the "Mind-cure movement" and also repeated its title as "New Thought." It was, James explained, "a deliberately optimistic scheme of life," and it possessed both "speculative" and "practical" sides. It had absorbed a series of cultural elements over "the last quarter of a century," so that it needed now to "be reckoned with as a genuine religious power." James found sources for the movement in the Christian gospels, in "Emersonianism or New England transcendentalism," in "Berkeleyan idealism," and in ideas of law, progress, and development that he attributed to "spiritism." He also looked to popular science for its optimistic evolutionary theory and even to Hinduism. James clearly had his finger on the cultural pulse as he pointed to roots and sources. From the perspective of the delight makers, we might say that the ghosts of Emerson, Bushnell, and Warren Felt Evans were all standing in the shadows, and so were those of Fourier and Davis.[36]

James attributed the widespread success of mind cure to its "practical fruits, and the extremely practical turn of character of the American people." Even though some of "the verbiage of a good deal of the mind-cure literature" was "so moonstruck with optimism and so vaguely expressed that an academically trained intellect finds it almost impossible to read it at all," it had its point. So the numbers it attracted needed to be studied "with respect." Nor was the respect only theoretical. James himself had been at least partially captivated by the movement—so much so that one year, on his son Henry's birthday, he gave the boy a copy of Ralph Waldo Trine's New Thought classic *In Tune with the Infinite*. Meanwhile, as he worked through his own attraction, James targeted the underside of human nature in its New Thought version. He cited mind-cure author Horace Fletcher with his newly minted word *"fearthought"* and a related criticism by New Thought people of the "misery-habit" and the "martyr-habit." For the committed, these were to be banished in the light of a "decidedly pantheistic" philosophy of the "spiritual" present in each person. New Thoughters saw themselves as "already one with the Divine without any miracle of grace, or abrupt creation of a new inner man."[37]

Pointing to Mary Baker Eddy's Christian Science as "the most radical branch of mind-cure in its dealings with evil" (James did not effectively distinguish it from New Thought), he reported that it viewed evil as "simply a *lie*." Still further, in a memorable turn of phrase that would prefigure the twentieth-century future, James connected mind-cure optimism to a theology of power based on the magnetic force of attraction. As I have already suggested, James had stated the "law" of attraction as it existed in New Thought, and the conclusion for him was clear. "One gets, by one's thinking, reinforcements from elsewhere for the realization of one's desires." "The great point in the conduct of life" was "to get the heavenly forces on one's side by opening one's own mind to their influx."[38]

At the same time, for James, the happiness bestowed by a religious belief afforded for people "a proof of its truth." Thus, feelings of happiness and delight became foundational for his pragmatism. "Such a belief ought to be true; therefore it is true—such, rightly or wrongly, is one of the 'immediate inferences' of the religious logic used by ordinary men." Nor, despite all James's tributes to the healthy-minded, was theirs the only path to bliss. The twice-born—those whom he had called the sick-minded—also had their ways to "rapturous sorts of happiness," and the "securest" of these lay through a pessimism more radical than James had yet explored. The new happiness arrived through the process called "redemption"—salvation by the "second birth" that granted a "deeper kind of conscious being" than the saved individual "could enjoy before." James had read Edwards carefully on the point, and he quoted him: "The conceptions which the saints have of the loveliness of God, and that kind of delight which they experience in it, are quite peculiar, and entirely different from anything which a natural man can possess, or of which he can form any proper notion." James went on to explain the bliss. "The most characteristic of all the elements of the conversion crisis," he declared, was "the ecstasy of happiness produced."[39]

By the time he published *A Pluralistic Universe* in 1909, James was using his model of manyness to cite twin paths to heaven's gate. The pursuit of happiness for both "evangelical Christianity" and "'mind-cure' religion or 'new thought'" opened onto "new ranges of life succeeding on our most despairing moments." Possibilities unknown to naturalism could "take our breath away." There existed "another kind of happiness and power, based on giving up our own will and letting something higher work for us." These seemed to "show a world wider than either physics or philistine ethics" could envision.[40] James, the secular and sophisticated Harvard professor, had affirmed a bliss consciousness pervasive in religion, and he was intent to argue its case and honor it.

Still more, the case he argued was at least implicitly aesthetic, and what stood out especially in the aestheticism was its emphasis on harmony. This despite the fact that, consciously, James had almost totally dismissed the theory of correspondence, beloved by his father and all Swedenborgians as well as by the other delight makers in this study thus far. As Perry stated categorically, James "could not sympathize" with the philosophy of "his father's contemporaries," since they "argued freely from analogy, took figures of speech literally, and produced a blend of poetry and science which was neither one nor the other." James himself was still more visceral in his war against rationalists and "anti-humanists" who insisted that "to be true, our thoughts must 'correspond.'" Not so, James argued. "The vulgar notion of correspondence here is that the thoughts must *copy* the reality." Yet it was "not self-evident that the sole business of our mind with realities should be to copy them."[41]

On the other hand, in an admiring critique of nineteenth-century German psychologist, philosopher, and physicist Gustav Theodor Fechner, James hailed the thinker's "great instrument" of "analogy" and found it "prodigious." In place of rationalistic arguments, Fechner raided the closet of correspondences that belonged to ordinary opinion. "The world is greater than my house, it must be a greater some one who built the world. My body moves by the influence of my feeling and will; the sun, moon, sea, and wind, being themselves more powerful, move by the influence of some more powerful feeling and will. I live now, and change from one day to another; I shall live hereafter, and change still more." Fechner could see difference, too, and obviously James was quick to approve. But his applause for Fechnerian analogy suggested that James's rejection of the theory of correspondence was tactical—a rhetorical strategy to distinguish himself from his father's world and from centuries of unexamined dogma. More than that, in his fascination with New Thought's law of attraction, James had actually come on board with a subcategory of the theory of correspondence. He admired the people who said that what you thought was what you got. Thus, with his weapon of language to battle rationalism and its "disdain for the particular, the personal, and the unwholesome," James championed "positive empirical evidence." There, analogies from a variety of sources, including religious experience, established, "when taken together, a decidedly *formidable* probability in favor of a general view of the world almost identical with Fechner's."[42]

Beyond Fechner and also New Thought, James's *Varieties* continued to argue for supernatural belief in terms of correspondence or analogy, now cast as "harmony." Characterizing religion in the "broadest and most general terms possible," he assessed that it consisted "of the belief that there is an unseen order, and that our supreme good" lay in "harmoniously adjusting ourselves thereto." When he explored saintliness, James discovered, amid other attributes, an emotional shift "towards loving and harmonious affections." And in part what gave his pragmatism a special power was that it might work as "a happy harmonizer of empiricist ways of thinking with the more religious demands of human beings." Existing unspoken beneath all of this, James's passion had orchestrated its own poetic logic. Within it, aesthetics lived and moved in an underground universe in which it had turned itself into an ethic of harmony. James may have rejected an inherited American moralism, as William Clebsch once argued, but the deeper ethic he embraced was turning the moral into the beautiful.[43]

We gain an important clue to the process from his youthful attraction to painting as a way of life—an attraction, Bjork has noted, that had already begun when James was around the age of ten. Although, as we recall, James walked away from art to embrace science, throughout his life the arts functioned as a continual source of delight. With his father's wide reading and acquaintance with literature and literary people, with his brother Henry a noted novelist, and with his sister, Alice, a diarist, we could say that the arts were a Jamesian family brand. For William James himself, as Bjork added, the walk away from a painter's life was not an outright abandonment of art for science but a "refocusing" of his "creative sight."[44]

More trenchantly, James's friend, the American author John Jay Chapman, came to the sometime conclusion that "James wanted to be a poet and artist, and that there lay in him, beneath the ocean of metaphysics, a lost Atlantis of fine arts." At times he thought James "really hated philosophy and all its works, and pursued them only as Hercules might spin or as a prince in a fairy tale sort seeds for an evil dragon." Meanwhile, another friend, Théodore Flournoy, James's Swiss psychology colleague, who wrote on spiritism and parapsychology, considered him an artist "in his extraordinarily vivid and delicate feeling for concrete realities, his penetrating vision in the realm of the particular." James read poetry actively throughout his life, and at the crucial time when Renouvier had inspired James's secular conversion experience, he also found solace in the poetry of Wordsworth. Perhaps summarizing the artist in his teacher best, James's student (and biographer) Perry wrote that he "retained the painter's sensibility, and something of the artist's detachment. He cultivated style in his scientific and philosophical writing, and was offended by its absence in others."[45]

James himself was decidedly conscious of the role of aesthetics in religion. His nineteenth lecture in *Varieties* called the "aesthetic motive" one of the unforgettable "buildings-out of religion." Contrasting the richness of traditional liturgical observance with the flatness of evangelical Protestantism, he was blunt. "To an imagination used to the perspectives of dignity and glory, the naked gospel scheme seems to offer an almshouse for a palace." More than that, steady immersion in James's essays—however philosophical their subject matter—yields a thick exposure to pictorial language. James spoke and wrote in metaphors, and he was not shy about tossing them to his audiences, whether learned or popular. In *A Pluralistic Universe*, for example, a lengthy exposition on intellectualism chastised "fixed" conceptual thought for its disconnect with the changing character of life. Concepts were "not *parts* of reality," James insisted, "but *suppositions* rather." His warning leapt from its page with metaphorical abandon. "You can no more dip up the substance of reality with them than you can dip up water with a net, however finely meshed."[46]

This sort of prose, constructed with an artist's eye and mind, appears throughout James's corpus—testimony to his creativity, yes, but also to its dense visual sensitivity, its painter's legacy. No reader of James's essays can get very far without encountering it and noticing its flavor and pungency. For all that, however, art was but one element of James's Platonic fusion. The good, the true, and the beautiful—the three founding fixtures of the Platonic philosophical world—functioned, for James, in combination. Despite his often-voiced ambivalence toward moralism, the fusion was nowhere clearer than in his verbal rebirthing of truth through the pragmatic theory. Truth was true because it was *good*. It was *"one species of good"* and not a separate category—*"the name of whatever proves itself to be good in the way of belief."* Truth put the pieces of people's worlds together and enabled them to move forward with a modicum of well-being. It remade life, one could say, *purposefully*. In this reading, value—the good—was primary. Moreover, value encompassed the aesthetic because of the presence of harmony linking the otherwise discontinuous parts of reality/life together. Indeed, professor of philosophy Gerald Myers thought that James "was prepared to assert" a relationship between ethics and aesthetics so "intimate" that the "morally ugly" would "almost always be aesthetically reprehensible." "Moral intuitions" were "not always easy to separate from aesthetic ones," and "moral and aesthetic premises in arguments" were "sometimes almost indistinguishable." To be sure, James's essay "The Moral Philosopher and the Moral Life"—an address from 1891 that he published in *The Will to Believe*—was his only exploration of theoretical ethics in print. But there he argued, not surprisingly, that value—the good—arose from individual interest. It was thus tied into the pragmatic matrix, which—one could argue—meant a harmonious linkage of parts and pieces so that ugliness (*pace* Myers) was dissipated and the beautiful abounded. In the Jamesian philosophical world, the Platonic triad proved impossible to disentangle.[47]

It needs to be added here that the good James sought—in all its truth and aesthetic power—existed not merely in present experience but also in a world on the other side of James's "thin veil." James was no Davis, with visitations from other worlds and planets. But he was obsessed, especially in his mature years, by accounts of spiritualist mediums—including the much-reported Leonora Piper—whose messages were now explored as so many psychic phenomena, using the received tools of science but also reinventing them. The Piper séances continued from 1885 through 1898, with James on a scientific but also intuitive trail to discover the spirit world from which she claimed to communicate. Far before that, though, from the early 1850s, James's sometime encounters with spiritualism captivated him. By the late 1860s as a medical student, and in the beginning of the next decade as a lecturer at Harvard College, he was so drawn to issues of mental pathology and spiritualism that he wrote several book reviews of works on these themes. When he visited England during the winter of 1882 and 1883, he became professionally linked to psychical research through friendships with members of the British Society for Psychical Research. Two years later, back in the United States, he threw himself into the founding of a sister organization, the American Society for Psychical Research.

Unfortunately for James, the American society self-destructed only two years later when scientific members of the organization balked, a situation that surely distressed James with his commitment to science *and* to something more. As Knapp's recent study has revealed, James's psychical research was intimately bound up with both his profession and his family, for James had met Piper in the context of the death of his year-old son Herman. The enticements of psychical research shaped James intellectually and enabled him to chisel out his core ideas. The will to believe, radical empiricism with its pluralistic readings of this world and any others, theories of the subconscious and its "mother sea," explorations of possible immortality—all found support through the psychical phenomena that so attracted him. For Knapp, the intellectual challenge of psychic phenomena moved James beyond easy divisions between natural and supernatural or normal and paranormal and set him, rather, on a path of reconciliation of opposites. It may be added that this "tertium-quid," or "third-thing," approach resonated strongly with James's own biographical experience.[48] It brought at least provisional resolution to the realities of his father's monism over against his own pluralism, his father's secure theological categories in contrast to his own leanings toward change, his father's universalism versus his own championship of the particular.

James had lived his life on the radical edge of religious commitment—thoroughly fascinated by those who had taken the plunge but ever, in some ways, holding back. He affirmed believers and cheered them on, writing voluminously to support their mental and spiritual worlds but never quite joining them completely. In that regard, Levinson has recounted the haunting detail that James "privately stopped by the church in Harvard Yard on his way to work every day." Spiritualism, whatever it represented, seemed to hold out hopes that one could begin to fathom what might be an "other side" and what might be there if it in fact existed. Not that James received any paternal corroboration for such ideas. The elder James displayed no sympathy for spiritualists; they were not useful, and so they could not be valuable. More than that, spiritualist phenomena came across for the father as decidedly banal, and he thought they could be dangerous for medical and moral reasons. Still, James Sr. did not disbelieve in the existence of spirits, and that fact could not have been lost on the son. The younger James, as Knapp has observed, came to a middle position in which he "strongly believed that Spiritualism ought to be investigated empirically," but—for all his advocacy of a science of spirit—"loathed an absolute reliance on scientific method." Its problem lay in its disregard for the worldview of spiritualists themselves.[49]

If the law of attraction was any arbiter, James's absorption in spiritualist phenomena told of a life lived in the middle. Despite his refusal to sign on to the theory of correspondence, he had moved easily and fluidly between Edwards and Emerson. He had unconditionally embraced the focus on experience that shaped both of them. At the same time, he had moved consciously away from an easy endorsement of the absolute that each of them upheld—whether as traditional Christian God or as Over-Soul. In fact, in *A Pluralistic Universe*, employing approaches he combined from psychology, psychical research, and religious experience, James thought that a superhuman consciousness might be either "polytheistically" or "monotheistically conceived of." Tilting toward the former, he found that the "only way to escape from the paradoxes and perplexities that a consistently thought-out monistic universe suffers from"—such as the existence of "evil," "universal determinism," and "the block-universe eternal and without a history"—was "to be frankly pluralistic." This meant assuming that "the superhuman consciousness, however vast" had "itself an external environment" and was as a consequence "finite."[50]

It was an astounding declaration in a culture that—for all its minor presence of polytheism from an elite openness to Hinduism and other possibilities—was still culturally embedded in Christianity and its Jewish roots. Within it, as Taves has written, the presence of psychology was persistent, with *Varieties* "the quintessential theoretical expression of the mediating tradition between psychology and religion." Still further, Taves targeted the concept of the "subconscious" as not only "a mediating term between science and religion, but also as a mediating term between divergent theological and metaphysical views." Use of the deliberately ambiguous "subconscious," she remarked, enabled James to "argue, as a scientist of religion" that, so far as it went, religious experience conveyed literal and objective truth.[51]

From another perspective, Bjork expanded the terms of the mediation. "The relational area between the fields," he stressed—"between art, natural science, medicine, aesthetics, psychology, and philosophy—became the great creative ground." In the postscript to his *Varieties*, James had identified himself with what he called "piecemeal supernaturalism"—a species of a "crasser" sort than the "refined supernaturalism" that was "universalistic." James had counted himself, despite his credentials, among the hoi polloi, the great unwashed of the ordinary world, and he embraced the location without quibbling. Writing in 1896 to Henry Rankin, a confirmed Christian correspondent, James rejected "historic Christianity" because it stood between him and "the imperishable strength and freshness of the original books." He had his own alternative calling: "I shall work out my destiny; and possibly as a mediator between scientific agnosticism and the religious view of the world (Christian or not) I may be more useful than if I were myself a positive Christian."[52]

Yet a stance of belief cannot be denied in James's evolving philosophical theology. Perry called James's position a "pluralistic pantheism," with God not an absolute being who experienced all things but the one who experienced the widest consciousness possible. The God James acknowledged was, as I have already remarked, finite. Yet for all the divine limits, this God could fuse with humans in a mystical state so that individual consciousness disappeared, leaving a co-consciousness shared between the divine and the human subject. James had not initially been comfortable with the term *pantheism*. With his concept of radical empiricism, however, he had a handle on the word, because radical empiricism banished dualism in favor of the facts of affection, which were neither subjective nor objective. So in James's version of pantheism, God became a being in the making, an Ultimate, but not an Absolute. The pluralistic consciousness enabled James to dispute the "absolute Mind of transcendental Idealism," with its "one integral Unit, one single World-mind." Instead—in what an Emersonian would consider a shocking suggestion—"there might be many minds behind the scenes as well as one."[53]

In his ongoing attempts to explain himself, James would straddle the polarities and opt for an ambiguous "pluralistic monism." The world was "neither a universe pure and simple nor a multiverse pure and simple." His "pragmatistic or melioristic type of theism," he thought, could be exactly what people needed in order to navigate "between the two extremes of crude naturalism on the one hand and transcendental absolutism on the other."[54] Nor by far was James the only delight maker to straddle polarities in favor of an ambiguous middle. Emerson had forged a path toward a new, nineteenth-century metaphysical consciousness. Even more, liberal Congregational minister Horace Bushnell had remained a beloved scion of the Hartford pulpit and denied the metaphysical leanings in his writings, but attracted the notice of Davis and other metaphysicians. Later, former Methodist minister Evans did something similar, reaching out to embrace esotericism yet continuing to pledge allegiance to Christianity, even in his role in mind cure.

The same could be said of Brisbane (with Fourier hovering behind him) and the spiritualist Davis. Brisbane, with Fourierist enthusiasm, had preached a gospel of social reform in economic terms that accepted the basics of nineteenth-century capitalism even as his communistic plans tilted it in socialist directions. He despised organized Christianity but learned to navigate its conventions carefully while he eased his way toward libertarian sexual reform in the shadow of the French Fourier. Davis, for his part, celebrated his visions, his conversations with spirits, and his trips to other planets, but also joined liberal and this-worldly causes for social reform—especially for the rights of women and a revolution in marriage law. A free-love advocate, he yet managed to tolerate the organized Christianity he hated, moving quite ironically to a theology that supported its views of an afterlife and the continuance of personal identity within it. With the realities of this evolving metaphysical culture behind him, James occupied a unique position as a scientist, then philosopher and psychologist, all as an elite professor at Harvard. More than that, his "tertium-quid" location placed him at a critical juncture for shepherding a traditional Christian past toward a growing mind-cure culture of positive thinking, which extended into the twentieth century and beyond.

Like some other pairings I have made, at first William James and Warren Felt Evans seem decidedly different from each other. Evans came from a rural home and modest financial means; James was born in the lap of luxury. Evans was a college dropout; James had all the advantages that wealth could produce for education abroad and at home. Evans shaped his devout religiosity in denominational terms, even as he stretched the envelope. James wanted nothing to do with denominations and lived his life as a searching agnostic. Evans was a country minister or ex-ministerial healer who shared his evolving metaphysics with others mainly through his books. James, as a teaching Harvard professor, forged a broad public avenue in new and evolving academic disciplines. Each, however, kept moving physically throughout his life, and the pilgrim qualities of their separate lives shaped their thought and helped give it flexibility. So each became preoccupied with the powers of mind, and each found ways to amplify those powers through their words and deeds. Especially, the convictions of both led them into mental territory beyond the conventions of their time, even as both saw the mind as a peerless tool to heal body and spirit. In short, each made his way into a metaphysical universe that would be strongly changed because of their interventions.

So, for example, the metaphysical fascination of both would set the stage for the late twentieth-century sayings of a channeled spirit entity called Seth. Then, too, with their homegrown process theology, the channeled teachings of Abraham would especially echo James in their announcement that divinity was in the making and continually expanding. It is not necessary, however, to turn to the late twentieth century and after to discover still further implications of Evans's and James's ideas. They were, after all, in many respects pronouncements of an everyday culture that they had replicated in a new theological key. Not that ordinary culture caused each of the two to think precisely as he did. That would surely be an overstatement. But in terms of the vague but helpful observation, ideas were in the air. Evans and James had run with them in their own intellectual and affectional worlds, and they had also learned from the culture around them and from the books they read. Perhaps because of the accidents of their biographies—their lives spent moving—they were free of a certain arrogance that often blinded "experts" who remained solidly fixed in one reality. So they had looked honestly at mind cure, even as they had looked at conversional and mystical states and perhaps came to experience them—true for Evans more than James. What this leaves out, though, is what was happening to mind cure as it experienced its own evolution into something other than it was at its start. As the nineteenth century waned and the twentieth century began, healing one's mind was already changing to become, of all things, curing one's personal finances—in a new message that became a metaphysical gospel of prosperity.

SECTION 5

Purses, Profits, and Futures Perfect

In 2013, Duke University's Kate Bowler published an important book. Evocatively called *Blessed*, the work's subtitle announced that it was *A History of the American Prosperity Gospel*. Bowler cited the gospel's many labels—for example, Word of Faith, Health and Wealth, Name It and Claim It. All of them signaled what became a widely known phenomenon among twentieth- and twenty-first-century American evangelicals, especially those Pentecostally inclined. Instead of the somewhat glib refrain "health and wealth and metaphysics," millions of Christian believers were cheering for "health and wealth and Jesus." As Bowler declared, the prosperity gospel constituted "a wildly popular Christian message of spiritual, physical, and financial mastery" that swept through "much of the American religious scene" and spread to churches globally as well.[1]

Bowler was surely aware of the larger story behind her historical narrative. Her introduction acknowledged "a transformation of popular religious imagination" that had "not yet ended." With faith, wealth, health, and victory as identifiable themes, she argued that the new gospel emphasized above all "demonstrable results." Still more, in a revealing first chapter, she wrote of its "core" message: "*Adherents, acting in accordance with divine principles, relied on their minds to transform thought and speech into heaven-sent blessings.*" Her book went on to identify "three distinct though intersecting streams," citing them as Pentecostalism, New Thought, and "an American gospel of pragmatism, individualism, and upward mobility."[2] We have been exploring some of the evidence for the last two among middle and late nineteenth-century Americans for whom metaphysical versions of an abundance theology flourished. All of this, though, leaves out the deep roots in an earlier time for what was happening for both evangelicals and metaphysicals. It leaves out, too, the story of how the prosperity gospel's emphasis on wealth was isolating one strand of what had been a multifaceted message. Whereas a Cotton Mather, or a Jonathan Edwards, or a Ralph Waldo Emerson could matter-of-factly understand material abundance as a sign of divine blessing (perhaps hardly think of it at all), they did so as part of an intricate web of meaning. They had committed their lives to a moral quest, an overarching theory of correspondence, a pursuit of beauty and delight, a love of nature, a devotionalism verging on the mystical, and a vitalism that permeated their way of being in the world. Now, however, new generations were targeting abundance with a single-minded passion that belied its previously complex history. The facet had become the fact, and the call of matter had grown hugely in importance.

For metaphysical believers, the abundance theology and practice grew stronger and louder. It flourished in ways that upstaged the evangelical version that Bowler tracked. Like a stream overflowing its banks, the metaphysical version of abundance found its way into new and astonishing corners of culture, becoming close friends with new arrivals and finding comfort among them. In what follows, I trace iconic examples of these new-old pursuits of desire and pleasure. Delight makers found new friends, true, and unexpected voices as well.

NINE

Minding Money and Market: Emma Curtis Hopkins and Elizabeth Towne

After years of male dominance and privilege, to enter the cultural world I explore now is to enter a territory inhabited and ruled largely by women. When women came to lead in metaphysics, Americans were already a prepared people. Women had been rising to new literary prominence by the middle of the nineteenth century, as an often-repeated anecdote from 1855 shows. Nathaniel Hawthorne had complained to his publisher about a "damned mob of scribbling women." These women were writing for other women in a rising urban middle class. Men were going off to business pursuits while their wives—freed from years of farm and industrial work as well as homespun industry—were presiding over fashionable households as part of a growing leisure class. But Hawthorne's women were novelists, and they plied a trade that, above all, reveled in romance. More to the point here, even as romance writers were scribbling, other women were achieving prominence as spiritualist mediums. Fragile and passive on their own, they became authoritative instruments claiming to be spoken through by spirits as mass spiritualism swept through the nation after 1848. A number of the mediums, too, began to take to public stages as trance speakers, bringing their listeners messages from the spirit world in commanding voices and demeanors. Ann Braude, in a now-classic work, has shown that it was only a matter of time before these mediums, newly empowered by spirit contact, began to speak in their own voices, moving into public leadership roles for reform causes, especially marriage and voting rights.[1] Significantly, in the same year that spiritualism began to catch fire, the first women's rights convention had been held in Seneca Falls, New York. Not two decades later, the devastating carnage of the Civil War laid waste to American home-and-family life. With huge numbers of their men killed or maimed, women perforce assumed new and greater roles.

With this prologue as background, the end-century, new-century women of my narrative here had set their sights on metaphysics. In general very much in sympathy with calls for social reform and female empowerment, they sought to change society one individual at a time. As we pursue their work and world, we witness the continuance of a slow shift from elitist theologizing (already apparent to an extent in earlier chapters) into a more user-friendly, hands-on version. Some, like Emma Curtis Hopkins, had surely read widely and integrated their sources into their new spiritual message. Others typically piggy-backed on the past or ignored it altogether to offer a present-time gospel featuring delight pre-packaged for easy consumption. Pragmatism and spirituality worked seamlessly together, so that delight makers could control their bodies, their destinies, and their environments. Out of the ruins of the war years, a new age of happiness was being born, and men, when they began to take part, usually did so as students or spirit visitants of women.

My story begins with Hopkins, born in 1849 in a farm community in Killingly, Connecticut. The oldest of nine, she had been raised as a Congregationalist and attended the local high school. Reportedly, several of her siblings died, and her father—a farmer and part-time realtor—lost a leg in the Civil War. The family apparently valued education, but Hopkins did more and taught herself, perhaps absorbing the classics in the world's most prominent religious traditions. The evidence suggests that she read voraciously, although in her writings the dazzling array of cited names and works points to her acquaintance with the publications of Warren Felt Evans and perhaps other secondary sources. Even though at least once Hopkins suggested a knowledge of Greek (like Evans), her work does hint broadly toward a superficial familiarity with the writers she named.[2]

Hopkins probably worked as a teacher for some time (she noted that role at least once in later writings), but the circumstances of her teaching are difficult to pin down.[3] Her domestic life is easier to track. She married George Irving Hopkins, a high-school English teacher, in 1874, and the couple had one child—John Carver Hopkins—who lived only until 1905, the victim probably of a flu epidemic. By then, though, John Carver had long been separated from his mother. The reasons were complex. Hopkins had displayed a growing feminism as she matured, and Gail Harley—who wrote the only academically credible book-length biography of Hopkins—called Margaret Fuller her lifelong role model. Meanwhile, Hopkins and her husband most probably experienced difficulties in their time together. By the 1880s, according to historian Beryl Satter, George Hopkins was in debt, and poverty stalked the household. Years after, Emma Hopkins in at least one letter also confessed her husband's abusiveness.[4] In October 1883, however, came the encounter that would change her life forever. She met Mary Baker Eddy when both she and Eddy were guests in the home of Mary F. Berry in Manchester, New Hampshire. Eddy spoke in an impromptu fashion on Christian Science healing, and shortly thereafter Hopkins apparently experienced a Christian Science healing from a breathing problem. By mid-December, she was making arrangements to join Eddy in Boston, even though she lacked the financial means. So began the consuming spiritual passion of her life, a passion that led to her departure from her son and the husband who eventually divorced her for "abandonment" in 1900.

Hopkins's "abandonment" began in earnest when, by the end of 1883, she enrolled in Eddy's class at the Massachusetts Metaphysical College, with an agreement to pay Eddy after she received her first fees as a Christian Science practitioner. Her certification as such came quickly (and, in fact, by January 1884, she had assisted in the healing of her husband as he suffered from a high fever, headache, and sore throat). The same year saw Hopkins resign from the Congregational Church and become a member of the First Church of Christ, Scientist, in Boston. Soon she was working without salary as editor of Eddy's *Journal of Christian Science*, and she seemed to be flourishing as a valued member of the Eddy organization. Success, though, was short. Under circumstances that are puzzling and defy clear explanation, Hopkins was fired as editor and ordered out of her (Christian Science) living quarters. Since Eddy herself hewed strictly to Christian and biblical sources, Hopkins's editorial breadth may have pushed the Christian Science founder too far. As a case in point, her 1885 piece "Teacher of Metaphysics" overflowed with mystical language, alluded to numerous world religious traditions, and—worse still—suggested that Hopkins was Eddy's peer, with a claim that like Eddy she knew God "face to face." On another front, much less theologically and more driven by politics, Hopkins's friendship with fellow student Mary Plunkett, who was seriously troubling Eddy, may have catalyzed the break.[5] Clear from this early period, though, were Hopkins's feminism, her theosophical universalism, her mystical theologizing, and her tolerance (unlike Christian Science) for widely diverse views.

After the rupture with Eddy (which Hopkins repeatedly tried to heal), she moved to Chicago, first working as editor of Andrew J. Swarts's *Mind Cure Journal* and then, with Plunkett in 1886, creating the Emma Curtis Hopkins College of Christian Science. A charismatic teacher, she attracted hundreds of students, among them so many of the future leaders of New Thought that she earned the title "Teacher of Teachers" and has been hailed by Harley as well as J. Gordon Melton as the "founder" of New Thought. She also traveled widely throughout the country—from San Francisco to Milwaukee, New York City, and Boston. Her students formed the Hopkins Metaphysical Association, which produced offshoots in a series of places. The association was so successful that by year's end in 1887, Hopkins groups numbered twenty-one and reached from Maine to California, in effect forming the first national New Thought organization.[6] Both Charles and Myrtle Fillmore, founders of the Unity School of Christianity, were Hopkins students. So was H. Emily Cady, author of *Lessons in Truth*, which functioned as Unity's definitive textbook and almost-Bible, and so, too, were Charles and Josephine Barton, publishers of the metaphysical *Life* magazine in Kansas City. Other students included Malinda Cramer, cofounder of Divine Science, and Kate Bingham, who taught Nona Brooks, also a cofounder of Divine Science. There were also poet and writer Ella Wheeler Wilcox; Annie Rix Militz, who founded the Homes of Truth on the West Coast; Ernest Holmes, who founded Religious Science; and many others. Significant here, the widely influential Helen Wilmans (1831–1907)—New Thought teacher, suffragist, and editor of the newsletter "Wilmans Express"—had begun her career as a Hopkins student. Wilmans left a strong imprint on Elizabeth Towne, New Thought's most active publisher, and likewise on William Walker Atkinson, author of more than a hundred books under various aliases (the work of both to be explored later).[7]

Hopkins's relationship with Plunkett proved ephemeral and ended in 1888, when Plunkett moved to New York to pursue her own rather flamboyant career as a Christian Science healer. Subsequently, she became involved in scandal, because—although already married—she entered a "spiritual marriage" with a man later allegedly exposed as a bigamist (with eight wives). Hopkins immediately severed any further association with Plunkett and so began her independent work with her college, which she now turned into a seminary. Reportedly, she hailed Christian Science as a "ministry" rather than "a business or profession," different from the practitioner model of Eddy's Christian Science.[8] Year after year, as she turned out graduates who became new ministers, she functioned as their bishop, ordaining those who had successfully completed their course of study. The Chicago work flourished for nine years from 1886 to 1895, but Hopkins herself—weary and discouraged by infighting at the seminary—relocated to New York City, where she remained until the end of her life in 1925. There she taught classes and did healing work, while she traveled, too, on the East Coast and to England and Italy.

Harley has pointed to the sharp disjuncture between the Hopkins of the Chicago era and the later Hopkins in New York City. The first Hopkins, she argued, followed Eddy's Christian Science theology, with its dismissal of matter into a realm of nonexistence. The second emphasized a mysticism that pointed to intense and continuing experience—as well as preoccupations similar to those of Warren Felt Evans, Theosophist Helena Blavatsky, and others of similar bent.[9] As I will show, however, even in the Chicago years, a new concern, not articulated by Eddy, found its way subtly but insistently into the Hopkins teaching. Now the healing of the body would become the prologue to very much else. In Hopkins's evolving language, the abolition of poverty and the cultivation of prosperity were surfacing on her theological agenda. If Hopkins was the "mother" or "founder" of New Thought, she was in fact creating its distinctive hallmark in a theology of abundance.[10]

Hopkins's publishing history was hardly orderly, with much of her early work appearing as pamphlets or as Bible lessons in the *Chicago Inter-Ocean* newspaper. *Class Lessons, 1888*—first issued in pamphlet form and available now only from devotional sources—began her Chicago writing career. At first glance, *Class Lessons* seems a replica of Eddy's Christian Science teaching. It was also thoroughly biblical overall, even though Hopkins invoked "hermetic philosophy, Chaldean inner laws, the Vedanta, Brahmin tenets and Pythagorean conclusions"—not to mention Ralph Waldo Emerson, Emanuel Swedenborg, and a wide array of others. As the text progressed, moreover, Hopkins began increasingly to refer to Asia and expand the list of problems the mind could obliterate. She declared to readers, for example, that "health and strength and perfect living are the desires of the heart. Desires are things sent before, signals thrown out, signs by the way of things that we have a right to." The subtle feminism and self-agency here were packaged carefully in a Christian Science envelope, but a new direction was already being charted. By the time Hopkins reached her fifth lesson, she had matter-of-factly inserted poverty into the list of maladies that the "scientific" mind could cure. "If you are in seeming poverty," she asserted, "deny poverty, and affirm your rightful and true supply." Denial of poverty and other maladies followed logically from Christian Science teaching because "Science" denied "the evidences of sense every time, and about everything."[11] Goodness, desire, and riches were forming an unorthodox trinity, though Hopkins stood firm with Christian Science theology, even as she began to undermine it with her casual inclusivity.

As she taught, Hopkins urged students to "declare the good of Spirituality" and then offered a veritable flood of examples that proceeded by way of denial. Prominent among them: "I do not believe in poverty or sorrow or sickness. I know that it is unscientific to be poor." She chastised the world's "wise teachers" who preached "that the sorrow and wrongs of the poor" existed "to teach the rich generosity and pity, and that the injustice, oppressions and exactions of the rich" were "to teach the poor humility, patience and long suffering." Rebuking conventional Christian teaching, she charged that "none of the talk about the loveliness of sorrow and the goodness of poverty" could warm "the limbs of the shivering," feed "the hungry," or loosen "the fangs of disease." As she summed up her lessons, she quoted (the unnamed) Job 22:25, "Thou shalt have plenty of silver."[12]

Given Hopkins's own struggle against poverty in the early years of her marriage, talk of abundance in her brand of Christian Science was not surprising. What is especially fascinating, though, is the kind of meticulous insistence she brought to the inclusion. Even in the speech she gave to her first graduating class in 1889, Hopkins reminded her students forcefully of concerns that moved beyond divine healing activity. Her graduates were "ministers of the gospel of The Good," following the work of Jesus in which "the poor were helped and fed." She counted her class among those who announced a "New Dispensation of the Holy Spirit," an order in which the poor might be "taught and befriended, women walk fearless and glad, and childhood be safe and free." Her Chicago Christian Scientists were among those who testified to "the omnipresence of God the Good" and denied "the presence or working power of any other Principle but the Good."[13]

In a formal lecture Hopkins gave during the Chicago years, the new strain in her teaching became yet more apparent. "How to Attain Your Good" started off with an Evans-style and theosophically inclined reference to the "fine etheric Substance pervading all the worlds of the universe," a "Cosmic Substance" that she also called "Mother," "Mother-Principle," and "God-Substance." The Motherhood of God already pointed the way to a vision of the divine being as a nurturer, like a mother feeding her child out of her own substance. In language that suggested her increasingly mystical evolution and her feminism (more on this later), Hopkins was pointing to the "Good-Substance." She went on to repeat, in mantra style, the affirmation that became increasingly identified with her: *"There is good for me, and I ought to have it."* What did the mantra intend for these aspiring students of Hopkins's Truth? After a series of more generic explanations, she found her way unmistakably to tangibility and profit. "You can make the connection between yourself and prosperity by saying that the good that is for you is love." When "love" was equated with God and "Good," as in the case of Jesus, blessing would pour down because of universal love.[14] With the New Thought Statement of Being affirming Good at its core, abundance on earth followed without controversy.

For all of her evolving Christian Science theology and her multiculturalism, however, Hopkins lived and taught as a devoted student of the Bible. Thus her lessons inserted expansive commitments into a traditional envelope. And the lessons were prolific. Hopkins began to write Bible lessons for her seminarians in 1891 and then, from 1893 to 1898, they appeared in the *Chicago Inter-Ocean* as a weekly column. Here as elsewhere, as Harley observed, prosperity was so integral to Hopkins's work that she did not "single it out" but rather interwove "the concepts of abundance and supply with her theology." One could say, in fact, that poverty had its pains and so required healing. Even a cursory glance at the first six series of lessons (from 1891 and 1892) points to just how seamlessly connected to the rest of her message the abundance theology was. In August of 1891, for example, Hopkins urged that if you believed in "the bounty of God" and kept close, you could dip "into his full waters of supply and by a metaphysical process catch the Prosperous Mind." Two weeks later she called God "Supreme giving" and "Supreme bounty"; if you praised him thus, you could "hand out and hand out and hand out, for back of you" was "infinite supply." The following week she pressed readers to give up their hard work and avoid the mistake of "Ben Franklin" who ran the belief in effort "into a saving up and hoarding state of mind that nearly warped the happiness out of the lot of nearly all the farmers' children of New England."[15]

So it went, as week after week her students and *Inter-Ocean* readers were, probably unawares, learning new lessons from scripture, lessons that seriously undercut the traditional Christian purchase on pain and suffering. Meanwhile, Hopkins continued steadfastly to support her emerging gospel in other writing from the 1890s. For example, her *Spiritual Laws in a Natural World* (1894) offered a metaphysical "treatment" against poverty as one of a series of interventions mostly dedicated to health of body. "The Almighty is my defense and I have plenty of silver," believers were taught to affirm. There was only one power—the "Good"—Hopkins declared, and so the poor had "plenty." The "miracle of abundant supply" was "ever being wrought," and Hopkins volunteered that she (with other New Thoughters) was "ready and glad to assist in dispensing the bread of life" to all "ready to listen."[16]

Hopkins's *Scientific Christian Mental Practice* offered a similar message. "*There is Good for me and I ought to have it,*" she wrote in her familiar catchphrase, as she repeated that the "first name of God" was "Good." Still more, as Hopkins followed the logic of her faith, she confided that the real "treatment" for prosperity was pleasure. "If a beggar child, looking . . . into a beautiful garden, is filled with pleasure," she explained, "forgetting his misery . . . he has given his own character a new vigor of goodness and has increased the strength of his life in some metaphysical relation of mind to life. He has unwittingly given himself a treatment for prosperity." Building on her mystical and metaphysical redefinitions to the earthly problem of lack, Hopkins called prosperity "the acknowledgment, either consciously or unconsciously, of the presence of God."[17]

Here was none of the flashiness that would come to mark a later New Thought pursuit of the prosperous, nor any of the mechanical quality that accompanied then-emerging practices of denial and affirmation. Hopkins had followed the Eddy pattern—first with heartfelt denials and then with a feeling-toned series of "universal affirmations," beginning with the ever-present "my Good is my God" and, as was her way, moving along increasingly mystical paths. Scientists should know neither poverty nor grief, she insisted. Instead, they should "talk for prosperity" and affirm *I believe in prosperity and success.* To be sure, Hopkins could serve up a negative example as well, sharing an anecdote about a pastor who "was very much pleased that he got his expenses paid by praying for them and had about $14.00 left over." Her somewhat disdainful moral to the story? "As all the wealth of the earth was offered him you can see that he was not especially honoring God by having such a little bit at his disposal."[18]

By the time Hopkins created *High Mysticism*—a process that occupied her over a series of years (Harley wrote of its production in stages from 1908 to 1915)—her increasing mysticism did not stifle the message of abundance, now repeated in another key. Citing "John the Revelator" in twelve visionary explorations that reworked material from a dizzying arsenal of traditions, Hopkins elevated the theology of supply to an important place in the mix. The "downward vision" she so much deplored was branded by "evil, matter, lack, pain, decay." The good news, instead, was that there was "no evil," "no matter with its laws," "no lack, no absence, no deprivation," "no power to hurt," and "neither sin nor sickness nor death." Even more to the point, Hopkins acclaimed the biblical King David. "'Prosper thou me!' commanded King David. 'Prosperity is of thee.' 'The silver and gold are thine.' 'Riches and honor come of thee.'"[19]

It was, veritably, a new age of the spirit that Hopkins was preaching, but what might be missed in her insistent gospel of prosperity is the now-familiar theory of correspondence that grounded it. Hopkins did not spend her pages on analogs and similes, and—as much as she admired Emerson—she did not follow him in consistently exploring nature and its spirit correlates. But any scrutiny of mind cure, now transformed into purse cure, would not be complete without acknowledging how changed the Hopkins version was. Instead of Emersonian words as signs of natural facts and natural facts as signs of spiritual ones, Hopkins had raised the mind to a commanding role. Now it no longer reflected the way things were. Rather, it *created* the way they were and made the conditions most desired tangibly present on earth. In other words, in Hopkins's telling, the law of correspondence had slid into a law of attraction with the human mind as the grand attracter. It was, truly, a *master* mind, as William Walker Atkinson, Napoleon Hill, and later New Thought teachers would insist. In this regard, her conclusions carried forward a message that would last into the twenty-first century. For all her biblical immersion, Hopkins had begun the subversive process that drew the contents of a higher self into an agenda that worked in the service of the ego.

Not that some of that had not been going on years before. Emerson, for one, had after all placed words in the mouth of his visionary poet at the end of *Nature*, implying that humans were now dormant giants with yet unused powers and possibilities. And under the banner of the law of attraction, Charles Fourier, Albert Brisbane, and Andrew Jackson Davis had declared that like not only replicated like but could also shape it. So they had already acknowledged the power of mind to incarnate one's fondest desires. Now, however, Hopkins was pursuing the principle with new awareness. She was intent on sharing her good news with Bible readers, even as she was undercutting a major part of the biblical message. In the Hopkins version of scriptural teaching, the law of attraction was drawing biblical readers with a vengeance. Hopkins's *Biblical Interpretations*, for example, explained to students that "as the magnetized bar draws steel filings, so does your determination to be cheerful draw cheerful conditions." In the same lesson, Hopkins added that "the Scriptures are a unit in telling that you attract more and more of things and people and powers like your thoughts. . . . If you keep your mind on prosperity, you will have that idea enrich and revive as a tree planted by living waters, or, as Jesus Christ said, more 'shall be given to him.'"[20]

When people were lucky, it was because they had "a mind that attracts luck." Accordingly, the Hopkins version of Christian Science taught, plainly and simply, "how to attract good." By contrast, only the bad idea "that got embedded into mind ages ago that man must labor in a material fashion" had "now made it almost impossible for the laboring classes to rest a moment without suffering for it." This "curse or lie concerning labor" had resulted in the "poor man's taxes" being "out of all proportion to the capitalist's taxes." Hopkins continued to hammer the point home, telling readers that there was "a law by which roses bloom according to their climate. Ideas in your home make a climate in which things and affairs spring up." What was the result? "A family always denying that they can afford this and that will fix their business affairs, so that it will some time be very apparent that they cannot have anything."[21]

Turned inside out, Hopkins's censures of poverty and lack become the pronouncements of a delight maker, an identity that her uninhibited prose in *High Mysticism* bore out. Still more, in a vitalism as far-reaching as anything seen so far, she announced in *Scientific Christian Mental Practice* that "your nature is God. Your possessions are power, wisdom, and substance." Like a reinvented René Descartes, she parsed philosophical words to reach a conclusion profoundly different from his dualism. "If I am, what must I be? Must I not be God in substance, nature, and office? And if the I AM of me is God, then that of me which is not God is not the I AM of me." Citing the "philosophers of antiquity," one Bible lesson used them as a springboard to land Hopkins in the mystical territory in which she loved to walk. A substance present in the universe filled "all things." It was "too fine" for the senses to perceive and could only be "touched" by the "understanding of the mind." But more—the "understanding of truth" was "the only touch fine enough to mold the substance," which was "truth itself." The result was not exactly intuitive. "Out of it" was "made happiness, peace, delight."[22] The substance was Truth and Truth was God: the pursuit of happiness had become an overarching mystical and vitalistic project.

Down from the heights, Hopkins could counsel her students that "to take the idea that there is nothing to hate is to enjoy life better." "Joy," she wrote, "gives mysterious potency to the hands visible, and to the hands invisible." So memorable was her gospel of joy that after Hopkins died, one of her students with a moneyed husband bought a large farm in Connecticut to carry on the Hopkins work—and called it "Joy Farm." It is important to note, too, that among the joyous while Hopkins was still alive, her New Thought followers were mostly white, middle class, and female. The underlying message of female power must have clearly resonated with them, as Hopkins's work as teacher of New Thought teachers attests. Already, while still writing for Eddy's *Journal of Christian Science* and supporting Eddy's role as God's messenger, she could announce triumphantly that "Woman's hour has struck." "The motherhood of God beats in the bosom of time, with waking energy, today."[23]

In fact, as Harley has shown, more than the often-cited Father-Mother God of Eddy, Hopkins emphasized a Mother God in a new way. Echoing the twelfth-century Joachim of Fiore's announcement of a coming New Age (or, very much later, the New Age anticipated by Swedenborg via Evans and even Madame Blavatsky), Hopkins looked forward to a coming millennium. She proclaimed the soon-to-be third age of the Holy Ghost—a Holy Ghost clearly feminine, closely aligned with the Hebrew Bible's Shekinah and with the New Testament's Holy Spirit. The future, in short, would be feminine, and women of Hopkins's era (as well as the men who followed her) could draw energy from it to vitalize current missions, plans, and projects.[24]

No surprise, then, that Hopkins—much more than Eddy—supported social reform efforts and saw them in terms of the mystical stratosphere in which she lived. To underline the point, Hopkins's Chicago years saw the publication of her pamphlet *The Ministry of the Holy Mother* in which the divine Mother was linked with the Spirit and the overall divine ministry. Her mystical statement also contained her declaration about service and her conviction that any true perception of the divine needed to include the feminine. Meanwhile, her ordination addresses from these years insistently called on the Mother God in the Holy Spirit.[25]

Hopkins, all the while, continued to use the language of Christian Science theology dutifully, keeping Eddy's Father-Mother God somehow still in charge. That said, however, more than in the New Thought of a later generation, when men took over the reins of leadership, the divine feminine provided the force for the earlier Hopkins-style abundance theology. Hopkins's move, though, was to blend her feminism with the prosperity principle, holding both in a mystical ever-ever land but somehow managing to bring both down to earth.

On the topic of money, as Satter has remarked, one way to explain the rapid rise of Christian Science in general lay in showing what healthy profits came from its practice in teaching, writing, and healing. Satter has noted that, when it came to New Thought, the price structure for classes varied widely. In the midst of this fluidity, for all her airiness, Hopkins's fee schedule was on the "high end." Her individual and group instruction cost fifty dollars per course. Nor did teaching exist alone as a source of income. There were also the perennial "treatments," and the treatments cost money for their receivers. Publications, too, could generate income, and then there was also the practice of lending out lesson transcripts to be copied—a rental arrangement—which brought in yet more dollars. As Satter has shown, one Hopkins student, F. S. Van Eps, taught a series of Christian Science lessons for only twenty-five dollars (promoting it as a combination package of enlightenment and Minnesota summertime vacation). Still more inexpensive was the well-known Ursula Newell Gestefeld's charge—simply a dollar per lesson or eight dollars for a nine-lesson term.[26]

Hopkins, clearly, was determined to be profitable. She did it, however, synthesizing for the most part the ideas of others—Emerson, Swedenborg,

Evans, and Eddy, to cite the most obvious (not to mention a slew of occult and theosophical sources). Yet it must be added that she reworked the material she borrowed as so much clay. Her mix brought together a mysticizing vitalism with its energy derived from a future feminine age *and* a tangible present reward system with its abundance theology. If there was a new prosperity gospel in late nineteenth-century America, Hopkins, more that many others, was its creator. In a process of change, though, the students she inspired went on to unyoke her teaching from its biblical base—this, ever so gradually. More and more, they used the Hopkins theology to refuel their own searches for financial success and the realization of desire in practical ways for the here and now. Mind had become a resource to corral, and its containment bred prosperity, contentment, and the pursuit of happiness. A salient case in point was Elizabeth Towne, enthusiastic follower of Hopkins's early student, Helen Wilmans.

Towne was born in Portland, Oregon, in 1865 as Elizabeth Lois Jones, one of only two major figures in this study not from the East Coast.[27] Even so, she eventually made her way east and died in Holyoke, Massachusetts, at the venerable age of ninety-five. Her childhood was apparently bumpy—Jones lost her mother when she was somewhere between nine and eleven, and she dropped out of school at fourteen to marry before her next birthday. Her nineteen-year-old husband was Joseph Holt Struble, and (perhaps unsurprisingly) the two at first lived with his parents. About two and a half years later, they and their year-old baby moved with the help of Elizabeth's father, a prominent lumber manufacturer who gave them $10,000 in money and property. Holt Struble himself worked unspectacularly as a clerk, and he felt he had "no money to throw away," as he and his spouse grew further apart but also added another child to their family. Meanwhile, Elizabeth—a member of the Mt. Tabor Methodist Episcopal Church—had heard a talk by the locally regarded Kate Williams, who claimed she had been cured of blindness by (Hopkins-style) "Christian Science." Williams was a woman of note, married to US Senator George H. Williams, and able to open their home to assist others in healing. Whether or not this was Elizabeth Struble's first introduction to New Thought, the session with Williams left its high-water mark. Not so for Holt Struble. In her somewhat autobiographical *Experiences in Self-Healing*, the later Towne reported that her first husband "held mental science and healers in utter contempt."[28] Finally, after at least sixteen years of marriage, she left him, taking her two children, Catherine and Chester, with her.

She did not sit idle after the separation. Already engaged in healing work, from 1898 she conceived the idea of publishing a New Thought paper supported with modest help from her father. So began her hugely successful

Nautilus Magazine, which would run from 1893 until 1953. By 1910, it would become the leading New Thought journal in the country, and by the 1920s, it would boast an average monthly circulation of 85,000. Not long after she launched it, the up-and-coming editor entertained a proposal of marriage from William E. Towne, a New Thought publisher in Holyoke, Massachusetts. Her separation from Holt Struble had become a divorce, and she accepted Towne's overture, relocating herself and her journal to Holyoke in 1900. There she continued to work as its editor with her obliging husband as associate. Eventually her son, Chester, also took on a managerial role. In Holyoke, Towne added to her run with success by beginning her own publishing company, writing numerous short works for it, and also putting into print a series of prominent New Thought authors, including the flamboyant Atkinson (see the next chapter).[29]

But this was not all. In addition to her New Thought life as publisher and author, Towne in her mature years became involved in feminist politics. She had already, in 1924, served as president of the International New Thought Alliance. Then, in 1926, she was elected Alderman-at-Large in Holyoke for the following year. She had been a strong voice in the woman's suffrage movement, which had led in 1920 to the Nineteenth Amendment and national voting rights for women. Now Towne would serve as the first female alderman in the mill town that was Holyoke, besting six male opponents by a solid majority. Apparently, voters were unfamiliar with the full range of her views, some of which they might have considered shocking or scandalous. Back in Oregon, she had, after all, been accused of sending obscene materials through the mail because of a published article endorsing extramarital sex for traveling businessmen. Holyoke voters probably did know, though, that she entertained unusual guests at her home—such as, according to Tzivia Gover, "Chinese diplomats, Indian religious leaders, and at least one newly released prisoner." She also smoked cigarettes (something no proper "lady" would do at the time), and she practiced meditation. Undeterred by her eccentricities and their likely effect on her political ambitions, Towne ran for mayor of Holyoke in 1928—a disappointment for Towne, however, as her bid ended in failure. According to Gover, it had been the most expensive and ambitious effort that Holyoke had witnessed in a local election, and Towne ran a contentious campaign in the process. With a record numbers of voters turning out, Towne's opponent, former Mayor John F. Cronin, beat her by a landslide. After that, the Depression in effect ended her political career.[30] Not so for her New Thought endeavors: Towne continued her publishing work and only gave up the *Nautilus* when she was in her eighties.

Towne's many short works—often actually pamphlets—were marked by her unmistakable style. They were written as more or less direct-address pieces, almost certainly aimed at women—with frequent pepperings of "dearie" and "sweetheart" in the midst of the prose. For someone who had dropped out of school at an early age, they displayed an impressive range of references and sometime quotations from prominent authors, many of them literary. It is not clear how much of the material Towne gleaned from secondary sources and how much came from her own primary-source reading, but the results suggest a writer who had wide-ranging acquaintance with numerous print sources. Themes and ideas—always simply and even repetitiously stated—made it clear that she was absorbing ideas and currents in the mental air at the time and refashioning them to her needs. She brought to her work the familiar theology of New Thought, even as she intertwined it with a kind of homespun rhetoric, with Emersonian allusions, and with continuing references to well-known Hopkins alumnae Helen Wilmans and Ella Wheeler Wilcox. She also occasionally published some of Walt Whitman's poetry. Not stopping there, she had clearly invested in Theosophy, spiritualism, and especially reincarnation beliefs. Still more, her vitalism—a continuing theme for the subjects of this study—led her to embrace the era's physical-culture movement exemplified by Benarr McFadden and others. Towne enthusiastically recommended fresh air, deep breathing, exercise, and vegetarian eating—all of a piece with New Thought, so far as she was concerned. She had even, by 1915, published a small book or pamphlet titled *Just How to Cook Meals without Meat*. Not to be dismissed, Towne's feminist posture continued apace, her interest in politics keen.

Add to this Towne's seemingly interminable focus on desire as the linchpin of her belief system. Providing an important background against which to understand Towne's thematic focus, Satter has argued for the centrality of desire among New Thought authors, a theme that shared center stage with concepts of mind, matter, and spirit. Especially in terms of sexuality and wealth, Satter shows, ideas about desire or its suppression preoccupied New Thought authors of the era.[31] What distinguished Towne in the debate, however, was the expansive and catch-all quality of her affirmation of desire. Not limited in expression, for Towne it colored all aspects of each individual's life situation. Moreover, whereas Emma Curtis Hopkins had immersed her prosperity ethic in a sea of biblical permission and had suffused it with mystical affirmation, Towne declared for an abundance theology that was much more direct. She had been influenced strongly by Helen Wilmans, the Hopkins student who later founded Mental Science and had gone on to carve her own highly successful New Thought organization in Florida.

And so, like Wilmans, Towne was less tethered to the Bible and to strictly Christian moorings.

As the unraveling and re-raveling process of change worked through Wilmans and then Towne, the satisfaction of desire provided *the* important path to living life purposefully. Wilmans had taught that matter was real and alive, included in a vast overarching Mind and part of a cosmos fused together by the law of attraction. In sync with the theory of evolution and the cosmic ambition of a Mind ever reaching for more, desire propelled everything. In short, it made the law of attraction work, and so inner desire—far from being suppressed—needed to be blessed and nurtured.[32] Towne took the Wilmans teachings to heart, blending them into her own eclectic mix and using them intensively in her writings. As I will show, the results prefigured the middlebrow process theology taught in our own time by figures such as Esther Hicks and her teachings of Abraham.

In shifting the rhetoric of New Thought from concepts of mind increasingly toward those of desire, Towne, like Wilmans, was moving into the territory of emotion. This was, of course, the same territory that had so clearly drawn William James, whose pragmatism in the end had been a siren call for desire. In fact, Towne's mirroring of a key James metaphor suggests an enthusiastic regard for his ideas, however she may have encountered them. James's "mother sea" into which consciousness ultimately merged was not far from Towne's "one great ocean" from which, she told readers, "personal wisdom and will" were "tossed," and to which they returned. Writing of her growing awareness of the oceanic current in the significantly titled *Joy Philosophy* (1903), she declared that we are "*conscious* only of that small portion of our intelligence represented by our bodies." There was, however, a "great sea of intelligence" that was "infinitely the larger part of us," and it acted "*sub-consciously*, or super-consciously." Later she told readers she now knew there were "UNSEEN *tides of spiritual force which work in and through us*, and which rise and fall, rise and fall, as do the tides of ocean." More apparently than James, though, Towne was interested in being in charge. Experience had shown her that the "more completely" she worked "*with* these spiritual tides of energy *the better control*" she had of them. Still, being a ready receiver was paramount. The mature Towne, in 1921, understood the "sea of thought" in James style as a "great sub-surface reservoir" through which came "telepathic messages from all corners of earth and heaven."[33]

Within Towne's cosmic sea, the Christian Bible held an honored but not ultimate place. Towne had "no blind faith" in it as "a special dispensation of a capricious God." Rather, it functioned as "the inspired utterance of many wise and devoted men," whose teachings she had "*proved to be invaluable.*"

She could have gotten the same information from "the One Source," she added, but she did not, and so she was grateful to the biblical authors. Still, for all the New Thought distance, she acknowledged that her Bible was "well thumbed" and "copiously underlined and annotated." Yet Towne's God was hardly personal in the biblical sense. In a conceptual frame that at first glance seemed to intersect negatively with her connection between divinity and desire, she could affirm that God's nature was "mind." God had "thought or spoke the universe into being," and was "still thinking this universe into greater being; thinking in and through you and me, and through all the lower forms of life as well." A second glance suggests, though, the expansive nature of a divinity whose calling card for Towne increasingly was desire. More provocative still, the expanding deity was imperfect. God was a process being, and evolution displayed "the bones of creatures God thought out and then abandoned for higher forms." The "fossil creatures" were "still preserved" so that humans might "see the mistakes God made before he succeeded in thinking out a satisfactory pattern of a man." Whatever the false starts, the nature of God and the universe proclaimed love. It was "the foundation principle of the world," and "the happiness of every one" was "in the long run absolutely certain."[34]

Thus, Towne's New Thought landed her squarely in the camp of emotion (as had the "mother sea"). In and through her own passional nature and that of others, she felt that she knew how joyous living worked and what it meant for prosperity. She had been clearly fascinated by the body's solar plexus—the radiating complex of nerves and ganglia in the pit of the stomach that is part of the sympathetic nervous system. Her pamphlet on using it became a popular part of her stock in trade (by 1915, she was advertising that it had "circulated by the hundreds of thousands"), and there she explored the powerful role of emotion in a decidedly physical way. "The Solar Plexus," she advised, was "the seat of emotion." "By proper exercise of the whole breathing apparatus you may gain such control of the Solar Plexus that anger, resentment, resistance, blues, discouragement and fear will be as foreign to you as are the awkward motions you used to make when you were first learning to walk or eat." More reflectively, she thought that conventional reason was an enemy. It boxed people in as "an endless labyrinth out of which no man emerged unaided by a higher wisdom than itself." It was "the original Chinese puzzle, forever unsolved." Instead, within the subconscious resided "the emotions or sympathies" that decided "our pitch." This "subconscious sea" swirled with the passions—so that the "secret of real enjoyment" lay in "perfect control of the emotional nature." There were "heights and depths and breadths of fun and joy which can never be touched except by the poised, controlled person," she told readers.[35]

Emotion, in the Towne universe, signaled a veritable New Thought quaternity in which desire initiated the working of the law of attraction, then satiated desire brought delight and happiness, and a continuing vitalism ran through it all. So the way to be a delight maker was to live in accord with the mighty engine of correspondence expressed by and in the law of attraction. In her early *Practical Methods for Self Development* (1904; "Dedicated to You, Sweet Heart"), Towne explained to her "dearie" reader that the "trouble with us" was that we wanted "the unseen powers, the Law of Attraction, or God, to work *our* way." Greater forces had been operating, though. Towne was convinced of the reincarnation of souls in new bodies because "desire in some previous state of existence" led them to new parents who acted as a "magnet." And so "disembodied souls" found, "by the working of the omnipresent Law of Attraction, their own particular place in the universe." In teachings that were on occasion confused, she circled connections between attraction and desire, sometimes equating the two and likewise calling desire "the will of the sub-self." Towne could also, at times, substitute "Love" for "Attraction." At one point, too, she demoted the law of attraction to only one of the principles by which the deity created. But in seeming contradiction, she hailed desire as "the primal force of Attraction inherent in every atom and in every organization of atoms through all creation," calling desire and gravitation "identical." With a "great Architect Dreamer of space and eternity," the way to be part of the "great dream" was "to make a magnet of one's self" that drew "every desirable thing."[36]

In point of fact, the many magnets of Towne's writings became ethical markers that guided New Thoughters on life's way. "Good Will to the unjust as well as to the just" functioned as "the magnetic power" enabling readers to attract what they desired. Opposite that, "all kinds of envy and criticism and fault-finding and ugly feeling DE-MAGNETIZE you so that you cannot attract the things you desire." If humans got exactly what they magnetically attracted, then the pursuit of happiness and delight could proceed apace *if* the good prevailed in what they sought and desired. Even more, within the (ethical) good that Towne taught, prosperity held a cardinal place. Every person must learn to make money, she urged. "It is the Law of your being which says 'I DESIRE it.' And Desire is the Law." "Oh, you dear dunce," she continued, "money is the MEASURE of the 'good' you can do mankind." Without it, you could do "nothing—but hire yourself out to some other man for bread and duds." Not that Towne promoted the life of a spendthrift.

Indeed, she instructed her followers on shrewd thinking and discipline on the path to success. She explained to readers that by putting more consideration into her own expenditures—"sleeping" on possible purchases before jumping in—she triggered "the beginning of opulence." "After a time," she divulged, "I found my desires growing stronger and more definite and less numerous. And at the same time I began to discover more money in my purse."[37]

Nor did a New Thoughter's abundance endanger others. "You can have all the money or air you can possibly use," Towne declared, "and you can have it without impoverishing anybody else"—a belief that the teachings of Abraham would later also express. Why did your wealth not impoverish others? Because money circulated. "The more pocket books it fills, and the fuller it fills them, the better for the whole world." Towne was on a roll. "Money flows, like blood; and as blood carries all needful and useful things to every atom in the body, so money carries all needful and useful things to every human atom." More practically, she confided to readers that "the spirit" always went shopping with her. "Nearly always the direct mental routes are open, so I have lots of fun shopping, never waste a lot of time at it, and I nearly always get just what I want, many times at bargain prices, though I almost never look at bargain ads in the papers."[38]

In Towne's brand of prosperity, a person had to work at it. She wrote memorably of the disciplined, step-by-step process she employed to heal her "emaciated and leaky purse." At first she had offered her healing work for free but then began to accept "free-will offerings." They simply did not add up to what she needed and wanted. The problem was that clients gave her money, but, she wrote, "the innate God of me did not want *gifts*. It wanted its RIGHTS." So Towne initiated her "'demonstration' over poverty" by charging for her services. She "set to work with good will to understand the law of wealth and *live* it," intending to make herself "a magnet which should draw gold and silver and greenbacks, instead of steel filings." She "meant to be so *right* with the kingdom of Good that good money would not only follow" but "*catch up*."[39]

Affirmations were key for a mindset that attracted money, and so was meditation—you meditated on what you desired, say, an easy $5,000—to jumpstart the enterprise. "The practice of prosperity"—a chapter title in her *Fifteen Lessons in New Thought*—meant that even marriage, whatever it was as a "sacred institution," needed to be a profitable material arrangement. "It should never be less on the material side than a good straight business arrangement between a man and a woman whereby a woman is given her living and some money which is her own, to spend exactly as she pleases."

Beyond prenuptial agreements to keep a woman's money coming, the ethic of flow and circulation did not deter a counter-ethic. A person made money "first by saving it." Dollars, Towne advised, "had attractive power as well as people," so that "to him who hath saved dollars more dollars shall flow." Meanwhile, the pursuit of money opened out into the pursuit of happiness, pointing the path toward the larger landscape. In a bit of hypothetical advice for children, Towne urged them to "*command your desires as well as your money*, and you will increase your happiness fourfold."[40]

Prosperity in the end merged into desire as one incarnation of the larger reality. Towne's books and pamphlets were aflood with the message—*right* desire always and ever led to delight and happiness as the law of attraction worked its work. Desire was "the voice of God," and simultaneously, contra an ethic of subservience to divine will, desire was "the unreasoning and unerring cry of the ego—every ego, from the original atom to the Christ man"—for "what was a necessity in the process of unfoldment." Over and over again, Towne reiterated the good news of desire and where it led. That was the homeland of delight and happiness. But you needed to live by the law of attraction to "reap happiness," she counseled readers. And it was all very clear for Towne in the way she read the Christian New Testament. "Jesus of Nazareth," she affirmed, had "announced the height of 'moral law,' the only immutable law of the Universe, the Law or Love, or Attraction, or Desire. 'Do unto others as ye would—*desire*—they should do unto you.'" The pragmatic result was inevitable. Experience taught, in Jamesian fashion, "that happiness, the one end and aim of creation, " could not "be attained except by living " in accord with "the Law of Love or Desire." Lessons could be learned from the young. "The key to heaven and happiness" was "held by a *little child*," who was "*natural*" and followed "with joy and trust his God-given inclinations." To the child, work was "*play*," and Towne began to emulate what she had begun to "see." "Since that time I have never *labored*. I *play* at all I do."[41]

Continuing in an autobiographical vein in other writings, Towne claimed that when she was "about twenty-seven," she "came into the experience called then [Methodist/Wesleyan] sanctification, now named cosmic consciousness." Here Towne was building on Richard Maurice Bucke's classic work *Cosmic Consciousness* (1901), which she cited explicitly, and she went on to rehearse the "truths" revealed to him by the "new consciousness." Among them were, "The foundation principle of the world is what we call love," and "The happiness of every one is in the long run absolutely certain." "Remember," she later exhorted, "that your chief end is to enjoy good in every day and hour of work"—a far cry from traditional Christian catechisms that instructed believers to know, love, and serve God in this world and be happy with him in the next. For Towne the heaven of the next life had migrated. "HEAVEN IS ANY PLACE WHERE PEOPLE LIVE CLOSE TOGETHER AND ENJOY EACH OTHER," she told readers.[42]

So there was God/desire/attraction, and there were humans, all together in the project of happiness. On the human side, the God that was desire and attraction could be discovered especially in vitalism. Living in a world in which, as Tzivia Gover remarked, the telegraph, telephone, and electricity had been introduced, "a philosophy that celebrated the forces of unseen streams of mental energy flourished." In that context, Towne's job description of thought rendered it as "vitalizing, energizing." Folding in the gospel of the physical-culture movement, she declared that "to a fully vitalized body, every act" was "joy." If your work was "drudgery," you needed to "stop short, call your thought home," and "take three or four very slow, full breaths of fresh air." "The supply of vital energy is really and truly UNLIMITED for every one of you," she taught her readers. "All you have to do is to inhale it with lungs and brain." A "sluggish mind" caused old age, but, contradicting that news, the mind itself was "never sluggish." It existed, Towne testified, as "the same free ethereal energy it was when you were young, and when the universe itself was but a baby." The problem was actually the body, which was "growing too dense, too heavy, to be readily used by mind." Enter, as ever, physical culture to upend the situation and ensure the success of the vitalistic project. For Towne, ever the pragmatist in her teaching, New Thoughters needed to work on both body and spirit to let the vital energy flow. Food was crucial. She suspected that "we really take the soul, the highest of its 'vibrations,' the least dense part of itself, the 'energy,' from what we eat." "No dirty sediment in happy cells," she declared.[43]

Attention to practical specifics, however, did not obscure the larger cosmology out of which Towne drew her message. All things—past, present, and future—were part of what she called the "Uncreate." Its nature was revealing. "The Uncreate," Towne affirmed, was "a limitless, pulsing sea of Energy, with currents and cross-currents, waves and ripples and depths of stillness." Even the stillness, though, moved incessantly. It was, in fact, "motion so intense, vibration so high, that ear nor eye nor nose nor tongue nor finger-tips" could "register it." From the "pulsing sea of energy" that was the "Uncreate," came "Create"—"as much of this energy" as had "become conscious of itself." "The friction of energy upon energy" produced "consciousness." The world as we knew it was a vitalistic masterwork, and within it humanity existed as "the most powerful concentrator of energy." With vibration as "Life" and "motion," she had bowed to the doctrine of correspondence yet again, and now she could reiterate that "the spiritual tides of the One-Power" flowed *"in all veins."* "We feel them, and respond," she wrote, "but we as yet only dimly understand."[44]

The vitalism could include the *"real* wisdom" that lurked "in the electric atmosphere . . . breathed by children and fools" and a testimony to life as a series of "fermentations"—like multiple risings of dough before baking bread. Especially, in Towne's fascination with physical culture, the vitalistic project recruited the solar plexus. It was "the point where *life is born*—where the Uncreate becomes Create." It inhaled "life and heat" and exhaled "magnetism." The physicality of all of this still led to the realm of spirit. Invoking "telephone, telegraph, and wireless" to make her point, Towne continued her extended analogy to declare her surety that "aspiration and inspiration" were "messages sent over the heaven-wire."[45] Like Cotton Mather's Nishmath-Chajim of old, an earthy physicality pervaded Towne's domain of spirit, but very much more than for Mather, it led to the home of ego, breath, and physical control. Towne had cast her vision into the heavens, but she always and steadily returned to a practical world in which she was calling the shots. Not waiting on a cosmic God or his biblical revelation, Towne had evaded the Christian strictures that had shaped Hopkins. Her project was more subversive and, as we will see in the case of Atkinson, it was opening the floodgates not to a Jamesian sea but to a resounding endorsement of secular profit and mastery in each situation, with the human will ever in control. Desire was surely governing destiny, but destiny was signaling less in erotic directions and, as in the American version of Fourierism, more in economic ones. New Thought was becoming truly new—a project now to enhance and empower the ego-self as the place where spirit had come home to rest—and to act.

TEN

Arcanes of Prosperity:
The Multiverses of William Walker Atkinson

Enter William Walker Atkinson—born in Baltimore in 1862 to a solidly middle-class family, whose grandfather and father were successful grocers and also involved with the city's school board, fire department, and politics. The younger Atkinson worked in his father's grocery store and attended public schools in the city. Later—at twenty-one and after a love that went unrequited—he experienced a breakdown, left the city, and, from a hotel in Philadelphia, sent suicide notes.[1] Little else is known about these years nor about his family's religious leanings or lack thereof. But not long after the breakdown, Atkinson became interested in esotericism and began to read works in Theosophy, until, by 1885, he was corresponding with early Theosophical Society leaders Thomas Moore Johnson and Elliott B. Page. Nearly a decade afterward, in 1903 in Chicago, he would become a member of the American Theosophical Society.

Long before, Atkinson had married Margaret Foster Black in 1889, experienced the death of their infant son, Joseph, in 1891, and was parenting a second son, William Courtney Atkinson, from 1894. The same year that his second son was born, Atkinson—who had studied law in Pennsylvania—passed the state bar. He began to practice successfully, mostly handling wills and estates. When he moved to a different town in Pennsylvania to join a law firm, however, he became involved in an imbroglio in which he was denied the transfer of his credentials. Unable to work for at least six months and waiting for the requisite period to retake the bar exam, he suffered a nervous breakdown and physical illness of an unspecified nature. Atkinson, already interested in Theosophy (even if not yet a member of the society), now read his way into New Thought under its then-prevailing name, Mental Science. It worked as a miracle drug. New Thought not only saved him personally but also gave him a compelling vocation as he began to turn out a prodigious list of close to one hundred books and seven hundred articles, publishing many under a series of pseudonyms in a staggering array of titles.

First, though, Atkinson moved to Chicago and perhaps traveled in the orbit of Emma Curtis Hopkins and, more arguably, of Helen Wilmans. He was drawn, with clearer evidence, to Prentice Mulford, based elsewhere, who was spreading news of a law of attraction as well as his own mantra, repeated in a book title: *Thoughts are Things* (1889). While claims regarding whose student Atkinson was or was not remain difficult to sustain, it could be said that, in an informal sense, the New Thought ideas of all three had surely mentored him. Indeed, Atkinson's first book had been dedicated to the memory of Mulford, and that in effusive terms. Meanwhile, by 1900 an energetic Atkinson was working as associate editor of a New Thought journal favoring hypnosis and called *Suggestion*, and he was also publishing his Mulford-influenced first book, significantly titled *Thought-Force in Business and Everyday Life*. Around the same time, he met the ambitious Sydney Flower, well-known as a New Thought publisher and entrepreneur. By the end of 1901, he had become editor of Flower's popular periodical *New Thought*, a post he held until 1905, when Flower's increasingly dubious schemes and criminal notoriety for illegal use of the mails led Atkinson to distance himself. Before that he had used the basement of Flower's Psychic Research Company for his own Psychic Club as well as his so-called Atkinson School of Mental Science.

Moving on from the Flower magazine, from 1907 Atkinson continued to churn out book after book, even as many of his numerous periodical articles began to appear under pseudonyms. Soon he apparently spun off these "authors," who began producing books of their own. There was the French Theron Q. Dumont, who was steeped in New Thought, will training, memory enhancement, magnetism, and salesmanship for white-collar workers. Meanwhile, the colorful Yogi Ramacharaka blended Atkinson's theosophical brand of Hinduism and occultism with physical-culture ideas on breathing and exercise to produce books apparently more successful than Atkinson's under his own birth name. Likewise bearing Indian names, Swami Bhakta Vishita and Swami Panchadasi appeared, both of whom curiously did not write on Hinduism. Other authorial entities included Magus Incognito, Three Initiates, and possibly Theodore Sheldon. There was also a series of four (later six) short "Arcane" books attributed to Atkinson, and, to top that, Philip Deslippe claims that he published under a dozen or more pseudonyms. Reasons for the aliases include, perhaps, Atkinson's own oversupply of titles that could make his market sag as well as freedom from previous contractual arrangements with publishers who stipulated continued publication with them. In the case of a few works that concerned themes like sexual regeneration, Atkinson was no doubt displaying caution about legal censorship for misuse of the mails[2]—something that had been a huge problem for Wilmans and had wrecked her publishing empire.

As if the catalog of works that he authored alone were not enough, Atkinson apparently co-wrote a series of books with Edward Beals on personal power, and he collaborated with the occultist Lauren William de Laurence for a least one work. He came to publish many of his writings and those of his stable of pseudonymous authors through the Yogi Publication Society and the Advanced Thought Publishing Company—which also produced *Advanced Thought*, a periodical that Atkinson edited from 1916 to 1919. Its debut issue told all—"A Journal of The New Thought, Constructive Occultism, Practical Psychology, Metaphysical Healing, Yogi Philosophy, Etc." Still more, he had become part of Elizabeth Towne's authorial list, most probably introduced to her by Sydney Flower. She not only published some of Atkinson's titles but also advertised and promoted his writing in the *Nautilus*. In the midst of all of this, he had managed to be admitted to the Illinois bar in 1903—although it is difficult to determine if he ever actually practiced law there. Later, in 1916, he would become an honorary president of the International New Thought Alliance. Except for a short time in Detroit, when he wrote the books with Beals, he seems to have devoted his mature years to alternating sojourns in Chicago and Los Angeles (he began during the Flower scandal), living in both cities and remaining finally on the West Coast. By this time, as Deslippe has remarked, Atkinson had left his mark on leaders whose names could provide "a table of contents in an encyclopedia of New Thought."[3] Finally, after the years of seemingly frenzied activity, Atkinson's health declined during the 1920s until he suffered a stroke in late 1931. He died outside Los Angeles in Pasadena almost a year later. Ironically—given the themes of success and prosperity in his many writings—Atkinson's family had to borrow money to provide for his funeral and burial.

What can be made of Atkinson and his career? For all his works and successes, he left no organization behind him, no society to carry on his name or ideas. So it is to his writing that we need to turn for clues. In that regard, even a cursory examination of his titles points to his habit of composition through mental templates on which he drew to repeat the themes and arguments that marked his brand. Sequences on the law of attraction, for example, are remarkably similar to each other from work to work. Yet they are not verbatim productions of previous material. Rather, they are statements of conviction from a person who felt rescued and wanted to spread the how-to news to others. Especially noteworthy, they are typically filled with exercises for the student to practice. Here was a no-nonsense approach to discipline that, Atkinson claimed, could transform the weak into the strong, the wimpy into the magnetic, and the spineless into almost superhuman examples of vital energy and success. Here, in sum, was the impeccable witness to the work of the law of attraction. All this and more, wrapped winningly in pragmatic, plain-prose writing.

Meanwhile, through the well-nigh compulsive writing that Atkinson published over the years, he functioned as a kind of reverse prism. He took refracted light from multiple sources and transformed them into one synthetic metaphysic unflaggingly oriented toward happiness and achievement. In so doing, he pointed the way for a cadre of later authors well outside the evangelical prosperity gospel. Those who came after him in turn offered their own increasingly secular message of fault-free good fortune. Among them were Napoleon Hill (*Think and Grow Rich*, 1937), Norman Vincent Peale (*The Power of Positive Thinking*, 1952), Rhonda Byrne (*The Secret*, 2006), and—to be noticed in chapter 11—trance channel Esther Hicks and the Abraham books. Atkinson's rainbow of sources strongly featured the New Thought teachings that had saved him at the time of his second nervous breakdown. It included, as much, Russian immigrant Helena Blavatsky's Theosophy, which had drawn him even before he turned to New Thought. In the mix, too, were popular renditions of psychology and science, most frequently drawn from theosophical sources as well as from the writings of William James, either through his many books of essays for lay audiences or through secondary sources. Hindu ideas also filtered steadily into his work, supported especially by his encounter and friendship in Los Angeles with one Baba Bharati, a Krishna devotee from Bengal. As important, Atkinson relentlessly espoused physical culture with views similar to those of Towne.

As the white light of the Atkinson prism became a beacon to draw students, his concept of the Master Mind characterized it above all. Atkinson had conveniently attributed the construct to his "French" alias, Theron Q. Dumont, but it was everywhere apparent in his writing. Napoleon Hill would later run with the Master Mind (as well as the Mulford-via-Atkinson news that thoughts were things), but it was Atkinson himself who had coined the Master phrase as well as all that it entailed. Here was the self-reliance of Ralph Waldo Emerson writ large, and here, too, were the occult powers that Theosophical Society cofounder Blavatsky promoted when she wrested herself from the passivity of spiritualist trance mediums. If one achieved Master-Mind status, everything else came as its spendthrift afterpiece. Salesmanship and business success were guaranteed, and they rested on the qualities that the Master Mind encompassed. Now the law of attraction reigned with no competition at all, even as Atkinson students worked to bolster their personal magnetism, their personal purchase on vitalism and energy, and their effective linkage of what Atkinson called Desire-Force and Will-Force. The Atkinson ideas had known a long and lingering history—from Emerson to Charles Fourier and Albert Brisbane, to James, and to Emma Curtis Hopkins and Elizabeth Towne. But it was Atkinson who fashioned the legacy into an imposing canon for control of individual destiny with a discipline that could not fail to succeed.

Atkinson's aliases gathered his separate rhetorics into thematic divisions more or less, stressing one or several emphases above others. But the aliases also had habits of straying into the territory of different aliases when and if they could. Hence the entire corpus of the Atkinson gospel reveals how the Master Mind that was Atkinson himself put it all together. If we begin with titles that he marketed under his own name, it is easy to see that, amid all the practicality, his vision of a grand cosmology of Mind worked at its foundation. He identified it in terms of the law of correspondence and frequently understood it through the familiar Jamesian trope of an ocean or sea. A *"great Ocean of Cosmic Mind"* filled *"all Space,"* Atkinson explained to readers, and words like "Gravitation" and "The Ether" pointed to "Something so far above human experience that the Mind of Man may grasp only its lowest shadings." To make yet more explicit Atkinson's reliance on the theory of correspondence, he appropriated its age-old formula. *"'As Above so Below—as Below so Above,'* says the Old Occult Maxim, and it may be found to operate on every plane." Following the theory, with uppercase insistence, he could declare for nature's "DYNAMIC MENTAL PRINCIPLE—A MIND-POWER—PERVADING ALL SPACE—IMMANENT IN ALL THINGS."[4]

For all the cosmic affirmations, however, the bottom line existed not in the far-flung stars but in the business emporium in which Atkinson, exceedingly savvy himself, assumed that his readers lived and breathed. "For the first time in the history of the world," he wrote enthusiastically, "Mind-Power is being employed for furthering commercial aims and ends." Still more, "mental treatments for wealth and success" were "commonly known and advertised," and "instructions in the use of suggestion for commercial purposes" were readily available. With his very first book, *Thought-Force in Business and Everyday Life* (1900), Atkinson had put success into action. Published in both Chicago and London by 1901, Atkinson engineered its reprint editions in Chicago and New York in 1903, and again in 1911 and 1913. By 1910, it was even available in Russian. According to Atkinson's own reckoning, the Sydney Flower edition of 1903 in New York was the eighteenth.[5]

Here, in what was essentially a full-blown success manual, Atkinson minced no words. He boldly reformulated mesmeric teaching (that invisible tides permeated all space) and spiritualist doctrine (that matter was actually a refined form of spirit), telling readers that matter was "but a grosser form of mind; mind but a finer form of matter." So thought waves traveled, and—no matter how far—they retained their connection with the sender and exerted an "influence" over self and others. In this context, he called himself "justified in regarding success as meaning the attaining of financial reward," and he hailed the "powers of Mental Control" that brought "not only Success, but also its material manifestation—Money." How did the student obtain it? Atkinson gave his ready and already familiar answer: "Success in life" depended "largely upon our ability to interest, attract, influence and control our fellow men."[6]

When a person wanted money, Atkinson explained in his larger work *Mind Power*, what was "really" wanted was "the things that money buys." So, he instructed, just as plants needed sustenance from earth and sun to thrive, it was "proper, desirable and praiseworthy" for humans to "insist upon" the "sustenance of life" they needed. Shifted to the mental realm, Atkinson's vision of a correspondence between plants and humans pointed to the spin-off law of attraction. Just as "Prentice Mulford (and Swedenborg before him)" had taught that "Thoughts are THINGS," so the New Thought person understood that, with "Right Thought," ideals of "Health, Happiness, and Prosperity" might be "realized" by the "proper exercise" of "mental powers." Indeed, as early as 1902, Atkinson had devoted an entire chapter in his book *The Law of the New Thought* to the law of attraction. Before that, in his first book, he had called it the "Adductive Quality of Thought." Now he confessed that the "law" (recall his lawyerly background) had "puzzled" him for "a long time," but at this point he apparently felt he had a handle on it. Once a person grasped "the idea of the Oneness of All," recognition would come regarding "why one part of the whole will affect another part of the whole, be that other part a person or a thing." Atkinson spoke for a seeming "great law of Nature whereby an atom attracts to itself that which is needed for its development," and he extrapolated from it his conviction that the force that brought such results manifested itself in "Desire." So attraction and desire could work seamlessly together, generating good or ill for each individual.[7]

Atkinson titled one chapter in his book *Thought Vibration* "The Attractive Power—Desire Force." Here he offered an expansive cosmology—a secular theology, if you will—predicated on the earlier magnetic and spiritualist version of Andrew Jackson Davis but now entwined with the affirmative, affective message of New Thought. And there was more good news for believers. Perhaps inspired by his orientalism and what he knew of South Asian notions of the "play" (Sanskrit *lila*) of the gods, he proclaimed a gospel of delight. "The things we see around us are the playthings of the Kindergarten of God," he explained. "If you don't see just what you want, ask for it," and "play, play, play, to your heart's content." The God principle was surely the source of all supply in the high theology of New Thought, but—with South Asia, life was all really a game, a play, a drama for the fun of it, like the play of a child who was drawn into a game for the sake of the game itself. If thoughts were real things, you were supposed to have fun with them in a desire-based universe—an admonition that, as we will see, the later "Abraham" would echo repeatedly.[8]

In yet another book, *Dynamic Thought*, Atkinson explained the connection between attraction and desire still further, surveying what he called "Radiant Energy" (meaning light, heat, electricity, and magnetism) and arguing that they "arose from the Motion of the Particles of Substance." Although science was "hazy" in explaining, Atkinson knew more, declaring without trepidation that the law of attraction was responsible. It was "the greatest Law in Nature," and—like other metaphysicians explored in this study—he found it demonstrated yet again in "Gravitation," "the Riddle of the Universe." Atkinson, though, could begin to solve the riddle. As he kept repeating, "Attraction" was "a form of 'Desire' or even 'Love.'" Desire hovered seemingly everywhere that attraction pulled. And always, desire was intertwined with material abundance. So in a repeated refrain, Atkinson's *Secret of Success* devoted a chapter to the law of attraction, a "great law" in "Nature" with workings of correspondence to track its operations. They were "uniform and constant," and we might "take the phenomena of one plane and thereby study the phenomena of another plane, for the same rule applie[d] in each case." That being so, one could know flatly that "the Law of Attraction" functioned as "an important part in the Secret of Success." Atkinson's advice? "Make yourself an atom of Living Desire," and the law of attraction would do the rest.[9]

Unpacking the secret of success still more, Atkinson proclaimed the power of a "magnetic" personality, the need to cultivate one through discipline, and its use for control of others and achievement of desire. He aimed to celebrate a "marriage of Occultism and Science," as he said in one book, and he called mesmerism a key example of how that could work—once laughed at and derided by science but later baptized and blessed as hypnotism. So magnetism in business, sales, and what have you had been embraced as part of a modern agenda and had now become an eminent aid to success. Atkinson would run cheerfully with science-based magnetism, but he also reinforced magnetic phenomena as parts of an older, occult world, steeped in the mysterious powers that drew all things. Desire functioned in tandem with these powers, causing the radiation of "the finer and more subtle mental and vital forces," which flowed "in all directions like the magnetic waves from the magnet."[10]

In a chapter in *Mind-Power* that he called "Personal Magnetism," Atkinson offered a foray into "occult history" to tout the virtues of the lodestone or "natural magnet," which, he wrote, "was known in China, India, and Persia thousands of years ago." Transposed to the early twentieth-century business world, it became *"the action of Mind-Power in the direction of powerfully influencing the imagination, desire, or will of another."* In short, it became an important piece of ammunition in the arsenal of success. (Atkinson ignored the conceptual problem of the positives and negatives needed for magnets to work.) Closely connected to the magnet for him was the role of a person's eye, "one of the most potent and effective instruments of suggestion." Taking on the near-legendary mesmeric gaze to help the would-be-successful, he offered targeted exercises in "Eye-Expression," assuring readers they would develop "the fascination of the eye." Accordingly, he instructed reader-students in the "Magnetic Gaze," or—better—the "Dynamic Gaze." So it went, as he worked away, guaranteeing a path to prosperity and success, ever making it clear that prosperity was the natural inheritance of humankind and the direction of one's thoughts was the way to attain it.[11]

Ratcheting up his claims, in one book that called magnetism a form of "Fascination" or "the manifestation of Mental Influence" when two people came together, he offered a calibrated method for "successful agents and salesmen" to use in "reaching their customers." The agent formed a thought about how much the other person desired the goods being hawked and then sent out "Thought-Waves that 'You desire my goods—you want them very much—you have an irresistible longing for them.'" Even more controlling, the agent could go further: "You will do as I say—will do as I say—you will yield to me fully and completely." Thought and projection would do the work and accomplish the result. Atkinson was certain.[12]

Meanwhile, as he traveled through the territory of attraction, desire, and its magnetic incarnation, Atkinson was also exploring the further reaches of nature. But the nature to which he subscribed was not a sense-based environmental landscape. Rather, it was an abstract cosmological construct that expressed the reality out of which law arose and functioned. With his legal background, Atkinson's enthusiasm for this second kind of nature made conceptual sense. But less logically connected, his grasp of law and *the* laws led not to courtroom-style details but to the murky domain between matter and spirit, to the in-between that Cotton Mather had long ago styled the Nishmath-Chajim, and to its vital force infusing the world. By the early twentieth century, it was an occult in-between, to be sure, but lawyer Atkinson had no qualms dwelling there. So—departing from scientific takes on "Force"—he saw all of it as "Vital-Mental Force." It was "an action of Mind upon Substance," and it caused "Motion." More elaborately, it was "Mind-Power"—namely, "that phase of mind" that was "aroused by desire-will" and that acted, preceding "Reason in evolution." As "something far more elemental and basic than intellect," it was "more nearly akin to the elemental life forces" personified "under the name of 'Nature.'"[13]

"Mind-Power" worked like electricity (Atkinson was happy to move in with scientists here); it was "vibratory," and it possessed "radio-activity, or radiant energy." Meanwhile, the brain—in quasi-Jamesian fashion—could be regarded as "in the nature of a 'transformer' of the Universal Mind-Power, or possibly as a 'converter' of the force into mentation." Atkinson declared that science itself held to a theory of etheric waves that "once set into motion" traveled until they contacted "matter capable of taking up their vibrations." If that were so, Mind-Power was "higher even than the finest ethereal substance," and it pervaded the ether. It followed that "vibrational activity set up in your mind, my mind, or the minds of thousands, pass[es] on [its] vibrations to the great ocean of Mind-Power, and produce[s] 'waves' or 'currents' of energy, which travel on until they reach the mental apparatus of other individuals." The news was that humans—as Atkinson's magnetic declarations had shown—were all connected in one grand web of influence, a moving, vibrating, vitalistic reality in which they all lived, like it or not. Atkinson himself, one could say, felt the "spirit"—confessing that he had "tried to infuse" what he wrote "with the strong, vital energy" that he felt "surging" through his being. For him, it bore witness, in the words of former Harvard president Charles W. Eliot (which Atkinson quoted in one of his books), to "the biological conception of a Vital Force."[14]

That vital force, however, had left the occult world to reside in early twentieth-century American business, re-branded in yet another way as a new psychology. In the small book he wrote for Towne, *The Psychology of Salesmanship*, for example, he argued that in order to succeed, "proper psychological principles" must be employed. Where did this lead? To the "imperative that the salesman should know something of the Mind of Man." Atkinson obliged by dissecting the mental states of both seller and buyer and resting his case on New Thought "right" vibrations as well as popular psychology. After a successful deal, the seller should keep a "balance" and not act toward the customer as "the recipient of alms." With thoughts of having done the customer "a good turn," the buyer would "catch these subtle vibrations." To encourage the success mentality of the seller, Atkinson readily quoted James on "an entire psychology of volition."[15]

In *Thought Vibration*, also with ample citations from James, Atkinson had already been entertaining the "new Psychology" with enthusiasm. It told people that they were "masters of their emotions and feelings," he affirmed, "instead of being their slaves." It told them, too, that "brain-cells may be developed that will manifest along desirable lines," while old and unpleasant "brain-cells" could be "placed on the retired list, and allowed to atrophy." Self-mastery, to be sure, was what Blavatsky had posited as the bedrock of Theosophy—the principle of control that had transformed her from passive spiritualist medium to active occult manipulator. But Atkinson's combinative focus, different from Blavatsky's version—linked success, magnetism, desire, vitalism, psychology, will-force, and occult control. It was perhaps never better expressed than in the works of Theron Q. Dumont, the Atkinson alias under which he published at least nine books. In what was apparently the first of these, *The Art and Science of Personal Magnetism* (1913), Dumont posed as a French teacher who had been instructing students in Paris for eighteen years. Subtitled *The Secrets of Mental Fascination*, the book trod intrepidly into an older occultism with a strong vitalistic component, even as it hailed the recent productions of scientists.[16]

"Personal magnetism," for Dumont, had a physical phase and was related to "nerve-force," with a description that was telling. "Nerve-force" was "that strange, mysterious form of energy, which controls all physical movements, and yet, at the same time, appears to be something higher than physical itself." Standard works in physiology did not understand the mystery and its "real nature," and so Dumont directed readers to "old occult writers of the past ages." Both old masters and new ones had "recognized the existence of a mighty subtle force of nature." Now Dumont could echo then-well-known Hindu Theosophist Rama Prasad and his exposition of the power of breath (*prana*) in *Nature's Finer Forces* (1894) by offering his own vitalistic reading of nerve-force. Occultists had given it names such as "vital force," "vital energy," "life force," "vital fluid," and "vital magnetism," even as "Orientals" had cited "prana" and "akashic energy." The point was clear—Dumont was in the now-familiar land of in-between, and he walked there comfortably. But the reason for the walk was not to admire the territory. Rather, Dumont aimed to provide a template for personal success and prosperity in whatever endeavor the student desired. So he explained painstakingly that "the magnetic energy of the person" tended to "run in currents and to be transmitted in waves." A person's own "atmosphere" was "composed of many waves of magnetic energy, circling around the confines of his aura." When they came in contact "with the mind of other persons, [the waves] set up a corresponding rate of vibration." In so doing, they produced a "mental state in them, corresponding to that of the person sending forth the magnetism."[17] The moral of the story was to develop one's personal magnetism, envelop the other in it, and so win the trophies that the magnetic emitter desired.

Dumont, like Atkinson without his alias, offered a cornucopia of exercises to develop one's magnetism, and as the exercises progressed, they became ever more controlling. One exercise, for example, counseled the student to send the message "I am stronger than you," accompanied by a forceful will. In another technique, called the "direct flash," he encouraged the magnetic student to issue a series of commands to another, among them, "I am your MASTER!"[18] In short, the burden of Dumont's teaching was how to control oneself and others, gaining complete mastery for what you wanted most. In some respects, he (and Atkinson in earlier works) was echoing Towne's focus on discipline, but in these new hands, discipline had become a sharp and even threatening tool for subduing others to one's own interests. This even if along the way Atkinson and Dumont had at times called for the ethical use of magnetic powers, avoiding harm to others.

As he hailed the "power of concentration" in one work so named, Dumont could quote Emerson ("Power to him who power exerts") and then go on to declare that "success to-day" depended "largely on concentrating on the Interior law of force." He replayed Atkinson's familiar themes yet again, holding up the power of desire—"a great creative force" if it was "pure, intense and sustained." Dumont exhorted readers to "concentrate on wealth," telling them "it was never intended that man should be poor." With a ready anecdote, he shared the story of an unprosperous prosperity lecturer who dressed poorly and held his lectures in shabby surroundings—to remind them that thoughts of wealth attracted wealth. Obviously, the lecturer was harboring another set of thoughts, and Dumont urged his students again to do better by concentrating on the fulfillment of their desires. He offered them a lengthy series of exercises to help. With a resounding endorsement of vitalism, then, Dumont predicted the day "when all business will employ highly developed persons to send out influences"—influences "so dominating" that employees would be "partly controlled by them" to their own good and profit.[19]

That rosy assessment had already, years earlier, been touted by Dumont in his book *The Master Mind*. Ever the disciplinarian, there Dumont/Atkinson announced that achieving the Master Mind demanded work. It was "consciously, deliberately, and voluntarily built up, cultivated, developed, and used." With a more psychological than occult orientation, here Dumont called the "Ego" the "Mind Master" and went on to name the "Will" as "the innermost, garment of the Ego." If Egos were asleep—the condition of "the masses of the race"—then the persons who owned them possessed "Slave Wills, subject to the influence, control, and direction of others," even if they were oblivious to the fact. Filled with exercises to remedy the situation, Dumont's work homed in on the role of emotions, which reached their "highest point" in the mental state called "Desire." It was "the great motive power of life," and the "fire" that produced "the steam of action" operating "like steam in a boiler." "Increase the intensity and degree [of desire], and the steam rushes out, and in a moment the pistons are moving and the wheels revolving." With the engine running full force, Dumont envisioned astounding results, especially as he looked to a future day. Humans were "rapidly evolving from the plane of physical power on to that of mental power." So "the man of the future" would be "as a super-man compared to the men of to-day." He would—formidably—"use the power of his mind so as to make the whole of Nature his slave." He assured readers, "the individuals of the Master Mind are the forerunners of these Supermen."[20]

Superhuman or not, perhaps no aliases better expressed the Dumont/Atkinson Master Mind than the three "Hindu" authors who were commanding his presses. Among them the clear overachiever was Yogi Ramacharaka. The author of some thirteen books, Ramacharaka produced works that, according to Deslippe, sold estimated millions of copies and were translated into languages including French, Spanish, German, Russian, and Japanese. Advertised in a range of New Thought periodicals from the beginning of the twentieth century, including Towne's *Nautilus*, all are in print today. The Ramacharaka persona was at least partially enabled by Atkinson's sometime acquaintance with Premananda Baba Bharati, whom I cited earlier. But more than that, the "Yogi" represented an ideal as incarnated in a person. Exoticized by the trappings of Hinduism and yoga, Ramacharaka exuded theosophical and occult knowledge, especially culled from Prasad's *Nature's Finer Forces* with its science of breath as well as yogic anatomy and cosmology. The science with which Ramacharaka seemed familiar also emanated from theosophical periodicals, even as his earliest writings introduced *Light on the Path* (1885), a well-known theosophical work by Mabel Collins. Still, at least two of his thirteen works—both from early 1907—were editions of existing translations of the *Bhagavad Gita* and the *Upanishads* (*The Bhagavad Gita; or, The Message of the Master* and *The Spirit of the Upanishads; or, The*

Aphorisms of the Wise). The yogi/Atkinson intended the two as introductions for an American readership.[21]

Beyond these identifiably South Asian works, it could be said, too, that Ramacharaka took the Hindu *siddhis*—the paranormal powers cultivated by yogic discipline, meditation, and practice—and repackaged them as the powers of mind in New Thought. So the Master Mind did not go away in the combinative agenda that Ramacharaka offered. Rather, it managed to manifest itself in yet another version. Especially strong in the new rendition was the role of physical culture. Indeed, for anyone familiar with the more or less standard postures of hatha yoga as they have been presented and practiced in Great Britain, Europe, and the United States, Yogi Ramacharaka's activity-inspired poses offered an expedition into a different universe. They emerged, in fact, as the prescribed physical-culture movements of which Atkinson—and Towne—were exceedingly fond. They were, in short, an early twentieth-century brand of calisthenics ("extend the arms straight out in front of you" and "swing back the hands until the arms stand out straight, sideways").[22] So they offered a transportable model that could be lifted from Ramacharaka's work to become a secular charter for cultivation of body and mind, ever with breath as the leading force to develop the student.

We can see how physical culture became yogic especially clearly in Ramacharaka's instruction manual *Hatha Yoga* from 1904. Subtitled *The Yogi Philosophy of Physical Well-Being (With Numerous Exercises, Etc.)*, the book defined hatha yoga as the part of "Yoga Philosophy which deals with the physical body—its care—its well-being—its health—its strength—and all that tends to keep it in its natural and normal state of health." This was an ambitious definition to be sure. With a long and convoluted Indian history, *hatha yoga* in the twentieth- and twenty-first-century Western world generally refers to systemic postural practice accompanied by a horizon of aspiration for physical and mental balance and well-being. By contrast, Ramacharaka's book fused physical culture in its American cultural subtext with Theosophy/occultism capped by a New Thought message of mind control. With this combinative triad for an agenda, Ramacharaka's embrace of vitalism was not hard to see. Titling his fourth chapter "Our Friend, the Vital Force," he declared for "a certain vital force" that resided "within every physical body." Hatha yoga, Ramacharaka wrote, was successful because it consisted of "methods best calculated to allow the Vital Force to work freely and without hindrance." "To clear the track of obstructions, and to give the chariot of the Vital Force the right of way on a smooth clear road" was "the aim of the Hatha Yogi."[23]

In keeping with the vitalism, Ramacharaka provided an abundance of breathing exercises to invigorate *prana*. Indeed, *prana* functioned as an integral part of the "cell-mind," which was "supplied from the Universal Mind—the great storehouse of 'mind-stuff.'" More than that, Ramacharaka explained with vitalistic enthusiasm, "occult authorities" taught that the "principle" the Hindus called *prana* existed as "the universal principle of energy or force." It was, he said, "Vital Force," with all things, therefore, "in vibration." That included matters sexual. With exceeding care, he provided instructions for "transmuting reproductive energy" through *pranayama* (breath control), raising energy from the spinal base to the crown of the head to aid meditation. "Keep the mind fixed on the idea of Energy, and away from ordinary sexual thoughts and imaginings," he cautioned with late-Victorian reserve. Less controversially, Ramacharaka ended his book by exhorting, "Let us return to nature" and "allow this great life to flow through us freely, and all will be well with us."[24]

Atkinson had scored with his combination of the physical-culture teaching of his time, Western occultism, and New Thought, all at the hands of a Hindu yogi—an authority not to be ignored by his readership. The program continued apace in Ramacharaka's exposition of raja yoga two years later. Raja—or royal—yoga had come to the United States with the celebrated Vivekananda, a devotee of the charismatic Indian mystic and religious leader Ramakrishna. Vivekananda had arrived to participate in the World's Parliament of Religions held in conjunction with the Columbian Exposition of 1893, and later his raja yoga had found its home with his founding, in 1896, of the monistic Vedanta Society in New York City. Here the message was that the true nature of individuals was divine, and it was each person's duty to develop the inner divinity. Ramacharaka proved to be thoroughly at home with Vedantist teaching, not unlike a number of Asian immigrants to the nation at the time. Still more, he wrote in a combinative space in which the influence of Theosophy could be read in his intertwined themes of raja yoga, *siddhi* powers, and *pranayama*.

No surprise, then, that in *Raja Yoga* Ramacharaka invoked a Hindu-cum-occult account of five hierarchical planes that surrounded each human, beginning from a vegetative one and ending with a final plane of Cosmic Knowing. The point of the planes, or sheaths, was to underline the theosophical and Atkinsonian theme of control, since from the vantage of the highest plane, knowledge became power—and most actively the power of the will. Thus, from the start, Ramacharaka's lessons insistently emphasized the "Will," which he identified with "the Power of the Ego—its birthright from the Absolute." This "Real Self of Man" was "the Divine Spark sent forth from the Sacred Flame." It was a convenient metaphysic—Ramacharaka early offered readers the affirmation that "'I' am Master of my mind, not its slave."

But there was more. The vitalistic connection—never far behind—was ever ready to be amplified. "Matter" (ourselves) proceeded "from Energy, and Energy from Mind," and all were "an emanation of the Absolute"—in a new trinitarian formula "three-fold in appearance but One in substance." Meanwhile, the Absolute was absolutely useful for one's plans and projects. One affirmation would have readers assert—in confused metaphors—that they were "resting on the bosom of the Great Ocean of Life." "Supporting" them, it would carry them "safely," even if storms and tempests raged. Warning against sloppy Western notions that, Ramacharaka cautioned, lumped all "out-of-conscious planes of mentation" together under rubrics such as the "sub-conscious," he sought to target the highest and the best. Thus, "I AM THE MASTER OF MY SOUL" read another affirmation, while one more asserted, "'I' am master over Body, Mind, Consciousness, and Sub-consciousness."[25] There were Emersonian encores aplenty in Ramacharaka's reference to the power of the will (Emerson's *Nature* in 1836 had long before announced its power). More than that, Ramacharaka had seamlessly connected a superficial acquaintance with Hinduism to the occult lore of Theosophy and to a nation exuberant with its success in taming a continent and taming human bodies, too, with exercise.

Ramacharaka's titles continued to dwell in an in-between land of combination, even including a book called *Mystic Christianity*.[26] Still, for all this productivity, Ramacharaka was not the only alias on Atkinson's Indian list, even if his writings had more to do with Hinduism than those of Swami Bhakta Vishita and Swami Panchadasi. Space precludes more than a passing nod for their works, but their titles alone speak volumes. Swami Bhakta Vishita's books, for example, seem thoroughly preoccupied with ghosts and spirits as well as seership, clairvoyance, telepathy, mediumship, and the like—in a staggering list of some thirty-two works, including at least six pamphlets. His *Genuine Mediumship; or, The Invisible Powers* (1908) is easy to obtain in reprints today. On the other hand, Swami Panchadasi played the role of literary pauper, with only three titles. All read like pages from a theosophical primer. His *Human Aura: Astral Colors and Thought Forms* (1912), for instance, clearly addressed the occult-oriented reader, while his *Clairvoyance and Occult Powers* (1916) ranged widely on clairvoyance, telepathy, psychometry, crystal gazing, astral-body travel, psychic influence, and magnetic healing. What was the Atkinson connection? Always control, control, and more control—so that will was fully developed and desires abundantly met.

As his topics grew more controversial, Atkinson also published anonymously. A significant case was his *Arcanes*, at first a single book called *The Arcane Teaching*, but then a set of four and—in a later version—six titles that formed a connected series. Its four-volume second appearance (1909) contained what would become six books by 1911, essentially by subdividing one of the earlier four. The works featured a huge and comprehensive vision that brought the occultism of Theosophy together with New Thought, both promoting Atkinson's gospel of dominion over self and circumstance. Significantly, everything seemed to start with the question of "How?"—ever and always Atkinson's concern. Still more, his legal mind surfaced strongly as he dissected his material, breaking it down in order to build it up. The "Arcanes," readers learned, were "a loosely organized body of men" who had "lived in all countries, in all times, since the days of the Ancient Greece, and probably for thousands of years before." Atkinson's background came to the fore again when he divulged "Arcane Teaching" concerning an "Absolute Supreme Power," that was known among the Arcanes as "The Law." Under the Law or "Lex," though—in an important twist—Arcane teaching targeted "Dominant Desire," balanced by its opposite pole of "Will." With Will in operation, a person remained under "Law" but could use it instead of "remaining passive to it."[27]

Exercises everywhere punctuated the *Arcanes*. Moreover, as Atkinson promoted "mentalism"—the Arcane teaching for obtaining success in manifesting *"whatever object in the outside world you wish,"* he did not fail to remind readers that *"Mental Images Materialize in response to the Law of Attraction."* As he moved into yet more occult territory, he titled a third Arcane book/pamphlet *Vril; or, Vital Magnetism*. Here, riding on the back of English occultist Edward Bulwer-Lytton's utopian novel *The Coming Race* (1871)—quoted in Blavatsky's *Isis Unveiled* (1877)—Atkinson forged his own manifesto on the mightiest force in the cosmos. Vril was "the universal principle of vital-energy, life-force, or vital magnetism." For ancient occultists, it was the "inherent usable energy" that, in Atkinson's time, was known as "human magnetism," even as the term originated in "ancient Atlantis." Explaining further, Atkinson told readers that vril was "a great cosmic principle of very fine energy permeating all forms of matter, and immanent in thought processes." It was also "the principle of inner vital power or energy . . . immanent in all forms of specialized matter, inorganic or organic." Vril lay at the heart of gravitation (read the law of attraction), and obtaining more of it became a fundamental human aim. It could be found naturally in food, drink, and breath. Absorbing ever more, though, was key. So the Arcane secret of vril absorption demanded the enlistment of the nervous system. According to Atkinson, it could *"be spurred to redoubled efficiency by the action of the mind directed upon it."* He obligingly offered directions to readers for applying vril-power in various situations and likewise for conserving it, finishing with an enthusiastic nod to what he called the "psychic" or "occult" phase of vril.[28]

The most controversial of the Arcane books that Atkinson had written anonymously (and probably the strongest reason for their anonymity) was his *Mystery of Sex*. After dispensing with obvious themes such as its universality and its expression of the law of opposites or polarity, he turned to sex in human life. Beyond its physical expression for "the reproduction of the species," Atkinson looked to its second aspect—the "vital, mental, moral and spiritual." This, he wrote, led "to planes of manifestation of which the animal world has no experience." There were, he acknowledged, some "roots" in the sexual life of "higher" animals, such as the love of mates and offspring. But reproduction was the form and function of sex—except for humans, who—misusing it—had "acquired the habit of employing the physical function of Sex for the purpose of sensual gratification alone"—contra nature. The "habits and practices of the human race," in short, were "unnatural and perverted." If this seemed like a throwback to a sexual ethic from a bygone era, Atkinson, as a delight maker, was hardly playing the renunciant. He was quick to condemn those who, decrying "ordinary sex relations" among humans, pronounced "all Sex impure" and led "the lives of ascetics."[29]

Rather, Atkinson welcomed sexual energy with enthusiasm and wanted to use it in keeping with his vitalistic quest. "Unquestionably existent" was "the peculiar vital force or energy, generally called Vital Magnetism," which possessed "features and phases of Sex." Everyone dwelled in their own "atmosphere," it was true, but there was "a particular phase of this Vital Magnetism" having "much to do with the relations of the two sexes." Atkinson was unabashed in calling it "Sex Magnetism," and he was ready to run with it. Beyond its proper use among married couples, though, it moved to a "Mental plane" when people of opposite sexes influenced one another with "inspiration and incitement to active thinking." Still higher was the "Spiritual Plane," to which men and women mounted "hand in hand, and by each other's help." But partners vanished when Atkinson moved to his capstone commentary. The "wonderful concentrated power" of sex could be used not just for generation but for self-regeneration. In other words, "the wonderful concentrated forces of the sexual functions" could "be used by the individual himself or herself in re-energizing, re-charging, or regenerating the vital powers within his or her own organism." So the "continence" of "occult brotherhoods and sisterhoods" had its point, and Atkinson was avid in promoting it to build one's "physical, mental and spiritual nature." Unlike an ascetic, who tried to "'kill out' the sexual nature," the continent American did not banish it but strove to "strengthen and develop it" (echoing the more reserved Ramacharaka). Transmutation—like the work of a *kundalini* yogi, who aimed to raise libidinal energy from the base of the spine to the "third eye" or the crown of the head—signaled using sexual energies "in accordance with the world-old occult and mystic teachings of Regeneration."[30] In the end, regeneration came from continence, continence came from control, and control—as ever in Atkinson's world—worked as the magic formula to guarantee success, prosperity, and delight. Desire denied had been transformed into desire fulfilled.

For a historian, it is obvious that sex and sexual suggestion could likely trigger repercussions for Atkinson in the wake of the Comstock laws from the 1870s, with their prosecution of "indecent" material carried through the mails. No alias could avoid that circumstance, and Atkinson, as a careful lawyer, was happy to avoid any incriminating pseudonym. He made up for that in spades with what would become the most popular of his works and would continue into the present as a metaphysical classic. This time the alias was triple. So it was that as the "Three Initiates" Atkinson wrote his *Kybalion* (1908). Deslippe has called it his "most significant work, and perhaps his best piece of writing." It continues to remain in print, with—as Deslippe has declared—"dozens, if not hundreds of different editions"—with translations into ten or more languages and even Braille. As Deslippe estimated, the book "directly or indirectly left its mark on the way millions of people viewed money, spirituality, the mind, success, and the nature of the universe itself."[31]

In what seems an obvious borrowing from Blavatsky's *Secret Doctrine* (1888)—with its nearly fifteen hundred pages announced as stanzas from the never-found "Book of Dzyan" and her own commentary—Atkinson offered a similar claim in a work of dramatically fewer pages. His book, he explained, was based on "the world-old Hermetic Teachings" to assist "earnest searchers after the Arcane Truths." Atkinson would give readers "an idea of the fundamental teachings of The Kybalion," so that—if they were true students—they could apply its wisdom. Thus, each chapter began—like Blavatsky's work—with a stanza (from his *Kybalion*) and followed it with Atkinson's interpretation. And as with Blavatsky's work, the source seems never to have existed. As Deslippe notes, the late-nineteenth-century Prentice Mulford—whom we have already met—was echoed within the *Kybalion*. Deslippe went on to point, too, to the use of the *Kybalion* as a "business tool" not long after Atkinson's death. For example, one classified ad from the *New York Times* (March 24, 1935) advertised the book as "seven powerful principals" [sic] for sales success. In another *Times* ad (March 31), "for fifty cents, aspiring salesmen in the midst of the Great Depression could learn commission-manifesting techniques from the ancient Egyptian magician Hermes Trismegistus in a cheaply rented, subdivided office space off of Broadway." In brief, for all its lofty metaphysical language, the *Kybalion* was teaching Americans how to achieve "money, success, and the best road to both."[32]

We have already met the *Kybalion*'s seven "Hermetic" principles in various ways before—mentalism, correspondence, vibration, polarity, rhythm, cause and effect, and gender. The work announced to readers that "mind"—like "metals and elements" could be "transmuted, from state to state; degree to degree; condition to condition; pole to pole; vibration to vibration." In that context, "Mental Transmutation" became "the art of CHANGING THE CONDITIONS OF THE UNIVERSE, along the lines of Matter, Force and Mind." It was the "Magic" of the ancients, and it was available to Americans now. It did not matter if a person used terms such as "psychic phenomena," or "mental influence," or "mental science," or "new-thought phenomena," the same one principle was working. So Atkinson told his readers, after his lesson on each of the principles, that the purpose of his writing was to "give the student a master-key" in order to "unlock the many doors leading into the parts of the Temple of Knowledge he may wish to explore."[33] Atkinson's news was old, and now he was drawing a line from an American present to the occult wisdom of the past—all in the service of desire fulfilled and delight attained through the powerful discipline of control. If the *Kybalion* was a rousing metaphysical success as a publication in the twentieth-century United States, its legacy would continue as well into the twenty-first. Now its metaphysical burden—transformed in an ever-changing cultural landscape—would become the stuff of trance channels and their abundance theology for Americans, promising them desire satisfied and prosperity always available.

ELEVEN

Channeling Delight and Destiny: The Coming of Seth and Abraham

To encounter trance channels in the late twentieth- and early twenty-first-century United States at first seems to be walking into a world that rhymes with spirit visits from the past. But as we will see, the rhymes were somewhat off, and a new poetic was afoot. Nineteenth-century mass spiritualism had operated on the premise of the special talent of the medium—usually a woman who was passive. The medium provided a necessary conduit for spirit entry into the world of the living in ritual-style séance settings. Spirits had names and birth and death dates. They were most frequently related to séance sitters around a parlor table. When unrelated spirits came to visit, they were often historical figures of great renown—a George Washington or an Isaac Newton, a Benjamin Franklin or a Thomas Jefferson. Sometimes, too, they were the spirits of American Indians, who often seemed to have forgiven whites for native genocide. Whoever these spirits were, however, they were beings who in previous times had lived on earth and who had died there.

Not so in the contemporary world of the last several decades inhabited by the new breed of trance channels. For one thing, they did not need to function in Protestant-style ritual settings like those of former-day séance circles. For another, the "spirits" who came to the new trance channels often rejected historicized accounts of previous earthly lives. They also disliked the term "spirits" and said instead that they were *entities*. If they had formerly dwelled on earth, it was during many times and numerous incarnations. A number claimed that they were not single entities at all, but *group entities*, with a collective name to signal the vibrational similitude that held them all together. Meanwhile, their obliging channels told different stories about their degree of conscious awareness during the channeling process. Some were off in a distant place, shut out from any conscious memory of what had happened during their channeling and needing to learn about it from those present. Others claimed to be conscious during the process and aware of what was going on.

Still further, even as old-style mediums persisted in small and self-contained settings—often spiritualist churches—throughout the twentieth century, the appearance of "channels" already pointed to something culturally new. So far as I am aware, the term reflected the evolving technological world that early became visible with the radio. As far back as 1934, it was used in the midst of emerging understandings of radio frequencies, when Guy Ballard published his fictionalized autobiography *Unveiled Mysteries* (under the pseudonym Godfré Ray King). As with radio waves, the "channels" received input from somewhere else, a somewhere that could be far away. Moreover, according to religious studies scholar Gordon Melton, the term *channel* gained particular currency during the 1950s. By that time, interest in unidentified flying objects (UFOs) was growing, along with speculation concerning extraterrestrials and "space commanders." Numbers of individuals were beginning to testify that they had been UFO contactees. Then, by the latter part of the twentieth century, "channels" had become straightforward conduits to operate television sets and, even more, to run sophisticated computer-age space technology. It was a gradual but easy glide, thus, to transform an old-fashioned medium into a New Age trance channel.[1]

Even in the high-science context of the space age and its connection with the mysterious messages of the new trance channels, though, it is worth recalling the careful theologizing of liberal Protestant theologian Horace Bushnell. He had pondered the metaphorical nature of language at length, even as he used it to construct his analogical framework regarding a world beyond this one. Old theological terms were familiar and comforting, but new statements, too, could point to the realms illuminated by Christian orthodoxy. Since all words were symbols and what they pointed toward was shrouded in mystery, the believer needed to be aware of the situation, tolerant of difference, and ready to yield the floor to a new language formula. Against this backdrop, for a working historian, the theological labors of a Bushnell and the more secular work of modern-day trance channels seem not so different as they first appear. Both versions are, in a sense, just-so stories. They are not built on the external evidence that would count in historiographical quarters. More, they involve intellectual and aesthetic formulas arising from intuitive beliefs about the nature of the world and the human place in it (might original theological constructs, Christian and other, also have been "channeled?"). At the same time, their messages reveal their connection to legacies of historical meaning that have gone before. Trance channels, like theologians, bring to their present the inherited pasts they carry with them. So, whether arising from a faith tradition or outside its reassuring (for many) boundaries, "proof" comes, as for William James, through resonance with the rest of an individual's and/or a community's life. Theologies succeed when they are able to pull major aspects of experienced reality together and render it intelligible, meaningful, and satisfying. A person knows that a belief is "true" because heart and head respond together; things click into place, and the flow of life seems better and stronger. In other words, imagination stirs feeling, and feeling tones the "objective" landscape of living in ways that—if it all works—yield greater joy and freedom, at least in some ultimate register.[2]

To place contemporary trance channels and their abundance theology in this older religious context is an important strategy for understanding what they are culturally about. If older theologies are a lot like trance productions of the present, and if these contemporary trance productions echo the historicizing work of past theologies, we have at hand a breakthrough opportunity for making sense of what they say and tell. From this perspective, we can look at the iconic gospel promoted by the still-active Esther Hicks, with the mysterious group entity called "Abraham," who at this writing speaks through her. In the domain of Abraham, as we will see, the law of attraction has reigned supreme as the one and only dominant law. It is a law of attraction that had been secularized by William Walker Atkinson and, after him, by Napoleon Hill—who reiterated ideas of attraction and a Master Mind found in Atkinson, along with generous doses of the work of Prentice Mulford. Especially, it is a cosmological message predicated on the prior work of trance channel Jane Roberts, who transmitted the teachings of an entity named Seth through a series of books and a following that, in her heyday, was robust.

"The spiritual teacher that launched the New Age"—so announced Roberts's book *The Seth Material* on the front cover of its 2001 edition.[3] Seth was channeled by Roberts (1929–1984) in an intense and ongoing process. The estimate of his significance was, to be sure, overstated, but it is also true that Seth has been widely credited with beginning the practice of channeling linked to the New Age movement in the 1970s. Roberts, who matriculated at Skidmore College from 1947 to 1950, was born and reared Catholic, although she later grew away from her church. Her childhood had been troubled, and there had been significant health problems. Nonetheless, in adulthood she emerged as a more or less successful writer of short stories, novels, and poetry in Elmira, New York. Then at one point her husband, artist Robert

Butts, somewhat teasingly encouraged her to produce a how-to book on developing extrasensory perception (ESP). The nudge, it turned out, became the gateway to a future neither could have envisioned. By 1963, Roberts had begun experimenting with a Ouija board, and out of the experiments came her first contacts with "the energy personality essence no longer focused in physical reality" who went by the name of Seth. Out of the experiments, too, came the first of the Seth books. But there had been an earlier paranormal or mystical experience before the Ouija board, and Roberts credited it as being the real beginning of what would later happen. It was, as she recalled, "a 'trip' without drugs." "Between one normal minute and the next," she wrote, "a fantastic avalanche of radical, new ideas burst into my head with tremendous force, as if my skull were some sort of receiving station turned up to unbearable volume." Still more: "Not only ideas came through this channel, but sensations, intensified and pulsating. I was tuned in, turned on—whatever you want to call it—*connected* to some sorce [sic] of energy." Seth would later confirm that this had been his first attempt to contact her.[4]

So began a channeling process that lasted more than twenty years, producing a book almost every year or two after 1970. Some were ascribed to Seth; others acknowledged Roberts as author; and two came from a student as a firsthand account of classes Roberts conducted with Seth. Roberts also published a book that she said was channeled from French impressionist artist Paul Cézanne and another from William James (distinctly unlike James's thinking and writing, although her own ideas might be called Jamesian). All told, easily several million copies of these works made their way into print. An Austin Seth Center was established in Texas from 1979 to continue the use of the Seth material, and Seth societies and conferences sprang up in a movement that kept going through many years (although now it is fair to say that it is declining). At least one religious studies scholar with a theological background began researching and writing on Sethian themes. Meanwhile, other trance channels began asserting that they, too, were communicating with Seth.[5]

Seth has stood out among later channeled entities toward the end of the twentieth century for the complex cosmology he offered—a cosmology that, as we will see, became a base for what Esther Hicks would transmit as the teachings of Abraham. The content of Seth's teachings suggested his familiarity with the American mediumistic tradition, in which key ideas bore a family resemblance to his own (although he insisted that terms like "spirit" and "medium" were "ridiculous" and people were simply using their "inner senses"). In keeping, too, with New Thought views and theosophical messages conveyed by Helena Blavatsky and others, Seth taught that consciousness created, even if he did so with new rhetorical flair. He echoed the vitalism of the tradition by employing a rudimentary "electrical" science to explain the emotional charge that he said made thought effective. "Thoughts formed and set out within the impulse range of emotion often succeed," he taught, "because of the peculiar nature of the emotional electrical impulses themselves," which possessed "a particularly strong electrical mass." Seth also repeated the inherited message of desire, speculating that "we may have been sparked on and off into consciousness and unconsciousness a million times, touched by desire, by yearnings toward creativity and perfection we barely understood." In fact, his own statement sounded very much like the law of attraction. "Intensity," he declared, was the "core about which the electromagnetic energy units form," with humans acting as vitalistic "transformers" to change energy into "physical objects." It followed that "the more intense the core, the sooner the physical materialization." This was the case "whether the mental image was a fearful one or a joyful one." Even more, Seth could toss out language about emanations from cells that followed "certain laws of magnetism." "Like definitely attracts like," he instructed, and the emanations were "actually emotional tones."[6]

As Seth pointed the way toward Abraham, he made it clear that creating your own reality came with a rider attached. It was co-creation, as Abraham would say. The way Seth put it, creation happened *"en masse,"* when humans (in Roberts's summary) formed matter "in order to operate in three-dimensional reality, develop our abilities and help others." Within this framework, the Sethian vista extended in new ways, as Seth spoke of what he called "the spacious present," a present "so precious" that it could not be "explored all at once." Humans had arbitrarily divided it "into large rooms of past, present and future." Within this vastness, there were multiple worlds and probable worlds, even as there were probable pasts, presents, and futures. The past, for example, was hardly unmalleable. It existed, instead, with vitalistic efficiency "as a series of electromagnetic connections" in the brain and the "nonphysical mind"—a past that could be changed and altered "not only before and during but *after* its occurrence." Meanwhile, in the present, individuals chose from "nonphysical probable events" with which they were in accord and brought them into "actuality." Following the law of correspondence from which the law of attraction had sprung, "when your ideas about yourself change[d]," so did "your experience." If you were "poor," your situation existed because "you chose that reality from many probable ones that did not involve poverty"—and that were "still open."[7]

Building on this cosmology, Seth taught theosophical concepts of reincarnation and karma, accepted without dispute the literal nature of lost continents called Atlantis and Lemuria (or Mu), and saw life—like Atkinson and occultists in general—as a schoolhouse for learning. Yet Seth brought a new self-consciousness to the process that was channeling. More sophisticated than the spiritualists of the past, he thought of it as "translation" and acknowledged its problems. He claimed (with Roberts more or less concurring) that her "consciousness" was not "blotted out during our communications" (although she acknowledged that at times her "Jane-self" was "far in the background"). Overall, her consciousness expanded, and there came "a projection of energy" that was "directed away from three-dimensional reality." He thought that what happened to Roberts was "normal rather than supranormal" and that "psychic ability" was "an outcropping or extension of creative abilities, inherent in each of us." In fact, he confided, the words that Roberts spoke were "not initially verbal at all." Seth's self-consciousness would be echoed by Abraham. Indeed, Seth paved the way for the group entity by telling Roberts that "as many layers of the self compose the whole self [entity], so many entities form a gestalt of which you know relatively little and of which I am not as yet prepared to tell you."[8]

Seth likewise emphasized the joy that would become Abraham's calling card. The "creative joy of play" held central place, as Seth asserted that "all creativity and consciousness" were "born in the quality of play, as opposed to work, in the quickened intuitional spontaneity." Encouraging such intuition as well as sleep and dreams, he told Roberts and her followers that there they could "perceive the joyfully changing nature" of their own and "any consciousness." He repudiated the "limiting" false belief that life was "a valley of sorrows." Instead, Seth combined joy with a vitalistic postscript on magnetism and the law of attraction, asserting that an effortless "joy of creativity" flowed through humans. It brought with it feelings compounded of "electromagnetic realities" that affected even the atmosphere. People grouped together "through attraction, building up areas of events and circumstances that finally coalesce," and they did so "either in matter as objects—or as events in 'time.'"[9] Seth, it turned out, was not only pursuing happiness; he was proclaiming its ever-abiding presence.

He had arguably learned from an American metaphysical past, with the prolific Atkinson delivering a similar message. He went well beyond Atkinson though, condemning "a lack of appreciation for those sensual joys with which you are surrounded." He also assured Roberts that "after-death environments" were "generally far more intense and joyful than the reality you now know"—a theme that Abraham would later take up and run with. Still more, in a teaching that anticipated ideas of universal expansion taught by Abraham, he assured Roberts and her followers that the "soul or entity" was "expanded through reincarnations, through existence and experience in probable realities." It existed in a "state of becoming."[10]

Finally, as we look ahead to Abraham, we can notice that Seth introduced the language and ideational base for "All That Is" (read "Source" or God) and underlined the role of desire and "contracted yearning" in generating life. Within this framework were new twists on the pluralistic worlds of James, with his doubting-Thomas innuendos regarding the unity of God and the universe. Here instead God became an "energy gestalt"—"ever-expanding" and "so secure in its existence" that it could "constantly break itself down and rebuild itself." This God ruled so emphatically by "desire" that "within *All That Is*," in effect, "the wish, desire, and expectation of creativity" had "existed before all other actuality." Seth, in short, was throwing a theological challenge to conventional belief and asking humans to step off a familiar world and into something definitively new. He was chasing the path of a process God instead of the "static one" that, he lamented, caused the "main theological difficulties" of humans.[11] Seth joined feeling and "pure energy" coming from "the core of BEING"—"from All That Is"—to teach that the "feeling-tone" with its energetic charge provided "the source of never-ending vitality." With God ever-changing and expanding, Seth could hail the grand significance of diversity (another recurring Abrahamic theme). Moreover, with the experience of this grand gestalt constantly changing and growing, Seth insisted on the essentiality of imbalance to drive life forward. He cautioned—like a spiritualizing quantum physicist—"When you say, 'This is God,' then God is already something else." "Consciousness and existence do not result from delicate balances so much as they are made possible by lack of balances," he emphasized.[12] In so many words, he had already proclaimed the "contrast" upon which the teachings of Abraham would be built.

With his often cosmological, even theological, declarations—building on a metaphysical past but synthesizing and elaborating it—Seth had paved a complex path. Yet it would open with seeming ease onto the simpler and more pragmatically focused teachings known from the 1980s as the teachings of Abraham. At first transmitted by Esther Hicks with the close collaboration of her late husband, Jerry Hicks, Abraham's ideas contain only veiled clues to the respective lives of the pair. Biographical details are sparse for the time before their meteoric rise in popular consciousness, but from various remarks in the front matter of some of their books as well as interview material, a rough picture emerges. Esther Hicks, the trance channel who has continued the Abraham work after her husband's death in 2011 from leukemia, was born in 1948 as Esther Weaver. Her parents lived in Coalville,

Utah, a small Rocky Mountain town. Henry "Bill" Emerson Weaver, her father, worked in the lumber trade, and apparently—unlike the rest of the family—did not identify as Mormon. Her mother, Ruth Blazzard Weaver, certainly did. The family included two other daughters, Jeanne and Rebecca, and—with a move to Park City, near Salt Lake City—the parents apparently provided a nurturing environment for the young Weavers. As part of it, though, Sunday school classes and Mormon culture in general transmitted suspicions of the paranormal and certainly of contact with the dead.[13]

Esther Weaver attended South Summit High School from 1962 to 1966. Family life was seriously impacted, however, when—while Esther was still a teen—her mother suffered a severe heart attack that left her more or less an invalid. We do not know the connection between this situation and Esther's marriage at twenty to Richard D. Geer, whom she later described as an authoritarian with whom it was difficult to live. The couple's daughter—Tracy Geer (now Ayers)—came along in Fresno, California, in 1971, in later years becoming part of Esther's emerging Abraham work. Five years afterward, in 1976, while Tracy was still a child, Esther Geer met Jerry Hicks when she was working as a secretary-bookkeeper for (most likely) his fourth wife. By August 1980 Esther had divorced her husband, and then she married Jerry. So began a saga that radically changed the lives of both, catapulting them into territory that—especially for Esther—seemed exceedingly alien and for both brought an abundance of wealth and fame.

Who was Jerry Hicks, the husband who turned metaphysical coach and transformed Esther's relationship to the dead, fostering her abilities as a trance channel? How did his admitted familiarity with Napoleon Hill's *Think and Grow Rich* (1937) and Jane Roberts's Seth books shape his and Esther's Abraham experience? And what kind of background did he bring to their joint endeavor? Born most likely in 1927—the oldest of three, with a brother and a sister—Jerry Hicks from his own report experienced a difficult childhood and an especially troubling relationship with his mother. His father, he claimed, had been in the US Navy, but when the father was present, he quarreled regularly with his wife. Jerry Hicks himself told interviewer Robert Chalmers that he had been raised in San Diego and Arkansas, spent two years in an orphanage, and eventually attended school in New Orleans. Elsewhere he reported that he had lived in eighteen homes in six states during his first fourteen years. If so, his adult life seemed equally itinerant, with sporadic jobs in the entertainment industry (he claimed two years in Cuba as an acrobat as well as twenty touring stateside as a musical master of ceremonies and comedian). Meanwhile, his marriages repeated the pattern—he spoke of at least four wives before he and Esther came together.

There were, he said, two children by his second wife, but he seemed to have no later relationship with them. His fortunes (or misfortunes) began to change, though, when through his fourth wife he became involved with the Amway Company—then in its heyday—and its multilevel marketing practices. He also had begun reading Hill, whose work, as we recall, was deeply influenced by the prior writings of Atkinson. Eventually he discovered Roberts's Seth.

Esther Hicks, with Mormon distress signals sounding, at first displayed considerable unease about her husband's metaphysical interests, and he in turn tiptoed around them in her presence so as not to upset her. But in time she came to listen to Jerry's readings from the Seth books and to read them with him. As a next step toward Abraham, the couple visited a trance channel named "Sheila," who claimed to speak for an entity called Theo. Sheila urged the pair to meditate, and she told Esther Hicks that she (Esther) would thereby meet her own spirit guide. Enter, in 1985, a distinctive entity named Abraham, whom Esther early described as a group of evolved, nonphysical teachers highly resonant with one another. Very much later, in 2013, Abraham in an identifying statement would declare much the same, but amplify the description to identify as "a Collective Consciousness, a vibration" and the "Source Energy that you are all extensions of." Significantly, Abraham added that "we ride on the momentum of the desire that all of you have already established, and then Esther translates our vibrations, our knowing, into words."[14]

The smoothness of the latter-day work had come after a rough beginning. Early transmissions from Abraham in the middle and late 1980s were ragged and also dramatic. At first, Esther Hicks wrote Abraham's messages with her nose, and when Abraham used her body and voice to speak, the tone was shrill, harsh, and distinctly foreign-sounding in accent. Time did its work, however, and summoning Abraham became an easy, seemingly effortless procedure. Nowadays, the foreign accent has almost entirely worn away, and Abraham often teaches and responds in repartee that is witty and ironic. Although Esther has disdained the term *channeling*, she continued to engage in the practice repeatedly, even—with a hiccup—after the death of her husband. In the years when the couple were in the midst of their greatest success, from 1987 on, they repeated the itinerant pattern of Jerry Hicks's earlier life. Like New Age circuit riders, they produced workshops in some sixty cities annually, becoming known for their monster bus—a forty-five-foot-long Marathon coach they drove from venue to venue—and that Esther claimed cost $1.4 million.

Meanwhile, together they published thirteen books—four of them so-called "Sara" books for children and the remaining nine for adults. Six of the nine were featured as *New York Times* best sellers, and one of them—*Money and the Law of Attraction*—climbed to first place on the *Times* list.[15] Still more, the number of books they have sold counts in the millions. Except for the often-cited *Ask and It Is Given*, which claims Abraham as deliberate author, all of the adult books mostly pass on from preliminary introductory material to transcribe the trance productions ascribed to Abraham at workshop sessions. The first two Abraham books, *A New Beginning I* and *II*, are no longer sold on the Abraham-Hicks website, but—orphan children that they apparently became for the enterprise—they are important because they reveal the gradual evolution of the Abraham message. Although both point in the direction of joy and happiness, they also echo the end-century millennial anxiety that preceded the year 2000. Nor were they ignored. *A New Beginning I*, subtitled *Handbook for Joyous Survival*, appeared in at least seven printings, beginning in 1988, while *A New Beginning II*, with its optimistic subtitle, *A Personal Handbook to Enhance Your Life, Liberty and Pursuit of Happiness*, could boast six from 1991. Here could be found apocalyptic notions of an earth shift, earthquakes, and the like—predictions that completely vanished in the later Abraham messages.[16]

These early writings were far eclipsed by what happened in the new century. With Abraham books now reaching *New York Times* best-seller lists, their teachings on the law of attraction sparked the imagination of Australian producer and New Age seeker Rhonda Byrne. Her small edited 2006 volume *The Secret* and video by the same name—with Esther Hicks's appearance in segments of its first version—garnered much more profit and attention than the Hicks's separate sales and recognition. A dispute over intellectual property rights, however, led to the withdrawal of Esther Hicks from the second edition of the video, even if, in keeping with the Abraham message, she did not pursue a court case.[17] In the aftermath of the break, the dispute caught the eye of Oprah Winfrey, and—already living the law of attraction herself—Winfrey gave Esther Hicks a platform to tell her side of the story. Oprah's turn to Abraham, with the clear message that Esther and Jerry Hicks had been teaching attraction for some twenty years before Byrne's *Secret* appeared, gave continuing approval and publicity to the Abraham teaching. Arguably, it was Winfrey's intervention that made Abraham even more of a leading name for a new and broadly based culture of seeking. Moreover, it was the subject of money that stood out as the most compelling part of the message.

The actual channeling process had always rested with Esther, but her husband played a pivotal role in what happened. Until the time of his death, Jerry Hicks enthusiastically involved himself, acting as the ever-ready prompt who called forth Abraham's teaching. Indeed, much of the early material in the Abraham books came in reply to his incessant questioning. Always present at workshops, he acted as a stenographer of sorts, even though the sessions were video recorded. Almost, it seems, Esther Hicks became Jerry's Scheherazade, continually re-engaging her husband by repeated renditions of the law of attraction in and through the transmissions of Abraham. Meanwhile, to repeat again, the law of attraction stood firmly in the metaphysical tradition as the latest and most self-interested version of the law of correspondence, the same law of correspondence that had been available from Puritan times and had been emphasized by Cotton Mather. Now, though, it had lost contact with all that—and with its mid-nineteenth-century Fourierist incarnation as well. If the law of attraction even offered a bow of acknowledgment to Atkinson, this was as far as memory traveled. Still more, as had happened so many times before, the law of attraction altered the magnetic metaphor—in which positives and negatives, in other words, *opposites*, attracted. Instead, here was a law in which like items gravitated toward one another, so that like was attracting like.

No matter for history and for science. The Hickses became fabulously wealthy as they traveled America in their monster bus, producing their workshops. They featured a plethora of other products, including CDs, DVDs, daily sayings (free) delivered via email, metaphysical playing cards, meditation instructions, and various other goods to enable devotees to achieve joy, well-being, and prosperity. After 2011 and the passing of Jerry, patterns had already been established and honed. The bus disappeared in favor of airlines, workshops became fewer and less frequent, but the message continued to be repeated with an enthusiastic following who came back again and again for more. From early on in the Abraham work, moreover, the making of money and what have you were seen as imperative not only for the pursuit of personal happiness but also for the workings of the universe. Echoing the cosmological orientation of Seth, Abraham produced a straightforward version of process theology, with expansion through human desire fundamental to cosmological well-being. Abraham signaled thorough comfort with evolution, telling followers that desires radiated "constantly" as "vibrational signals" that were "received and answered by Source." "In that moment," declared Abraham, the universe was "expanding." More explicitly, Abraham repeated that "because of your exposure to your specific experience, which causes your specific desire to be formulated within you, and because Source hears and answers your request—the Universe, in which we are all focused, expands."[18]

Put another way, creation was what humans did—either by deliberate intent (consciously focusing thoughts as guided by emotional feedback toward pleasant ones) or by default (letting thoughts and feelings—negative or positive—operate without intervention). Humans as physical beings were manifestations of what Abraham called the Nonphysical, possessing an older, wiser inner being in contact with Abraham or Source or God. By incarnating in the physical realm, humans took on the "leading-edge" task of expanding Source, and they were thus, according to Abraham, at the tipping point of the process by which God grew. In this situation, they took upon themselves what the Hickses and Abraham called the "contrast." When they thereafter encountered the negative environment that flourished among many/most of the physically existent, they generated strong desire about what they wanted instead. So humans, by virtue of their temporary embodied state, launched "rockets of desire," and these "rockets"—whether they led to fulfillment or not on the physical plane—expanded the Source energy by which life continued. Thus, the universe could be endlessly enhanced and enlarged. So however humble and seemingly insignificant, the desire of any human held a lofty place in the eternal order of things. It moved the God process forward, and therefore its significance was huge.

Abraham scolded humans for generally not being in on the joy of continuous creation. Humans worried and stressed out, acted in anger or thought of revenge, gave up in depression and hopeless despair, or lived out other negative feelings that kept them from the delight that engagement in the creative process could bring. Yet according to Abraham, they *never* got it wrong. Each misfortune or disappointment caused them to launch yet another "rocket of desire" that expanded the universe—from Abraham's point of view a very good thing. Likewise, humans never got it done. Each successfully fulfilled desire gave only short-term satisfaction before yet another series of rockets was fired into metaphysical space. And so forth, on and on. Here action was transferred from the physical world that humans called "reality" to the substrate in which an individual's imagination conjured up delights already come and desires fully gratified. Abraham explained to devotees that imagination was the power grid, so to speak—not the flesh-and-blood world of real money, real lovers, real health, and the like. It was only by taking delight in the happy-ever-after narrative conjured by a person's mind that physical manifestations could be generated. The trick was to live fully and delightedly in the world as imagined and not to worry about dreams that were not coming true.

Still more, the ever-solicitous Abraham—with the active involvement of Esther Hicks—taught that humans possessed an emotional guidance system, and when they experienced negative emotion, their feelings were telling them that they had fallen off-course. How to get from off-base to on? From depths to heights? Abraham explained that an emotional sliding scale revealed to each person how close to or far from Source they were operating, and so how close they might be to the fulfillment of their desires. If they asked for the bliss of fulfilled desire from Source but immediately blocked the request with their own negativity and lack of alignment, miracles could not happen, and wishes could not come true.

At the very bottom of the scale were feeling states of "Fear/Grief/Depression/Despair/Powerlessness." Next rising upward came "Insecurity/Guilt/Unworthiness," followed by "Jealousy," then "Hatred/Rage," and next "Revenge." Further up came "Anger," "Discouragement," "Blame," "Worry," and "Doubt," then "Disappointment," "'Overwhelment,'" and "Frustration/Irritation/Impatience." Still rather negative were "Pessimism" and "Boredom," but by the seventh step glimmers of emotional light appeared with "Contentment," then "Hopefulness," and then "Optimism." As a person rose yet higher on the scale came "Positive Expectation/Belief," succeeded next by "Enthusiasm/Eagerness, Happiness," then "Passion," and finally, at the top of the scale, "Joy/Knowledge/Empowerment/Freedom/Love/Appreciation."[19] If the list seemed to replicate Esther Hicks's own values and to appear somewhat idiosyncratic, we can notice that location on it was to a large extent governed by an emotion's relationship to energy. More precisely, greater energy made an emotion better. Depression was worse than revenge or anger, because the latter two were more active states. Passion was better than contentment because tranquility was less energetic than passion. Happiness seemed to be less important than empowerment.

Be that as it might, Abraham did not leave humans struggling as they tried to climb the emotional guidance scale. Rather, twenty-two processes were offered, designed to help humans ascend to their vibrational heights as they worked from negative emotions to positive. Determining one's emotional set-point and its range were basic to finding and using an appropriate process. So, for example, someone with a set-point between "Anger" and "Fear/Grief/Depression/Powerlessness" could use Process #22—termed "moving up the emotional scale." Abraham explained that the task was really one of "deliberate creation," which meant "*deliberately* achieving an emotional state." The first example offered, significantly enough, focused on a lack of money. In this situation, Abraham advised that the distance to be traveled was "not the distance between not enough money to enough money," but rather "the distance between a feeling of insecurity to a feeling of security." The way to reach a feeling of security lay in a person's use of declarative statements that gradually grew less powerless as the individual moved up the scale—not to its top at this stage—but instead to more active negative states like anger.[20] Abraham, in other words, was a gradualist.

The processes themselves were more or less calibrated to emotional states that occupied a close range of set-points on the emotional guidance scale, say from fifth through tenth. In many cases, their names suggested the activity to be accomplished—names such as "turning it over to the manager," "pivoting," "wouldn't it be nice if . . . ?" "the prosperity game," and "the magical creation box." At the very top of the list of processes, the so-called "rampage of appreciation" beckoned the lucky few—suitable for persons with a set-point range between the very first—"Joy/Knowledge/Empowerment/Freedom/Love/Appreciation" and the fifth—"Optimism." Rampages heightened praise for an object, a situation, or an event, escalating higher and higher as if to incarnate the greater good desired.[21] Occasionally in workshops, at an attendee's prompting, Esther/Abraham would demonstrate. Abraham's precision in recommending—and enthusiasm for—the exercises echoed earlier New Thought practices along these lines, if we recall Towne and, especially, Atkinson. But Abraham brought a playfulness to the processes, even as they rested on difficult emotional and psychological work. What the teachings lacked in metaphysical complexity, they compensated for in a pragmatism of detail.

How could the pragmatic agenda draw intense and devoted followers, and, more, how could it positively work in their behalf? As I have already begun to suggest regarding the emotional guidance scale and its successful operation, Abraham had an inherited vitalistic answer. Humans were vibrational beings living in a similarly vibrational universe. As they went about thinking and feeling, they set up vibratory rates that attracted to themselves those elements that resonated in alignment with their thinking-feeling states. "The *Law of Attraction* and its magnetic power reaches out into the Universe and attracts other thoughts that are vibrationally like it," Abraham declared. Every thought possessed "magnetic attracting potential," but thoughts accompanied by "the feeling of strong emotion" were "the most powerful." Still further, the magnetic universe enacted in the law of attraction moved beyond the solitary individual into a huge web of interaction. The Abraham group proclaimed a process theology: Thoughts that were "vibrationally similar to one another" were "drawn magnetically to one another through the powerful *Law of Attraction*." Likewise, "people who feel a certain way" were "drawn to one another, magnetically, through this *Law*." So each person operated "*like a powerful magnet, attracting*," and humans always and ever kept attracting more of the same—more of what they were thinking and feeling.²² It followed that the law of attraction (correspondence in new clothes) became the fundamental means by which the universe expanded—either in the direction that human creators thought they desired, or, conversely, in the direction of what their *unconscious* thought vibrations were conjuring up.

Every subject was "actually two subjects," Abraham said—the wanted and the unwanted. Thus, humans, by their lack of conscious focus, their absence of deliberate creation, could attract unwanted elements into their lives. That was why Abraham had supplied the guidance scale and supplemented it with a series of practices to help humans toward its top. All of this had crystallized, for Abraham, into a three-step process by which the universe operated and through which humans could achieve their desires. "You ask," and then immediately "the answer is given" (the work of Source and always affirmative); finally, "the answer, which has been given, must be received or allowed (you have to let it in)." It was, Abraham kept reminding devotees, their own negative emotions—their own ways of living at the bottom of the emotional guidance scale—that prevented the positive fulfillment of Source from operating in their world.²³

The implications did not stop there. Since, according to Abraham, the most important thing for any human was to feel good, and since imagining and fulfilling desire were key to good-feeling states, the human *self* stood at the apex of the Abraham ethic. In books and workshops, Abraham taught the importance of being completely selfish. Echoing Ralph Waldo Emerson in his often-cited "Self-Reliance," Abraham promoted the centrality of self and its satisfaction. Continually the Abraham group refused to stand down on the issue. To place "such emphasis on the value of your feeling good" had been seen by some as tantamount to teaching selfishness. "And we acknowledge," Abraham announced without embarrassment, "that true selfishness is at the very core of our teaching." "If you are not selfish enough, if you do not care how you feel, if you are not willing to continually redirect your thoughts to the direction of feeling good, you cannot come into alignment with the Source within you." Abraham insisted that each person, when in a nonphysical state, knew "that this physical world was not broken and in need of repair" and that an individual "did not come forth to fix it." The group underlined the high virtue of selfishness unapologetically and did so again and again. "Indeed, we do teach selfishness, for if you are not selfish enough to deliberately align with the Energy of your Source, you have nothing to give anyway." There was an "art" to selfishness, and—Abraham added—"*the not allowing of self is usually where the not allowing of others comes forth.*"²⁴ The pursuit of happiness entailed the selfish art.

Still further, if the ethic of selfishness dominated, it had an unlikely companion in an Abrahamic social ethic. Because, in Abraham's teaching, the "law" of allowing was basic to an achieved creative process, it became a societal template. Diversity proved intrinsic to the expanding nature of the universe. So humans who allowed—who let others be, even if their thought-and-feeling worlds were dramatically different enough to evoke moral indignation and condemnation—were aligning themselves with their Source. Paradoxically, in so doing they created the conditions that led to the manifestation of their own private dreams.

On the other side of diversity and its de facto social ethic, Abraham's moral register moved in antinomian directions. Abraham negated the value of much human law and condemned it for being governed by fear, by a lack of tolerance for difference, and by an insistence that others adopt personally and culturally predominant patterns and behaviors. The suspicion of law and its enforcement was especially notable in Abrahamic advice on parenting and child-rearing. Imposing parental norms on the young continually met a stern rebuke from Abraham, who saw infants and toddlers as much more in touch with their nonphysical Source than their elders. Let the little ones be, Abraham enjoined; let the little ones develop their own ways of living in the world. When parents interfered with choices their children were making, they deprived their offspring "temporarily of the contrast that they came to live." Parents harangued their children so that the parents themselves could "feel good." They were implicitly saying that "when I look at you, I want to feel good, which means you need to perform in ways that make *me, me, me, me* feel good." Still more, the dialog went, "I don't want *you* to feel selfish. You need to behave in ways that make *me* (I'm your selfless mother) feel good."[25] It is fair to add that these celebrations of diversity and injunctions to antinomianism stood in Abraham's world without criticism, without exploration of the limits of both in the lived reality of human societies. Utopia could not unravel if one lived in resonance with the emotional guidance system and acted in accord with the law of (positive) attraction. Still, an observant person did not need to look far to see dystopias all around.

Again and again, however, the Abrahamic message proclaimed that when humans entered the physical world, they intended to live in joy. Abraham had come to teach them how to do it. "*Well-Being is the basis of the Universe. Well-Being is the basis of All-That-Is. It flows to you and through you. You have only to allow it. Like the air you breathe, you have only to open, relax, and draw it into your Being.*" Organized religions were all right if they enabled these results, but Esther/Abraham harbored a deep suspicion, especially, of

Christianity. Perhaps because of Esther's Mormon upbringing, or perhaps for other reasons, Abraham—like the long-ago Andrew Jackson Davis and like Helena Blavatsky and Theosophists in general—displayed a coolness and, if you will, hostility to Christianity. In one memorable workshop exchange regarding Jesus and his crucifixion on Good Friday, Esther/Abraham snapped in so many words that the day was the one in which Jesus was most out of alignment. Overall, there was little reverence in Abraham's universe for organized religion, even if the group acknowledged—as James had done—that religions could work for people in positive and helpful ways.

Finally, though, after a lifetime of living by the law of attraction in all its vitalistic dimensions, of allowing the good to enter and rule a person's life, the time of transition would come when the devotee wanted it to happen. Ultimately, death was not to be feared since it signaled emergence into "pure positive energy." "We do not see what you call your 'death' experience as the end of anything," Abraham stated flatly. "You are an Eternal Being who has no end." Each person was *"Eternal Consciousness"* and expressed *"an endless, glorious dance of Consciousness."*[26] The Abraham teaching about never getting it wrong came full circle in the death event.

As my summary here already suggests, the teachings of Abraham easily disclosed themselves to be footnotes to Seth, along with the pragmatic and economic concerns (more on these later) that came from Hill and, before him, William Walker Atkinson. As I have already suggested, too, it was Seth who told students that they were creating their own reality and—in accord with the metaphysical tradition—that they attracted what came into their lives. It was Seth who repeated notions again and yet again concerning a grander, fuller series of worlds beyond the everyday concerns of those who visited him. It was Seth who emphasized feelings and their generative importance. Seth likewise taught the same process of channeling—emotionally tinged thought blocks that got translated by the channel—that Esther Hicks's Abraham did. This, even if Esther, unlike Roberts, insisted that she was always a conscious channel and never went away during the channeling process. Seth taught the contrast that Abraham repeatedly underlined. Seth taught joy (although Abraham taught it more), and Seth—with his probable worlds—surely taught diversity. Finally, it was Seth who sketched out a horizon on which the mysterious All That Is hovered ever distant—yet ever available through the practices that he (Seth) taught through Roberts.

For his part, the never-entranced and Atkinson-revisited Hill encouraged Jerry (and so Esther) Hicks toward things practical—the simplification of cosmological schemes and probable worlds, and always money and what it could buy. Prosperity fueled the Abrahamic law of attraction, even if Jerry

Hicks—and so Esther—inserted its desire and fulfillment into a worldview that had become transcendental. The pursuit of money was, in fact, the default activity that nudged the law of attraction into free-swinging operation, with all other concerns—health, relationships, sex, what have you—playing an apparent second fiddle. Still more, a large swath of Americans wanted to find out more about how to get money, if the book *Money and the Law of Attraction*'s number-one position on the *New York Times* best-seller list provides any clue. Its highly repetitive text of channeled messages has offered abundant evidence for workshop listeners and then readers seeking wealth and, from it, happiness. In his preface to the work, Jerry Hicks remarked that the outcome of his "personal *Think and Grow Rich* experience" convinced him that "the achievement of success was something that could be *learned*." When the Abraham group came on stage, followers were told that, on first entering the physical world, humans "remembered that the basis of everything" was "*vibration*." The law of attraction responded to vibrations, organizing them and "bringing things of like vibrations together while holding those not of like vibrations apart." This, of course, was the continually reiterated Abraham message, as we have already seen. Here, though, we can notice that in this context Abraham urged that "*you cannot feel poor (and vibrate poor) and thrive. Abundance cannot find you unless you offer a vibration of abundance.*" Abraham observed that money was "not absolutely essential to your experience" but went on to observe that "to most people *money* and *freedom*" were "synonymous." Abraham would show followers "how to utilize the leverage of Energy" available to them to achieve their desires. People got what they thought and felt about, so they needed to be ever aware of their "vibrations" and change them so that they felt different as they thought their thoughts.[27]

Abraham worked as perennial preacher, enjoining followers over and over again on the operation of the law of attraction to experience true prosperity. "*You have to find a way of feeling the essence of what you desire before the details of that desire can come to you. In other words, you have to begin to feel more prosperous before more prosperity can come.*" Indeed, Abraham reminded, "*An improved feeling of prosperity, even if your current reality does not justify the feeling, will always bring more prosperity to you. Paying attention to the way you feel about money is a much more productive activity than noticing how others are doing.*" How could followers be sure of the difference? Abraham had an answer at the ready, emphasizing one more time the importance of the feelings that accompanied their thoughts. "*When you are thinking of money in the way that will make it come to you, you always feel good. When you are thinking of money in the way that keeps it from coming to you, you always feel bad*." Financial success, according to Abraham, did not come from hard work but instead required *"alignment of thought."* "All of the money that you want is available for you to receive," Abraham exhorted. "All you have to do is *allow* it into your experience." Still more, to the criticism that the desire for money and prosperity was unspiritual, Abraham had a straightforward answer. People needed to remember that they were "here in this very physical world where Spirit has materialized." They were living in "very physical bodies on this very physical planet"—a situation in which "that which is Spirit and that which is physical or material blend." It followed, for Abraham, that *"all of the magnificent things of a physical nature that are surrounding you are Spiritual in nature."*[28]

Physical and spiritual well-being went hand in hand in Abraham's world. Workshop attendees and followers read the transcripts, purchased excerpts on CDs, or downloaded daily messages via the Internet so that they could ever be reminded. They also meditated with a CD that established a breathing pattern by using a minimalist musical background. They needed the reminders because they were convinced that negative thoughts and feelings perennially bedeviled them in their everyday lives. So they turned repeatedly to Abraham for one more infusion of gospel truth, one more reiteration of the abundance theology by which they were trying to live in pursuit of prosperity and happiness. The message went on and still does.

My story leaves off here—trailing to be sure. What needs to be added, though, is that, when Americans began learning about trance channels in a late-century, new-century New Age climate, they were arguably ready to hear about them. Although relatively few became devotees of the channels, many more were at least peripherally acquainted with their existence and operation. And although probably even fewer had even heard of Cotton Mather, seriously read Ralph Waldo Emerson, acknowledged so much as the names of Horace Bushnell, Charles Fourier, or Andrew Jackson Davis, let alone Warren Felt Evans—Americans unawares stood in their lineage. Ideas regarding the law of correspondence had provided an alternate way of organizing the world from Puritan days. So had a sense of the divine in nature—even if the landscape spirituality of many Puritans later gave way to a predominantly abstract and cosmological view of nature in the tradition I have been pursuing. Mystical experience likewise became transformed, and so, too, vitalism and its continuing magnetic expression. The delights of fulfilled desire ran through the centuries. Delight makers in generation after generation were ready to tell Americans how they might rejoice in their fondest wishes come true and effectively pursue the happiness the Founding

Fathers had begun to champion. Prosperity became an American calling card, and the abundance theology, with its implicit process message, only flourished the more as years passed. Within it all, an aesthetic of intuition and felt sensitivity prevailed.

This, of course, is a partial reading of American culture, even of American metaphysical culture—as admitted from the first. But the reading tangibly engages a reality that is an American legacy. An Anglo-American metaphysic speaks in the public arena, and its voice is identifiable even among those who would not now call themselves Anglo-American (or even shudder at the thought). Perhaps what has come to happen would terrify the first generations, but the processes of change do their work and do their will. The ghosts of Puritans past cannot go home again. They have acquired new clothes, new words, new ways. That is the labor of history.

AFTERWORD

And Crowned Thy Good?

Michio Kushi and Herman Aihara had arrived in the United States from Japan separately. Both, however, came with a similar intention—to spread the teachings of Japanese reformer, food philosopher, and cultural nationalist George Ohsawa in their later twentieth-century time. Kushi brought with him a mixed religious background and in his home country had joined the Japanese Protestant Christian Association. Aihara, however, had a sparser acquaintance with Christianity and an innocence regarding major Christian themes. The two men ended up on opposite sides of the nation, Kushi eventually in the Boston area, and Aihara in Oroville, California. But in his co-written book *The Gospel of Peace* (1992) Kushi told the story of an invited visit that both made to the mountain home of a California friend.[1]

There, sleeping arrangements by their host put Kushi in the house and Aihara in a separate shrine on the grounds. After both had gone off to their assigned places, Kushi heard an anxious knock at his door. He opened to an Aihara in a considerable state of turmoil regarding his temporary bedroom. "A horrible thing is there! I can't sleep there," he lamented to his friend. Kushi recounted what happened next. "I went with him up the mountain to the shrine to see what it was that had disturbed my friend so much. As I entered the shrine, I saw nothing, until in the candlelight I saw on the wall a picture of Jesus hanging from the cross, suffering, bloody, tormented. I was so shocked. Of course, Herman cannot sleep there, I thought. I wouldn't be able to sleep there either. Some frightful spirit is coming from that picture." Kushi then segued into a prolonged censure of Christian history as it unraveled under the sign of the cross. "Such horrible things have happened because people have become fixated or attached to the horrible aspect of the crucifixion." "Why do so many people, not just Christians," he continued more broadly, live with "horrible hells inside of them[?] Why do they want to suffer?" "If people were released from this delusion, then they would become very happy."[2]

"What kind of mind or mentality could pray in front of such a picture?" Kushi asked rhetorically. "Instead of peaceful, merry, happy thoughts, there could be nothing but horror, shock, and guilt." Pictures like this one brought "images of fear into your mind. Only thoughts of punishment could be engendered. Or perhaps revenge. This kind of mentality creates big trouble."[3] The shock value of Aihara's and Kushi's naive perspective is manifest. Kushi's blunt questions and declarations—so stark in their rebuke of the gospel of suffering—had landed him squarely in the domain of the delight makers who have populated this study. I place his questions here because of their unvarnished reproof of a major religious project of the West, and—in this instance—the United States. They show in their harsh declaration what had been afoot more subtly when metaphysical ideas and ideologies began their work of undercutting religious orthodoxy. Indeed, among the metaphysically inclined, a strain of anti-Christian sentiment could be discerned in the nation from the nineteenth century on.

Ralph Waldo Emerson hated the Unitarian church services that he famously found "corpse-cold," even as he preferred his Sunday walks in nature. Neither Charles Fourier, nor Albert Brisbane, nor Andrew Jackson Davis could offer kind words about the organized Christianity of their time. Horace Bushnell tried to have his theology both ways—in concert with the organized Congregational church but also ever-so-friendly to the metaphysicians who were undermining it. Warren Felt Evans read and thought himself out of Methodism, ending his life in an esoteric Christianity that stretched his Swedenborgian conversion to its limits. William James spoke and wrote ambivalently on Christian right and wrong, while the trance channels wholeheartedly turned from organized Christian teaching. Delight makers, in short, largely earned their livings by sapping Christianity in favor of a newer, more expansive vision of reality that they said they knew. They were, of course, dealing with their own partial reading of Christianity, but a reading that flourished in an American culture still largely Christian in ambience. More, it was a culture that continued to push an aspect of Christianity into a worldview underlining the suffering that was part of human life and calling it redemptive.

The implications of their critical reading can be found in selected sites throughout American religious history. Even Puritan thinkers like Cotton Mather and Jonathan Edwards had trod carefully, keeping to orthodoxy and yet digging trenches around and under it to accommodate an embryonic way of thinking that began to filter in. Mather had nurtured his vitalistic preoccupation, flattening the theory of correspondence to accommodate his Nishmath-Chajim. Edwards's Calvinistic God strayed from his heavenly territory to work within nature and communicate through its processes. By the turn of the nineteenth century, perhaps surprisingly, some of these perceptions melded with those of identified freethinkers such as, for one example, Elihu Palmer. After studying to be a Presbyterian minister at Dartmouth College, Palmer had quickly turned to deism and published the anti-Christian *Principles of Nature* by 1801. Well before that, though, he was already sermonizing in the style of the delight makers. In the late 1780s, passing through Sheffield, Massachusetts, he preached that the most effective way to thank the creator for his largesse was to enjoy it, taking conscious delight in the natural world. Rather than haranguing his temporary congregation on sin and suffering, he encouraged listeners to take joy in the day "in innocent festivity, and to render themselves as happy as possible." Intriguing, too—especially in the shadow of the deism of Thomas Paine and his *Age of Reason*—was Palmer's expansive vision, in his book at least, of the unity of the material world, which was permeated by a life force that echoed European vitalism and its physiology.[4]

To make the point clear, Mather and Edwards were letting in the possibility of a different grasp of the universe, of nature, of correspondence, of the human place in it all. They were, in their own way, doing corrective work on the legacy they had inherited. Later comers would take their insights and erode the Christian base on which they were grounded. The transgressive nature of their overtures would emerge ever more strongly. Increasingly independent of the orthodox past, new metaphysicals could look at the long cultural tradition that had fostered the glorification of suffering under the cross of Jesus. They could look at it and then look away—preferring *not* to see each human life as lived in a vale of tears and instead as an opportunity for prosperity, pleasure, and the pursuit of happiness. This is, of course, a partial reading of a complex cultural move, but—as I have explained—this enterprise rests on partial readings. Such readings, I hope, will allow us to see in a different way the cultural possibilities for Anglo-Americans and fellow travelers. Beyond that, these readings seek to see the possibilities in slow motion as they transformed themselves through processes of historical encounter and change.

Given all of this, here is the "good" the deity seemed to be crowning: Although the deterioration of organized Christianity over the centuries did leave much to lament and brought in its wake considerable existential confusion, it did allow room for the emergence of a new narrative about human life that prioritized joy and blessing over pain and suffering. Such was the obvious message of the small army of positive thinkers who spread out across the American cultural landscape from the nineteenth century on. "There is a crack in everything God has made," Emerson was reputed to have written, even though he excepted reason. Much more recently, in an often-quoted line, singer/songwriter Leonard Cohen observed that the "crack in everything" was "how the light gets in."[5] So a cracked and heavily challenged Christianity—an organized tradition that left more than a passport for the late twentieth-century emergence of American secularists and agnostics—could also leave an opening for a new kind of spiritual light. Metaphysicians were providing an alternate reality system that, in its own way, confronted not only a culturally Christian society with its elevation of a crucifixion more than a resurrection. It also implicitly confronted Buddhist and other Asian views that taught detachment, the quenching of desire, and the virtue of life lived with as little emotional stir as possible.

Supplanting West and East in its brash proclamation of a vital, magnetic life that pursued happiness under the law of attraction (the former correspondence), this alternative-reality system worked as an American original. The theology of abundance, of delight through fulfillment, of sensuous and economic well-being with a body functioning in perfect health—all this beckoned with fresh promise for culture-weary humans who had earlier absorbed a more grievous message. The abundance theology could build self-esteem, enhance confidence, and create mentalities that augured success in a wide range of endeavors. It could also lay a foundation for an everyday system that instructed believers to shut the proverbial door and keep out evil, to prefer sunshine living, expansive in its embrace of the pleasure principle.

If that was the good news of the new gospel, there was more to be noticed. In keeping with the truism, "The bigger the front, the bigger the back," we need to look again. Never mind that, as I remarked earlier, the magnetic rendering of the law of attraction rested on a fundamental conceptual flaw. That is, explanations of magnetism had detailed from the first that the attractive power of the lodestone required an *opposite* magnetic pole—an observation expressed in the well-known platitude that opposites attract. Yet in the affirmative teaching that came with New Thought and similar cultural labor, it was *like* that attracted like. "*There is good for me, and I ought to have it,*" Emma Curtis Hopkins had insisted. Writers and practitioners in her tradition—like William Walker Atkinson with a vengeance—had urged the importance of thought manipulation, of a form of conjuring in which one envisioned as already accomplished what one desired. This quasi-magical process was basic to success. So the newly minted revelation backed away from the accepted science of positives and negatives that attracted. It placed itself instead in a more intuitive world that used scientific-sounding language to establish its own "vibratory" law of cosmological and emotional action. Making sense of revelation involved something different from/more than logical process.

Still further, in the new ethic of delight and the pursuit of happiness, things strayed ever further from commonsense readings of natural roots and processes. Environmental and physiological landscapes gave way before the vastness of skies and stars—and the urgency of the accumulation of wealth. Once the law of correspondence had been reinvented as the law of attraction, the beauty that had beguiled an Edwards, an Emerson, and a Bushnell faded into a delight in acquisition. Add to this the clear evidence that Americans began overtly substituting economic interest for Fourierist passion. The business of America was, indeed, business. Still—underlying the aggressive drive for business success—without the beauty of nature to partner with it, a half-hidden passion beyond economics remained. The teachings of Abraham continued to declare that desire moved the universe, that it was the heartbeat and pulse of Source that kept life expanding and made it eternal. But it is difficult to conceive the core of such incessant desire in thoroughly economic ways. A Freudian would have a field day with the Hicks-Abraham continual allusion to "rockets of desire." So even in the wealth-oriented version of desire that lay at the core of the abundance theology lurked the return of the repressed. In the end, Fourierist eroticism and passion did not evaporate. They simply got dressed in new clothes to function as the feeling and imagination out of which creation rose. This was, in itself, neither good nor bad, but it is worth noticing.

Meanwhile, to underline an observation already assumed here, the Anglo-Americana of the delight makers ran through late twentieth-century and twenty-first-century culture—middle class, ethnically diverse, mixed race, and more, even though—as I will suggest below—White supremacy pervaded the mix. Secularization has meant the growth of ever-burgeoning ranks of the non-religiously-affiliated. Besides, with the new technologies that grew, a common middle-of-the-road language dominated the public space. Metaphysics as a distinct tradition folded into a fuzzier set of lifestyle assumptions. All of this suggests more than enough ambiguity in the ethical world of delight makers and their pursuit of happiness. To bring the matter to a head, consider, if you will, historian Nell Irwin Painter's riveting judgment that none other than Ralph Waldo Emerson functioned as "the philosopher king of American white race theory." With an argument largely based on his collection of lectures published in 1856 as *English Traits*, she contended that Emerson had articulated "the earliest full-length statement of the ideology later termed Anglo-Saxonist." He had provided his audiences a synthesis of "all the salient . . . concepts of American whiteness." Once *English Traits* appeared in print, she told readers, after only three months there were 24,000 copies of the book in the United States and Great Britain, with positive reviews abounding. She called out the work for its "blatant English/Saxon chauvinism" and promotion of a "rampant Anglophilia." Not confining herself to *English Traits*, she also offered a dismal estimate of Emerson's famed essay "Self-Reliance," faulting it for its "tortured analysis" of class. But in the end it was *English Traits* that carried the most weight in her assessment. "Emerson created a white racial ideal that was both virile and handsome," she wrote. "His thinking, as they say, became hegemonic."[6]

For those literary, philosophical, and religious studies scholars who have cut their teeth on a more sanguine version of Emerson, Painter's work comes as a shock—and, on reflection, a reformative shock. Even a cursory reading of *English Traits* more than supports her scathing analysis of these collected lectures. We learn that the English are "a powerful and ingenious race." With the racial issue, for Emerson, a highly significant factor in human culture, it operated as "a controlling influence in the Jew," and "in the negro" was of "appalling importance." In Emerson's judgment, "queries concerning ancestry and blood" might "be well allowed," because no prosperity seemed "more to depend on the kind of man than British prosperity." "Only a hardy and wise people could have made this small territory great." Things got even more appalling as Emerson proceeded. The "English face" showed "combined decision and nerve, with the fair complexion, blue eyes, and open and florid aspect." "The fair Saxon man," declared Emerson, was "not the wood out of which cannibal, or inquisitor, or assassin" was formed. By contrast, he was "moulded for law, lawful trade, civility, marriage, the nurture of children, for colleges, churches, charities, and colonies." In fact, in England existed "the best stock in the world, broad-fronted, broad-bottomed, best for depth, range, and equability, men of aplomb and reserves, great range and many moods, strong instincts, yet apt for culture."[7]

Clearly, within Emerson's praise for the English, White supremacy loomed large. Still more, if we use Emerson's statement as a searchlight for questioning delight makers as a cohort, problems grow. How much of the gospel of happiness and abundance is predicated on a certain class and kind of people, secure in the privilege that comes with whiteness and also displaying a related series of other markers? How does it work if you are born among people of color, people also dealing with poverty, family dysfunction, neighborhood decay, police and government abuse and indifference, school and workmates who encourage misery and even criminality? How does it operate if you are born not in the United States at all but in a refugee camp in Syria, or among members of drug cartels in Central America, or among masses waiting at the Mexican border to enter the United States, or in disease-ravaged Brazil or India? How does it explain draughts, wildfires, hurricanes, floods, tornadoes, cyclones, monsoons, volcanic eruptions, and other climactic catastrophes? What is its answer for plague, pestilence, and pandemic? What does it say about victims of crime and violence? How does it respond to unprovoked war, with millions fleeing from bombarded homes—as in the Ukraine? The list goes on. Hicks-Abraham, at least, would insist that each person who enters the world in a particular time and place has chosen these circumstances and that the contrast can spur a definitive turn away from suffering and toward a better path. But the pronouncements ring hollow after any daily broadcast of national and planetary news.

Still more, it could be argued that delight makers have exhibited a solipsism that has belied their testimony to a web of connection in a universe in which all express one eternal mystery of consciousness and love. The pursuit of the selfish may honor diversity and choice among all beings, but it is hardly a call to action in a mission for social justice. By contrast, Christianity with its "offensive" crucifixion has many times spurred the zeal of social reformers. The cross can be a statement not so much about suffering glorified as about the power of love and forgiveness. Suffering could, in effect, become a transcendent and powerful redemptive tool. Love could overcome fear and hate, and the cross of Jesus could be seen as a clear break in the hate chain that held humanity bound. Love could lead to violent death *and* to emancipation and freedom, with nascent possibilities for a human race saved and reborn. As historian of religions Mircea Eliade wrote in his classic *Cosmos and History*, "one of the great superiorities of Christianity, compared with the old Mediterranean ethics, was that it gave value to suffering and even to a seeking out of pain for its salutary qualities."[8]

A myriad of late twentieth- and twenty-first-century demonstrations come to mind to underline the power seen in Christian suffering. For an example here, let the late US Congressman from Georgia, John R. Lewis, be a stand-in. The great-grandson of a slave and son of a tenant farmer in Alabama, he found in his Christian faith a conviction that suffering was redemptive and that he was called to endure it in the cause of nonviolent revolution. Historian Jon Meacham's study has tracked the faith-filled trajectory of Lewis from seminary days in Nashville through his leadership in early sit-ins and freedom rides in which he was continually bruised and beaten, and kept on going back for more. Always he responded to hatred and physical violence with a discipline calling out love and compassion for perpetrators. Elected chair of the Student Nonviolent Coordinating Committee by acclamation in 1963, two years later in Selma, Alabama, he marched across the Edmund Pettus Bridge on notorious "Bloody Sunday," clubbed, tear-gassed, unconscious, and bleeding, with a concussion and a fractured skull. Lewis survived. Years later, before his death from pancreatic cancer in July 2020, he looked back on the movement of the 1960s and the role he had played in it. He asked a new generation to get into "good trouble." He reminded them that within the movement led by Martin Luther King Jr., Lewis and his fellow activists had told elected officials and the nation, "We *can* change. We *can* help create the Beloved Community. We *can* help redeem the soul of America."[9] For Lewis and those like him, no good could be crowned without the cross.

How to square Lewis's steadfast conviction, his gospel of suffering and redemption through violence, with the theology of abundance and the affirmative gospel of the delight makers? There are no easy answers here, and piecing together the stark alternatives requires acts of cognitive stretching that are, in themselves, painful. Add to the problem that the abundance theology can be especially harsh on the unsuccessful, the unhealed, and the emotionally broken. If positive mental processes attract the good that people desire, then those whom the law of attraction eludes are easily scorned for failure. Hubris can reign, and a blame-the-victim ideology can judge them as at best misfits, or ignoramuses, or ne'er-do-wells. The abundance theology hails the law of attraction and human alignment with it. If we do not at first catch hold in the merry-go-round of life, delight makers insist that with discipline, faith, and positive imagining we can jump on. If we do not, *we* are responsible for the bad results.

The huge irony here is that makers of delight clearly show up in their own ways among the suffering—with their good, like Lewis's, not crowned without pain and distress. Even before their agenda was more fully developed in the nineteenth century, Mather endured the deaths of wives and numerous children as well as years of political angst and uncertainty. Edwards was dismissed from his pastorate at Northampton and later alienated yet another congregation at Stockbridge. With an apparently irascible temperament, he waged theological war over the revivals he came to champion. Bushnell's professional life, in the mid-nineteenth century, was lived amid voluminous criticism of his writings, a denominational "heresy" trial, and years of ill health with his infamous "throat trouble." Emerson, meanwhile, felt the pain of loss when his young wife and first-born son both died. Brisbane suffered woes of his own making as he failed in successive marriages and failed yet more grandly to execute his strongly advocated plans for social reform. Davis functioned as a cantankerous twit, even as he attracted a steady following for his free-love ideas and pronouncements regarding spirits. Relegated to an extremist role in society, he experienced a success that was never quite successful and lived with a huge chip on his shoulder toward conventional religion especially.

Far more painful was Evans's life journey, as his search for divine union brought him into anguished mystical territory at the same time his chronic illnesses followed him. James shared Evans's mental anguish but for different reasons, living through suicidal thoughts and years of depression that belied his professional façade of success. Hopkins felt the sting of rejection when she was fired by Mary Baker Eddy and an even more stinging conflict when her seminary became a source of continual infighting. Elizabeth Towne had her failed first marriage to point to as well as her struggles with almost-poverty and her later political defeat in Holyoke. Atkinson experienced two nervous breakdowns and a lifetime of overproduction, as if he had to keep chasing success or fall into some great chasm. Jane Roberts was plagued by ill health throughout her life and was also greatly troubled in her continual and exhausting interactions with Seth. Jerry Hicks, who so admired her, after his own itinerant life and marital adventures, died of leukemia—with a large challenge to the teachings of Abraham. Esther Hicks probably fared best, bearing the brunt of her husband's death but finding her own inner resources to continue her work without him.

Lest this amount to a near-dismissal of the American theology of abundance and a withering condemnation, it needs to be said that—as the results I earlier identified show—it has been a multivalent project. The concerted effort to deny and banish suffering has existed as one example of a human predilection for denial that people engage when they want something to go away. And as historians remind us, people live in their own cultural worlds—some vastly better off than the worlds of others. Cultural bubbles protect and insulate. They largely prevent visionary wanderings over the horizon of circumstance. Pondering these issues makes it difficult to throw the first stone.

On another matter, like all human creations—as I have tried to show—the abundance theology evolved and changed over the years. If it beckoned more aesthetically and holistically before the law of attraction began to dominate it, we can also observe that even at its most crass and banal, an underlying vision of good abided. Whatever its condition, the metaphysical pursuit of happiness in America does shine a light on its vision of the sacrality of the material world. In a kind of sacramentalism that, in its own way, harks back to classical Christian ideas about the physical gifts of the creation and its imputed creator, delight makers found in their quests for wealth, health, and happiness resonances with the expanding processes of a vast universe. They were mimicking an eternal and unending order, and so they could celebrate materiality instead of simply using it as so many crutches to move beyond into a world of spirit. As they did so, they went about the task of creating meaning for themselves and their own lives—this very much before they could look to the lives and circumstances of others.

William James in his *Varieties of Religious Experience* had judged the religion of the "sick-minded" to be more complete than that of the "healthy-minded." His judgment meant more than a hiccup for an unadulterated embrace of the abundance theology. But as he also recognized, overbeliefs and commitments to the "more" could vary from person to person. So again as a working historian, I have to notice that where and when individuals are born, what class, and race, and gender they represent, and all the other particulars that can be named have more than a casual bearing on what sense they make of life and how they live it. That acknowledged, my remarks here have not been intended to pull the rug out from under the delight makers—especially after the deep searching of my readings. These reflections are only meant to frame their project with its creativity but also its wobbles—and with the sharpness of its juxtaposition to inherited alternatives. With all their ethical quandaries, delight makers cannot be pushed back into some deep American closet. For good or ill, they have something important to say. They are a voice in the public square, and they offer lessons in living that should not be silenced.

ACKNOWLEDGMENTS

First, I owe a large debt to those long-ago citizens of Yellow Springs, Ohio, who first introduced me to modern-day metaphysics and provided a full-throttle education on its themes. Since I have been writing in the area of metaphysical religion for a while now, I also need to acknowledge my own previous work. Like Johann S. Bach, Georg F. Handel, Giacomo Rossini, and other composers whose music I love, I freely borrowed from previous books and articles I wrote, adding, subtracting, and repurposing in ways that made sense for my current project. These adaptations have been cheerfully acknowledged in the notes and are all used with permission.

That said, there is very much more here that I had not figured out in previous work, and so I acquired newer debts. To aid me in writing this book, I need to thank the University of California, Santa Barbara, which made it possible for me to have an ongoing sabbatical without a designated end date. Retirement from such a generous institution has been a wonderful experience. UCSB's Davidson Library, with its Interlibrary Loan Department, has come through again and again with rare sources that I needed and online access to still others. So has the Internet, with its further wealth of digitized sources that in another era would be unusable except through extensive travel. The coronavirus pandemic, too, with its lockdowns and health restrictions, has enabled me to double down on research and writing with new intensity. Meanwhile, UCSB has honored a research fund from the time of my retirement that has supported incidental publishing expenses.

Over the years, Philip Deslippe provided research assistance and, much more recently, generously shared with me his own writing—both published and unpublished—on William Walker Atkinson. For Warren Felt Evans, James F. Lawrence of the Swedenborgian House of Studies, at Pacific School of Religion in the Graduate Theological Union at Berkeley, provided important feedback and details. Independent scholar Keith McNeil likewise pointed me toward a wealth of details regarding Evans from his own research. At the University of Chicago Press, Alan G. Thomas has been patient and encouraging for more years than I want to own up to in public. Meanwhile, Kyle Wagner, who has recently come aboard as editor, has graced me with his sharp eyes and incisive comments that were just right. The two anonymous readers for the press also provided me with valuable insights. Finally, I have dedicated this book to all the teachers and students from whom I have learned over the years—some of them in official academic settings and others through the serendipities of passing events, friends, and acquaintances. I am more than ever ready to admit to the web of influences that makes each of my projects in reality a community affair, and I remain humbled by all the intellectual and personal good that has come out of that reality.

NOTES

INTRODUCTION

1. For a full discussion of these themes, see Catherine L. Albanese, *A Republic of Mind and Spirit: A Cultural History of American Metaphysical Religion* (New Haven, CT: Yale University Press, 2007).
2. For more on vitalism, see Sebastian Normandin and Charles T. Wolfe, eds., *Vitalism and the Scientific Image in Post-Enlightenment Life Science, 1800–2010* (Dordrecht: Springer, 2013).
3. William A. Clebsch, *American Religious Thought: A History* (Chicago: University of Chicago Press, 1973).

SECTION ONE

1. Robert Calef, *More Wonders of the Invisible World* (1700), as quoted in Kenneth Silverman, *The Life and Times of Cotton Mather* (1984; reprint, New York: Welcome Rain, 2002), 110.
2. Jonathan Edwards, "Sinners in the Hands of an Angry God" (1741), in Clarence H. Faust and Thomas H. Johnson, eds., *Jonathan Edwards: Representative Selections, with Introduction, Bibliography, and Notes* (New York: Hill and Wang, 1962), 164.

CHAPTER ONE

1. For the summary material expressed here, see Richard F. Lovelace, *The American Pietism of Cotton Mather: Origins of American Evangelicalism* (Grand Rapids, MI: Christian College Consortium, 1979), esp. 27; Cotton Mather, *Paterna: The Autobiography of Cotton Mather*, ed. Ronald A. Bosco (Delmar, NY: Scholars' Facsimiles & Reprints, 1976), iv–ix; and Otho T. Beall Jr. and Richard H. Shryock, *Cotton Mather: First Significant Figure in American Medicine* (Baltimore, MD: Johns Hopkins University Press, 1954), 123–24. For general treatments, see Robert Middlekauff, *The Mathers: Three Generations of Puritan Intellectuals, 1596–1728* (1971; reprint, New York: Oxford University Press, 1976); and Kenneth Silverman, *The Life and Times of Cotton Mather* (1984; reprint, New York: Welcome Rain, 2002).
2. A. Whitney Griswold, "Three Puritans on Prosperity," *New England Quarterly* 7, no. 3 (1934): 478–79; Sacvan Bercovitch, "'Delightful Examples of Surprising Prosperity': Cotton Mather and the American Success Story," *English Studies: A Journal of English Letters and Philology* 51, no. 1 (1970): 41, 43.

3. Cotton Mather, *A Christian at His Calling: Two Brief Discourses. One Directing a Christian in His General Calling; Another Directing Him in His Personal Calling* (Boston: B. Green & J. Allen for Samuel Sewall Jr., 1701), 21, 24, 37–39, 45, 48, 60, 70. Italics in text quotations from Mather throughout are always transcribed from sources. In biblical quotations, I have transcribed material as it appears in the King James Version.
4. Cotton Mather, *Bonifacius: An Essay upon the Good, That Is to Be Devised and Designed, by Those Who Desire to Answer the Great End of Life, and to Do Good While They Live* (Boston: B. Green, 1710), 136–37, 140–41. For the scriptural quotations, cf. Eccles. 11:1 and Prov. 3:9–10.
5. Cotton Mather, *The Way to Prosperity: A Sermon Preached to the Honourable Convention of the Governour, Council, and Representatives of the Massachuset-Colony in New-England, on May 23. 1689* (Boston: R. Pierce for Joseph Brunning, Obadiah Gill, and James Woode, 1690), 9. Mather cites and quotes 1 Chron. 22:11 ("My son, the LORD be with thee; and prosper thou, and build the house of the LORD thy God"); Cotton Mather, *A Town in Its Truest Glory: A Brief Essay upon a Town Happy, and Glorious; Recommending, Those Things, by which a Town May Come to Flourish with All Prosperity* (Boston: B. Green for Daniel Henchman, 1712), 12–13; Cotton Mather, *A Man of Reason: A Brief Essay to Demonstrate, That All Men Should Hearken to Reason* (Boston: John Edwards, 1718), 30.
6. David Levin, *Cotton Mather: The Young Life of the Lord's Remembrancer, 1663–1703* (Cambridge, MA: Harvard University Press, 1978), esp. 256–65; Cotton Mather, *Parentator: Memoirs of Remarkables in the Life and the Death of the Ever-Memorable Dr. Increase Mather, Who Expired August 23, 1723* (Boston: Printed by B. Green for Nathaniel Belknap, 1724), 83; Levin, *Cotton Mather*, 258.
7. Kate Bowler, *Blessed: A History of the American Prosperity Gospel* (New York: Oxford University Press, 2013), 30; Cotton Mather, *The Minister: A Sermon, Offer'd unto the Anniversary Convention of Ministers, from Several Parts of New-England* (Boston: n.p., 1722), 14; Middlekauff, *Mathers*, 191–208.
8. Middlekauff, *Mathers*, 245–46; Cotton Mather, *Pia Desideria: Or, The Smoking Flax, raised into a Sacred Flame; In a Short and Plain Essay upon those Pious Desires* (Boston: S. Kneeland for S. Gerrish, 1722), 6, 7.
9. Middlekauff, *Mathers*, 303.
10. Lovelace, *American Pietism of Cotton Mather*, 5, 53, 28.
11. Cotton Mather, *The Christian Philosopher: A Collection of the Best Discoveries in Nature, with Religious Improvements* (London: Eman. Matthews, 1720). I have read Mather's work in the modern edition: Mather, *The Christian Philosopher*, ed. Winton U. Solberg (Urbana: University of Illinois Press, 1994). See 237, 318. Solberg reads *The Christian Philosopher* with clear attention to Mather's pietism. See his introduction, esp. xci, cix–cx.
12. Ralph Boas and Louise Boas, *Cotton Mather: Keeper of the Puritan Conscience* (New York: Harper, 1928), 259, 266; Levin, *Cotton Mather*, 75.
13. I. Woodbridge Riley, *American Philosophy: The Early Schools* (New York: Dodd, Mead, 1907), 197–99; for Miller, see Perry Miller, "From Edwards to Emerson," in *Errand into the Wilderness* (1956; reprint, New York: Harper & Row, 1964), 184–203.
14. Woodbridge Riley, *American Thought: From Puritanism to Pragmatism and Beyond* (1915; reprint, New York: Greenwood Press, 1969), 174–75. Winton Solberg details this line of interpretation in his introduction to *The Christian Philosopher*, extending his observations to Kenneth B. Murdock; see Solberg, ed., "Introduction," in Mather, *Christian Philosopher* (1994), cvi–cvii.

15. Mather, *Christian Philosopher*, 191.
16. Cotton Mather, cited and quoted in Lovelace, *American Pietism of Cotton Mather*, 121.
17. Mather, "An Appendix Touching Prodigies in New-England," in *Way to Prosperity*, (unnumbered) 9.
18. Mather, "Appendix," 10–12.
19. Mather, *Paterna*, 236. Bosco's transcription is in typeface, and the underlinings are probably approximations of Mather's emphases (typically expressed as italics in sources published in Mather's own day).
20. Levin, *Cotton Mather*, 52.
21. For a helpful account of Mather's *Magnalia Christi Americana*, see Silverman, *Life and Times of Cotton Mather*, 156–66.
22. Cotton Mather, *Magnalia Christi Americana; or, The Ecclesiastical History of New-England, in Seven Books*, 2 vols. (Hartford, CT: Silas Andrus & Son, 1853), 1:25; the translation from Virgil's *Aeneid* is my own, based on the Latin text in Charles Knapp, ed., *The Aeneid of Vergil*, rev. ed. (Chicago: Scott, Foresman, 1951), 139.
23. Mather, *Magnalia*, 1:25; 2:6.
24. Mather, *Magnalia*, 2:6.
25. Mather, *Magnalia*, 2:6, 341–42. See also the account in Silverman, *Life and Times of Cotton Mather*, 157.
26. Mather, *Magnalia*, 2:343, 6.
27. Mather, *Magnalia*, 2:355, 357–61.
28. Mather, *Magnalia*, 2:361–62; Cotton Mather, BRONTOLOGIA SACRA: *The Voice of God in the Thunder; Explained and Applied in a Sermon Uttered by a Minister of the Gospel in a Lecture to an Assembly of Christians Abroad, at the Very Same Time When the Thunder Was by the Permission and Providence of God Falling upon his Own House at Home* (London: John Astwood, 1695).
29. Mather, *Magnalia*, 2:364.
30. Mather, *Magnalia*, 2:425.
31. Mather, *Magnalia*, 2:448.
32. Mather, *Magnalia*, 2:448–49, 449, 450, 452, 453, 456–65.
33. Mather, *Magnalia*, 2:456–59.
34. For a pertinent discussion of metaphysical religiosity, see Catherine L. Albanese, *A Republic of Mind and Spirit: A Cultural History of American Metaphysical Religion* (New Haven, CT: Yale University Press, 2007), 6–10; for references to astrology and fortune tellers, see Mather's biography of William Phips, the first royally assigned governor of Massachusetts Bay, in Mather, *Magnalia*, 1:222–23.
35. Cotton Mather, *Batteries upon the Kingdom of the Devil: Seasonable Discourses upon Some Common, but Woful, Instances, Wherein Men Gratifie the Grand Enemy of Their Salvation* (London: Nath. Hiller, 1695), 41; Lovelace, *American Pietism of Cotton Mather*, 188.
36. Lovelace, *American Pietism of Cotton Mather*, 189; Silverman, *Life and Times of Cotton Mather*, 125.
37. Cotton Mather, *Diary*, as quoted and cited in Silverman, *Life and Times of Cotton Mather*, 127–28; Mather, *Paterna*, 109.
38. Mather, *Paterna*, 110–13.
39. See the account in Silverman, *Life and Times of Cotton Mather*, 129.
40. Silverman, *Life and Times of Cotton Mather*, 169; see also Lovelace's summary—somewhat different from this—in *American Piety of Cotton Mather*, 190.
41. Cotton Mather, *Diary*, 2:365–66, as quoted in Lovelace, *American Pietism of Cotton Mather*, 246–47.

42. Cotton Mather, *A Discourse on Witchcraft*, in *Memorable Providences, Relating to Witchcrafts and Possession* (Boston: R. P. and Joseph Brunning, 1689), 5; Boas and Boas, *Cotton Mather*, 198; on the cosmological connection, see Levin, *Cotton Mather*, 152.
43. Cotton Mather, *Diary*, 1:81, 83, as quoted in Lovelace, *American Pietism of Cotton Mather*, 125; Lovelace, *American Pietism of Cotton Mather*, 144; Mather, *Paterna*, 122, 126.
44. Lovelace, *American Piety of Cotton Mather*, 145.
45. Silverman, *Life and Times of Cotton Mather*, 171–72.
46. Mather, *Christian Philosopher*, 19, 88, 89.
47. Mather, *Christian Philosopher*, 111, 121.
48. Gen. 2:7. All biblical quotations hereafter are from the King James Version, the biblical translation familiar to metaphysicians for most of the history this narrative explores.
49. Middlekauff, *Mathers*, 318.
50. Cotton Mather, quoted in Silverman, *Life and Times of Cotton Mather*, 122, 133.
51. Silverman, *Life and Times of Cotton Mather*, 122.
52. Cotton Mather, *Coheleth: A Soul upon Recollection; Coming into Incontestible Sentiments of Religion, such as All the Sons of Wisdom Will and Must Forever Justify* (Boston: S. Kneeland for S. Gerrish, 1720), 16.
53. Solberg, ed., "Introduction," in Mather, *Christian Philosopher*, l, lvi, lxxi, lxxxii.
54. Cotton Mather, *The Angel of Bethesda: Visiting the Invalids of a Miserable World* (New-London[, CT]: Timothy Green, 1722); Beall Jr. and Shryock, *Cotton Mather*, 53–54; Cotton Mather, *The Angel of Bethesda*, ed. Gordon W. Jones (Barre, MA: American Antiquarian Society and Barre Publishers, 1972); Cotton Mather, *The Threefold Paradise of Cotton Mather: An Edition of "Triparadisus,"* ed. Reiner Smolinski (Athens: University of Georgia Press, 1995), with an introduction and full scholarly apparatus. Mather revisited the "Triparadisus" in 1726/1727, but it remained unpublished until this 1995 edition. *The Angel of Bethesda* as a longer treatise (1724) at last appeared in print in 1972 under the auspices of the American Antiquarian Society, edited by medical doctor Gordon W. Jones. Kenneth Silverman calls it "the only comprehensive American medical work of the entire colonial period" in *Life and Times of Cotton Mather*, 406.
55. Beall and Shryock, *Cotton Mather*, 64.
56. Mather, *Angel of Bethesda* (1722), 1; Silverman, *Life and Times of Cotton Mather*, 92.
57. Silverman, *Life and Times of Cotton Mather*, 408–9; Mather, *Angel of Bethesda* (1722), 4, 10.
58. Mather, *Angel of Bethesda* (1722), 12.
59. Mather, *Angel of Bethesda* (1972), 28–38, 29–30 (Mather's proposed subtitle for his new, more comprehensive *Angel of Bethesda* was *An ESSAY upon the Common Maladies of Mankind*); Gordon W. Jones, ed., "Introduction: Part II"), in Mather, *Angel of Bethesda* (1972), xvii; Mather, *Angel of Bethesda* (1972), 5.
60. Mather, *Angel of Bethesda* (1722), 11.
61. Middlekauff, *Mathers*, 321; Mather, *Threefold Paradise*, 122–26.
62. Emanuel Swedenborg, *Heaven and Its Wonders and Hell: From Things Heard and Seen* (1758), trans. J. C. Ager (1852; reprint, New York: Swedenborg Foundation, 1964), 17–22; Andrew Jackson Davis, *The Principles of Nature, Her Divine Revelations, and a Voice to Mankind*, 34th ed. (Boston: Colby and Rich, 1881), 674–77 (there is evidence this was actually the 17th ed.); Mather, *Threefold Paradise*, 123. See also Mather, *Angel of Bethesda* (1722), 5–6, and Mather, *Angel of Bethesda* (1972), 31.

CHAPTER TWO

1. This brief biographical sketch relies on many sources, including, from latest to earliest, Philip F. Gura, *Jonathan Edwards: America's Evangelical* (New York: Hill and Wang, 2005); George M. Marsden, *Jonathan Edwards: A Life* (New Haven, CT: Yale University Press, 2003); Edward M. Griffin, *Jonathan Edwards* (Minneapolis: University of Minnesota Press, 1971); Perry Miller, *Jonathan Edwards* ([New York]: William Sloane Associates, 1949); Ola Elizabeth Winslow, *Jonathan Edwards, 1703–1758* (New York: Macmillan, 1940); Henry Bamford Parkes, *Jonathan Edwards: The Fiery Puritan* (New York: Minton, Balch, 1930); Alexander V. G. Allen, *Jonathan Edwards* (Boston: Houghton, Mifflin, 1889); Samuel Miller, "Life of Jonathan Edwards," in Samuel Miller and William P. O. Peabody, *Lives of Jonathan Edwards and David Brainerd* (Boston: Hilliard, Gray, 1837); Sereno Dwight, ed., *The Works of President Edwards: With a Memoir of His Life*, vol. 1 (New York: S. Converse, 1829); [Samuel Hopkins], *The Life of the Late Reverend, Learned and Pious Mr. Jonathan Edwards* (Boston: S. Kneeland, 1765) (also available as Samuel Hopkins, *Memoirs of the Life, Experience and Character of the Late Rev. Jonathan Edwards, A. M., President of the College, at Prince-town, in New-Jersey*, in Edward Williams and Edward Parsons, eds., *The Works of President Edwards*, vol. 1 [1817; reprint, New York: Burt Franklin, 1968]).
2. On influences for Edwards's "Of Being," see E. Brooks Holifield, "Edwards as Theologian," in Stephen J. Stein, ed., *The Cambridge Companion to Jonathan Edwards* (New York: Cambridge University Press, 2007), 146; see also Jonathan Edwards, "Of Being," in John E. Smith et al., eds., *The Works of Jonathan Edwards*, vol. 6, *Scientific and Philosophical Writings*, Wallace E. Anderson, ed. (New Haven, CT: Yale University Press, 1980), 203, n. 3; and Jonathan Edwards, *The "Miscellanies"*, in Thomas A. Schafer, ed., *The "Miscellanies"*, a-500, vol. 13 of Smith et al., *Works* (1994).
3. Edwards, "Of Being," 203.
4. Jonathan Edwards, Entry No. 194, in Edwards, *"Miscellanies"*, 334–35; Edwards, "Of Being," 202, 206.
5. Jonathan Edwards, "The Mind" (ca. 1723), in Anderson, ed., *Scientific and Philosophical Writings*, 336, 337, 354.
6. E. Brooks Holifield, *Theology in America: Christian Thought from the Age of the Puritans to the Civil War* (New Haven, CT: Yale University Press, 2003), 104–5.
7. Edwards, "Mind," 333–35; Marsden, *Jonathan Edwards*, 79.
8. Edwards, "Mind," 337–38; John E. Smith, Harry S. Stout, and Kenneth P. Minkema, "Editors' Introduction," in Smith, Stout, and Minkema, eds., *A Jonathan Edwards Reader* (New Haven, CT: Yale University Press, 1995), xiii.
9. Jonathan Edwards, "Personal Narrative" (ca. 1739), in George S. Claghorn, ed., *Letters and Personal Writings*, vol. 16 of Smith et al., *Works* (1998), 791–94.
10. Edwards, "Personal Narrative," 790–91, 794–95.
11. Edwards, "Personal Narrative," 795, 796, 793, 801.
12. Winslow, *Jonathan Edwards*, 139; Smith, Stout, and Minkema, "Editor's Introduction," xxxiii; Edwards, Entry No. 189, in Edwards, *"Miscellanies"*, 332.
13. Perry Miller, "Introduction," in Jonathan Edwards, *Images or Shadows of Divine Things*, ed. Perry Miller (1948; reprint, Westport, CT: Greenwood Press, 1977), 36; Edwards, *Images or Shadows*, 79 (no. 79); William A. Clebsch, *American Religious Thought: A History* (Chicago: University of Chicago Press, 1973), 17–18.
14. Jonathan Edwards, "A Divine and Supernatural Light," in Mark Valeri, ed., *Sermons and Discourses, 1730–1733*, vol. 17 of Smith et al., *Works* (1999), 410 (emphasis in original), 413, 414–15; Winslow, *Jonathan Edwards*, 137.

15. Jonathan Edwards, *Heaven Is a World of Love*, sermon 15 of *Charity and Its Fruits* (1738), in Paul Ramsey, ed., *Ethical Writings*, vol. 8 of Smith et al., *Works* (1989), 368 (emphasis in original), 369–71, 385–86.
16. Jonathan Edwards, *Two Dissertations: Dissertation I, Concerning the End for Which God Created the World*, in Ramsey, ed., *Ethical Writings*, 433–35, 441.
17. Edwards, *Images or Shadows*, 61 (no. 57); Clarence H. Faust and Thomas H. Johnson, "Introduction," in Faust and Johnson, eds., *Jonathan Edwards: Representative Selections, with Introduction, Bibliography, and Notes* (New York: Hill and Wang, 1962), xcvi; Jonathan Edwards, "Beauty of the World" (1725), in Anderson, ed., *Scientific and Philosophical Writings*, 305–6.
18. Marsden, *Jonathan Edwards*, 463; Edwards, *End for Which God Created the World*, 531; Parkes, *Jonathan Edwards*, 65, 36; Miller, *Jonathan Edwards*, 292; Faust and Johnson, "Introduction," cv. The passage, found in Edwards's "Personal Narrative," 793–94, concerns Edwards's disclosure that after his conversion experience, his "sense of divine things gradually increased" so that "God's excellency" appeared in "everything; in the sun, moon and stars; in the clouds, and blue sky; in the grass, flowers, trees; in the water, and all nature."
19. Miller, "Introduction," 38.
20. Riley, *American Philosophy*, 153; Clebsch, *American Religious Thought*, 50, 54; Jonathan Edwards, *Two Dissertations: Dissertation II, The Nature of True Virtue*, in Ramsey, ed., *Ethical Writings*, 539, 540–41, 543, 548, 619 (emphases in original).
21. Paul Ramsey, "Editor's Introduction," in Ramsey, ed., *Ethical Writings*, 5; Edwards, *End for Which God Created the World*, 432–33, 435 (emphases in original).
22. Edwards, "Mind," 332, 344, 362, 380, 363.
23. Jonathan Edwards, *A Treatise concerning Religious Affections*, ed. John E. Smith, vol. 2 of Smith et al., *Works* (1959), 96–98 (emphasis in original).
24. For the influence of John Locke on Edwards, see the summary discussion in Morton White, *Science and Sentiment in America: Philosophical Thought from Jonathan Edwards to John Dewey* (London: Oxford University Press, 1972), 9–29, 49–54; Edwards, *Religious Affections*, 101, 132.
25. Edwards, *Religious Affections*, 201; White, *Science and Sentiment*, 49.
26. Roland A. Delattre, *Beauty and Sensibility in the Thought of Jonathan Edwards: An Essay in Aesthetics and Theological Ethics* (1968; reprint, Eugene, OR: Wipf and Stock, 2006), vii, 1; Karl Barth, *Church Dogmatics*, vol. 2, part 1 (Edinburgh: T. & T. Clark, 1957), 651, as quoted in Delattre, *Beauty and Sensibility*, 119–20.
27. Delattre, *Beauty and Sensibility*, 145.
28. Alan Heimert, *Religion and the American Mind: From the Great Awakening to the Revolution* (Cambridge, MA: Harvard University Press, 1966), 95, 103–4; Marsden, *Jonathan Edwards*, 259; Holifield, *Theology in America*, 105.
29. Holifield, *Theology in America*, 122–23; Mark A. Noll, *America's God: From Jonathan Edwards to Abraham Lincoln* (New York: Oxford University Press, 2002), 23.
30. Jonathan Edwards to Lady Mary Pepperrell, Stockbridge, MA, 28 November 1751, in Claghorn, ed., *Letters and Personal Writings*, 415, 417; Jonathan Edwards, Entry No. *a*, in Edwards, "*Miscellanies*," 163; Edwards, "Personal Narrative," 796; Marsden, *Jonathan Edwards*, 44, 505.
31. Miller, "Introduction," 40; Edwards, *Images or Shadows*, 44 (no. 8).
32. On Edwards and "mechanical philosophy, see Avihu Zakai, "The Age of Enlightenment," in Stein, ed., *Cambridge Companion*, 85, 87; Edwards, *Images or Shadows* 69 (no. 70).

33. Allen, *Jonathan Edwards*, 68; on the theory of correspondence among the Transcendentalists, see Catherine L. Albanese, *Corresponding Motion: Transcendental Religion and the New America* (Philadelphia: Temple University Press, 1977).
34. Edwards, *Images or Shadows*, 109 (no. 156); Marsden, *Jonathan Edwards*, 77; Edwards, "Mind," 353; Marsden, *Jonathan Edwards*, 80.
35. Jonathan Edwards, "Of the Prejudices of the Imagination," in Anderson, ed., *Scientific and Philosophical Writings*, 196–97.
36. Edwards, *Images or Shadows*, 94 (no. 117); Edwards, "Beauty of the World," 305–6.
37. See the *Catholic Encyclopedia* at http://www.newadvent.org/cathen/14254a.htm, and the classic, if dated, Evelyn Underhill, *Mysticism: A Study in the Nature and Development of Man's Spiritual Consciousness* (New York: Dutton, 1911). A 12th edition of this latter work was published in 1955 by World Publishing.
38. Edwards, "Beauty of the World," 306; Allen, *Jonathan Edwards*, 24; Riley, *American Philosophy*, 126–27, 153.
39. Riley, *American Thought*, 28, 31.
40. White, *Science and Sentiment*, 33; Parkes, *Jonathan Edwards*, 39–40; Gura, *Jonathan Edwards*, 66–67; Winslow, *Jonathan Edwards*, 76–78.
41. Miller, *Jonathan Edwards*, 193.
42. Edwards, "Personal Narrative," 790, 792, 793.
43. Richard Maurice Bucke, *Cosmic Consciousness: A Study in the Evolution of the Human Mind* (Philadelphia: Innes, 1901); Edwards, "Personal Narrative," 794, 801.
44. Edwards, "Personal Narrative," 801–4.
45. Edwards, "Divine and Supernatural Light," 413, 421–22.
46. Edwards, "Divine and Supernatural Light," 424.
47. Edwards, *"Religious Affections,"* 132, 197 (emphasis in original), 200.
48. Edwards, *"Religious Affections,"* 201–2, 205–6.
49. Edwards, *End for Which God Created the World*, 527–28.
50. Edwards, *End for Which God Created the World*, 531 (emphases in original).

SECTION TWO

1. Ralph Waldo Emerson, "Self-Reliance," in Joseph Slater, Alfred R. Ferguson, and Jean Ferguson Carr, eds., *Essays: First Series*, vol. 2 of *The Collected Works of Ralph Waldo Emerson* (Cambridge, MA: Harvard University Press, Belknap Press, 1979), 33.
2. Ralph Waldo Emerson, quoted in Perry Miller, "From Edwards to Emerson," in Miller, *Errand into the Wilderness* (1956; reprint, New York: Harper & Row, Harper Torchbooks, 1964), 188; Miller, "From Edwards to Emerson," 184–203.

CHAPTER THREE

1. Thomas W. Higginson, *Contemporaries* (Boston: Houghton, Mifflin, 1899), 2:1; Moncure Daniel Conway, *Emerson at Home and Abroad* (Boston: R. Osgood, 1882), 35; Ralph L. Rusk, *The Life of Ralph Waldo Emerson* (New York: Charles Scribner's Sons, 1949), 7–9; Ralph Waldo Emerson, "New England Reformers," in Joseph Slater, Alfred R. Ferguson, and Jean Ferguson Carr, eds., *Essays: Second Series*, vol. 3 of *The Collected Works of Ralph Waldo Emerson* (Cambridge, MA: Harvard University Press, Belknap Press, 1983), 153. Biographical material summarized here is also taken from a variety of sources, including Rusk, *Life of Ralph Waldo Emerson*; Catherine L. Albanese, "Charon and the River: The Changing Religious Symbols of Six American Transcendentalists" (PhD diss., University of Chicago, 1972), and *Corresponding Motion: Transcendental Religion and the New America* (Philadelphia: Temple University Press,

1977); and https://www.notablebiographies.com/Du-Fi/Emerson-Ralph-Waldo.html. Biographical treatments of Emerson, often themed, abound. From the 1970s on, for example, these include Stephen E. Whicher, *Freedom and Fate: An Inner Life of Ralph Waldo Emerson*, 2d ed. (Philadelphia: University of Pennsylvania Press, 1971); Edward Wagenknecht, *Ralph Waldo Emerson: Portrait of a Balanced Soul* (New York: Oxford University Press, 1974); Joel Porte, *Representative Man: Ralph Waldo Emerson in His Time* ((New York: Oxford University Press, 1979); Gay Wilson Allen, *Waldo Emerson: A Biography* (New York: Viking Press, 1981); David Robinson, *Apostle of Culture: Emerson as Preacher and Lecturer* (Philadelphia: University of Pennsylvania Press, 1982); John McAleer, *Ralph Waldo Emerson: Days of Encounter* (Boston: Little, Brown, 1984); Evelyn Barish, *Emerson: The Roots of Prophecy* (Princeton, NJ: Princeton University Press, 1989); Donald L. Gelpi, *Endless Seeker: The Religious Quest of Ralph Waldo Emerson* (Lanham, MD: University Press of America, 1991); Robert D. Richardson, *Emerson: The Mind on Fire—A Biography* (Berkeley: University of California Press, 1995); Ronald A. Bosco and Joel Myerson, *Emerson in His Own Time: A Biographical Chronicle of His Life* (Iowa City: University of Iowa Press, 2003); and Len Gougeon, *Emerson and Eros: The Making of a Cultural Hero* (Albany: State University of New York Press, 2007).
2. Hovering in the background of this assessment is Sherman Paul's classic study, *Emerson's Angle of Vision: Man and Nature in American Experience* (Cambridge, MA: Harvard University Press, 1952).
3. Ralph Waldo Emerson, "Circles," in Joseph Slater, Alfred R. Ferguson, and Jean Ferguson Carr, eds., *Essays: First Series*, vol. 2 of *The Collected Works of Ralph Waldo Emerson* (Cambridge, MA: Harvard University Press, Belknap Press, 1979), 179–81.
4. Emerson, "Circles," 186, 188.
5. Emerson, "Circles," 188–89.
6. Emerson, "Circles," 190; Ralph Waldo Emerson, *Nature*, in Robert E. Spiller and Alfred R. Ferguson, eds., *Nature, Addresses, and Lectures*, vol. 1 of *The Collected Works of Ralph Waldo Emerson* (Cambridge, MA: Harvard University Press, Belknap Press, 1971), 7 (emphasis in original).
7. Emerson, *Nature*, 7, 9, 10.
8. Emerson, *Nature*, 12–13, 17, 23, 42–43, 45 (emphases in original); Richard Holmes, *Coleridge: Darker Reflections, 1804–1834* (New York: Pantheon, 1999), 361.
9. Erik Ingvar Thurin, *Emerson as Priest of Pan: A Study in the Metaphysics of Sex* (Lawrence: Regents Press of Kansas, 1981); Ralph Waldo Emerson, "History," in Slater, Ferguson, and Carr, eds., *Essays: First Series*, 22; Gougeon, *Emerson and Eros*, 5, 7.
10. Ralph Waldo Emerson, *The Journals and Miscellaneous Notebooks of Ralph Waldo Emerson*, vol. 9, 1843–1847, ed. Ralph H. Orth and Alfred R. Ferguson (Cambridge, MA: Harvard University Press, Belknap Press, 1971), 381, 339. Conrad Wright, "Emerson, Barzillai Frost, and the Divinity School Address," in Wright, *The Liberal Christians: Essays on American Unitarian History* (Boston: Beacon Press, 1970), 42–44, 49–50, 53. Wright quoted Emerson's journals.
11. Ralph Waldo Emerson, "The Divinity School Address," in Spiller and Ferguson, eds., *Nature, Addresses, and Lectures*, 76, 79–81, 85–86.
12. Emerson, "Divinity School Address," 90, 92–93.
13. William A. Clebsch, *American Religious Thought: A History* (Chicago: University of Chicago Press, 1973), 74, 192, n. 24; Emerson, "History," 8, 21; Ralph Waldo Emerson, "Self-Reliance," in Slater, Ferguson, and Carr, eds., *Essays: First Series*, 31, 37, 40; Ralph Waldo Emerson, "Compensation," in Slater, Ferguson, and Carr, eds., *Essays: First Series*, 71.

14. Ralph Waldo Emerson, "Love," in Slater, Ferguson, and Carr, eds., *Essays: First Series*, 99–100, 105–6.
15. Emerson, "Love," 109.
16. Ralph Waldo Emerson, "Friendship," in Slater, Ferguson, and Carr, eds., *Essays: First Series*, 121–22; Thurin, *Emerson as Priest of Pan*, 172; Ralph Waldo Emerson, "Clubs," in Ronald A. Bosco and Douglas Emory Wilson, eds., *Society and Solitude*, vol. 7 of *The Collected Works of Ralph Waldo Emerson* (Cambridge, MA: Harvard University Press, Belknap Press, 2007), 115, 122, 114; Ralph Waldo Emerson, "Inspiration," in Joel Myerson, ed., *Letters and Social Aims*, vol. 8 of *The Collected Works of Ralph Waldo Emerson* (Cambridge, MA: Harvard University Press, Belknap Press, 2010), 163.
17. Ralph Waldo Emerson, "The Over-Soul," in Slater, Ferguson, and Carr, eds., *Essays: First Series*, 159–60; Ralph Waldo Emerson, "Art," in Slater, Ferguson, and Carr, eds., *Essays: First Series*, 216.
18. Ralph Waldo Emerson, "The Poet," in Slater, Ferguson, and Carr, eds., *Essays: Second Series*, 3–4, 16, 13, 9.
19. Gougeon, *Emerson and Eros*, 13, 117, 223, n. 175; Ralph Waldo Emerson, "Beauty," in Barbara L. Packer, Joseph Slater, and Douglas Emory Wilson, eds., *The Conduct of Life*, vol. 6 of *The Collected Works of Ralph Waldo Emerson* (Cambridge, MA: Harvard University Press, Belknap Press, 2003), 155–56; Thurin, *Emerson as Priest of Pan*, 167.
20. Ralph Waldo Emerson, "Books," in Bosco and Wilson, eds., *Society and Solitude*, 95; Ralph Waldo Emerson, "Domestic Life," in Bosco and Wilson, eds., *Society and Solitude*, 65–66; Emerson, "Inspiration," 160.
21. Thurin, *Emerson as Priest of Pan*, 3.
22. Emerson, "Inspiration," 152–53, 154.
23. Emerson, "Inspiration," 154–55.
24. Richardson, *Emerson*, 23.
25. Ralph Waldo Emerson, "Demonology," in Robert E. Spiller and Wallace E. Williams, eds., *Human Life*, vol. 3 of *The Early Lectures of Ralph Waldo Emerson, 1838–1842* (Cambridge, MA: Harvard University Press, Belknap Press, 1972), 151, 156, 157, 167.
26. Emerson, "Demonology," 168–69.
27. Emerson, "Demonology," 169–70.
28. For a full-length biography of Emanuel Swedenborg, see Inge Jonsson, *Emanuel Swedenborg*, trans. Catherine Djurklou (New York: Twayne, 1971); for a briefer view, see Jane K. Williams-Hogan, "Swedenborg: A Biography," in Erland J. Brock et al., eds., *Swedenborg and His Influence* (Bryn Athyn, PA: Academy of the New Church, 1988), 3–27; and Sig Synnestvedt, "Life of Emanuel Swedenborg," in Synnestvedt, ed., *The Essential Swedenborg: Basic Teachings of Emanuel Swedenborg, Scientist, Philosopher, and Theologian* (New York: Twayne, 1970).
29. Ralph Waldo Emerson, "Swedenborg; or, the Mystic," in Wallace E. Williams and Douglas Emory Wilson, eds., *Representative Men: Seven Lectures*, vol. 4 of *The Collected Works of Ralph Waldo Emerson* (Cambridge, MA: Harvard University Press, Belknap Press, 1987), 77, 79–80, 65, 69.
30. Emerson, "Swedenborg; or, the Mystic," 65–66, 69, 75, 71–72; Swedenborg's controversial book is available in English as Emanuel Swedenborg, *The Delights of Wisdom Pertaining to Conjugial Love after Which Follow the Pleasures of Insanity Pertaining to Scortatory Love* (1768), trans. Samuel M. Warren and rev. trans. Louis H. Tafel (1856; reprint, New York: Swedenborg Foundation, 1980).
31. See https://qz.com/1099800/average-size-of-a-us-family-from-1850-to-the-present/ ; on Puritans and sexuality, see, for example, Edmund S. Morgan, "The Puritans and

Sex," *New England Quarterly* 15, no. 4 (1942): 591–607; Lelan Ryken, *Worldly Saints: The Puritans as They Really Were* (Grand Rapids, MI: Zondervan, 1986); and Richard Godbeer, *Sexual Revolution in Early America: Gender Relations in the American Experience* (Baltimore: Johns Hopkins University Press, 2002); Thurin, *Emerson as Priest of Pan*, 113; Emerson, "Love," 109.

32. Ralph Waldo Emerson, "The Individual," in Stephen W. Whicher, Robert E. Spiller, and Wallace E. Williams, eds., *The Philosophy of History*, vol. 2 of *The Early Lectures of Ralph Waldo Emerson, 1836–1838* (Cambridge, MA: Harvard University Press, Belknap Press, 1964), 181; Clebsch, *American Religious Thought*, 79, 95.
33. Emerson, "Over-Soul," 167, 159, 160, 166–67, 168.
34. J. August Higgins, "The Aesthetic Foundations of Religious Experience in the Writings of Jonathan Edwards and Ralph Waldo Emerson," *American Journal of Theology and Philosophy* 38, nos. 2–3 (2017): 164–66; Emerson, *Nature*, 45; Higgins, "Aesthetic Foundations," 166.
35. Ralph Waldo Emerson, "The Uses of Natural History," in Stephen W. Whicher and Robert E. Spiller, eds., *Science*, vol. 1 of *The Early Lectures of Ralph Waldo Emerson, 1833–1836* (Cambridge, MA: Harvard University Press, Belknap Press, 1966), 24–26; Thurin, *Emerson as Priest of Pan*, 4–5.
36. Emerson, "Natural History," 2–3
37. Emerson, "Natural History," 21–23. The full last-line sentence in the essay references Emerson's unexamined arrogance and racism, since he cites not only the "child" and "unschooled farmer's boy," but first the "idiot" and the "Indian."
38. Emerson, *Nature*, 8; Emerson, "Demonology," 158, 170; Emerson, *Nature*, 16, 10, 17, 1 (emphasis in original).
39. Swedenborg, quoted in Emerson, "Swedenborg, or the Mystic," 60–61 (emphasis in original), 65.
40. Ralph Waldo Emerson, "Wealth," in Packer, Slater, and Wilson, eds., *Conduct of Life*, 54, 60; Emerson, "Domestic Life," 55; Ralph Waldo Emerson, *The Journals and Miscellaneous Notebooks of Ralph Waldo Emerson*, vol. 7, 1838–1842, ed. A. W. Plumstead and Harrison Hayford (Cambridge, MA: Harvard University Press, Belknap Press, 1969), 142; Emerson, "Wealth," 67–68.
41. Ralph Waldo Emerson, "Art," in Bosco and Wilson, eds., *Society and Solitude*, 20; Gertrude Reif Hughes, *Emerson's Demanding Optimism* (Baton Rouge: Louisiana State University Press, 1984), 147 155 (emphasis in original; Hughes cited Sherman Paul's classic *Emerson's Angle of Vision* [1952] to her point regarding dynamism).
42. Emerson, "Compensation," 57.
43. Emerson, "Compensation," 58, 63, 59, 64, 70, 59.
44. Clebsch, *American Religious Thought*, 105–6; Ralph Waldo Emerson, *The Journals and Miscellaneous Notebooks of Ralph Waldo Emerson*, vol. 4, 1832–1834, ed. Alfred R. Ferguson (Cambridge, MA: Harvard University Press, Belknap Press, 1964), 314; Emerson "Friendship," 116.
45. Higgins, "Aesthetic Foundations"; Clebsch, *American Religious Thought*, xvi; Emerson, "Poet," 5; Emerson, "Friendship," 114; Ralph Waldo Emerson, "Spiritual Laws," in Slater, Ferguson, and Carr, eds., *Essays: First Series*, 77.
46. Emerson, "Art," in Slater, Ferguson, and Carr, eds., *Essays: First Series*, 213; Emerson, "Divinity School Address," 77; Gougeon, *Emerson and Eros*, 4; Emerson, "Love," 106, 104.
47. Emerson, *Nature*, 15–17.
48. Emerson, "Beauty," 153–54, 161–63.

49. Emerson, *Nature*, 10; Emerson, "Over-Soul," 166–67.
50. Emerson, "Over-Soul," 173–74.

CHAPTER FOUR

1. This reading of Horace Bushnell has been freely adapted from "Horace Bushnell among the Metaphysicians," *Church History* 79, no. 3 (2010): 614–53 (© American Society of Church History, 2010; adapted with permission), and—for Bushnell's relation to Emanuel Swedenborg—from my introduction to *The Spiritual Journals of Warren Felt Evans: From Methodism to Mind Cure* (Bloomington: Indiana University Press, 2016), 38–40, again with permission. Biographical material on Bushnell has been culled from a number of sources, including Mary Bushnell Cheney, *Life and Letters of Horace Bushnell* (New York: Harper & Brothers, 1880); Theodore T. Munger, *Horace Bushnell: Preacher and Theologian* (Boston: Houghton, Mifflin, 1899); Barbara M. Cross, *Horace Bushnell: Minister to a Changing America* (Chicago: University of Chicago Press, 1958); Robert L. Edwards, *Of Singular Genius, of Singular Grace: A Biography of Horace Bushnell* (Cleveland, OH: Pilgrim Press, 1992); Robert Bruce Mullin, *The Puritan as Yankee: A Life of Horace Bushnell* (Grand Rapids, MI: William B. Eerdmans, 2002).
2. See Catherine L. Albanese, *A Republic of Mind and Spirit: A Cultural History of American Metaphysical Religion* (New Haven, CT: Yale University Press, 2007). For a brief overview, see Catherine L. Albanese, *America: Religions and Religion*, 5th ed. (Boston: Wadsworth, Cengage Learning, 2013), 184–87.
3. For earlier scholarship, see J. Stillson Judah, *The History and Philosophy of the Metaphysical Movements in America* (Philadelphia: Westminster, 1967), esp. 21, 11; and Charles S. Braden, *Spirits in Rebellion: The Rise and Development of New Thought* (Dallas: Southern Methodist University Press, 1963), esp. 4. On contemporary scholarship about metaphysical religiosity, see Albanese, *Republic of Mind and Spirit*, esp. 21–118, for a full discussion of this summary; Leigh Eric Schmidt, *Restless Souls: The Making of American Spirituality* (San Francisco: HarperSanFrancisco, 2005), although Schmidt does not employ the term *metaphysical*; and the special issue of the *Journal of the American Academy of Religion* 75, no. 3 (2007): 582–677, with essays by Courtney Bender, John Lardas Modern, and Pamela Klassen, and an introduction by Albanese. For an early American version, see Jon Butler, *Awash in a Sea of Faith: Christianizing the American People* (Cambridge, MA: Harvard University Press, 1990).
4. See Winthrop S. Hudson, *Religion in America* (New York: Charles Scribner's Sons, 1965), 175–78; Cheney, *Life and Letters*, 195; Munger, *Horace Bushnell*, 43; Cross, *Horace Bushnell*, 28; Edwards, *Singular Genius*, 295; Mullin, *Puritan as Yankee*, 6.
5. Cheney, *Life and Letters*, 108; Letter of Ralph Waldo Emerson to George Partridge Bradford, August 28, 1854, in Ralph L. Rusk, ed., *The Letters of Ralph Waldo Emerson* (1939; reprint, New York: Columbia University Press, 1966), 4:460 (and see Edwards, *Singular Genius*, 61, who reads the ambiguous reference this way).
6. Theodore Parker, *A Discourse on the Transient and Permanent in Christianity: Preached at the Ordination of Mr. Charles C. Shackford, in the Hawes Place Church in Boston, May 19, 1841* (Boston: B. H. Greene and E. P. Peabody, 1841); Theodore Parker, *A Discourse of Matters Pertaining to Religion* (Boston: Charles C. Little and James Brown, 1842); Horace Bushnell, *Nature and the Supernatural, As Together Constituting the One System of God* (1858; reprint, London: Alexander Strahan, 1864), 352 (and see the references to Parker on 94–96, 108–9, 228, 233, 237, 249–50, 280, and 355).
7. Bushnell, *Nature and the Supernatural*, 41 (see also 97–98, where Emerson is condemned along with Thomas Carlyle).

8. Bushnell, *Nature and the Supernatural*, 23–24.
9. Horace Bushnell, "Inspiration by the Holy Spirit," in [Mary Bushnell Cheney, ed.] *The Spirit in Man: Sermons and Selections*, centenary ed. (New York: Charles Scribner's Sons, 1907), 15–16.
10. Samuel Taylor Coleridge, *Aids to Reflection*, ed. James Marsh (Burlington, VT: Chauncey Goodrich, 1829); Cheney, *Life and Letters*, 203 (emphasis in original). On Bushnell and Gibbs, see Donald A. Crosby, *Horace Bushnell's Theory of Language: In the Context of Other Nineteenth-Century Philosophies of Language* (The Hague: Mouton, 1975), 50–55; and David L. Smith, ed., *Horace Bushnell: Selected Writings on Language, Religion, and American Culture* (Chico, CA: Scholars Press, 1984), 8–9.
11. See Philip F. Gura, *The Wisdom of Words: Language, Theology, and Literature in the New England Renaissance* (Middletown, CT: Wesleyan University Press, 1981), 53, where he called Bushnell a "Christian Transcendentalist." Gura was following the model suggested by Ronald V. Wells in *Three Christian Transcendentalists: James Marsh, Caleb Sprague Henry, Frederic Henry Hedge* (New York: Columbia University Press, 1943); see also Crosby, *Bushnell's Theory of Language*, 153.
12. Horace Bushnell, *God in Christ: Three Discourses Delivered at New Haven, Cambridge, and Andover, with a Preliminary Dissertation on Language* (1849; reprint, New York: Charles Scribner's Sons, 1876), 25–26; Ralph Waldo Emerson, *Nature*, in Robert E. Spiller and Alfred R. Ferguson, eds., *Nature, Addresses, and Lectures*, vol. 1 of *The Collected Works of Ralph Waldo Emerson* (Cambridge, MA: Harvard University Press, Belknap Press, 1971), 17.
13. Bushnell, *God in Christ*, 30 (uppercase in original), 78.
14. Bushnell, *God in Christ*, 46–47, 80, 92–93.
15. Horace Bushnell, "Revelation," in Smith, ed., *Horace Bushnell*, 29–30; Edwards, *Singular Genius*, 58–60. On the language of hieroglyphs in the American Renaissance (language employed by both Bushnell and Emerson), see John T. Irwin, *American Hieroglyphics: The Symbol of the Egyptian Hieroglyphics in the American Renaissance* (New Haven, CT: Yale University Press, 1980).
16. Horace Bushnell, *Christ in Theology: Being the Answer of the Author before the Hartford Central Association of Ministers, October, 1849, for the Doctrines of the Book Entitled "God in Christ"* (Hartford, CT: Brown and Parsons, 1851), 15 (uppercase in original), 37–38.
17. Horace Bushnell, "Our Gospel a Gift to the Imagination," in Conrad Cherry, ed., *Horace Bushnell: Sermons* (New York: Paulist Press, 1985), 97, 99, 105, 98, 101. The entire essay appears in Horace Bushnell, *Building Eras in Religion* (New York: Charles Scribner's Sons, 1881), 249–85.
18. Thomas C. Upham, *Life and Religious Opinions and Experience of Madame de La Mothe Guyon: Together with Some Account of the Personal History and Religious Opinions of Fénelon, Archbishop of Cambray*, 2 vols. (New York: Harper, 1846).
19. On Mary Bushnell's written recollections, as well as Cheney's own, see Cheney, *Life and Letters*, 191–92, 64, 46; and see the short accounts in Edwards, *Singular Genius*, 96–97, and Mullin, *Puritan as Yankee*, 128–30, 41.
20. Cheney, *Life and Letters*, 76, 276–77, 516 (emphasis in original).
21. Cheney, *Life and Letters*, 516; Horace Bushnell, *Christian Nurture* (1860; reprint, New York: Charles Scribner, 1867), 197 (this is an expanded version of the *Discourses on Christian Nurture* of 1847 and is an ultimate version containing a series of earlier ones); Bushnell, *God in Christ*, 147 (emphasis in original); Bushnell, *Nature and the Supernatural*, 127 (emphasis in original); Bushnell, "Our Gospel a Gift," 102.

22. Horace Bushnell, "Christ the Form of the Soul," in Bushnell, *Spirit in Man*, 39–40; Horace Bushnell, "The Immediate Knowledge of God," in Bushnell, *Sermons on Living Subjects* (New York: Scribner, Armstrong, 1872), 115, 122; Horace Bushnell, "Our Advantage in Being Finite," in Bushnell, *Sermons on Living Subjects*, 340; Horace Bushnell, "God Preparing the State of Glory," in Bushnell, *Spirit in Man*, 226–27.
23. Bushnell, "Revelation," 30; Letter of Horace Bushnell to Cyrus Bartol, April 11, 1849, in Cheney, *Life and Letters*, 220.
24. William Alexander Johnson, *Nature and the Supernatural in the Theology of Horace Bushnell* (Lund, Sweden: CWK Gleerup, 1963), 13, 231; Crosby, *Bushnell's Theory of Language*, 161–63. The fear of being labeled a pantheist had apparently not troubled Bushnell until after he wrote *God in Christ*, since the term appears neither in that work nor in his earlier one on Christian nurture.
25. Ralph Waldo Emerson, "The Divinity School Address," in Robert E. Spiller and Alfred R. Ferguson, eds., *Nature, Addresses, and Lectures*, vol. 1 of *The Collected Works of Ralph Waldo Emerson* (Cambridge, MA: Harvard University Press, Belknap Press, 1971), 81; Emerson, *Nature*, 43. On the miracles question, see William R. Hutchison, *The Transcendentalist Ministers: Church Reform in the New England Renaissance* (Boston: Beacon Press, 1959), 52–97.
26. Emerson, *Nature*, 43; Bushnell, *Nature and the Supernatural*, 23.
27. Bushnell, *Nature and the Supernatural*, 234, 325–27.
28. Bushnell, *Nature and the Supernatural*, 333–34.
29. Bushnell, *Nature and the Supernatural*, 335–38.
30. Perry Miller, "From Edwards to Emerson," in Miller, *Errand into the Wilderness* (1956; reprint, New York: Harper & Row, Harper Torchbooks, 1964), 202.
31. Frank B. Carpenter, "Studio Talks with Dr. Horace Bushnell," *The Independent* 52, no. 2667 (1900): 117, 117–19; on "Brama," or "Brahma" and "Brahminism [sic]," see, for example, the references in Bushnell, *God in Christ*, 140, 173; Bushnell, *Nature and the Supernatural*, 42, 51, 249–50, 290; Horace Bushnell, "The War of Our Desires" (1848), in Bushnell, *Spirit in Man*, 369; and Horace Bushnell, "Death Abolished" (1849), in Bushnell, *Spirit in Man*, 286.
32. "Obituary Record of the Graduates of Bowdoin College and the Medical School of Maine for the Year Ending 1 June 1893," *Bowdoin College Library Bulletin*, No. 4, Second Series: 138; B. F. Barrett, *A Cloud of Independent Witnesses to the Truth, Value, Need, and Spiritual Helpfulness of Swedenborg's Teachings* (Philadelphia: Swedenborg Publishing Association, 1891), 171.
33. Bushnell, *Nature and the Supernatural*, 321.
34. Munger, *Horace Bushnell*, 177; Bushnell, "God Preparing the State of Glory," 220, 222; Horace Bushnell, "God's One Family," in Bushnell, *Spirit in Man*, 341–43.
35. According to Howard A. Barnes (*Horace Bushnell and the Virtuous Republic* [Metuchen, NJ: American Theological Library Association and Scarecrow Press, 1991], 139), Andrew Jackson Davis later published this material in 1852 as *The Approaching Crisis: Being a Review of Dr. Bushnell's Recent Lectures on Supernaturalism* (New York: Published by the Author, 1852). See, in a still later edition, A. J. Davis, "A Letter to Rev. Dr. Bushnell" (Hartford, Dec. 15, 1851), in Andrew Jackson Davis, *The Approaching Crisis: Being A Review of Dr. Bushnell's Course of Lectures, on the Bible, Nature, Religion, Skepticism, and the Supernatural* (Boston: Colby & Rich, 1868), 7–8 (emphasis in original).
36. Bushnell, *Nature and the Supernatural*, 9, 40.
37. Horace Bushnell, "Unconscious Influence," in *Sermons for the New Life* (New York: Charles Scribner, 1858), 197, 202 (and see Smith, *Symbolism and Growth*, 49–57, for

a useful discussion of this sermon); Horace Bushnell, "Life, or the Lives," in Bushnell, *Work and Play: Or Literary Varieties* (New York: Charles Scribner, 1864), 268 (emphasis in original); see Davis, *Approaching Crisis* (1868), 239. For magnetism, see Franz Anton Mesmer, *Physical-Medical Treatise on the Influence of the Planets (1766)*, in Mesmer, *Mesmerism: A Translation of the Original Medical and Scientific Writings*, trans. George J. Bloch and introduced by Ernest R. Hilgard (Los Altos, CA: William Kaufmann, 1980), 1–20.

38. Bushnell, *Nature and the Supernatural*, 9, 97, 123.
39. Bushnell, *Christian Nurture*, 26, 118, 31.
40. On Bushnell's organicism, see Conrad Cherry, "The Structure of Organic Thinking: Horace Bushnell's Approach to Language, Nature, and Nation," *Journal of the American Academy of Religion* 40, no. 1 (1972): esp. 3; Horace Bushnell, "The Age of Homespun," in Bushnell, *Work and Play*, 380–81, 392–93 (and see Mullin, *Puritan as Yankee*, 10–11, on the oration).
41. Bushnell, *God in Christ*, 212; Bushnell, "Work and Play," in Bushnell, *Work and Play*, 10, 13 (emphasis in original), 14–15; Cross, *Horace Bushnell*, 27.
42. Horace Bushnell, "The Spirit in Man," in *Sermons for the New Life*, 31; Bushnell, "War of Our Desires," 368–69; Horace Bushnell, "Christ Regenerates Even the Desires," in Bushnell, *Sermons on Living Subjects*, 192–93.
43. Bushnell, *Christian Nurture*, 211; Horace Bushnell, "Prosperity Our Duty," in Bushnell, *Spirit in Man*, 135–58, 139.
44. Cheney, *Life and Letters*, 15, 524.
45. Bushnell, *Christian Nurture*, 393, 401; Bushnell, *Christ in Theology*, 249, 338.
46. Bushnell, *God in Christ*, 106, 48 (emphasis in original), 50 (emphasis in original), 52, 55, 73, 77.
47. Bushnell, *God in Christ*, 93–95, 347, 106.
48. Bushnell, *God in Christ*, 137–39.
49. Bushnell, *Christ in Theology*, 16–17, 39–40.
50. For example, Emma Curtis Hopkins, the major teacher of New Thought teachers, had been Congregationalist when she began the odyssey from the Christian Science of Mary Baker Eddy (with Eddy's own Congregational roots) to what came to be called New Thought. Myrtle Fillmore, cofounder of Unity School of Christianity, had been Methodist. H. Emilie Cady, author of Unity's basic textbook, *Lessons in Truth*, was a homeopathic physician with a Presbyterian background, who for a time followed the New York City work of A. B. Simpson, founder of the Christian and Missionary Alliance, with excitement. La Roy Sunderland—who began a journal on magnetism, combined magnetism with phrenology, incorporated spiritualism, and celebrated the laws of mind—had been a Methodist minister and charismatic preacher of revival before his transformation. Warren Felt Evans, a major early New Thought theologian, served as a Methodist minister for twenty-five years and was drawn to proto-Holiness and Oberlin perfectionism before sending back his ordination credentials, becoming a Swedenborgian, a spiritualist, and then a "mind-cure" healer. Tithing practices in New Thought churches like Unity and Religious Science parallel those in conservative Protestant ones. The ethos of worship in New Thought churches is usually exuberant and enthusiastic, a style associated with much of American evangelicalism.
51. Bushnell, *Christ in Theology*, 340, 131–32.
52. For a succinct and pithy overview, see *The Westminster Dictionary of Church History*, ed. Jerald C. Brauer (Philadelphia: Westminster Press, 1971), s.v. "Sin"; see also Piet

Schoonenberg, *Man and Sin: A Theological View*, trans. Joseph Donceel (Notre Dame, IN: University of Notre Dame Press, 1965).

53. Volumes from the English translator of Plato Thomas Taylor were available from at least 1804, and Taylor continued to write in a Neo-Platonizing vein. See, for example, Arthur Versluis, *The Esoteric Origins of the American Renaissance* (New York: Oxford University Press, 2001), 145; and John McAleer, *Ralph Waldo Emerson: Days of Encounter* (Boston: Little, Brown, 1984), 160.
54. Bushnell, *Nature and the Supernatural*, 21; Johnson, *Nature and the Supernatural*, 103; Bushnell, *Nature and the Supernatural*, 58, 69–70.
55. Bushnell, *Nature and the Supernatural*, 92, 111, 125.

SECTION THREE

1. Courtney Bender, *The New Metaphysicals: Spirituality and the American Religious Imagination* (Chicago: University of Chicago Press, 2010), 4–5, 122.
2. Walt Whitman, *Leaves of Grass: The Original 1855 Edition* (np: np), 17.

CHAPTER FIVE

1. For biographical information on Albert Brisbane, see—as primary sources—his (not to be totally trusted "as-told-to") autobiography—Redelia Brisbane, *Albert Brisbane: A Mental Biography with A Character Study* (1893; reprint, New York: Burt Franklin, 1969); Albert Brisbane, *The European Travel Diaries of Albert Brisbane, 1830–1832: Discovering Fourierism for America*, ed. Abigail Mellen and Allaire Brisbane Stallsmith (Lewiston, NY: Edwin Mellen Press, 2005); Albert Brisbane, *Letters of the American Socialist Albert Brisbane to K. A. Varnhagen von Ense*, ed. Terry H. Pickett and Françoise de Rocher (Heidelberg: Carl Winter Universitätsverlag, 1986). See also Richard Norman Pettitt Jr., "Albert Brisbane: Apostle of Fourierism in the United States, 1834–1890" (PhD diss., Miami University, 1982); Lloyd E. Rohler Jr., "The Utopian Persuasion of Albert Brisbane, First Apostle of Fourierism" (PhD diss., Indiana University, 1977); Arthur Eugene Bestor Jr., "Albert Brisbane—Propagandist for Socialism in the 1840's," *New York History* 28, no. 2 (1947): 128–58; and—for a contemporary synopsis from the 1840s—"Albert Brisbane," *The United States Magazine and Democratic Review* 11, no. 51 (1842): 302–4.
2. R. Brisbane, *Albert Brisbane*, 118.
3. Albert Brisbane, *Social Destiny of Man; or, Association and Reorganization of Industry* (1840; reprint, New York: Burt Franklin, 1968).
4. Brisbane, *European Travel Diaries*, 23, n. 55.
5. Jonathan Beecher and Richard Bienvenu, trans. and eds., *The Utopian Vision of Charles Fourier: Selected Texts on Work, Love, and Passionate Attraction* (Boston: Beacon Press, 1971), 3. Other sources on the life and teaching of Fourier include the hagiographic early biography in French by his physician, Charles Pellarin, *Charles Fourier, sa vie et sa théorie* (Paris:Librairie de L'École Societaire, 1843); also in French, much more recently, Pascal Bruckner, *Fourier* (Paris: Seuil, 1975); and, in English, Parke Godwin, *A Popular View of the Doctrines of Charles Fourier* (1844; reprint, Philadelphia: Porcupine Press, 1972); Nicholas V. Riasanovsky, *The Teaching of Charles Fourier* (Berkeley: University of California Press, 1969). The definitive biography is Jonathan Beecher, *Charles Fourier: The Visionary and His World* (Berkeley: University of California Press, 1986).
6. See Beecher, *Charles Fourier*, 26, and Charles Pellarin, *The Life of Charles Fourier*, 2nd ed., trans. Francis Geo. Shaw (New York: William H. Graham, 1848), 8.

7. Beecher and Bienvenu, *Utopian Vision*, 8.
8. For a full account of the Fourier bibliography, see Beecher, *Charles Fourier*, 571–79.
9. Beecher, *Charles Fourier*, 83, 81–84, 207–8
10. R. Brisbane, *Albert Brisbane*, 53.
11. Rohler, "Utopian Persuasion," 159; R. Brisbane, *Albert Brisbane*, 72; Brisbane, *European Travel Diaries*, 176.
12. R. Brisbane, *Albert Brisbane*, 109, 146, 155; Brisbane, *European Travel Diaries*, xi.
13. Brisbane, *European Travel Diaries*, 52.
14. R. Brisbane, *Albert Brisbane*, 55–56.
15. Rohler, "Utopian Persuasion," 151, 15–17; Carl J. Guarneri, *The Utopian Alternative: Fourierism in Nineteenth-Century America* (Ithaca, NY: Cornell University Press, 1991), 32.
16. Guarneri, *Utopian Alternative*, 32–33.
17. Albert Brisbane, *Association; or, A Concise Exposition of the Practical Part of Fourier's Social Science* (1843; reprint, New York: AMS Press, 1975); Parke Godwin, *A Popular View of the Doctrines of Charles Fourier* (1844; reprint, Philadelphia: Porcupine Press, 1972); Guarneri, *Utopian Alternative*, 94, 355; for the "New Amorous World," or *Le Nouveau monde amoureux*, see Beecher and Bienvenu, *Utopian Vision*, xiii, 54. Parke Godwin (1816–1904) was an American journalist strongly interested in Fourierism. A year after he published his *Popular View*, he became critical of Brisbane.
18. Guarneri, *Utopian Alternative*, 353, 355 (the Hempel work was *The True Organization of the New* [Swedenborgian] *Church*); Charles Fourier, *The Social Destiny of Man; or, Theory of the Four Movements*, trans. Henry Clapp Jr., with *A Treatise on the Functions of the Human Passions*; and Albert Brisbane, *An Outline of Fourier's System of Social Science* (1857; reprint, New York: Gordon Press, 1972); Brisbane, *Outline*, 161.
19. Albert Brisbane and Charles Fourier, *Sociological Series, No. I: General Introduction to Social Science* (1876; reprint, Westport, CT: Hyperion Press, 1976); and Charles Fourier and Albert Brisbane, *Sociological Series, No. II: Theory of Social Organization* (1876; facsimile ed., Ann Arbor, MI: University of Michigan, University Microfilms, 1967); Brisbane and Fourier, *Sociological Series, No. I*, iii–iv; Fourier and Brisbane, *Sociological Series, No. II*, 244–51.
20. Albert Fried, *Socialism in America: From the Shakers to the Third International—A Documentary History* (Garden City, NY: Doubleday, 1970), 7. For a brief and helpful discussion of the Newton-Fourier relationship, see Guarneri, *Utopian Alternative*, 334–35n.
21. R. Brisbane, *Albert Brisbane*, 192–93 (emphases in original).
22. Brisbane, *Social Destiny of Man*, 24.
23. Brisbane, *Social Destiny of Man*, 202, 185–86, 245, 249 (emphases in original).
24. Rohler, "Utopian Persuasion," 43, 127; Brisbane, *Social Destiny of Man*, 348; Michael Fellman, *The Unbounded Frame: Freedom and Community in Nineteenth-Century American Utopianism* (Westport, CT: Greenwood Press, 1973), 5; Brisbane, *Association*, 15, 17.
25. R. Brisbane, *Albert Brisbane*, 210.
26. Guarneri, *Utopian Alternative*, 187.
27. Pettitt, "Albert Brisbane," 75–78; Charles Fourier, quoted in Brisbane, *Association*, 43 (emphases in original).
28. Brisbane, *Social Destiny of Man*, vii, 113, 459.

29. Albert Brisbane, *Fundamental Principles of Fourier's Theory of Social Science*, bound with Fourier, *Social Destiny of Man*, 117, 119.
30. Brisbane, *Fundamental Principles*, 161–62.
31. Brisbane, *Fundamental Principles*, 168–70.
32. Albert Brisbane and Charles Fourier, *Sociological Series, No. I: General Introduction to Social Science* (New York: C. P. Somerby, 1876), 26–31.
33. Fourier, *Social Destiny of Man*, iv, ix.
34. Fourier, *Social Destiny of Man*, 103, 117–18, 120–21 (emphases in original).
35. Fourier, *Social Destiny of Man*, 122, 126, 127.
36. Beecher and Bienvenu, *Utopian Vision*, 398; Charles Fourier, *The Theory of the Four Movements*, trans. Ian Patterson and ed. Gareth Stedman Jones and Ian Patterson (Cambridge, UK: Cambridge University Press, 1996), 45.
37. Rohler, "Utopian Persuasion," 51–52; R. Brisbane, *Albert Brisbane*, 245; Rohler, "Utopian Persuasion," 146.
38. Brisbane, *Association*, 3; Brisbane, *Social Destiny of Man*, 209; Guarneri, *Utopian Alternative*, 94.
39. Brisbane, *Social Destiny of Man*, 209; Brisbane, *Fundamental Principles*, 117.
40. Brisbane, *Social Destiny of Man*, 158, 202, 244.
41. See, for example, Rohler, "Utopian Persuasion," ii; R. Brisbane, *Albert Brisbane*, 190.
42. Brisbane, *European Travel Diaries*, 73–74.
43. Brisbane, *European Travel Diaries*, 176.
44. Regarding Fourierist mysticism, see, for example, William Hall Brock, "Phalanx on a Hill: Responses to Fourierism in the Transcendental Circle" (PhD diss., Loyola University, 1995), 233; R. Brisbane, *Albert Brisbane*, 208–9.
45. R. Brisbane, *Albert Brisbane*, 256 (emphasis in original).
46. Guarneri, *Utopian Alternative*, 278 (emphasis in original); Brisbane, "Preface," in *Social Destiny of Man*, trans. Clapp, x.
47. See Carl Guarneri, "Foreword," in Brisbane, *European Travel Diaries*, ix, Guarneri, *Utopian Alternative*, 60.
48. Rohler, "Utopian Persuasion," 145; Guarneri, *Utopian Alternative*, 79–80, 11; Fellman, *Unbounded Frame*, 16.
49. Guarneri, *Utopian Alternative*, 11.
50. Guarneri, *Utopian Alternative*, 353, 355.
51. Guarneri, *Utopian Alternative*, 215; on Brook Farm, see Lindsay Swift, *Brook Farm: Its Members, Scholars, and Visitors* (1900; reprint, Secaucus, NJ: Citadel Press, 1961).
52. Letter of Ralph Waldo Emerson to Thomas Carlyle, October 30, 1840, in Joseph Slater, ed., *The Correspondence of Emerson and Carlyle* (New York: Columbia University Press, 1964), 283; Ralph Waldo Emerson, journal entry, October 17, 1840, in *The Journals and Miscellaneous Notebooks of Ralph Waldo Emerson*, vol. 7 (1838–1842), A. W. Plumstead and Harrison Hayford, eds. (Cambridge, MA, Belknap Press of Harvard University Press, 1969), 408; Ralph Waldo Emerson, *Uncollected Writings: Essays, Addresses, Poems, Reviews, and Letters* (1912; reprint, Port Washington, NY: Kennikat Press, 1971), 72, 74, 154.
53. Letter of Ralph Waldo Emerson to Lidian Emerson, March 3, 1842, in Ralph L. Rusk, ed., *The Letters of Ralph Waldo Emerson* (New York: Columbia University Press, 1966), 3:21; Letter of Ralph Waldo Emerson to Lidian Emerson, March 1, 1842, in Rusk, *Letters*, 3:18; Ralph Waldo Emerson, journal entry, ca. August 25, 1843, in *The Journals and Miscellaneous Notebooks of Ralph Waldo Emerson*, vol. 9, 1843–1847, Ralph H.

Orth and Alfred R. Ferguson, eds. (Cambridge, MA: Belknap Press of Harvard University Press, 1971), 8; Brock, "Phalanx on a Hill," 207–8.
54. Guarneri, *Utopian Alternative*, 72
55. Guarneri, *Utopian Alternative*, 116–17.
56. Godwin, *Popular View*, 106.

CHAPTER SIX

1. Davis's account of his own life may be found in Andrew Jackson Davis, *The Magic Staff: An Autobiography* (New York: J. S. Brown, 1859), and Andrew Jackson Davis, *Beyond the Valley: A Sequel to "The Magic Staff": An Autobiography* (Boston: Colby and Rich, 1885); see also Ernest Isaacs, "A History of Nineteenth-Century American Spiritualism as a Religious and Social Movement" (PhD diss., University of Wisconsin, 1975), 26–56. I have gleaned what follows from an adaption of material from three previous publications (all adapted with permission): Catherine L. Albanese, "On the Matter of Spirit: Andrew Jackson Davis and the Marriage of God and Nature," *Journal of the American Academy of Religion* 60, no. 1 (1992): 101–17 (used by permission of Oxford University Press [https://global.oup.com/academic]; for permission to reuse, please visit http://global.oup.com/academic/rights); Catherine L. Albanese, *A Republic of Mind and Spirit: A Cultural History of American Metaphysical Religion* (New Haven, CT: Yale University Press, 2007), esp. 206–20, 190–93 (used by permission); and Catherine L. Albanese, "Historical Imagination and Channeled Theology; or, Learning the Law of Attraction," in Cathy Gutierrez, ed., *Handbook of Spiritualism and Channeling* (Leiden: Brill, 2015), 480–502 (used by permission).
2. Gibson Smith, *Clairmativeness; or, Human Magnetism with an Appendix* (New York: np, 1845). Davis himself wrote that the correct title was *Clairlativeness*, referring to a "clear production" by a spirit; see Andrew Jackson Davis, *The Present Age and Inner Life: A Sequel to Spiritual Intercourse* (Hartford, CT: S. Andrus, 1853), 153.
3. Davis, *Magic Staff*, 227–41, 242–43.
4. Andrew Jackson Davis, *The Principles of Nature, Her Divine Revelations, and a Voice to Mankind* (New York: S. S. Lyon and W. Fishbough, 1847).
5. John C. Spurlock, *Free Love* (New York: New York University Press, 1988), 84. On "conjugial love," see Emanuel Swedenborg, *The Delights of Wisdom Pertaining to Conjugial Love after Which Follow the Pleasures of Insanity Pertaining to Scortatory Love* (1768), trans. Samuel M. Warren and rev. trans. Louis H. Tafel (1856; reprint, New York: Swedenborg Foundation, 1980).
6. Andrew Jackson Davis, *The Great Harmonia*, 5 vols. (Boston: Benjamin B. Mussey, 1850–59). Individual volumes carry different subtitles, and there are short titles for each volume as well: vol. 1, *The Physician*; vol. 2, *The Teacher*; vol. 3, *The Seer*; vol. 4, *The Reformer*; vol. 5, *The Thinker*.
7. See Davis, *Magic Staff*, 494–95, 545–52; Davis, *Beyond the Valley*, 94–114, 203–4.
8. Andrew Jackson Davis, *The Principles of Nature, Her Divine Revelations, and a Voice to Mankind*, 34th ed. (Boston: Colby and Rich, 1881), 1–4 (emphases, uppercase, and exclamation point in original). Subsequent citations of this work are from this edition, which is actually more likely the seventeenth than the thirty-fourth edition; see Slater Brown, *The Heyday of Spiritualism* (1970; reprint, New York: Pocket Books, 1972), 97n, which argues on solid evidence that a printer's error was exploited in later editions.
9. Franz Anton Mesmer, *Physical-Medical Treatise on the Influence of the Planets* (1766), in Mesmer, *Mesmerism: A Translation of the Original Medical and Scientific Writings,*

trans. George J. Block and intro. Ernest R. Hilgard (Los Altos, CA: William Kaufmann, 1980), 3, 6, 14, 20.
10. Mesmer, *Physical-Medical Treatise*, 19 (uppercase in original).
11. Davis, *Principles of Nature*, 323.
12. Davis, *Principles of Nature*, 326–27, 121 (emphases, uppercase, and exclamation point in original).
13. Davis, *Principles of Nature*, 131 (uppercase in original).
14. Emanuel Swedenborg had elaborated on his spirit visits to other planets in the solar system and beyond in *Concerning the Earths in Our Solar System, Which Are Called Planets; and Concerning the Earths in the Starry Heaven; Together with an Account of Their Inhabitants* (1758); for a recent translation, see Emanuel Swedenborg, *Life on Other Planets*, trans. John Chadwick (West Chester, PA: Swedenborg Foundation, 2006); Davis, *Principles of Nature*, 675–76.
15. Emanuel Swedenborg, *The True Christian Religion, Containing the Universal Theology of the New Church*, trans. John C. Ager, 2 vols. (1853; reprint, New York: Swedenborg Foundation, 1970), 1:367; Swedenborg's detailed descriptions of visits to heaven and hell may be found in Emanuel Swedenborg, *Heaven and Its Wonders and Hell: From Things Heard and Seen* (1758), trans. J. C. Ager (1852; reprint, New York: Swedenborg Foundation, 1964), and for an ample summary of Swedenborg's experiences of heaven, see Colleen McDannell and Bernhard Lang, *Heaven: A History* (New Haven, CT: Yale University Press, 1988), 181–227, esp. 191–99; Davis, *Principles of Nature*, 47 (emphasis in original), 674–75 (emphases in original).
16. Andrew Jackson Davis wrote extensively on the Summerland in *Death and the After-Life: Eight Evening Lectures on the Summer-Land*, rev. and enlarged (Boston: Colby & Rich, 1865).
17. Davis, *Principles of Nature*, 643–76; 676.
18. Andrew Jackson Davis, *Being a Philosophical Revelation of the Natural, Spiritual, and Celestial Universe*, vol. 2 of *The Great Harmonia* (*The Teacher*, 1851) (reprint, Boston: Bela Marsh, 1862), 253–54 (emphases in original).
19. Davis, *Principles of Nature*, 328, 489 (emphasis in original), 511, 557.
20. Davis, *Principles of Nature*, 145 (emphases in original).
21. Davis, *Principles of Nature*, 734, 776–78 (emphasis, uppercase, and exclamation point in original).
22. Davis, *Principles of Nature*, 714, 734, 736–37 (emphases and uppercase in original).
23. Davis, *Principles of Nature*, 683, 684 (emphasis in original), 690, 691–92, 694–99; for the attack on the clergy, see 699–728.
24. Davis, *Principles of Nature*, 729–30, 733 (emphasis and uppercase in original), 734–37 (emphases in original).
25. Davis, *Principles of Nature*, 738 (emphasis in original), 741–43.
26. Davis, *Principles of Nature*, 746–47, 749–50.
27. Davis, *Principles of Nature*, 766–68 (emphasis in original).
28. Davis, *Principles of Nature*, 771, 774.
29. Davis, *Principles of Nature*, 776–79, 781–82.
30. Letter of A. R. Bartlett, March 31, 1847, in William Fishbough, "Scribe's Introduction," to Davis, *Principles of Nature*, ix–x; Brown, *Heyday of Spiritualism*, 101.
31. Swedenborg, *Delights of Wisdom Pertaining to Conjugial Love*, 114 (emphasis in original), 235–36.
32. Davis, *Principles of Nature*, 63, 95, 97, 119, 100, 217, 267, 269, 309, 87, 131, 463 (uppercase in original).

33. Andrew Jackson Davis, *The Penetralia; Being Harmonial Answers to Important Questions* (Boston: Bela Marsh, 1857), 191–92 (accessed at https://books.google.com/books/about/The_Penetralia.html?id=k3U_AAAAYAAJ); Andrew Jackson Davis, *Answers to Ever-Recurring Questions from the People: A Sequel to the "Penetralia"*, 7th ed. (Boston: Banner of Light Publishing, 1869?), 182.
34. Davis, *Penetralia*, 254–55; see also Davis, *Answers to Ever-Recurring Questions*, 124.
35. Davis, *Magic Staff*, 497; Davis, *Great Harmonia*, 2:203 (emphasis in original); Andrew Jackson Davis, *Concerning Physiological Vices and Virtues, and the Seven Phases of Marriage*, vol. 4 of *The Great Harmonia*, (*The Reformer*, 1855) (reprint, Boston: Bela Marsh, 1859), 306 (emphasis in original).
36. Davis, *Magic Staff*, 501; Davis, *Great Harmonia*, 4:233–34, 235; Davis, *Great Harmonia*, 2:200 (emphasis in original); Davis, *Great Harmonia*, 4:230–32, 237; Davis, *Great Harmonia* 2:182; Davis, *Great Harmonia*, 4:242, 241, 248 (emphasis in original); Davis, *Answers to Ever-Recurring Questions*, 253, 270–72.
37. Cf. Davis, *Magic Staff*, 469.
38. My discussion here has been adapted from Catherine L. Albanese, "Horace Bushnell among the Metaphysicians," *Church History* 79, no. 3 (2010): 614–53 (© American Society of Church History, 2010; adapted with permission). According to Howard A. Barnes (*Horace Bushnell and the Virtuous Republic* [Metuchen, NJ: American Theological Library Association and Scarecrow Press, 1991], 139), Andrew Jackson Davis first published this material in 1852 as *The Approaching Crisis: Being a Review of Dr. Bushnell's Recent Lectures on Supernaturalism* (New York: Published by the Author, 1852). All references in what follows, however, are to a more conventional edition, which appeared in 1868. See Davis, "A Letter to Rev. Dr. Bushnell" (Hartford, December 15, 1851), in Andrew Jackson Davis, *The Approaching Crisis: Being a Review of Dr. Bushnell's Course of Lectures, on the Bible, Nature, Religion, Skepticism, and the Supernatural* (Boston: Colby & Rich, 1868), 5, 7–8 (emphasis in original), 261 (emphasis in original).
39. Davis, *Approaching Crisis*, 15–16 (emphasis in original), 30, 33–34 (emphases and uppercase in original).
40. Davis, *Approaching Crisis*, 40, 46, 47 (emphases and uppercase in original).
41. Davis, *Approaching Crisis*, 52, 61–62 (emphases and uppercase in original).
42. Davis, *Approaching Crisis*, 85–86, 87 (emphasis in original), 105–6 (emphases in original).
43. Davis, *Approaching Crisis*, 115–17 (emphases in original).
44. Davis, *Approaching Crisis*, 132–33, 135–36 (emphases and uppercase in original), 140.
45. Davis, *Approaching Crisis*, 161, 185.
46. Davis, *Approaching Crisis*, 195, 212–15 (emphases and uppercase in original).
47. Davis, *Approaching Crisis*, 217–22, 239–40 (emphases in original), 250–51 (emphasis in original)

SECTION FOUR

1. George M. Beard, *American Nervousness: Its Causes and Consequences* (New York: G. P. Putnam's Sons, 1881).
2. Beard, *American Nervousness*, vi–vii.
3. Beard, *American Nervousness*, viii–ix.
4. Beard, *American Nervousness*, ix.

CHAPTER SEVEN

1. Evans made this assertion in the "Chronology of My Life" that preceded the second volume of his manuscript journal. See Catherine L. Albanese, ed., *The Spiritual Journals of Warren Felt Evans: From Methodism to Mind Cure* (Bloomington: Indiana University Press, 2016), 123. In the material that follows, I draw heavily on my introduction to this publication (1–45), as well as Catherine L. Albanese, *A Republic of Mind and Spirit: A Cultural History of American Metaphysical Religion* (New Haven, CT: Yale University Press, 2007), esp. 303–13; both sources used with permission.
2. William J. Leonard, "Warren Felt Evans, M.D.: An Account of His Life and His Services as the First Author of the Metaphysical Healing Movement," *Practical Ideals* 10, no. 3 (1905): 21. Leonard produced a four-part series in the New Thought periodical *Practical Ideals* from September–October 1905 through January 1906.
3. Charles S. Braden, *Spirits in Rebellion: The Rise and Development of New Thought* (1963; reprint, Dallas: Southern Methodist University Press, 1984), 90–91.
4. The traditional account carried forward by New Thought authors that Phineas P. Quimby was Evans's mentor and doctor has been thoroughly discredited with prodigious evidence by independent scholar Keith McNeil in *A Story Untold: A History of the Quimby-Eddy Debate* (Carmel, IN: Hawthorne, 2020), vol. 3, esp. 1071–73, 1095–97, 1160–73. For my own synopsis and research, see Albanese, ed., *Spiritual Journals*, 6–10.
5. Leonard, "Warren Felt Evans, M.D.," 17–18 and n. 11.
6. See Braden, *Spirits in Rebellion*, 126–28; Beryl Satter, *Each Mind a Kingdom: American Women, Sexual Purity, and the New Thought Movement, 1875–1920* (Berkeley: University of California Press, 1999), 70; Albanese, *Republic of Mind and Spirit*, 313 and 566, n. 129.
7. Warren Felt Evans, Journal II (November 4, 1865), in Albanese, ed., *Spiritual Journals*, 247.
8. For the prevalence of quietism among nineteenth-century Americans, particularly those inclined to the holiness movement, see Patricia A. Ward, *Experimental Theology in America: Madame Guyon, Fénelon, and Their Readers* (Waco, TX: Baylor University Press, 2009), esp. 6, 10.
9. Warren Felt Evans, Journal II (January 3, 1859), in Albanese, ed., *Spiritual Journals*, 137.
10. It is interesting to note that Evans's unpublished manuscript (in the National Library of Medicine in Bethesda) suggests the continuing significance of the idealism of Berkeley in Evans's own thinking. The manuscript exists in two notebooks with Evans's tentative title for each: "A Practical Application of the Ideal Philosophy to the Cure of Disease" and "Occult Science of Medicine: A Practical Application of Idealism to the Cure of Disease."
11. Warren Felt Evans, Journal I (June 3, 1853), in Albanese, ed., *Spiritual Journals*, 59–60.
12. W. F. Evans, *The Happy Islands; or, Paradise Restored* (Boston: H. V. Degen, 1860), 3, 14–15, 18–19.
13. Evans, *Happy Islands*, 26–27, 39.
14. Evans, *Happy Islands*, 39–40.
15. Evans, *Happy Islands*, 40–42.
16. Phoebe Palmer, *The Way of Holiness* (New York: Palmer and Hughes, 1845), 60–70; Evans, *Happy Islands*, 43–45.
17. Evans, *Happy Islands*, 167–68; Evans, Journal II (December 14, 1858), in Albanese, ed., *Spiritual Journals*, 135–36; Evans, Journal I (July 26, 1850), in Albanese, ed., *Spiritual Journals*, 52.

18. Evans, *Happy Islands*, 175, 179; Ralph Waldo Trine, *In Tune with the Infinite*; or, Fullness of Peace, Power, and Plenty (1897; reprint, Indianapolis: Bobbs-Merrill, 1970), e.g., 167, 47; Ralph Waldo Emerson, "The Over-Soul," in Joseph Slater, Alfred R. Ferguson, and Jean Ferguson Carr, eds., *Essays: First Series*, vol. 2 of *The Collected Works of Ralph Waldo Emerson* (Cambridge, MA: Harvard University Press, Belknap Press, 1979), 159–60; Evans, *Happy Islands*, 259–60.
19. Evans, *Happy Islands*, 246–48.
20. As a significant clue, Keith McNeil has pointed out in personal correspondence that Evans habitually listed his previously published titles in the front matter for each new book, beginning with his third, *Celestial Dawn*. There, the sequence lists *Happy Islands* first and *Divine Order* second.
21. Warren Felt Evans, *Divine Order in the Process of Full Salvation* (Boston: Henry V. Degen, 1860), 3, 9, 13, 17–18, 23.
22. Palmer, *Way of Holiness*, 60–70; Evans, *Divine Order*, 45; William E. Boardman, *Higher Christian Life* (Boston: Hoyt, 1858).
23. Evans, *Divine Order*, 35, 33, 34.
24. Evans, *Divine Order*, 38–39, 41.
25. Palmer herself had claimed an experience of entire sanctification in 1837.
26. Evans, *Divine Order*, 46–47.
27. Evans, Journal II (December 2, 1861), in Albanese, ed., *Spiritual Journals*, 194–95 (emphasis in original).
28. W. F. Evans, *The Celestial Dawn; or, Connection of Earth and Heaven* (Boston: T. H. Carter, 1864).
29. W. F. Evans, *The Celestial Dawn; or, Connection of Earth and Heaven* (Boston: James P. Magee, 1862), 79, 72, 74, 76, 127. All future references to *Celestial Dawn* are to the 1862 edition. Besides citing Boardman, Evans quoted at length from Charles G. Finney's *Guide to the Savior; or, Conditions of Attaining to and Abiding in Entire Holiness of Heart and Life* (Oberlin, OH: James M. Fitch, 1848), in its third edition by 1855. Finney's words appear nowhere in Evans's journals.
30. Evans, *Celestial Dawn*, 15, 42, 53–54, 188–89.
31. Evans, *Celestial Dawn*, 195, 264.
32. Evans, Journal II (December 14, 1858), in Albanese, ed., *Spiritual Journals*, 136 (emphasis in original); W. F. Evans, *The New Age and Its Messenger* (Boston: T. H. Carter, 1864), 35, 19 (emphasis in original). Evans's work was published simultaneously in London by Charles P. Alvey. Pythonism historically referred to the ambiguous form of prophecy attributed to the famed Greek oracle of Apollo at Delphi. The "Stygian lake" is the River Styx, which flowed through the underworld of Greek mythology.
33. Ralph Waldo Emerson, *Nature*, in Robert E. Spiller and Alfred R. Ferguson, eds., *Nature, Addresses, and Lectures*, vol. 1 of *The Collected Works of Ralph Waldo Emerson* (Cambridge, MA: Harvard University Press, Belknap Press, 1971), 17–18; Evans, *New Age*, 21–22.
34. Evans, *New Age*, 25, 94 (emphasis in original).
35. W. F. Evans, *The Mental-Cure, Illustrating the Influence of the Mind on the Body, Both in Health and Disease and the Psychological Method of Treatment* (Boston: H. H. & T. W. Carter, 1869); McNeil, *Story Untold*, 3:1506, n. 225.
36. Evans, *Mental-Cure*, 28, 55, 79–80, 62–63; for spirits, see, e.g., 79–80, 181, 288, 360; for Brittan, 291; for spiritual spheres, 70; for death, 108; for magnetism, 272–73.
37. Evans, *Mental-Cure*, 58–59, 62–63 (emphases in original).

38. W. F. Evans, *Mental Medicine: A Theoretical and Practical Treatise on Medical Psychology* (Boston: Carter and Pettee, 1872); for Phineas Quimby's Swedenborgianism, see J. Stillson Judah, *The History and Philosophy of the Metaphysical Movements in America* (Philadelphia: Westminster, 1967), 149–50.
39. Evans, *Mental Medicine*, 145, 210 (emphasis in original), viii–ix.
40. W. F. Evans, *Soul and Body; or, The Spiritual Science of Health and Disease* (Boston: Colby and Rich, 1876), 3–4, title page, 22–23, 30 (emphases in original). The French title of Kardec's widely influential work is *Le livre des esprits contenant les principes de la doctrine spirite*. Evans's "phrenopathy" meant cure of the body by the mind.
41. W. F. Evans, *The Divine Law of Cure* (Boston: H. H. Carter, 1881); see Braden, *Spirits in Rebellion*, 99, for the list, although the characterizations are my own.
42. Evans, *Divine Law of Cure*, 153–54, 164,168–69 (emphasis in original), 252.
43. W. F. Evans, *The Primitive Mind-Cure: The Nature and Power of Faith; or, Elementary Lessons in Christian Philosophy and Transcendental Medicine* (Boston: H. H. Carter and Karrick, 1885). I have used the 5th edition here and in what follows (Boston: H. H. Carter and Karrick, 1886), which to all appearances and in keeping with nineteenth-century habitual practice was actually a reprint. For Berkeley, see, e.g., Evans, *Primitive Mind-Cure*, 1, 12; for Emerson, see 20,26, 93, 138; for Al-Ghazali, see 20.
44. H. P. Blavatsky, *Isis Unveiled: A Master-Key to the Mysteries of Ancient and Modern Science and Theology*, 2 vols. (1877; reprint, Los Angeles: Theosophy Company, 1975); Evans, *Primitive Mind-Cure*, 138–39, 143–44 (emphasis in original).
45. Evans, *Primitive Mind-Cure*, 5, 7 (emphasis in original).
46. Evans, *Primitive Mind-Cure*, 165–98, 194–97, 168–69 (emphasis in original), 171.
47. W. F. Evans, *Esoteric Christianity and Mental Therapeutics* (Boston: H. H. Carter and Karrick, 1886); A Christian Scientist, "Evans's Esoteric Christianity," *Christian Science Journal* 4, no. 5 (1886): 105–6.
48. Evans, *Esoteric Christianity*, 5, 11–21, 15.
49. Evans, *Esoteric Christianity*, 46, 17 (emphasis in original).
50. Evans, *Esoteric Christianity*, 46–47, 28, 23 (emphases in original).
51. Evans, *Esoteric Christianity*, 16, 114.
52. R. Laurence Moore, "The Occult Connection? Mormonism, Christian Science, and Spiritualism," in Howard Kerr and Charles L. Crow, eds., *The Occult in America: New Historical Perspectives* (Urbana: University of Illinois Press, 1983), 135.

CHAPTER EIGHT

1. This narrative is informed by material from the following biographies of William James: Robert D. Richardson, *William James: In the Maelstrom of American Modernism—A Biography* (Boston: Houghton Mifflin, 2006); Linda Simon, *Genuine Reality: A Life of William James* (New York: Harcourt Brace, 1998); Daniel W. Bjork, *William James: The Center of His Vision* (New York: Columbia University Press, 1988); Gerald E. Myers, *William James: His Life and Thought* (New Haven, CT: Yale University Press, 1986); Gay Wilson Allen, *William James: A Biography* (New York: Viking Press, 1967); and the important earliest biography by James's student Ralph Barton Perry, *The Thought and Character of William James—Briefer Version* (1948; reprint, New York: George Braziller, 1954).
2. Louis Menand, *The Metaphysical Club* (New York: Farrar, Straus and Giroux, 2001), 93.
3. For James's psychical interests, see Krister Dylan Knapp, *William James: Psychical Research and the Challenge of Modernity* (Chapel Hill: University of North Carolina Press,

2017); and Deborah Blum, *Ghost Hunters: William James and the Search for Scientific Proof of Life after Death* (New York: Penguin Books, 2007).
4. Henry James Sr., quoted in Allen, *William James*, 17.
5. Simon, *Genuine Reality*, 40.
6. William James, Diary, quoted in Myers, *William James*, 46.
7. Myers, *William James*, 46; William James, quoted in Perry, *Thought and Character of William James*, 121; Perry, *Thought and Character*, 153; William James, quoted in Perry, *Thought and Character*, 153. For more on Renouvier, see William Logue, *Charles Renouvier, Philosopher of Liberty*. (Baton Rouge: Louisiana State University Press, 1993); and John I. Brooks, *The Eclectic Legacy: Academic Philosophy and the Human Sciences in Nineteenth-Century France* (Newark: University of Delaware Press, 1998).
8. William James, *The Will to Believe and Other Essays in Popular Philosophy* (New York: Longmans, Green, 1897).
9. James, *Will to Believe*, 9, 11, 17.
10. James, *Will to Believe*, 24, 29.
11. Knapp, *William James*, 175 (emphasis in original); Allen, *William James*, 508; Simon, *Genuine Reality*, xxii.
12. James, *Will to Believe*, 12 (emphasis in original); William James, *Pragmatism* (1907) *and Four Essays from "The Meaning of Truth"* (1909), ed. Ralph Barton Perry (Cleveland: World Publishing, Meridian Books, 1955), 45.
13. James, *Pragmatism*, 78, 142–43 (emphasis in original).
14. William James, *The Meaning of Truth: A Sequel to Pragmatism* (1909; reprint, West Valley City, UT: Editorium, Waking Lion Press, 2006), x, 37, 42 (emphases in original); William James, *A Pluralistic Universe: Hibbert Lectures at Manchester College on the Present Situation in Philosophy* (1909; reprint, Lincoln: University of Nebraska Press, 1996), 250–51, 260.
15. William James, *Essays in Radical Empiricism*, ed. Ralph Barton Perry (1912; reprint, Lincoln: University of Nebraska Press, 1996), 42 (emphasis in original), 93.
16. William James, *Human Immortality: Two Supposed Objections to the Doctrine* (1898), 2d ed. (1899; reprint, New York: Dover Publications, 1956), 15–17 (emphasis in original), 25–27; Ralph Waldo Emerson, *Nature*, in Robert E. Spiller and Alfred R. Ferguson, eds., *Nature, Addresses, and Lectures*, vol. 1 of *The Collected Works of Ralph Waldo Emerson* (Cambridge, MA: Harvard University Press, Belknap Press, 1971), 43.
17. Bjork, *William James*, 77–78; James, quoted in Perry, *Thought and Character*, 147 (emphasis in Perry).
18. James, *Will to Believe*, 17; James, *Pragmatism*, 47; James, *Will to Believe*, 61.
19. William James, *The Varieties of Religious Experience: A Study in Human Nature* (1902), intro. Reinhold Niebuhr (1961; reprint, London: Collier-Macmillan, 1969), 29, 377, 396 (emphasis in original).
20. James, *Pragmatism*, 84 (emphases in original), 89, 141, 167 (emphases in original).
21. James, *Meaning of Truth*, 46, 48 (emphasis in original), 107; James, *Pluralistic Universe*, 212, 253, 263, 289.
22. James, *Varieties*, 99; William James, *The Principles of Psychology*, 2 vols. (New York: Henry Holt, 1890); Henry Samuel Levinson, *The Religious Investigations of William James* (Chapel Hill: University of North Carolina Press, 1981), 44.
23. Levinson, *Religious Investigations*, 202.
24. James, *Will to Believe*, 74.

25. James, *Pluralistic Universe*, 176; William James, "The Energies of Men" (1907), in John J. McDermott, ed., *The Writings of William James: A Comprehensive Edition* (Chicago: University of Chicago Press, 1977), 674 (emphases in original); Emerson, *Nature*, 42.
26. Myers, *William James*, 37; Bjork, *William James*, 67; Perry, *Thought and Character*, 146; William James to Alice Gibbens James, September 3 and 5, 1895, quoted in Bjork, *William James*, 201 (emphasis in original).
27. William James to Alice Gibbens James, July 9, 1898, quoted in Bjork, *William James*, 230; Simon, *Genuine Reality*, xix.
28. Perry, *Thought and Character*, 275; James, *Will to Believe*, 44; William James, quoted in William A. Clebsch, *American Religious Thought: A History* (Chicago: University of Chicago Press, 1973), 161 (emphasis in original). The German Walpurgisnacht, from April 30 to May 1, is the night when, according to inherited belief, witches engaged in a huge celebration as they awaited the coming of spring.
29. James, *Varieties*, 299–300.
30. James, *Varieties*, 305–6.
31. Richardson, *William James*, 397; James, *Varieties*, 323, 331 (emphasis in original), 333–34.
32. James, *Varieties*, 334; Ann Taves, *Fits, Trances, and Visions: Experiencing Religion and Explaining Experience from Wesley to James* (Princeton, NJ: Princeton University Press, 1999), 283–84; James, *Varieties*, 335.
33. William James to Henry Rankin (June 16, 1901), quoted in Richardson, *William James*, 406 (emphasis in original); William James, "A Pluralistic Mystic," *Hibbert Journal* 8 (July 1910), quoted in Allen, *William James*, 495.
34. James, *Varieties*, 54–57 (emphasis in original).
35. Allen, *William James*, viii; James, *Varieties*, 78, 141.
36. James, *Varieties*, 87–88, 89–90.
37. James, *Varieties*, 91; Levinson, *Religious Investigations*, 9; James, *Varieties*, 92–94. Ralph Waldo Trine's book is *In Tune with the Infinite; or, Fullness of Peace, Power, and Plenty* (1897; reprint, Indianapolis: Bobbs-Merrill, 1970).
38. James, *Varieties*, 99 (emphasis in original).
39. James, *Varieties*, 78, 126, 135, 188–89, 207.
40. James, *Pluralistic Universe*, 305.
41. Perry, *Thought and Character*, 39; James, *Meaning of Truth*, 40 (emphasis in original).
42. James, *Pluralistic Universe*, 151, 309–10 (emphasis in original).
43. James, *Varieties*, 59, 221; James, *Pragmatism*, 55; Clebsch, *American Religious Thought*, 1.
44. Bjork, *William James*, 8, 31.
45. John Jay Chapman, , *Memories and Milestones* (New York: Moffat, Yard, 1915), 26, quoted in Bjork, *William James*, 178; Théodore Fournoy, "Artistic Temperament," quoted in Simon, *Genuine Reality*, xx; Richardson, *William James*, 87, 147; Perry, *Thought and Character*, 62.
46. James, *Varieties*, 358; James, *Pluralistic Universe*, 253 (emphasis in original).
47. James, *Pragmatism*, 59 (emphases in original); Myers, *William James*, 419; Perry, *Thought and Character*, 221, James, "The Moral Philosopher and the Moral Life," in *Will to Believe*, 184–215.
48. Knapp, *William James*, 2, 7–8.
49. Levinson, *Religious Investigations*, 26; Knapp, *William James*, 38, 58.
50. James, *Pluralistic Universe*, 310–11.

51. Taves, *Fits, Trances, and Visions*, 271, 286.
52. Bjork, *William James*, xvii; James, *Varieties*, 403; William James to Henry Rankin, June 1896, quoted in Richardson, *William James*, 365.
53. Perry, *Thought and Character*, 333–34; James, *Pragmatism*, 106, 111, and see the discussion in Levinson, *Religious Investigations*, 202; James, *Human Immortality*, 58, n. 5.
54. James, *Pragmatism*, 23, 101, 193.

SECTION FIVE

1. Kate Bowler, *Blessed: A History of the American Prosperity Gospel* (New York: Oxford University Press, 2013), 3.
2. Bowler, *Blessed*, 7, 11 (emphasis in original).

CHAPTER NINE

1. Ann Braude, *Radical Spirits: Spiritualism and Women's Rights in Nineteenth-Century America*, 2nd ed. (Bloomington: Indiana University Press, 2001).
2. Sources for Hopkins used in this study include Gail M. Harley, *Emma Curtis Hopkins: Forgotten Founder of New Thought* (Syracuse, NY: Syracuse University Press, 2002); Catherine L. Albanese, *A Republic of Mind and Spirit: A Cultural History of American Metaphysical Religion* (New Haven, CT: Yale University Press, 2007); Beryl Satter, *Each Mind a Kingdom: American Women, Sexual Purity, and the New Thought Movement, 1875–1920* (Berkeley: University of California Press, 1999); and John S. Haller Jr., *The History of New Thought: From Mind Cure to Positive Thinking and the Prosperity Gospel* (West Chester, PA: Swedenborg Foundation Press, 2012).
3. See Harley, *Emma Curtis Hopkins*, 9.
4. Harley, *Emma Curtis Hopkins*, 29; Satter, *Each Mind a Kingdom*, 81, 274, n. 5. J. Gordon Melton also explored Hopkins's feminism and sometime encouragement of social activism on behalf of women in "Emma Curtis Hopkins: A Feminist of the 1880s and Mother of New Thought," in Catherine Wessinger, ed., *Women's Leadership in Marginal Religions: Explorations Outside the Mainstream* (Urbana: University of Illinois Press, 1993): 88–101.
5. Emma Curtis Hopkins, "Teacher of Metaphysics," *Christian Science Journal* (September 1885), in J. Gordon Melton, ed., *New Thought: A Reader* (Santa Barbara, CA: Institute for the Study of American Religion, 1990), 90; Harley, *Emma Curtis Hopkins*, 18–20.
6. Gary Ward Materra, "Women in Early New Thought: Lives and Theology in Transition from the Civil War to World War I" (PhD diss., University of California, Santa Barbara, 1997), 136–37; on Hopkins as the "founder" of New Thought, see—besides Harley—J. Gordon Melton, "New Thought's Hidden History: Emma Curtis Hopkins, Forgotten Founder," *JSSMR: The Journal of the Society for the Study of Metaphysical Religion* 1, no. 1 (1995): 5–40.
7. See, for example, the list in Harley, *Emma Curtis Hopkins*, 67–68; and Melton, "Emma Curtis Hopkins," 95–96.
8. Materra, "Women in Early New Thought," 140.
9. Harley, *Emma Curtis Hopkins*, 35–129.
10. The claim of Hopkins as "founder" of New Thought seems strained at best. Many of her ideas were clearly derivative, and she was building on a coalescence of mind-cure and theosophical work that had come before. Moreover, she herself never founded a lasting organization. Rather, many organizations and projects sprang from her work through the independent ministries of her students.

11. Emma Curtis Hopkins, *Class Lessons of 1888* (Portland, OR: Wise Woman Press, 2006), 27, 44, 66.
12. Hopkins, *Class Lessons*, 105–8, 166.
13. Emma (Curtis) Hopkins, "C. S. Ordination Address," *Christian Science* 1, no. 7 (1889): 173–75. I have found at least five Hopkins ordination addresses, with similar content, in Ida Nichols's Chicago-based *Christian Science* journal.
14. Emma Curtis Hopkins, "How to Attain Your Good (n.d.)," in Melton, ed., *New Thought*, 96–100 (emphasis in Melton and most probably in the original).
15. Harley, *Emma Curtis Hopkins*, 69; Emma Curtis Hopkins, "Bible Lesson III. Christ at Samaria," August 2, 1891, in *Bible Interpretations: Lessons One to Seventy-Five (1892–1892)* (Las Vegas: McAllister Editions, 2017), 23; Hopkins, "Bible Lesson V. Feeding the Starving" August 16, 1891, in *Bible Interpretations*, 30; Hopkins, "Bible Lesson VI. The Bread of Life," August 23, 1891, in *Bible Interpretations*, 33.
16. Emma Curtis Hopkins, *Spiritual Laws in a Natural World* (1894; no ed., Las Vegas: n.p., 2020), 139, 6, 62.
17. Emma Curtis Hopkins, *Scientific Christian Mental Practice* (1958; reprint, Marina del Rey, CA: DeVorss, n.d.), 17–18 (emphasis in original), 48, 50. The work was of uncertain date but a product of the Chicago years, if probably published posthumously.
18. Hopkins, *Scientific Christian Mental Practice*, 57, 73, 90 (emphasis in original), 93.
19. Emma Curtis Hopkins, *High Mysticism: A Series of Twelve Studies in the Wisdom of the Sages of the Ages* (Marina del Rey, CA: DeVorss, [1974]); Harley, *Emma Curtis Hopkins*, 2; Hopkins, *High Mysticism*, 27, 32, 74.
20. Hopkins, "Bible Lesson XXXVIII. Psalm 1:1–6. Realm of Thought," April 3, 1892, in *Bible Interpretations*, 186, 190.
21. Hopkins, "Bible Lesson XLIX. Review. See Things As They Are," June 19, 1892, in *Bible Interpretations*, 242–44; Hopkins "Bible Lesson LXVI. Acts 10:1–20. Faith in Good to Come," October 16, 1892, in *Bible Interpretations*, 341.
22. Hopkins, *Scientific Christian Mental Practice*, 71, 120; Hopkins, "Bible Lesson XXV. Isaiah 11:1. A Golden Promise," January 3, 1892, in *Bible Interpretations*, 128.
23. Hopkins, *High Mysticism*, 255; Charles S. Braden, *Spirits in Rebellion: The Rise and Development of New Thought* (Dallas: Southern Methodist University Press, 1963), 147 (the student was Ethelred Folsom Hellung).
24. Harley, *Emma Curtis Hopkins*, 82–83; Melton, "Emma Curtis Hopkins," 93–95.
25. Emma Curtis Hopkins, *The Ministry of the Holy Mother* (Cornwall Bridge, CT: Emma Curtis Hopkins Fund, n.d.).
26. Satter, *Each Mind a Kingdom*, 85.
27. Much of the material in this account of Towne's life is drawn from her own autobiographical remarks in Elizabeth Towne, *Experiences in Self-Healing* (1905; reprint, New York: Cosimo, 2007). The other figure is Esther Hicks (born Weaver).
28. Towne, *Experiences in Self-Healing*, 28.
29. See Satter, *Each Mind a Kingdom*, 234, 249, 326, n. 53.
30. See Tzivia Gover, "Mrs. Elizabeth Towne: Pioneering Woman in Publishing and Politics (1865–1960), *Historical Journal of Massachusetts* 37, no. 1 (2009): esp. 53, 55, 60–62.
31. Satter, *Each Mind a Kingdom*, 9, 14–17.
32. Satter, *Each Mind a Kingdom*, 167–68.
33. Elizabeth Towne, *The Life Power and How to Use It* (1906; reprint, Monee, IL: McAllister Editions, 2017), 90; Elizabeth Towne, *Joy Philosophy* (New York: Sydney Flower, 1903), 5–6 (emphases in original); Towne, *Experiences in Self-Healing*, 29,

38 (uppercase and emphases in original); Elizabeth Towne, *Fifteen Lessons in New Thought; or, Lessons in Living from the Principles of Creation to the Principles of Health and Prosperity* (1921; Monee, IL: McAllister Editions, 2017), 49.
34. Towne, *Experiences in Self-Healing*, 47 (emphasis in original); Towne, *Joy Philosophy*, 9; Towne, *Fifteen Lessons*, 4, 22, 37.
35. Elizabeth Towne, *Just How to Wake the Solar Plexus: Awaken Your Sun Center and Live at Full Potential* (1907; Las Vegas: n.p. 2020), 21; Towne, *Fifteen Lessons*, 1, 49–50; Elizabeth Towne, *How to Use New Thought in Home Life: A Key to Happy and Efficient Living for Husband, Wife, and Children* (Holyoke, MA: Elizabeth Towne, 1921), 114. For Towne's circulation claim regarding *Just How to Wake the Solar Plexus*, see William Walker Atkinson, *New Thought: Its History and Principles; or, The Message of the New Thought* (Holyoke, MA: Elizabeth Towne, 1915), 36.
36. Elizabeth Towne, *Practical Methods for Self Development: Spiritual, Mental, Physical* (Holyoke, MA: Elizabeth Towne, 1904), 6 (emphasis in original); Elizabeth Towne, *You and Your Forces; or, The Constitution of Man*, enlarged ed. (Holyoke, MA: Elizabeth Towne, 1905), 27, 44; Towne, *Life Power*, 47; Towne, *Fifteen Lessons*, 11. 17, 24, 30.
37. Towne, *How to Use New Thought*, 97 (uppercase in original); Elizabeth Towne, *How to Grow Success* (1904; Monee, IL: McAllister Editions, 2017), 27, 42 (uppercase in original).
38. Towne, *Practical Methods*, 31; Towne, *Life Power*, 49.
39. Towne, *Experiences in Self-Healing*, 58, 62–63 (emphasis and uppercase in original), 65 (emphases in original).
40. Towne, *Joy Philosophy*, 48; Towne, *How to Use New Thought*, 46, 64 168 (emphasis in original).
41. Towne, *You and Your Forces*, 33; Towne, *Practical Methods*, 7; Towne, *You and Your Forces*, 48 (emphasis in original); Towne, *Experiences in Self-Healing*, 37 (emphases in original).
42. Towne, *Fifteen Lessons*, 36–37 (Towne was referring to Richard Maurice Bucke, *Cosmic Consciousness: A Study in the Evolution of the Human Mind* (1901; reprint, New York: E. P. Dutton, 1940); Towne, *Fifteen Lessons*, 59; Towne, *How to Use New Thought*, 3 (uppercase in original).
43. Gover, "Mrs. Elizabeth Towne," 51; Towne, *How to Grow Success*, 34, 72 (uppercase in original); Towne, *Practical Methods*, 41–42, 47, 49.
44. Towne, *You and Your Forces*, 13, 16, 68; Towne, *Life Power*, 98; Towne, *Experiences in Self-Healing*, 30 (emphases in original).
45. Towne, *Joy Philosophy*, 14 (emphasis in original); Towne, *Just How to Wake the Solar Plexus*, 6 (emphasis in original), 13; Towne, *Fifteen Lessons*, 41–42.

CHAPTER TEN

1. Philip Deslippe, "The Hidden Sage: Willian Walker Atkinson and His Legacy" *New Dawn* 13, no. 5 (2019): 63.
2. Deslippe, "Hidden Sage," 65; Three Initiates [William Walker Atkinson], *The Kybalion: The Definitive Edition*, ed. Philip Deslippe (New York: Jeremy P. Tarcher/Penguin, 2008), 28.
3. Deslippe, "William Walker Atkinson and the First Issue of *New Thought* Magazine," *New Thought* 98, no. 1 (2013): 23.
4. William Walker Atkinson, *Dynamic Thought; or, The Law of Vibrant Energy* (Los Angeles: Segnogram, 1906; reproduced in another format, Monee, IL: n.p., 2020), 116,

107, 125 (emphases in original); William Walker Atkinson, *Mind-Power: The Secret of Mental Magic* (Chicago: William Walker Atkinson, 1912), 7 (uppercase in original).

5. Atkinson, *Mind-Power*, 70; William Walker Atkinson, *Thought-Force in Business and Everyday Life: Being a Series of Lessons in Personal Magnetism, Psychic Influence, Thought-Force Concentration, Will Power and Practical Mental Science* (Chicago: William Walker Atkinson, 1900; reprints, Chicago: Psychic Research, 1901; London: L. N. Fowler, 1901; Chicago: New Thought, 1903; New York: Sydney Flower, 1903; Chicago: A. C. McClure, 1911; Chicago: A. C. McClure, 1913). The Russian edition was title *Sila Mysli* (1910; reprint, Orel: Obshchestvo "Kniga," 1992).
6. Atkinson, *Thought-Force* (1900), 57, 59, 14.
7. Atkinson, *Mind-Power*, 430–31; William Walker Atkinson, *New Thought, Its History and Principles; or, The Message of the New Thought—A Condensed History of Its Real Origin with Statement of Its Basic Principles and True Aims* (Holyoke, MA: Elizabeth Towne, 1915), 27 (uppercase in original); Atkinson, *Thought-Force*, 59; William Walker Atkinson, *The Law of the New Thought: A Study of Fundamental Principles and Their Application* (Chicago: Psychic Research, 1902), 23.
8. William Walker Atkinson, *Thought Vibration; or, The Law of Attraction in the Thought World* (Chicago: New Thought, 1906), 84–89, 104. On *lila* and the play of the gods in Hinduism, see Jonathan Z. Smith, ed., *The HarperCollins Dictionary of Religion* (San Francisco: HarperSanFrancisco, 1995), s.v. "lila."
9. Atkinson, *Dynamic Thought*, 79–80; William Walker Atkinson, *The Secret of Success* (Chicago: Advanced Thought, 1908), 53, 56 (an imprint of this work appeared in 1907 in Auckland, Australia, under the auspices of the Floating Press).
10. Atkinson, *Dynamic Thought*, 2–3; Atkinson, *Secret of Success*, 58.
11. Atkinson, *Mind-Power*, 121–23, 134 (emphasis in original), 193, 196–206, 201–3.
12. William Walker Atkinson, *Practical Mental Influence and Mental Fascination: A Course of Lectures on Mental Vibrations, Psychic Influence, Personal Magnetism, Fascination, Psychic Self-Protection, Etc., Etc.* (Chicago: Advanced Thought, 1908), in Atkinson, *The Wisdom of William Walker Atkinson* (Redford, VA: Wilder, 1907), 80, 82.
13. Atkinson, *Dynamic Thought*, 65; Atkinson, *Mind-Power*, 31–32, 78.
14. Atkinson, *Mind-Power*, 301, 303–4, 440.
15. William Walker Atkinson, *The Psychology of Salesmanship* (Holyoke, MA: Elizabeth Towne, 1912; reproduction, Las Vegas: Mystical World, 2015), 7, 87–88.
16. Atkinson, *Thought Vibration*, 77; Theron Q. Dumont [William Walker Atkinson], *The Art and Science of Personal Magnetism: The Secrets of Mental Fascination* (Chicago: Advanced Thought, 1913; reproduction, Monee, IL: Timeless Wisdom Collection, 2020), 3.
17. Dumont, *Art and Science of Personal Magnetism*, 19–20, 66.
18. Dumont, *Art and Science of Personal Magnetism*, 72–75 (case and punctuation original).
19. Theron Q. Dumont [William Walker Atkinson], *The Power of Concentration* (Chicago: Advanced Thought, 1918), in Atkinson, *Wisdom*, 128, 153, 161, 162, 183, 169–80, 189.
20. Theron Q. Dumont [William Walker Atkinson], *The Master Mind; or, The Key to Mental Power Development and Efficiency* (Chicago: Advanced Thought, 1913; reproduction, Monee, IL: Pantianos Classics, 2020), 6, 18–19, 76–77, 152–53.
21. Deslippe, "William Walker Atkinson as Yogi Ramacharaka" (Unpublished paper, n.d.), 3–6.
22. Yogi Ramacharaka [William Walker Atkinson], *Hatha Yoga; or, The Yogi Philosophy of Physical Well-Being* (Oak Park, IL: Yogi Publication Society, 1904), 195.

23. Ramacharaka, *Hatha Yoga*, 9, 23–24, 28. For an illuminating study that puts hatha yoga into historical and contemporary perspective, see Mark Singleton, *Yoga Body: The Origins of Modern Posture Practice* (New York: Oxford University Press, 2010).
24. Ramacharaka, *Hatha Yoga*, 139, 151, 159, 232, 243.
25. Yogi Ramacharaka [William Walker Atkinson], *A Series of Lessons in Raja Yoga* (Chicago: Yogi Publication Society, 1906), 197–220, 2, 46, 71, 122, 193–95, 221 (uppercase in original), 247.
26. Yogi Ramacharaka [William Walker Atkinson], *Mystic Christianity; or, The Inner Teachings of the Master* (1908).
27. Anonymous [William Walker Atkinson], *The Arcane Teaching* (Chicago: Arcane Book Concern [A. C. McClung], 1909), reproduced in Atkinson, *The Arcanes: The Complete Four Books* (Monee, IL: Timeless Wisdom Collection, 2016), 3, 5, 89, 91–92.
28. Anonymous [William Walker Atkinson], *The Arcane Formulas; or, Mental Alchemy* (Chicago: Arcane Book Concern [A. C. McClung], 1909), reproduced in Atkinson, *Arcanes*, 213, 215 (emphases in original); Anonymous [William Walker Atkinson], *Vril; or, Vital Magnetism* (Chicago: Arcane Book Concern [A. C. McClung], 1909), reproduced in Atkinson, *Arcanes*, 216, 217, 218–19, 221, 258 (emphasis in original), 261–72. Blavatsky cites *Vril* in H. P. Blavatsky, *Isis Unveiled: A Master-Key to the Mysteries of Ancient and Modern Science and Theology*, 2 vols. (New York: J. W. Bouton, 1877), 1:616.
29. Anonymous [William Walker Atkinson], *The Mystery of Sex; or, Sex Polarity* (Chicago: Arcane Book Concern [A. C. McClung], 1909), reproduced in Atkinson, *Arcanes*, 275–79, 299, 305, 315.
30. [Atkinson], *Mystery of Sex*, 315–17, 319, 321, 325.
31. Three Initiates [William Walker Atkinson], *The Kybalion: A Study of the Hermetic Philosophy of Ancient Egypt and Greece* (Chicago: Yogi Publication Society, 1908). The high-quality contemporary edition I am using in what follows is Deslippe, ed., *Kybalion*, cited in n. 1 above; see 12, 42–44.
32. Deslippe, ed., *Kybalion*, 51, 55, 17, 30, 43–44.
33. Deslippe, ed., *Kybalion*, 63–73, 75, 77 (uppercase in original), 78, 77.

CHAPTER ELEVEN

1. Godfré Ray King [Guy Warren Ballard], *Unveiled Mysteries* (Chicago: St. Germain, 1934); J. Gordon Melton, personal communication, July 14, 2010.
2. My remarks here and in a good part of what follows are based on my article "Historical Imagination and Channeled Theology; or, Learning the Law of Attraction," in Cathy Gutierrez, ed., *Handbook of Spiritualism and Channeling* (Leiden: Brill, 2015), 480–502, used with permission.
3. Jane Roberts, *The Seth Material* (1970; reprint, Manhasset, NY: New Awareness Network, 2001).
4. Jane Roberts, *How to Develop Your ESP Power* (New York: F. Fell, 1966); reissued as *The Coming of Seth* (Cutchogue, NY: Buccaneer Books, 1966); Roberts, *Seth Material*, 4, 10–11 (emphasis in original).
5. J. Gordon Melton, "Seth," in J. Gordon Melton, ed., *New Age Encyclopedia* (Detroit, MI: Gale Research, 1990), 274. The theologian is Paul Giurlanda of St. Mary's College of California.
6. Roberts, *Coming of Seth*, 212, 92; Jane Roberts, *Seth Speaks: The Eternal Validity of the Soul* (1972; reprint, San Rafael, CA: Amber-Allen, 1994), xvii–xviii, 67, 41; Roberts, *Seth Material*, 293.

7. Roberts, *Seth Material*, 109; Roberts, *Seth Speaks*, 6 (emphasis in original); Roberts, *Seth Material*, 112; Roberts, *Coming of Seth*, 55; Roberts, *Seth Material*, 195–205, 218, 220 (emphasis in original); Jane Roberts, *The Nature of Personal Reality: Specific, Practical Techniques for Solving Everyday Problems and Enriching the Life You Know* (1974; reprint, San Rafael, CA: Amber-Allen and New World Library, 1994), 274–75, 233 (underline in original).
8. Roberts, *Seth Speaks*, 32, 22–23; Roberts, *Nature of Personal Reality*, 23, 10.
9. Roberts, *Seth Material*, 77; Roberts, *Seth Speaks*, 13; Roberts, *Seth Material*, 13, 156–57.
10. Roberts, *Seth Speaks*, 137, 120, 71.
11. Roberts, *Seth Material*, 241–42, 237, 241 (emphasis in original), 244.
12. Roberts, *Nature of Personal Reality*, 12–13; Roberts, *Seth Material*, 240–44, 214.
13. Sources for the brief (probable) biographies of Esther Hicks and Jerry Hicks include Robert Chalmers, "Interview: The Couple Who Claim They Can Make You Rich beyond Your Wildest Dreams," *The Independent* (UK), July 8, 2007, available at https://culteducation.com/group/1289-general-information/8820-interview-the-couple-who-claim-they-can-make-you-rich-beyond-your-wildest-dreams.html; David Stone, Blog, "Why Jerry Hicks's Biography Makes Too Short a Story (December 5, 2018), available at https://david-stone-writer.blog/2018/12/05/jerry-hicks-bio/ (Stone is a self-described skeptic and extremely opinionated); "Esther Hicks," *Wikipedia*, available at https://en.wikipedia.org/wiki/Esther_Hicks; Esther Hicks and Jerry Hicks, *Introducing Abraham: The Secret behind "The Secret"* (DVD, Carlsbad, CA: Hay House, 2007); Jerry Hicks, "Introduction," in Esther Hicks and Jerry Hicks, *The Law of Attraction: The Basics of the Teachings of Abraham* (Carlsbad, CA: Hay House, 2006). 3–8; Esther Hicks, "An Introduction to Abraham," in Esther Hicks and Jerry Hicks, *Ask and It Is Given: Learning to Manifest Your Desires* (Carlsbad, CA: Hay House, 2004), xxi–xxxi. My explanation in what follows is often a digest of writings common (repetitively so) in all the Abraham books, and, unless specifically cited, material in quotation marks is reiterated language to be found throughout.
14. Wayne W. Dyer and Esther Hicks, *Co-Creating at Its Best: A Conversation between Master Teachers* (Carlsbad, CA: Hay House, 2014), 5–7.
15. The *New York Times* best sellers were Esther Hicks and Jerry Hicks, *Money and the Law of Attraction: Learning to Attract Wealth, Health, and Happiness* (Carlsbad, CA: Hay House, 2008); Hicks and Hicks, *Ask and It Is Given*; Esther Hicks and Jerry Hicks, *The Amazing Power of Deliberate Intent: Living the Art of Allowing* (Carlsbad, CA: Hay House, 2006); Hicks and Hicks, *The Law of Attraction*; Esther Hicks and Jerry Hicks, *The Astonishing Power of Emotions: Let Your Feelings Be Your Guide* (Carlsbad, CA: Hay House, 2007); and Esther Hicks and Jerry Hicks, *The Vortex: Where the "Law of Attraction" Assembles All Cooperative Relationships* (Carlsbad, CA: Hay House, 2009).
16. Jerry Hicks and Esther Hicks, *A New Beginning I: Handbook for Joyous Survival* (San Antonio, TX: Abraham-Hicks Publications, 1988); and Jerry Hicks and Esther Hicks, *A New Beginning II: A Personal Handbook to Enhance Your Life, Liberty and Pursuit of Happiness* (San Antonio, TX: Abraham-Hicks Publications, 1991). Again, these consist largely of material channeled as Abraham.
17. Rhonda Byrne, *The Secret* (New York: Simon & Schuster, 2006); Hicks and Hicks, *Introducing Abraham*.
18. Hicks and Hicks, *Ask and It Is Given*, 17, 30.
19. Hicks and Hicks, *Ask and It Is Given*, 114
20. Hicks and Hicks, *Ask and It Is Given*, 294 (emphasis in original), 295.
21. Hicks and Hicks, *Ask and It Is Given*, 141–46.

22. Hicks and Hicks, *Law of Attraction*, 32–33 (emphasis in original), 83 (emphasis in original).
23. Hicks and Hicks, *Ask and It Is Given*, 49, 47.
24. Hicks and Hicks, *Vortex*, 187; Hicks and Hicks, *Ask and It Is Given*, 82, 104; Hicks and Hicks, *Law of Attraction*, 140 (emphasis in original).
25. Hicks and Hicks, *Money and the Law of Attraction*, 220–21 (emphases in original).
26. Hicks and Hicks, *Ask and It Is Given*, 14 (emphasis in original); Hicks and Hicks, *Amazing Power of Deliberate Intent*, 9 (emphases in original).
27. Jerry Hicks, "Preface," in Hicks and Hicks, *Money and the Law of Attraction*, xv (emphasis in original); Hicks and Hicks, *Money and the Law of Attraction*, 9, 12 (emphasis in original), 61 (emphases in original), 62–63.
28. Hicks and Hicks, *Money and the Law of Attraction*, 67 (emphasis and underline in original), 70 (emphasis and underline in original), 84 (emphasis and underline in original), 86–87 (emphases in original), 91–92 (emphasis and underline in original).

AFTERWORD

1. Michio Kushi and Alex Jack, *The Gospel of Peace: Jesus's Teachings of Eternal Truth* (New York: Japan Publications, 1992).
2. Kushi and Jack, *Gospel of Peace*, 156–57.
3. Kushi and Jack, *Gospel of Peace*, 157.
4. Elihu Palmer, *Principles of Nature; or, A Development of the Moral Causes of Happiness and Misery among the Human Species* (1801); see the account of the sermon in Kirsten Fischer, *American Freethinker: Elihu Palmer and the Struggle for Religious Freedom in the New Nation* (Philadelphia: University of Pennsylvania Press, 2021), 53, and of Palmer's vitalism in Fischer, *American Freethinker*, 57–67.
5. The lines are from Cohen's song "Anthem," which appeared in his 1992 album *The Future*.
6. Nell Irwin Painter, *The History of White People* (New York: W. W. Norton, 2010), 151, 166, 173, 183.
7. Ralph Waldo Emerson, *English Traits* (1856), in Emerson, *Essays and English Traits*, ed. Charles W. Eliot (New York: P. F. Collier, 1937), 331, 338, 341, 348, 382–83.
8. Mircea Eliade, *Cosmos and History: The Myth of the Eternal Return*, trans. Willard R. Trask (New York: Harper & Row, 1959), 96.
9. Jon Meacham, *His Truth Is Marching On: John Lewis and the Power of Hope* (New York: Random House, 2020), 248–49.

INDEX

Abraham (entity), 10, 289, 295–306; *Ask and It Is Given*, 296; books, 295–96; correspondence (law/theory) and, 301; early transmissions of, 295; emotional guidance scale, 299–300; law of attraction and, 289; *Money and the Law of Attraction*, 296; nature and, 305; New Thought and, 300; organized religion and, 303; prosperity and, 300, 303, 304–5; vitalism and, 300, 303
abundance theology, 5, 8, 10, 12, 68, 127, 243–44, 251, 285, 305–6, 310–11, 314–16; channels and, 289; Edwards and, 68; Hopkins and, 249, 255–56; Mather and, 21; Towne and, 258–59
aesthetics, 10, 11, 67–68, 306, 315; Bushnell and, 101, 119, 288; channels and, 288; Clebsch and, 11, 94; Edwards and, 46, 52, 55–57, 88–89, 94; Emerson and, 88–89, 94; James and, 233–36, 238; Mather and, 23–25, 26, 27–28, 29–30, 31, 32, 36, 42
Aihara, Herman, 307–8
Allen, Alexander, 58, 60
Allen, Gay Wilson, 230
altar theology, 193
American Nervousness (Beard), 183–85
Angel of Bethesda, The (Mather), 39, 40, 41–42
Approaching Crisis, The (Davis), 115
Art and Science of Personal Magnetism, The (Atkinson), 276–77
Ask and It Is Given (Abraham [entity]), 296
association, 136, 137, 140–41, 147, 164–67, 169–71, 179
association, law of, Davis and, 166–68
Association; or, A Concise Exposition of the Practical Part of Fourier's Social Science (Brisbane), 137
Associationism, 137–38, 139, 143, 150–52, 154
Atkinson, William Walker, 7, 8, 10, 253, 289, 310; anonymous Arcane books of, 281–83; *The Art and Science of Personal Magnetism*, 276–77; career summary of, 269–70; correspondence (law/theory) and, 271–73, 285; Desire-Force and, 271; *Dynamic Thought*, 273; early background of, 267–68; law of attraction and, 272, 273; *The Law of the New Thought*, 272; magnetic personality and, 273–77; *The Master Mind*, 277–79; Master Mind concept of, 270–71, 289; mentalism and, 282–83; *Mind Power*, 271–72, 274–75; mysticism and, 181, 284; nature and, 271, 272, 273, 274, 275, 276, 278, 280, 283; New Thought and, 267–68, 270, 273, 275, 278, 279, 280, 282, 285; power of concentration and, 277; prosperity and, *269*, 270, 274, 276–77, 284; pseudonyms of, 268–69, 271; *The Psychology of Salesmanship*, 275–76; as reverse prism, 270–71; sexual energy and, 283–84; spiritualism and, 272; suffering and, 315; *Thought-Force in Business and Everyday Life*, 268,

Atkinson, William Walker (*cont.*) 271; *Thought Vibration*, 272-73, 276; vitalism and, 271, 275, 276-77, 279-81, 283; Will-Force and, 271

attraction, law of, 10, 127, 128, 287, 310-11, 315-16; Atkinson and, 268-70, 272-73, 282; Brisbane and, 136, 138-40, 146; Bushnell and, 115-17; Davis and, 173, 181; Evans and, 191, 196, 207, 213; Hicks and, 300-301, 303-4, 310-11, 315-16; Hopkins and, 253; James and, 224, 232, 234, 237; Mather and, 36-37; Roberts and, 289, 291-92, 296-97; Towne and, 259, 261, 263; attractive industry, 128, 136, 140-42, 143, 146, 154, 168-69

Bach, Johann Sebastian, 46, 47
Bailey, Alice, 11
Bandelier, Adolph, 3
Barrett, Benjamin Fiske, 113
Barth, Karl, 55
Bartlett, Reverend A. R., 172
Bartol, Cyrus, 102
Barton, Charles and Josephine, 248
Baxter, Richard, 198
Beall, Otho, 39
Beard, George M., 183-85
beauty, 9, 11, 12, 311; Brisbane/Fourier and, 135, 136, 142; Bushnell and, 104, 105, 107, 116, 118, 122; Clebsch and, 94-95; Davis and, 164, 171, 177, 179; Edwards and, 44, 45, 46, 48, 49-51, 52-57, 64-65, 67, 118, 127; Emerson and, 73, 76-82, 88, 89, 91, 94-96; Evans and, 191; James and, 227; Mather and, 23, 24, 32
Beecher, Jonathan, 132, 133-34, 146-47
Bender, Courtney, 128, 129
Bercovitch, Sacvan, 18
Berkeley, Bishop George, 190
Berry, Mary F., 247
Bhakta Vishita, Swami (pseudonym of Atkinson), 281
Bharati, Premananda Baba, 278
Biblical Interpretations (Hopkins), 253
Bienvenu, Richard, 132, 133, 146-47
Bjork, Daniel, 232, 234, 236, 238, 244, 248
Blavatsky, Madame Helena, 7, 191, 205, 249, 270, 276, 290
Blessed (Bowler), 243

Blood, Benjamin Paul, 230
Boardman, William E., 190, 195, 196, 197
Boas, Ralph and Louise, 34
Boehme, Jakob, 61, 83, 203
Bowler, Kate, 243
Braude, Ann, 245
Brisbane, Albert, 7, 8, 9, 128, 201, 239, 253; acceptance of Fourier's law of universal analogy, 147; Amatory Harmony, theory of, 144; appreciation of arts and, 135; *Association; or, A Concise Exposition of the Practical Part of Fourier's Social Science*, 137; Associationism and, 151; attraction, law of, and, 136, 138-40, 146; attractive industry and, 140-41, 154; beauty and, 135, 136, 142; bond with Fourier, 134-35; correspondence (law/theory) and, 135, 138, 140, 142, 146, 147-49; early background of, 129-30; flaw of, 152; Fourierist system and, 131-32, 136, 138-44, 151-52; labor and, 141-42; *A Mental Biography*, 132, 134-35, 149; mysticism and, 148, 150-51; nature and, 134, 135, 150; organized religion and, 149-50, 239; phalanxes and, 130, 131, 139, 140, 141, 143, 146, 151, 152-54, 170; prosperity and, *146*; on relationship of man and nature, 134-35; social conscience of, 135-36; *The Social Destiny of Man (versions)*, 130, 136-37, 140-42, 147-49; Swedenborg and, 154
Brittan, Samuel Byron, 158, 201
Brook Farm (Massachusetts), 152, 153
Brooks, Nona, 248
Brown, Sir Thomas, 105
Brown, Slater, 172
Bucke, Richard Maurice, 62, 263
Burroughs, George, 15-16
Bushnell, Horace, 6, 8, 9, 69, 119, 127, 190, 239, 288; and attraction, law of, 115-17; Barrett critique of, 113; beauty and, 104, 105, 107, 116, 118, 122; *Christian Nurture*, 107, 117, 118; Christian nurture and, 115-16, 117; *Christ in Theology*, 100, 105, 120; correspondence (law, theory) and, 101, 103-4, 106, 108, 111, 120, 122, 209; Davis and, 176-81; divine thought in nature and, 104-5; dualism of, 109-10; early background of, 99-100; Edwardsian strain in, 118;

Emerson and, 123–24; Evans and, 209–10; *God in Christ*, 100, 105, 107, 116, 119; magnetists and, 114–15; metaphysical reading of, 123; metaphysical religiosity and, 101–2; miracles and, 110–12; mysticism and, 100, 101, 102, 106, 107–8, 119, 120; nature and, 100, 101, 102, 106, 107–8, 119, 120; *Nature and the Supernatural*, 100, 102–3, 104, 107, 108–9, 114–15, 121–22; negative theology and, 120–21, 122; pantheism and, 109, 113–14, 210; Pentecostalism and, 202, 210; prosperity and, *117*; quietism and, 106, 209; New Thought and, 111, 118, 119, 120; "Preliminary Dissertation on Language," 103–4; religious language and, 119; Samuel Taylor Coleridge as literary hero, 103; spiritualism and, *107, 108*, 113, 114; suffering and, 314; term *analogy* and, 103; unrevealed God and, 119–20; vitalism and, 107, 117; words with faces, 105, 120–21

Bushnell, Mary Apthorp (wife of Horace Bushnell), 106, 108

Byrne, Rhonda, 270, 296

Cady, H. Emily, 248

Calef, Robert, 15, 37

Calvinism, Mather-and-Edwards brand of, 5

Carpenter, Frank (Francis) B., 113

Celestial Dawn, The (Evans), 197–98

Chambers, Robert, 160

channels, 1, 7–8, 10, 11, 59, 287–89, 295, 304, 305; abundance theology and, 289; Atkinson and, 285; Davis and, 159; Emerson and, 81, 83; Evans and, 240; Hicks and, 270, 293–94, 295–96, 303; James and, 240; Roberts and, 289–90; Seth (entity) and, 292, 303

Chapman, John Jay, 234

Charity and Its Fruits (Edwards), 50

Cheney, Mary Bushnell, 101, 102, 118

Christianity, delight makers and, 146, 308–10

Christian Nurture (Bushnell), 107

Christian Philosopher, The (Mather), 23–26, 31, 36

Christian Science, 232

Christian suffering, power seen in, 313–16

Christ in Theology (Bushnell), 100, 105

Clapp, Henry, Jr., 138, 143, 144–45

Class Lessons, 1888 (Hopkins), 249

Clebsch, William, 11, 49, 52, 79, 88, 94–95, 234

Cloud of Independent Witnesses, A (Barrett), 113

Collins, Mabel, 278

Concerning the End for Which God Created the World (Edwards), 65–66

Corpus Hermeticum (Trismegistus), 100–101

correspondence (doctrine, law, theory, worldview), 4, 10, 27, 90, 305, 310, 311; Abraham (entity) and, 301; Atkinson and, 271–73, 285; Brisbane/Fourier and, 135, 138, 140, 142, 146, 147–49; Bushnell and, 101, 103–4, 106, 108, 111, 120, 122, 209; Davis and, 160, 162, 165, 169, 173, 174, 178, 180; Edwards and, 51, 57–59, 67, 118; Emerson and, 87, 89–94, 309; Evans and, 190, 191–94, 199–200, 203, 206, 207–8, 209, 212; Hicks and, 297; Hopkins and, 252–53; James (Henry) Sr. and, 217; James (William) and, 233–34, 237; Mather and, 24–26, 28–29, 31, 36–37, 69, 309; Mesmer and, 165; Seth (entity) and, 291; Swedenborg and, 86, 90, 113, 154, 155, 190, 203, 209; Towne and, 261, 265; Transcendentalists and, 6

Cosmic Consciousness (Bucke), 263

Cousin, Victor, 129

Cramer, Malinda, 248

Davis, Andrew Jackson, 6, 8, 9–10, 75, 108, 146, 154, 155, 191, 201, 239–40, 253; anticlericalism of, 158, 165, 176–77, 240; *The Approaching Crisis*, 115, 176; association, law of, and, 166–67; associative arrangements and, 169–70; attraction, law of, and, 173, 181; beauty and, 164, 171, 177, 179; Bushnell and, 114, 176–81; domestic bliss in associative arrangements and, 170–71; correspondence (law/theory) and, 160, 162, 165, 169, 173, 174, 178, 180; early background of, 157–58; education of, 172–73; evil and, 179–80; Fourier and, 158, 159, 160, 164, 165–71, 175–81; Galen and, 158; *The Great Harmonia*, 159; Great Positive Mind, 162–63, 165, 168, 173–75; human history

Davis, Andrew Jackson (*cont.*)
and, 165–66; influences on, 160–71; Levingston and, 157–58; love and, 158; marital adventures of, 158–59; marriage and, 174–76; mysticism and, 162–63, 174; nature and, 159, 160, 161–63, 165, 166, 168, 169, 170–71, 173, 174–75, 177–80; New Thought and, 167; phalanxes and, 169; *The Principles of Nature, Her Divine Revelations, and a Voice to Mankind*, 158, 159–60, 161, 165–66, 172, 173–74; sources of human action for, 167–68; spiritual republicanism and, 176; spiritualism and, 42, 74, 103, 114, 146, 154, 157, 159, 174, 176, 178; suffering and, 315; "superior association" and, 171–72; Swedenborg and, 158, 163–64, 171, 172–73; theology of materialism and, 171–72; vitalism and, 172

Delattre, Roland, 55–56

delight makers, Anglo-American, 311; explaining global problems and, 312–13; method of earning livings, 308; solipsism of, 313; suffering and, 314–15. *See also specific individual*

Delight Makers, The (Bandelier), 3

desire and delight, theology of, 5, 8, 10; Mather and, 21–23

"Divine and Supernatural Light, A" (Edwards), 49, 58, 63, 118

Divine Law of Cure, The (Evans), 204–5

Divine Order in the Process of Full Salvation (Evans), 195, 196, 197

Dodge, Catherine DeWolf, 158, 174

Dumont, Theron Q. (pseudonym of Atkinson), 277–79

Dynamic Thought (Atkinson), 273

Eddy, Mary Baker, 232, 247

Edwards, Jonathan, 5, 8, 9, 11, 15–16, 88, 127, 244, 308–9; abundance theology and, 68; aesthetics and, 46, 52, 55–57, 88–89, 94; beauty and, 44, 45, 46, 48, 49–51, 52–57, 64–65, 67, 118, 127; *Charity and Its Fruits*, 50; *Concerning the End for Which God Created the World*, 65–66; correspondence (law/theory) and, 51, 57–59, 67, 118; as delight maker, 44–50; "A Divine and Supernatural Light," 49, 58, 63, 118; divine delight and, 47–48; divine sovereignty and, 47; emanation/remanation and, 68; eros and, 49–50; family background of, 43–44; fondness for typology, 57–58; gospel of sweetness of, 50–51; "Images of Divine Things," 118; *Images or Shadows of Divine Things*, 49, 57; "The Mind," 45; ministerial life of, 44; mysticism and, 44, 60–67; *The Nature of True Virtue*, 52, 54; at Northampton, 44; nature and, 49, 50, 57, 58, 59, 60, 62, 309; New Thought and, 52, 66; "Of Being," 44, 45, 46; pantheism/panentheism and, 52, 60, 66; "Personal Narrative," 47, 52, 57, 61; prosperity and, 68; at Stockbridge, 44; Transcendentalists and, 58–59; *A Treatise concerning Religious Affections*, 54; vitalism and, 54, 68; water and, 59–60

Emerson, Mary Moody, 84, 87–88

Emerson, Ralph Waldo, 6, 8, 9, 11, 69, 110, 127, 128, 239, 244, 249, 252, 253, 270, 310; aesthetics and, 88–89, 94; "Art" essay, 92–93; Jakob Boehme and, 83–84; beauty and, 73, 76–82, 88, 89, 91, 94–96; "Books" essay, 82; Bushnell and, 123–24; Calvinist roots of, 87–89; "Circles" essay, 74–77; "Clubs" essay, 80–81; "Compensation" essay, 79, 93; correspondence (law/theory) and, 87, 89–94, 309; *The Conduct of Life*, 82, 96; "Demonology" lecture, 84–85; doubts on Fourierism, 153; dualism and, 93–94; early career, 72–73; eroticism and, 83; *Essays: Second Series*, 81–82; exploration of conversations by, 80–81; family background, 71–72; "Friendship" essay, 80, 95; "History" essay, 90–91; *Letters and Social Aims*, 82–83; literary record of, 73–74; "Love" essay, 80; mysticism and, 74, 77, 83, 84, 87, 97; as naturalist, 97; nature and, 73, 74–76, 78–80, 82, 83, 85, 87, 88–92, 94, 96, 97, 123, 145, 222; *Nature (book)*, 91, 95–96, 103, 104; "The Over-Soul" essay, 81, 86, 96–97; as philosopher king of White race theory, 311–12; prosperity and, 312; Puritan heritage of, 87–89; *Representative Men*, 91–92; "Self-Reliance" essay, 79, 312; suffering and, 314–15; Swedenborg and, 91–92; "The Divinity School Address,"

78–79; Transcendentalism and, 69, 83, 84, 87, 97, 103, 123, 153; Unitarian church services and, 308; vitalism and, 75–82, 84, 86, 87, 93, 95, 96, 222
English Traits (Emerson), 311–12
Esoteric Christianity and Mental Therapeutics (Evans), 206–7
Essays in Radical Empiricism (James), 216, 221
evangelicalism, Mather and, 22
Evans, Warren Felt, 7, 8, 10, 239, 246, 249; affirmation and, 199; attraction, law of, and, 191, 196, 207, 213; beauty and, 191; belief in mind cure, 194–95; break with Methodism, 188; Bushnell and, 209–10; *The Celestial Dawn*, 197–98; comprehensive vision of, 198–99; correspondence (law/theory) and, 190, 191–94, 199–200, 203, 206, 207–8, 209, 212; *The Divine Law of Cure*, 204–5; *Divine Order in the Process of Full Salvation*, 195, 196, 197; early background of, 187–88; *Esoteric Christianity and Mental Therapeutics*, 206–7; *The Happy Islands*, 192–94; influence of medieval saints and mystics on, 190; James and, 240–41; journals tracing spiritual and intellectual changes of, 189–90; *The Mental-Cure*, 201–2; *Mental Medicine*, 202–3; metaphors of rushing waters and, 194; metaphysical world of, 210–12; mysticism and, 189, 190–92, 196, 198, 203–4, 205, 208, 213; nature and, 191, 194, 206, 210, 213; *The New Age and Its Messenger*, 199–200; New Thought and, 188, 194, 196, 200, 201, 202, 205, 212; panentheism/pantheism, and, 208; perfectionism and, 190, 195–96; *The Primitive Mind-Cure*, 205–7; quietism and, 190, 196; as religious seeker, 208–9; sanctification and, 195–96; *Soul and Body*, 203–4; spiritualism and, 190, 199, 201–2, 203–4, 205; suffering and, 315; Swedenborg and, 190–91, 199–201; themes and concerns in writings of, 191; Theosophy and, 191; Transcendentalism and, 58–59; vitalism and, 191, 202, 203, 205, 206, 207, 213
evil, problem of, 12

Faust, Clarence, 51
Fechner, Gustav Theodor, 233–34

Fellman, Michael, 141
Fénelon, François de (archbishop), 106, 190, 193, 196, 197, 200
Fifteen Lessons in New Thought (Towne), 262–63
Fillmore, Charles, 7
Fillmore, Charles and Myrtle, 248
Fishbough, William, 158
Fletcher, Horace, 232
Flournoy, Théodore, 235
Flower, Sydney, 268
Fourier, Charles, 7, 9, 86, 128, 130, 132–33, 202, 239, 253; association and, 136, 137, 140–41, 147; Associationism and, 137–38, 139, 143, 150–52, 154; attraction, law of, and, 136, 138–40, 146; correspondence (law/theory) and, 135, 138, 140, 142, 146, 147–49; Davis and, 166; hostility toward Christianity and, 136, 308; mysticism and, 132; nature and, 147; phalanxes and, in America, 130, 131, 139, 140, 141, 143, 146, 151, 152–54, 170; social harmony, natural law of, 144–45; Swedenborg and, 154–55; *Theory of the Four Movements*, 145, 147, 151; *Treatise on Domestic and Agricultural Association*, 130, 133; writings of, 133–35
free love, 6–7, 128, 146
Frost, Reverend Barzillai, 77
Fuller, Margaret, 246

Gibbs, Josiah, 103
God in Christ (Bushnell), 100, 105, 107, 116
Godwin, Parke, 137, 155
Gospel of Peace, The (Kushi), 307
Gougeon, Len, 77, 95
Gover, Tzivia, 264
Great Awakening, 44
Great Harmonia, The (Davis), 159
Great Positive Mind, 173–75, 183
Grew, Nehemiah, 39
Grimes, J. Stanley, 157
Griswold, Whitney, 18
Guarneri, Carl, 136–37, 141, 147–48, 151, 152, 154
Gura, Philip, 61

Happy Islands, The (Evans), 192–94
Harley, Gail, 246, 248, 251, 252, 254

Harmonialism (Davis), 158, 162, 167, 173, 174, 175, 176, 177–80; Evans and, 201, 204
Harvey, William, 39
Hawthorne, Nathaniel, 245
Heimert, Alan, 56
Helmont, Jean Baptiste van, 39, 41
Hempel, Charles Julius, 137, 154
Hicks, Esther, 7, 8, 10, 270, 289, 290, 293–95; Abraham (entity) and, 10, 289, 295; abundance theology and, 289, 305–6; attraction, law/theory of, and, 300–301, 303–4, 310–11, 315–16; business enterprises of, 297; channeling process of, 296–97; correspondence (law/theory) and, 297, 301; *Money and the Law of Attraction*, 300–301; suffering and, 315; prosperity and, 300, 303, 304–5; Winfrey, Oprah, and, 296
Hicks, Jerry (husband of Esther), 293, 294–95, 296; business enterprises of, 297; suffering and, 315
Higgins, J. August, 88–89, 94
Higher Christian Life (Boardman), 195
High Mysticism (Hopkins), 252, 254
Hill, Napoleon, 7, 253, 270, 289
Holifield, E. Brooks, 45–46, 56
Holmes, Ernest, 248
Hopkins, Emma Curtis, 7, 8, 10, 258, 268, 310; abundance theology and, 249, 250–51, 255–56; attraction, law of, and, 253; Bible and, 251; *Biblical Interpretations*, 253; censures of poverty by, 254; Christian Science and, 247; *Class Lessons, 1888*, 249; correspondence (law/theory) and, 252–53; early background of, 246–47; Emerson and, 252; emphasis on Mother God, 254–55; *High Mysticism*, 252, 254; language of Christian Science theology and, 255; lessons of, 249–50; luck and, 253–54; *The Ministry of the Holy Mother*, 255; money and, 255–56; move to Chicago, 247–48; move to New York City, 248–49; mysticism and, 247, 249, 250, 252, 254–55, 256; nature and, 252; New Thought and, 247–48, 250, 251, 252, 253, 255; Plunkett and, 248; prosperity and, 249–53, 255, 256; publishing history of, 249; rupture with Eddy, 247–48; *Scientific Christian Mental Practice*, 251–52, 254; social reforms and, 255; *Spiritual Laws in a Natural World*, 251; spiritualism and, *258*; suffering and, 315; as teacher, 247–48; vitalism and, 254, 256
Hopkins, George Irving (husband of Emma), 246–47
Hopkins, John Carver (son of Emma), 246–47
Hudson, Winthrop S., 101
Hughes, Gertrude Reif, 93

"Images of Divine Things" (Edwards), 118
Images or Shadows of Divine Things (Edwards), 49, 57
In Tune with the Infinite (Trine), 194, 232
Isis Unveiled (Blavatsky), 205

James, Henry, Sr., 138; influence on son William, 216–18
James, William, 7, 8, 10, 11, 138, 202, 270; aesthetics and, 233–36, 238; attraction, law of, and, 224, 232, 234, 237; correspondence (law/theory) and, 233–34, 237; early life and education of, 215–16; "The Energies of Men" essay, 226; *Essays in Radical Empiricism*, 216, 221; Evans and, 240–41; experience and, 219–22; free will and, 223–24; happiness and, 232–33; healthy-mindedness and, 231; influence of father on, 216–18; *The Meaning of Truth*, 224; medical materialism and, 223; mind cure and, 219, 230–32; mysticism and, 226, 227–30, 239, 241; nature and, 221, 226–28, 231; New Thought and, 225, 230, 231, 232, 233, 234; pantheism and, 239; pluralistic monism and, 239; *A Pluralistic Universe*, 216, 224, 233, 235, 238; *Pragmatism*, 220; pragmatism of, 220, 222–23; *The Principles of Psychology*, 225; psychical research of, 236–37; as public intellectual, 216; pursuit of happiness and, 230–31; radical empiricism and, 219, 221, 225, 227, 228, 239; religious experiences and, 225; spiritualism and, 236–37; sick-mindedness and, 231; spiritualism and, 236–38; suffering and, 315; Transcendentalism and, 220, 231; truth, pragmatic theory of, 220–21; *The Varieties of Religious Experience*, 216, 219, 223, 227, 229–30, 234, 316; vitalism

and, 219, 222–25; *The Will to Believe*, 218–19, 220
John of Parma (Brother), 61
Johnson, Thomas, 51
Johnson, William A., 109, 121
Joy Philosophy (Towne), 259

Knapp, Krister Dylan, 219
Kushi, Michio, 307–8

Law of the New Thought, The (Atkinson), 272
Leaves of Grass (Whitman), 128
Lechevalier, Jules, 130
Lessons in Truth (Cady), 248
Levin, David, 20–21
Levingston, William, 157–58
Lewis, John R., 313–14
López, Gregorio, 198
Losa, Francisco de, 198
Love, Mary Fenn, 159
Lovelace, Richard F., 21, 35, 36
Lyon, Silas Smith, 158

Magnalia Christi Americana (Mather), 26–31
Markham, Della E., 159
Marsden, George, 46, 51, 56, 57, 58–59
Master Mind, The (Dumont/Atkinson), 277–79
materialism, theology of, Davis and, 171–72
Mather, Cotton, 5, 8, 9, 15, 75, 127, 244, 308–9; abundance theology, and, 21; aesthetics and, 23–25, 26, 27–28, 29–30, 31, 32, 36, 42; *The Angel of Bethesda*, 39, 40, 41–42; angels, view of, 32–34; attraction, law of, and, 36–37; *The Christian Philosopher*, 23–26, 31, 36; correspondence (law/theory) and, 24–26, 28–29, 31, 36–37, 69, 309; desire and delight, theology of, 21–23; evangelicalism and, 22; family background, 17–18; journal-keeping of, 34–35; "machinery of prayer" and, 35–36; *Magnalia Christi Americana*, 26–31; mysticism and, 17, 23, 32–34, 37; nature and, 23–24, 25, 38, 309; New Thought and, 35, 167, 200, 243; Nishmath-Chajim and, 37–42, 68, 75, 127, 172, 265, 275, 309; pietism and, 22; "plastic spirit" and, 38–39; principle of magnetism and, 36–37; prosperity and, 18, 20–21, 25, 42; reformed tradition and, 32–33; spiritualism and, 42; suffering and, 314; tithing and, 19–20; vitalism and, 34, 37–40, 68, 308; *The Way to Prosperity*, 20, 25
McDougal, Henry Clay, 131
Meacham, Jon, 313–14
Mead, Richard, 160, 161
Meaning of Truth, The (James), 224
Mental Biography, A (Brisbane), 132, 134–35, 149
Mental-Cure, The (Evans), 201–2
Mental Medicine (Evans), 202–3
Mesmer, Franz Anton, 86, 115, 160–61, 191, 203; vitalism and, 172
metaphysics, 3–4, 101, 311
Middlekauff, Robert, 21–22
Militz, Annie Rix, 248
Miller, Perry, 49, 52, 57, 61–62, 69; criticism of Bushnell, 112–13
"Mind, The" (Edwards), 45
mind cure, 241; Evans and, 188, 194, 199, 203, 205, 239; Hopkins and, 252; James and, 219, 224, 230, 231
Mind Power (Atkinson), 271–72, 274–75
Ministry of the Holy Mother, The (Hopkins), 255
Minkema, Kenneth P., 46–47, 48
Money and the Law of Attraction (Hicks-Abraham), 296, 304
Moore, R. Laurence, 211–12
Muir, John, 6
Mulford, Prentice, 268, 284, 289
Mullins, Robert Bruce, 102
Munger, Theodore, 114
Myers, Frederic, 216
Myers, Gerald, 218, 226, 236
mysticism, 6, 60, 100–101, 106, 305; Atkinson and, 281, 284; Brisbane and, 148, 150; Bushnell and, 100, 101, 102, 106, 107–8, 119, 120; Davis and, 162–63, 174; Edwards and, 44, 60–67; Emerson and, 74, 77, 83, 84, 87, 97; Evans and, 189, 190–92, 196, 198, 203–4, 205, 208, 213; Fourier and, 132; Hopkins and, 247, 249, 250, 252, 254–55, 256; James and, 226, 227–30, 239, 241; Mather and, 17, 23, 32–34, 37; Roberts and, 290; Swedenborg and, 6, 172, 200

Nature (Emerson), 91, 95–96, 103, 104
nature (environment and cosmological principle), 6, 123, 305, 309, 311; Abraham (entity) and, 305; Atkinson and, 271, 272, 273, 274, 275, 276, 278, 280, 283; Brisbane and, 134, 135, 150; Bushnell and, 6, 9, 101, 102–4, 106, 107, 109–10, 111, 118, 121, 122, 123, 210; Davis and, 159, 160, 161, 162–63, 165, 166, 168, 169, 170–71, 173, 174–75, 177–80; Edwards and, 49, 50, 57, 58, 59, 60, 62, 309; Emerson and, 73, 74–76, 78–80, 82, 83, 85, 87, 88–92, 94, 96, 97, 123, 145, 222; Evans and, 191, 194, 206, 210, 213; Fourier and, 147; Hopkins and, 252; James and, 221, 226–27, 231; Mather and, 23–24, 25, 38, 309; Puritans and, 5; Transcendentalists and, 6, 9
Nature and the Supernatural (Bushnell), 100, 102–3, 104, 107, 108–9, 114–15
Nature of True Virtue, The (Edwards), 52, 54
Nautilus Magazine (Towne), 256–57
negative theology, 120–21, 122
New Age, 2, 7, 200, 254, 288, 289, 295, 296, 305
New Age and Its Messenger, The (Evans), 199–200
Newman, Francis W., 231
New Thought, 7, 10, 265, 310; Abraham (entity) and, 300; Atkinson and, 267–68, 270, 273, 275, 278, 279, 280, 282, 285; Bushnell and, 111, 118, 119, 120; Davis and, 167; Edwards and, 52, 66; Evans and, 188, 194, 196, 200, 201, 202, 205, 212; Hopkins and, 247–48, 250, 251, 252, 253, 255; James and, 225, 230, 232, 233, 234, 254; Mather and, 35, 167, 200, 243; Seth (entity) and, 290; Towne and, 256–58, 259–62, 264
Nishmath-Chajim (Mather), 37–42, 68, 75, 127, 172, 265, 275, 309
Noll, Mark, 56
Norton, Andrews, 110

"Of Being" (Edwards), 44, 45, 46
Ohsawa, George, 307
Olcott, Henry Steel, 7
orthodox Christianity, hostility toward, 189, 308–9; Abraham (entity) and, 302–3; Brisbane and, 139–40, 149–50, 239, 308; Davis and, 158, 165, 176–77, 240, 308; Fourier and, 136, 308

Painter, Nell Irwin, 311–12
Palmer, Elihu, 309; vitalism and, 309
Palmer, Phoebe, 190, 193, 195, 196, 197
Panchadasi, Swami (pseudonym of Atkinson), 281
panentheism, Edwards and, 60, 66; Evans and, 208
pantheism, Bushnell and, 109, 113–14, 210; Edwards and, 60, 66; Evans and, 208; James and, 239
Parker, Theodore, 102, 110
Parkes, Henry Bamford, 52, 61
Peale, Norman Vincent, 7, 270
Pentecostalism, 10, 243; Bushnell and, 202, 210
perfectionism: Evans and, 190, 195, 198; Oberlin and, 190, 197; Phoebe Palmer and, 193
Perry, Ralph Barton, 228, 233, 236, 239, 243, 245, 249
"Personal Narrative" (Edwards), 47, 52, 57, 61
phalanxes, Brisbane/Fourier and, 130, 131, 139, 140, 141, 143, 146, 151, 152–54, 170; Davis and, 169
Piper, Leonora, 10, 236, 237
Plunkett, Mary, 247, 248
Pluralistic Universe, A (James), 216, 224, 233, 235, 238
Popular View of the Doctrines of Charles Fourier, A (Godwin), 137, 155
Practical Methods for Self Development (Towne), 261
pragmatism, 8, 243, 246; Abraham (entity) and, 300; James and, 220, 222, 223–24, 232, 234, 259
Pragmatism (James), 220
Prasad, Rama, 276
Primitive Mind-Cure, The (Evans), 205–7
Principles of Nature (Elihu Palmer), 309
Principles of Nature, Her Divine Revelations, and a Voice to Mankind, The (Davis), 158, 161, 165–66, 172, 173–74
Principles of Psychology, The (James), 225
prosperity, 5, 256, 285; Atkinson and, 269, 270, 274, 276–77, 284; Brisbane and, 146; Bushnell and, 117; Edwards and,

68; Emerson and, 312; Hicks/Abraham [entity] and, 300, 303, 304–5; Hopkins and, 249–53, 255; Mather and, 18, 20–21, 25, 42; Towne and, 258, 260–63
prosperity gospel, 10, 146, 241, 243–44
Psychology of Salesmanship, The (Atkinson), 275–76
Puritans, 5, 15–16; business as divine calling and, 18; delight and, 5; nature and, 5

Quimby, Phineas P., 7, 201, 202–3

Ramacharaka, Yogi (pseudonym of Atkinson), 278–81
Rankin, Henry, 238
Ray, John, 38, 40
Reed, Sampson, 87, 90
Richardson, Robert D., Jr., 84, 228
Riley, I. Woodbridge, 23–24, 52, 60–61, 64
Ripley, George, 102, 110
Roberts, Jane, 7, 8, 10, 289; early background of, 289–90; mysticism and, 290; Seth (entity) and, 289–93; *The Seth Material*, 289–90; suffering and, 315; vitalism and, 291–92
Rohler, Lloyd, 134, 136
Rolle, Richard, 61

Saint-Simon, Claude-Henri Rouvroy de, 130
sanctification, 5–6
Satter, Beryl, 246, 255, 258
Scientific Christian Mental Practice (Hopkins), 251–52, 254
Seth (entity), 10, 289–93; New Thought and, 290; vitalism and, 291–92
Seth Material, The (Roberts), 289–90
Shryock, Richard, 39
Silverman, Kenneth, 32, 33, 37, 39
Smith, John E., 46–47, 48
Smith, Joseph, 108
Social Destiny of Man, The (Brisbane), 130, 136–37, 140–42, 147–49
Soul and Body (Evans), 203–4
spiritualism, 6, 9, 10, 101, 107, 108, 122, 173, 245; Atkinson and, 272; Bushnell and, 107, 108, 113, 114; Davis and, 42, 74, 103, 114, 146, 154, 157, 159, 174, 176, 178, 272, 288, 292; Evans and, 190, 199, 201–2, 203–4, 205; Hopkins and, 258; James and, 236–37; Mather and, 42
spiritualist mediums, 236, 245, 287
Spiritual Laws in a Natural World (Hopkins), 251
Spurlock, John, 158
Stout, Harry S., 46–47, 48
Struble, Joseph Holt, 256
suffering, Christian, 313–16
Swedenborg, Emanuel, 6, 75, 85–87, 90, 112–13, 154, 249; correspondence (law/theory) and, 86, 90, 113, 154, 155, 190, 203, 209; Davis and, 163–64, 171, 172–73; Evans and, 190–91, 199–201; Fourier and, 154–55; mysticism and, 6, 172, 200; vitalism and, 173

Taves, Ann, 238, 239, 248
Teachings of Abraham (entity), 240, 259, 262, 290, 293, 303, 311, 315. See also Abraham (entity)
Theory of the Four Movements (Fourier), 145, 147, 151
Theosophy, 7, 111, 122, 191, 205, 207, 208, 258, 267, 270, 276, 279, 280, 281, 282
Thoreau, Henry David, 6
Thought-Force in Business and Everyday Life (Atkinson), 268–69, 271
Thought Vibration (Atkinson), 272–73, 276
Thurin, Erik Ingvar, 77, 83
Towne, Chester (son of Elizabeth), 257
Towne, Elizabeth, 7, 8, 10, 248, 269; abundance theology of, 258–59, 262; affirmations and, 262–63; Bible and, 259–60; centrality of desire and, 258–59; correspondence (law/theory) and, 261, 265; cosmic consciousness and, 263–64; early background of, 256–57; emotion and, 260–61; ethical markers in writings of, 261–62; feminist politics and, 257; *Fifteen Lessons in New Thought*, 262–63; happiness project of, 264; *Joy Philosophy*, 259; *Nautilus Magazine*, 256–57; New Thought and, 256–58, 259–62, 264; pamphlets of, 258; *Practical Methods for Self Development*, 261; prosperity and desire for, 263; prosperity and, 258, 260–63; suffering and, 315; "the Uncreate" and, 264–65; vitalism and, 258, 261, 264–65

Transcendentalism, American, 6, 9, 23, 52, 72, 73, 80, 102, 105, 110, 118, 131, 137, 146, 204; Edwards and, 58–59; Emerson and, 69, 83, 84, 87, 97, 103, 123, 153; James and, 220, 231; nature and, 6, 9
Treatise concerning Religious Affections, A (Edwards), 54
Treatise on Domestic and Agricultural Association (Fourier), 130, 133
Trine, Ralph Waldo, 7, 194, 232
Trismegistus, Hermes, 100–101, 105

Varieties of Religious Experience, The (James), 216, 219, 223, 227, 229–30, 234, 316
Vestiges of Creation (Chambers), 160
vitalism, 4–5, 182, 244, 305; Abraham (entity) and, 300, 303; Atkinson and, 271, 275, 276–77, 279–81, 283; Bushnell and, 107, 117; Davis and, 172; Edwards and, 54, 68; Emerson and, 75–82, 84, 86, 87, 93, 95, 96, 222; Evans and, 191, 202, 203, 205, 206, 207, 213; Hopkins and, 254, 256; James and, 219, 222–25; Mather and, 34, 37–40, 68, 308; Mesmer and, 172; Palmer (Elihu) and, 309; Seth (entity) and, 291–92; Swedenborg and, 173; Towne and, 258, 261, 264–65

Walsh, Thomas, 198
Way of Holiness, The (Phoebe Palmer), 193
Way to Prosperity, The (Mather), 20, 25
White, Morton, 55
White supremacy, 311–13
Whitman, Walt, 6; free love and, 128
Wilcox, Ella Wheeler, 248
Williams, Kate, 256
Will to Believe, The (James), 218–19, 220
Wilmans, Helen, 248, 256, 268
Winfrey, Oprah, 296
Winslow, Ola Elizabeth, 48–50, 61
Wright, Conrad, 77

Yellow Springs, Ohio, 1–2
Yonut, Captain, 110–11, 113

www.ingramcontent.com/pod-product-compliance
Lightning Source LLC
Chambersburg PA
CBHW022027290426
44109CB00014B/779